COMMUNICATION
AND EXPRESSION
IN HOOFED MAMMALS

ANIMAL COMMUNICATION

EDITORS

Jean Umiker-Sebeok
Thomas A. Sebeok

COMMUNICATION AND EXPRESSION IN HOOFED MAMMALS

Fritz R. Walther

INDIANA UNIVERSITY PRESS
BLOOMINGTON

Manufactured in the United States of America

Library of Congress Cataloging in Publication Data
Walther, Fritz R.
Communication and expression in hoofed mammals.
(Animal communication)
Bibliography: p.
Includes index.
1. Ungulata—Behavior.   2. Animal communication.
3. Mammals—Behavior.   I. Title.   II. Series.
QL737.U4W25   1983   599.3'0451   82-49011
ISBN 0-253-31380-5
1 2 3 4 5 87 86 85 84 83 84

To my wife

Contents

Foreword

In 1961, Friedrich Kainz, a Professor of Psychology at the University of Vienna, published a 322-page book, *Die "Sprache" der Tiere*, within the compass of which he comfortably managed to fit all available data pertinent to his inquiry. Furthermore, he also indulged himself in a restless activity much beloved by Teutonic academics of those times, untranslatably called *Problemschau*, as well as a fair measure of polemic theorizing, suggestively epitomized by quotation marks confining the word "language" in his title. Thus, less than a quarter of a century ago, the speculative era of animal communication studies came to a neat culmination, while their empirical pursuit was already being vigorously embarked upon, in many workshops on both sides of the Atlantic, mainly as a part of comparative psychology and ethology.

These empirical researches drew variously upon several branches of the natural sciences, for instance, acoustic physics, the diverse life sciences, of course, and the cycle of semiotic disciplines, the latter leading to the coinage as far back as 1963 of the convenient one-word nominal designation "zoosemiotics." This, in turn, spawned a family of new terms, such as "anthroposemiotics," contrastively referring to man's total—nonverbal and verbal—communicative repertoire, and the novel heuristic brainchild "phytosemiotics," which already has elicited scientific studies on the arguably lively nonverbal communication of plants.

By 1965, an internationally manifested need persuaded the Wenner-Gren Foundation for Anthropological Research to convene the first Symposium on animal communication, with seventeen participants, in Burg Wartenstein, Austria. The resulting essays and discussions were published in two books and separately, e.g., in *Science*, late in that decade. In 1968, one of the undersigned edited, for the Indiana University Press, the first reference work ever to appear on the subject, *Animal Communication: Techniques of Study and Results of Research*. This ran to 686 pages, and appeared later, in full or in part, in several other languages as well. The book rapidly sold out, but the demand for it continued and the Press sought to reprint it. However, the "field"—for that is what it had grown into—had in the meantime experienced such rapid global development that, in our judgment, the preparation of an entirely fresh reference tool had become necessary. Hence *How Animals Communicate* was published, by the same Press, in 1977; this version was 1,128 pages in length, yet even then was far from all-encompassing.

By 1980, when *How Animals Communicate* was nearly sold out, the scope of animal communication studies had become so vast that no single compendium could do it justice. The Press therefore decided, upon the recommendation of the undersigned, to launch a series of separate books, by the world's leading authorities on animal communication, each of which would not only report the latest research but also summarize everything that is known about the communicative behavior of a particular species or grouping of species. The selection of species to be covered in this new series—simply entitled *Animal Communication*—would obviously depend upon the current availability of scientific information about different animals, but the format of the series would provide the flexibility needed to achieve its ultimate goal of representing most of the millions of animal species that inhabit the earth.

Whether about dogs, fireflies, or elephants, books in the series are written in a jargon-free style, with all specialized terms clearly defined, so that, while of high scientific value, they will be accessible to a wide variety of readers from various related disciplines as well as to interested persons from outside the academic world. Comprehension is further enhanced by a rich selection of photographs and drawings, and a selective bibliography as a guide to further study.

Fritz R. Walther's excellent book, *Communication and Expression in Hoofed Animals*, opens the *Animal Communication* series with a vivid account of the communicative patterns of an impressive variety of even- and odd-toed ungulates. Professor Walther is one of the world's leading experts on ungulate behavior and this book, the fruit of years of careful and painstaking empirical study, will no doubt prove to be a vital contribution to man's understanding of the lives of hoofed animals. The author brings to his work the keen and finely honed powers of observation of the best of detectives as well as those of a fine artist. Through his clear, concrete reports of ungulate communication by tactile, olfactory, visual, and auditory means in natural and quasi-natural conditions, Professor Walther succeeds in sharing with us the excitement of decoding the seemingly mysterious gestures, movements, sounds, and other expressions of horses, deer, antelopes, and many other fascinating creatures. A labor of love as well as a disciplined scientific exercise, this book allows the reader to achieve, through acquaintance with accurate and objective empirical facts, a deeper appreciation and admiration for the unique and complex ways in which hoofed animals exchange information with one another and with other animal species in their environment.

THOMAS A. SEBEOK
JEAN UMIKER-SEBEOK

Preface

A wise man once said that an author, when writing the preface to his book, should spend less time trying to convince the readers of the objectivity of his approach toward the subject, and more time giving them some information about his very subjective background, since this may contribute much more to their understanding of the book than anything else. The more I later learned about scientific and philosophical literature, the more convinced I became that this man was right. Since I intend in this preface to follow his advice, I now have to make a few "confessions."

To put it in a nutshell: I am an animal lover, a painter and photographer, a concretist and empiricist, and, at least occasionally, a pedant, and in my case, all these points are closely linked with each other.

Being an animal lover, my approach toward animals is not principally different from that toward foreign humans. I wish to learn and to know their names, what country they come from, and, above all, what they look like and what they do. If possible, I try to live with them for some time and to learn their language—and the "language" of animals is their expressive behavior.

Love is always limited to relatively few objects. Therefore, I mistrust people who say they are enthusiastic about the entire animal kingdom. There are about one million recent species, and I doubt whether such an inflation of love and enthusiasm is psychologically possible in one human. At least it is not for me. Although I realize that there are many fine animals in this world, deep in my heart I believe that true animals have horns or at least hooves, and my devotion primarily belongs to them. This goes back to the days when I was a boy, and—as with all true love—I cannot tell how I came to it.

Likewise, I cannot say how I came to draw and to paint. I always enjoyed it, although quite a number of my art products did not turn out as beautifully as I had intended. However, I draw animals not to compete with Leonardo da Vinci but to make sure that I have seen them correctly. As one of my anatomy teachers phrased it: you have only seen something when you have made a sketch of it.

Because I liked hoofed mammals so much, I made many drawings of them, both in zoological gardens and in the wild. In the course of time, however, I became somewhat tired of sketching them as they stood, grazed, or rested, and began to look for more special postures and movements. This was my path to the study of behavior. For a long time the behavioral "data" I gathered were mainly drawings in my sketchbook, and my first scientific publication, twenty-five years ago, was the direct result of such sketches. Even nowadays, when I observe a behavior that is new to me, I do not feel happy until I have sketched it. In addition, it contributes to my peace of mind to have taken a few good photos of it which—particularly in a later publication—often document the events in a more convincing way than drawings can do.

One of my teachers in human psychology once said I was the perfect example of a concretist—and a psychologist is always right. He did not exactly mean this as a compliment, since he defined a concretist to be someone with a rather low IQ who always sticks to things he has seen, heard, smelled, or touched, and who never makes a break-through to the heights of abstract thinking. (Critics of this book and its author are advised to make a note of this point.) Consequently, I am primarily interested in behavioral phenomena, i.e., the movements, postures, gestures, vocalizations, etc., of the animals. What certain people think about these behaviors and how they fit their hypotheses is, at best, of secondary interest to me. Insofar as I myself have theorized, it never amounted to much more than adding two and two. In most cases I am content when I know, in as much detail as possible, what a given behavior looks like, the situations in which it occurs, and its possible effects upon partners. Neither do I ask much of the physiological underlying mechanisms, nor of the biological metaphysics "behind the behavior" such as adaptiveness, selection pressure, fitness, "selfish" or "altruistic" genes, etc. In short, I am an empiricist, but neither a causal-analytical nor a teleological thinker. (Again, this is a statement which I highly recommend for negative reviews.)

When describing or discussing animal behavior, I strongly rely on species and behaviors I have watched myself (which does not necessarily imply that I was always the first and only author to describe them). This last statement reveals the weakness and the possible strength of this book. Since the number of hoofed mammals is great, I have not watched them all—which nobody regrets more than I. Consequently the reader will find gaps, occasionally even in cases where publications by other authors are available, and sometimes perhaps also in the case of a species or a behavior in which the reader is particularly interested. However, the communicative and expressive behaviors of the animals under discussion are often so subtle that one simply has to have first-hand knowledge to present and interpret them adequately or to correctly use the findings of other authors. Therefore, I would rather be blamed for a certain incompleteness than risk provoking the accusation that I had written about animals or behaviors without knowing what I was talking about.

Nowadays, unfortunately, it is not particularly unusual for people to write about ungulate behavior without knowing it well enough. Due to space limitations, and also because I wish to end my days in peace, I resist the temptation to provide a list of contemporary scientists who have made more or less serious mistakes in their behavioral descriptions (not to mention their interpretations), and/or who completely misquoted the originally correct reports of other researchers, obviously because they had no idea what the animals and/or their behaviors look like.

Of course, to err is human, and even with the best factual base one can still arrive at the wrong conclusions. Mistakes of this type certainly have to be corrected, but they may also be forgiven. However, when a scientist makes definite statements about something which he does not know for sure, it is a crime against the spirit of science. The famous anatomist Ferdinand Hochstetter used to say: "Wenn einer über etwas schreibt, was er nicht selbst gesehen hat, so ist das unanständig" (When somebody writes about something which he has not seen himself, this is obscene). I embrace these royal words, and I wish to keep this book free of such sins. In short, this is my apology for largely restricting the discussions to species and behaviors which I know from my own observations: at least as far as the facts are concerned, the reader can rely on the information.

It is for methodological reasons that I predominantly consider the behavior of nondomestic animals under natural or, at least, seminatural conditions (such as in zoos with large enclosures or on game ranches) in this book. Experiments in a laboratory necessarily restrict the reactions of the animal, often to an extreme extent, whereas, with respect to the investigation of communicative and expressive behavior, it is a major requirement that the animal be able to show its full behavioral repertoire.

All domestic animals have originated from wild ancestors. Thus, the behavior of the wild species is the basis for that of the domestic forms. It has frequently been presumed that domestication has changed these behaviors (although I personally have the impression that the frequency as well as the extent of such changes has often been overestimated). Whether such changes have taken place and, if so, what has been changed in detail, cannot be recognized before the behavior of the wild species is known. The investigation of the behavior of the wild ungulates therefore appears to be of primary importance.

When Simenon's immortal Inspector Maigret was asked what he

thought about a case he was investigating, he used to answer: "I never think." I cannot quite give such a proud answer, since I sometimes think. However—and here my pedantic nature comes into play—this thinking primarily concerns problems of definitions, classifications, and related matters. Apparently not too many of my colleagues in behavioral science share this habit; one of them once actually said to me that one should not worry about terms and definitions. Although I can understand how somebody may arrive at this attitude, I cannot agree with it. It is true that defining and classifying are awkward businesses and that truly good definitions and classifications are and will remain rare in spite of all the effort we may put into them. However, we cannot get around the use of terms in science. When undefined, a term almost necessarily remains vague and gives rise to misunderstandings. Moreover, after the terms have become established, they channel our thinking. Thus, when they are inadequate or poorly defined, our thinking may easily go in the wrong direction. It is the same with classification. To name one example out of hundreds; aggression is sometimes said to consist of those behaviors by which an animal attempts to inflict injuries upon an opponent. If this definition were correct, all the many threat displays and all the numerous fighting techniques that largely, or even completely, exclude bloodshed would not belong to aggressive behavior. Obviously, this is nonsense; some more thinking about definition and classification would have been desirable in such a case. Generally, it is the same as with drawing: even when the results are not as satisfactory as we would have wished them to be, the efforts which we put into problems of definitions and classifications are not lost. At least they help to clarify our views.

Admittedly, the location in this book of the chapters with mainly theoretical considerations gave me a headache. On the one hand, they contain many conclusions that follow from the facts described, so it would be logical to place them after the presentation of the facts: at the end. On the other hand, these theoretical considerations provide the key for the organization of the material in this book. Therefore, they should be placed at its beginning. Finally I decided to begin the book with three theoretical chapters, which of course has the disadvantage that the reader may not or at least not fully understand certain statements in these chapters before he has read the later ones. To a minor extent, however, this is true for all chapters in the book. For example, one cannot fully understand what is said about advertising presence and position until one has read the discussion on threat and dominance displays, and vice versa. I have no better solution to this dilemma than to repeat the perhaps somewhat arrogant but certainly very true advice of the philosopher Arthur Schopenhauer in the preface to his principal work: "One must read the book twice."

From the "confessions" above the reader may easily conclude what is to be expected from this book. It deals with (wild) hoofed mammals and their communicative and expressive behavior insofar as it can be observed in intact animals under natural conditions. Its primary goal is to make known certain facts, and it sometimes tries to contribute to the clarification of definitions and to the classification of behaviors. Otherwise, the theorizing is moderate and remains on the level of comments about the described phenomena. If the reader wishes to advance to more abstract speculations, he may do so on his own.

Finally, I should perhaps explain why I think that the behavior of animals such as hoofed mammals may be of special importance to general conceptions of communication and expression. A correct understanding of (human) communicative and expressive behavior appears to be essential to man, judging from the number of publications on these subjects throughout history, and nobody will doubt that these have raised a variety of difficult problems. Comparison is one of the best ways, if not the only way, to approach and to illuminate such difficult problems. Of all the things in creation animals are closest to man, particularly with respect to behavior. Thus, for an approach toward fundamental problems of communication and expression, it is imperative to compare the situation in man to that in animals; we do not have any choice in the matter. Consequently, writings on principal aspects of human communication or expression usually contain more or less elaborate comparisons to animal behavior. However, most of these comparisons are anything but masterpieces of the human mind.

In principle, one can compare anything to almost anything; it is certainly not difficult to draw comparisons, but it may be very difficult to make the comparison fruitful and meaningful. In the first place, in any reasonable comparison the two things compared must be of equal category level. One can compare a Jeep to a Land Rover, but it does not make sense to compare the Jeep to the motorcar, because "the motorcar" is a much broader category than "the Jeep," comprising in addition to the Jeep many other different types and models of cars. In the second, even when the two subjects are of equal category level, the comparison can only be fruitful when they are neither too similar nor too different. If they are too similar, a comparison will hardly reveal new fundamental insights. If they are too different, the comparison cannot teach us anything but a difference that was to be expected from the beginning. Apparently no one has investigated these questions of "too similar" and "too different" to a satisfactory extent, or set up concrete rules for an "optimal realm" of comparison—at least, I could find no evidence to the contrary in the literature available to me.

It must be said that many people, particularly philosophers, theologians, human psychologists, sociologists, and linguists, almost habitually violate at least one if not both principles mentioned above while comparing such subjects as communication or expression in man and in animals; often not even the publications of animal psychologists and zoologists are free of such faults.

In the worst case, "the human being" is compared to "the animal." This is a clear violation of the principle that only subjects of equal category level can be compared; man is one species (or at least one genus—there are differences of opinion among the experts) in the taxonomic sense, whereas "the animal" is an incomparably (!) broader and more abstract term, comprising about one million recent species of such different physical and behavioral organization as houseflies and elephants. Not only is, say, a dog much closer to a human in its physical and behavioral organization than it is to an earthworm (yet dog and earthworm are lumped together as "animals"!), but it is simply impossible to extrapolate a picture of the behavior of "the animal" out of these one million species, and the authors of such books do not even try to do so. When one takes a closer look at such publications, it usually turns out that "the human being" is a professor, while "the animal" is a bee or a rat. Other authors may take into account four or five species more—let us say a locust, a goldfish, a bat, a canary, and a dolphin in addition to the rat and the bee—and by selecting a few behavioral features from each, they construct a monster which they name "the animal." When, then, "the animal" is compared to "the human being," the result is always that there is a big difference, and that man's position is absolutely unique— surprise, surprise. It would be a waste of time and paper to discuss such "literature" in detail, but it is numerous.

However, even books and papers that deserve to be taken more seriously frequently suffer from weaknesses and biases in regard to the comparisons. In part this goes back to certain peculiarities of the historical development of ethology. In its beginning and for a long time thereafter, ethological research focused predominantly or even exclusively on the behavior of birds, fish, and certain insects. It is primarily this part of ethology which has found its way into the recent books and papers of philosophers, sociologists, etc. Said ethological studies doubtless have their great scientific merits; however, particularly in such subtle fields as communication and expression, one can hardly think of a more inadequate approach than the comparison of human behavior to that of honey bees, sticklebacks, or herring gulls. Even when one leaves man outside the discussion and tries to establish a picture "only" of vertebrate behavior on the basis of birds and fish, as ethologists often do, it still will be inadequate.

Insofar as mammals are taken into consideration for behavioral comparison with humans, the facts most frequently quoted come from studies either of (white) mice and rats or of primates such as rhesus monkeys and chimpanzees—the rats still being pretty far away from man in their physical and behavioral organizational level, the primates being our very closest relatives in the animal kingdom—and between these two extremes there is a big gap. Because of this gap, scientists who predominantly or exclusively consider primates often fall victim to the presumption that this or that behavior is a prerogative of primates when, in truth, it is much more widespread among mammals. Sometimes one may also get the impression that problems of animal communication only become interesting to some experimenters when they have occasion to teach a human communication code to the animals (for example, when a captive chimpanzee learns the American sign language), and they do not seem to realize that such cases are artifacts which, while they may be of interest and have their scientific merits, are otherwise absolutely inadequate to teach us anything about the animals and their communication.

In short, in attempting to illuminate fundamental and general problems of communication and/or expression, one is certainly on the right course when one takes the situation in animals into consideration. However, it is important that the right animals be selected for purposes of comparison. When they are as close to man as primates are, the contrast may often not be great enough to reveal basic new insights. If they are as far away from man as butterflies, sticklebacks, songbirds, or rats are, the comparison will almost necessarily end with the statement of a difference which, when taken as representative for animals in general, will lead to an overestimation of that difference. Carnivores or ungulates, on the other hand, are different enough from man to allow a pronounced contrast, and at the same time close enough to make the comparison meaningful in that it may bring more than the sterile statement of a difference. To provide some material for such fruitful comparisons is one of the major goals of this book.

At this point I am afraid that I may have lost a few readers. At least, I can imagine that somebody may have had reservations when I said that there are animals, such as primates, that are too close to humans for a fruitful comparison. Nevertheless, it is true—at least with respect to such fields as communication and expression. For example, in humans as well as in apes and monkeys, the facial expressions play a prominent role in (visual) communication. Thus, when one compares man only to other primates, there is the danger (and I do think that quite a number of scientists have fallen victim to it) of remaining unaware that facial expressions comprise only a small portion of expressive behaviors, are very special cases of expression, and, phylogenetically as well as phenotypically, are by no means the most original ones. The truly basic expressions are movements and postures of the body, the neck, and the head—as is so strikingly and beautifully demonstrated by animals such as hoofed mammals.

Another, in my opinion, misleading trend in comparative literature on communication has developed, apparently under the influence of linguistics. Of course, a linguist primarily deals with the human language and its derivatives (writing, Morse code, sign language for the deaf-mute, etc.). This is his job and there is nothing wrong with that. However, when discussing problems of human (!) communication, the thinking of linguists seems often to be so thoroughly focused on human language that they, at best, consider a few nonverbal, human vocalizations and largely "forget" the postures, gestures, and facial expressions. That is, they usually mention them—somewhere in the introduction—but they neither consider them nor incorporate them to any extent into their conclusions and conceptions. Correspondingly, the vocalizations of animals (e.g., the songs of birds) often play a great role in comparative discussions on communication, obviously because they are at least acoustical, and thus some people apparently presume they come relatively close to human communication. I think this is a mistake. Of course, human communication has reached its greatest perfection in the acoustical realm—i.e., with the development of a verbal language—whereas our gestures and posture are more or less auxiliary means of communication and thus may appear to be only of secondary importance to many people concerned with theories of human communication. However, in at least a considerable number of animal species, it is precisely the opposite, i.e., vocalizations are more or less supplemental, while gestures and postures are the most important means of communication. In short, gestures and postures are the "language" of animals, and animal communication has reached its greatest perfection in this field. Consequently—as strange as it may sound to some—it is not animal communication by means of vocalizations but animal communication by means of gestures and postures that provides us with the best parallels to human communication and the best material for a fruitful comparative discussion.

To illustrate the points above by at least one simple, concrete example (which I will later describe in detail): when the "master bull" (alpha animal) of a migratory herd of oryx antelope leaves the group, walks 200 yards back to a straggler, passes him, stops him from moving farther away from the herd by blocking his path in broadside position, turns toward him, threatens him by presenting his horns, and makes him hurry back and join the herd, this "master bull" has done something that comes much closer to human communication than anything a white rat, songbird, or honey bee may do— including, I dare say, the latter's famous "waggle run."

Furthermore, within the hoofed mammals, there are more primitive suborders (Ceratomorpha in odd-toed ungulates, Nonruminantia in even-toed ungulates) and more advanced suborders (Hippomorpha in odd-toed, Tylopoda and Ruminantia in even-toed ungulates). Even within these suborders there are pronounced differences with respect to the evolutionary levels of physical organization. Thus, the study of hoofed mammals offers a remarkable opportunity to relate certain forms of communication to different levels of advancement in physical organization.

Finally, since some ungulate species have been domesticated for thousands of years, and others have frequently been kept in zoological gardens, their study can make essential contributions to the discussion of problems of man-animal communication.

The acknowledgments would become excessively long if I named here all the many people who supported my studies in different ways and thus directly or indirectly contributed to this book. However, I think I can keep the list short, since most of these people fall into only two categories: those who like me and those who do not. People who dislike me will have only one more reason for their negative judgment when I do not mention them here, and my friends will forgive me anyway. Thus, it does not matter too much if I omit them.

This book is a revision and an elaboration of a chapter on behavior of Artiodactyla in the now out of print How Animals Communicate, edited by T. A. Sebeok (1977). I was invited to write this book by Prof. T. A. Sebeok and Dr. J. Umiker-Sebeok, and I thank them for their trust and encouragement. Eleven colleagues from the Texas A&M University and the New Mexico State University kindly corrected my occasionally somewhat "Teutonic" English in the manuscript, each of them one to three chapters. Furthermore, I am very grateful to all the authors who allowed me to reprint figures or tables from their publications in this book and/or kindly sent me originals of their photos. (Their names are given in the captions to the figures.) I also thank the publishers who gave me permission to use these illustrations. These publishers or publishing institutions were: E. J. Brill,

Leiden (*Behaviour*); Duncker und Humblot, Berlin (*Zoologische Bei-träge*); Gustav Fischer, Jena (*Der Zoologische Garten*); Walter de Gruyter & Co., Berlin (*Handbuch der Zoologie*); Juris Druck A.G., Zürich; Paul Parey, Hamburg (*Zeitschrift für Tierpsychologie*); Department of Agriculture and Nature Conservation of South West Africa (*Madoqua*); Institute of Arctic Biology of the University of Alaska, Fairbanks; International Union for Conservation of Nature and Natural Resources, Morges; and the publishers of the *Journal of Mammalogy*, Lubbock, and *Zoologica Africana*, Capetown.

While writing the book, I was employed by Texas A&M University and the Texas Agricultural Experiment Station (College Station). My field work in previous years was supported by grants from Fritz Thyssen Stiftung (Köln), Deutsche Forschungsgemeinschaft (Bad Godesberg), Zoologische Gesellschaft von 1848 (Frankfurt a. M.), Gertrud Rüegg Stiftung (Zürich), Smithsonian Institution (Washington), Research Council of the University of Missouri (Columbia), and Caesar Kleberg Research Program in Wildlife Ecology (College Station). I was privileged to work in the following national parks, conservation areas, and zoological gardens: Serengeti National Park (Tanzania), Ngorongoro Conservation Area (Tanzania), Tarangire National Park (Tanzania), Nairobi National Park (Kenya), Kruger National Park (South Africa), Etosha National Park (South West Africa—Namibia), Chaibar (Israel), Yellowstone National Park (U.S.A.), National Bison Range (Montana, U.S.A.), Camp Cooley Ranch (Texas, U.S.A.), Y.O. Ranch (Texas, U.S.A.), King Ranch (Texas, U.S.A.), Zoo Frankfurt a. M. (Germany), Zoo Hannover (Germany), Münchener Tierpark Hellabrunn (Germany), G. von Opel-Freigehege (Kronberg, Germany), Giardino zoologico di Napoli (Italy), Giardino zoologico di Roma (Italy), Zoo Basel (Switzerland), and Zoo Zürich (Switzerland). I feel deeply obliged to the directors and the staff of these national parks and zoological gardens.

As mentioned above, the number of persons to whom I owe gratitude is very extensive. Thus, an individual word of thanks can go here only to those four who repeatedly gave me such crucial help that I could never have made my way without them. These are Prof. Dr. Dr. H. Hediger (Zürich), Prof. Dr. Dr. B. Grzimek (Frankfurt a. M.), Dr. R. Faust (Frankfurt a. M.), and my wife, Elisabeth M. Walther.

COMMUNICATION
AND EXPRESSION
IN HOOFED MAMMALS

1. AN INTRODUCTION TO HOOFED MAMMALS

Neither the term "hoofed mammals" nor its synonym, "ungulates," is really very scientific. If extended to mean all mammals with somewhat hooflike structures on their feet, this group could also include elephants (Proboscidea) and hyraxes (Hyracoidea), and considering all aspects of phylogenetic relationships (Thenius 1969), it could be further extended to include aardvarks (Tubulidentata), sea cows (Sirenia), and possibly even whales (Cetacea). Commonly, however, only odd-toed ungulates (Perissodactyla) and even-toed ungulates (Artiodactyla) are regarded as "hoofed mammals," and it is in this latter sense that the term "hoofed mammals" (or "ungulates") is used in this book.

Whether and to what degree odd-toed and even-toed ungulates are related to each other is a difficult problem of paleontology. Some earlier paleontologists (e.g., Schlosser 1887, Simpson 1945) felt that both Perissodactyla and Artiodactyla could ultimately be traced back to the same group of fossil mammals, the Condylarthra, and they related these Condylarthra to another group of fossil mammals, the Creodontia, which were considered to be the ancestors of the recent beasts of prey, the carnivores. Thus, according to this view, odd-toed and even-toed ungulates ultimately are of a more or less mutual phylogenetic origin, and this origin is not too far from that of the recent carnivores.

However, some modern paleontologists have a different opinion. For example, Thenius (1969), a contemporary master in this field, uses the term "Condylarthra" only in quotation marks because quite a number of fossil species have been united under this name, and they form several groups within the "Condylarthra" which are much more heterogeneous than earlier authors supposed them to be. Thus, it might have been a mistake to unite them under the same name. With respect to the recent odd-toed and even-toed ungulates, it seems probable that they have evolved from two very different and distant groups of "Condylarthra." Thus, according to this view, the recent Perissodactyla and Artiodactyla are of different phylogenetic origin. Consequently, when one unites them under the term "hoofed mammals" it is only a matter of tradition and convenience and does not imply any genuine relationships.

1

Since I am no paleontologist, I cannot take a position in these controversies. Behaviorwise—modern paleontologists may or may not forgive me—there are trends and features in Perissodactyla and Artiodactyla that appear to be related to each other, and sometimes there are even resemblances to the behavior of certain carnivores. I ask the reader to keep these aspects in mind. On the other hand, in accordance with the results of recent paleontological work as well as the modern zoological classification system, we must consider odd-toed and even-toed ungulates as being separate and independent orders.

The order of recent odd-toed ungulates (Perissodactyla) is taxonomically divided into two suborders: the—in terms of evolution—more primitive Ceratomorpha and the more advanced Hippomorpha. The Ceratomorpha comprise two families: the tapirs (Tapiridae) with one genus and four species, and the rhinoceroses (Rhinocerotidae) with four genera and five species. The Hippomorpha comprise only one family, the horses (Equidae), with one genus and six species.

The order of recent even-toed ungulates (Artiodactyla) is taxonomically divided into three suborders: the (more primitive) Nonruminantia, the Tylopoda (which still seem to represent a comparatively original group of Artiodactyla), and the (advanced) Ruminantia. The Nonruminantia comprise three families: the swine (Suidae) with five genera and eight species, the peccaries (Tayassuidae) with one genus and two species, and the hippos (Hippopotamidae) with two genera and two species. The Tylopoda consist of only one family: the camels and llamas (Camelidae), with two genera and four species. The Ruminantia comprise five families: the mouse deer (Tragulidae) with two genera and four species, the deer (Cervidae) with eleven genera and thirty-two species, the giraffe-related animals (Giraffidae) with two genera and two species, the pronghorns (Antilocapridae) with one genus and one species, and the horned ungulates (Bovidae) with forty-two genera and ninety-nine species. Except for the (primitive) tragulids, the aforementioned Ruminantia families form the infraorder Pecora. (For more details of zoological classification, see the classification list at the end of this book.)

Numbers of genera and species (as well as subfamilies and tribes) vary somewhat with different classification systems. I have followed here the classification of Haltenorth (1963), which is very concise. Thus, the numbers of genera and species given above may represent the minimum. But even when we restrict this discussion to odd-toed and even-toed ungulates, and when we use a very concise classification system, the term "hoofed mammals" still includes 169 species with considerable differences in size, body structure, life habits, and social organization, inhabiting a great variety of terrestrial habitats in North and South America, Africa, Europe, Asia, and even the Arctic. Some species, both wild and domestic, have been introduced by man to Australia, New Zealand, and other countries where they have not been endemic. In the following account I present a sketchy outline of general body characteristics, habitats, and social organization in the ungulate families as far as it may be necessary for a better understanding of the later chapters on communication and expression.

Of the odd-toed ungulates, tapirs (Tapiridae) live in the dense tropical forests and jungles of South America and Malaya, and they frequently take to the water. They have a keen sense of smell, their hearing is relatively good, but their eyesight is poor. They are unsociable loners. At maximum, three animals may occasionally be seen together (Frädrich 1968). Very much the same is true for the rhinoceroses (Rhinocerotidae), especially the Asiatic rhinoceroses, except for the Indian rhino (*Rhinoceros unicornis*), in which group sizes can be somewhat greater (Schenkel and Lang 1969). The African rhinos are found in comparatively open woodlands of the African "bush" type, and they may also venture into the open plains. Their habitat is considerably dryer than that of the Asiatic species. In all the tapir and rhino species, the animals stay in rather circumscribed areas for long periods; however, nothing is known of territoriality in most of the species, or, rather, different authors have different opinions about it. Territorial behavior is definitely known only in adult males of the square-lipped or white rhino (*Ceratotherium simum*— Owen-Smith 1975). The owners of territories tolerate the presence of a few subordinate males, and they are temporarily visited by cows in their territories.

By contrast, all the horse-related species (Equidae) are gregarious animals with quite good eyesight. They inhabit open grasslands, some species even deserts in Africa and Asia. (The famous mustangs of the American plains are feral descendants of domestic horses.) In some areas, horses or their relatives may also be found in woodland, but never in truly dense forests. Plains zebra (*Equus quagga*), mountain zebra (*Equus zebra*), and probably also the wild horse (*Equus przewalskii*) are not territorial (Klingel 1967, 1968, 1972). They form permanent harem groups (one adult stallion with several mares and their young) and all-male groups. Larger herds are temporary and unstable associations of such harems and all-male groups. Grevy's zebra (*Equus grevyi*), African wild ass (*Equus asinus*), and probably also Asiatic wild ass (*Equus hemionus*) live in unstable groups of either one or both sexes. Some of the stallions become territorial and are temporarily visited by female groups in their territories. They tolerate other nonterritorial males, but fight their territorial neighbors under certain conditions (Klingel 1969, 1974).

Among the even-toed ungulates, the swine (Suidae) generally inhabit rather dense forests and thickets, preferably with water close by, in Europe, Asia, and Africa. Only the African warthog (*Phacochoerus aethiopicus*) stays in open grasslands. The peccaries (Tayassuidae) are found in corresponding habitats in South America and the southern parts of North America. Some of the species can adapt to very different ecological conditions. For example, the collared peccary (*Tayassu tajacu*) lives in the deserts of Arizona as well as in the tropical rain forests of South and Central America. Vision is poor in swine, but the senses of smell and hearing are very acute. Old males are solitary; otherwise swine usually live in small groups of at most thirty to forty members. The groups often remain in relatively circumscribed areas, but apparently they are not territorial. Quite a number of the species are nocturnal, but not all of them. For example, the warthog is strictly diurnal, and spends the night sleeping in aardvark dens. Male swine possess specialized weapons in their long canines which show great species-specific variations as to size and shape. The canines of the upper jaw are curved upward in all the swine, but not in peccary.

Recent hippopotamuses (Hippopotamidae) are restricted to Africa. Pygmy hippo (*Choeropsis liberiensis*) live solitarily, i.e., singly or in pairs, in swampy forests. They are good swimmers, although far less aquatic than their huge relatives. The latter (*Hippopotamus amphibius*) are found in streams and lakes bordered by grassland. They are semiaquatic, gregarious animals, which form "schools" of five to about thirty that may occasionally join together in larger herds. Different observers (e.g., Hediger 1951, Verheyen 1954) have expressed different views on the social organization of these groups and about territorial behavior in hippo, and it thus appears inopportune to make definite statements on these subjects here. With their elongated incisors, the lower ones pointing straight forward, fighting bulls can inflict deep wounds on the opponent's body (Hediger 1951).

In the Tylopoda or Camelidae, respectively, only a few two-humped camels still exist in the wild (Gobi Desert). The two domestic forms of camels, the Bactrian camel (*Camelus bactrianus*) and the dromedary (*Camelus dromedarius*), live in desert regions of Asia and North Africa. They have also been introduced to other continents, particularly Australia. The other Tylopoda, the llamas (*Lama*), are restricted to the highlands of South America. Hearing and sight are well developed. The sense of smell is mainly used for objects at close range. In vicuna (*Lama vicugna*), territorial behavior is combined with harem behavior (Koford 1957, Franklin 1974); that is, a territory is inhabited by one adult male with a group of females and their young. Nonterritorial males form bachelor herds. The social organization of guanaco (*Lama guanicoe*), the other wild llama species (there are also domesticated forms), seems to be similar.

The mouse deer and their relatives (Tragulidae) are the most primitive of the recent Ruminantia. These little creatures, solitary and nocturnal, live in dense tropical rain forests in Asia and Africa. The upper canines of the males are elongated and play a role in fighting (Ralls et al., 1975, Robin 1979).

Similar elongated upper canines protruding from the mouth are also found in males of the two antlerless Cervidae species, the musk deer (*Moschus moschiferus*) and the Chinese water deer (*Hydropotes inermis*), as well as in muntjac (*Muntiacus muntjak*) whose males possess small antlers.

The continent with the most cervid species is Asia. In Europe and North America, cervids also are prominent game animals. One species, the reindeer (*Rangifer tarandus*), ranges up to the Arctic. A few cervid species are found in South America. In Africa, only a subspecies of red deer (*Cervus elaphus*) occurs in the Atlas region. Two taxonomic groups are distinguished in Cervidae on the basis of differences in the bony structure of the forelegs: the Telemetacarpalia and the Plesiometacarpalia. The Telemetacarpalia comprise nearly all the North and South American cervids except the elk (*Cervus canadensis*), and they also include the moose (*Alces alces*), the reindeer, and the roe deer (*Capreolus capreolus*). All the many other Asiatic and European cervids as well as the American elk belong to the Plesiometacarpalia. Although some deer species may locally venture into grasslands, they are predominantly forest animals and their habitats range from dense tropical forests to park-like forests in the temperate zone. They are water dependent and thus are not found in dry countries. Some of them are well adapted to live in swamps. Although quite a number of the species can go quite high up in the mountains, none of them, perhaps excepting the musk deer, can be said to be a typical mountain animal. The reindeer is in more than one respect an exception among the cervids: it is not only the most northern species, but it also inhabits the tundra, which is an absolutely open landscape. Moreover, it is by far the most gregarious species of all the cervids, with herds of hundreds of animals. It is the single cervid species in which the females as well as the males possess antlers, and the single one which has been domesticated by man (besides the existence of wild forms). In all the other deer species (with the exception of the antlerless musk deer and water deer) only the males possess antlers, which are bones (usually ramified) that are shed and grow again, surrounded by velvet, every year. These antlers are special weapons for intraspecific fighting, and they are of very different species-specific size and shape.

Hearing is particularly good in cervids, but eyesight and the sense of smell are also well developed. Strictly solitary life habits are as rare as the formation of very large herds. Most commonly, cervids form relatively small groups, ranging from two to about thirty or forty members. Except during the rutting season and—in northern countries—the wintertime, the sexes commonly live separated, forming bands of females with their offspring, and all-male groups. During the rutting season, usually, one adult male is together with one female or a bunch of females. During winter, cervids often form relatively large herds of both sexes (mixed herds). Territorial behavior has up to now been found for sure only in male roe deer (Hennig 1962). Territoriality has been presumed for more deer species by several authors; however, these apparently were errors. Although some of the cervid species have not yet been investigated in this regard, we may safely say that most of them are not territorial.

Pronghorn (*Antilocapra americana*), the single living species of the Antilocapridae, is restricted to the western plains of North America. Pronghorn are unique among recent Artiodactyla in that they possess bony structures on their heads resembling the antlers of deer, but such a bone is surrounded by a horn sheath, and it is not the bone, but this horn sheath, which is shed every year. Eyesight seems to be particularly good in pronghorn, but olfaction also plays a role in their lives and their hearing is at least adequate. Pronghorn are gregarious and form female and all-male groups as well as larger mixed herds. Adult bucks seasonally become territorial and are temporarily visited by female herds. Occasionally a female herd may stay for a longer while with a male in his territory.

The Giraffidae are presently restricted to Africa. The okapi (*Okapia johnstoni*) lives solitarily in a relatively limited area of the dense, central African rain forests. Among the senses, hearing seems to play a prevailing role. Male okapi have short bony structures on their heads which are not shed, but are surrounded by skin throughout the animal's life. It is only in old males that the skin is gone at the tips, and the bare bone occurs. Giraffe (*Giraffa camelopardalis*) have similar "horns" on their heads in both sexes. In contrast to the okapi, giraffe are gregarious, forming all-male groups, female groups, and mixed herds up to about fifty head. They are not territorial. Their major habitat is relatively open woodland, but they also venture locally into grasslands and, on the other hand, can sometimes also be seen in forests with dense vegetation. Sight prevails among the senses.

With at least ninety-nine species, the horned ruminants (Bovidae) are the largest family of the recent even-toed ungulates. They are characterized by the possession of true horns, which means that the corresponding bones (os cornu) on the skull are surrounded by permanent horn sheaths and are not shed throughout the animal's life. As with the antlers of the cervids, these horns are specialized weapons for intraspecific fighting but play a minor role, if any, in defense against predators. They show a tremendous species-specific variety in size, weight, and shape. In some species only the males have horns; in others both sexes possess horns, but the horns of females are considerably smaller and/or of different shape than those of males. In other species, the horns of males and females are—roughly speaking—equal, although the female horns are almost always somewhat weaker than those of males. About 70 percent of the recent species live in Africa, and another 20 percent in Asia. The rest are found in Europe and North America up to the Arctic. There are no endemic horned ungulates in South America. The bovid species inhabit almost all terrestrial habitats. Some of them, such as the small duikers (Cephalophinae) live in dense tropical rain forests. Quite a number of bovids are very dependent on water and occur mainly in thickets or forests near rivers, pools, or lakes. These include the majority of wild oxen (Bovinae) and some of the so-called antelopes such as waterbucks and reedbucks (Reduncinae), bushbuck (*Tragelaphus scriptus*), etc. Sitatunga (*Tragelaphus spekei*) is even semiaquatic. Other species, such as greater and lesser kudu (*Tragelaphus strepsiceros* and *Tragelaphus imberbis*), sable antelope (*Hippotragus niger*), and roan antelope (*Hippotragus equinus*), live in subtropical open woodland. Many Bovids, such as the wildebeests (*Connochaetes*), hartebeests (*Alcelaphus*), topis (*Damaliscus*), oryx antelopes (*Oryx*), and a considerable number of gazelle species (*Gazella*) and their relatives, populate the subtropical open plains with all their variations ranging from high-grass areas to semiarid short grass plains. The musk ox (*Ovibos moschatus*) inhabits the Arctic tundra. In contrast to the deer family (Cervidae), certain bovid species such as addax antelope (*Addax nasomaculatus*), dorcas gazelle (*Gazella dorcas*), and Loder's gazelle (*Gazella leptoceros*), have adapted to desert conditions, and others, such as wild goats and sheep (*Capra and Ovis*), chamois (*Rupicapra rupicapra*), and the American mountain goat (*Oreamnos americanus*), are typical animals of the high mountain range. Sense of smell, hearing, and eyesight generally are well developed with usually one or two of the senses prevailing in the single species.

Particularly small species such as duikers (Cephalophinae) and dwarf antelopes (Neotraginae) live singly or in pairs. Small groups from three to thirty or fifty animals are common in many species. Herds of hundreds and thousands of animals occur mainly with typical open plains animals such as wildebeest, Thomson's gazelle (*Gazella thomsoni*), springbuck (*Antidorcas marsupiallis*), or American bison (*Bison bison*). All-male bands and groups of females with their offspring occur in all the gregarious or at least semigregarious species. Mixed herds are especially typical of species that form larger herds, but may occasionally be seen in almost any species. The permanent harems so typical of horses, plains zebra, or vicuna are not found in bovids. What comes closest to the idea of harems is the occasional association of a female group with a territorial male throughout his territorial period in certain species under certain local conditions (Walther 1972a). However, in most cases when one adult bovid male is seen together with females, it is a territorial male being visited by a group of females which will leave him alone after a short time (pseudoharem). Presumably about 50 percent of the bovid species are not territorial; this is true mainly of the wild oxen, sheep, goats, and some related species such as chamois or mountain goat, and furthermore, of some of the bigger forest antelopes such as greater and lesser kudu, nyala (*Tragelaphus angasi*—Anderson 1980), but also eland antelope (*Taurotragus oryx*), etc.

In territorial bovid species, Estes (1974a) distinguished the territorial/solitary type and the territorial/gregarious type. The territorial/solitary type is mainly found in small antelopes such as Kirk's dikdik (*Rhynchotragus kirki*), klipspringer (*Oreotragus oreotragus*), and (presumably) the duikers. Here, the animals live singly or—apparently more commonly—in pairs in territories which are kept for long periods, under favorable conditions possibly for a lifetime (Hendrichs and Hendrichs 1971). In the territorial/gregarious type, which is much more common in bovids than the territorial/solitary type, only males become territorial, each of them holding his territory for a limited period. This period varies with species and local conditions. Most commonly, it ranges from a few weeks to a few months per year. These territorial males are then temporarily visited by female groups (usually for only a few hours per day).

If someone had written a book on communicative and expressive behavior of ungulates about thirty years ago, he would not have needed much more than thirty pages, provided that he kept the discussion strictly to the subject. By contrast, our knowledge has tremendously increased during the last decades. However, it is still far from being complete, and a lot of research is still needed. Some information is available on some of the rhino and tapir species, on the hippos, tragulids, peccaries, and certain swine. However, of the thirty-two cervid species, only about seven have been studied intensively enough to allow description and discussion of the phenomena and problems of communication and expression. Relatively good information is available on the behavior of the horse-related, the camels and llamas, the giraffes, and the pronghorn; however, each of these groups contains only a few species. More investigations of communicative and expressive behavior have been carried out on bovid species than on the species of all the other groups together, but even here the approximately thirty species investigated make up less than one-third of all bovid species.

Information from studies on the behavior of hoofed mammals is usually rather good on visual displays (postures and gestures), considerably less so on acoustical and olfactory behavior, and poor on tactile communication. (This is provided that one takes the "communication" seriously and does not consider every form of bodily contact to be communication.) Further difficulties are given by general problems of expressive behavior and intraspecific communication, which will be discussed in detail in separate chapters.

A few remarks on organs and parts of the body that play a role in the expressive behavior of ungulates will complete this introductory discussion. Hoofed mammals are primarily pantomimers. In particular, the positions of the head relative to the neck and those of the neck relative to the body (stretched forward, erected, lowered, etc.) often have very definite meanings and can signal a multitude of information to conspecific partners (Schloeth 1961a). In some species, the torso can also show special postures (e.g., lordosis or kyphosis of the back).

Two aspects of the physical structure of animals of the ungulate type are noteworthy with respect to orientation of the entire animal, or at least its head, toward the addressee. First, the eyes of these animals are located much more laterally on the head than, say, in humans, monkeys, or certain carnivores. For this reason, a broadside position or a sideward turn of the head in hoofed mammals does not necessarily result in loss or avoidance of eye contact with the partner. It often is one-eyed fixation of the other animal. Even when such an animal turns its body or head so far that it almost faces away from its partner, this movement is functionally comparable to only a slight sideways inclination of the human head.

Second, these animals present their full breadth when standing in lateral position to an addressee, whereas they offer a relatively small silhouette when standing in frontal orientation. In humans the situation is just the opposite. Linked with the broadside position is the presentation by some species of striking color patterns (such as black or white stripes and bands) and/or additional structures such as beards and manes (which sometimes are extended over the entire back and can be erected).

Movements of the legs come after the postures of the head, the neck, and the torso with respect to importance in communication. Bending or stretching the legs can contribute to the appearance of body postures; and a slow-motion walk—sometimes combined with an exaggerated lifting of the forelegs—and various forms of (symbolic) kicking with the forelegs and stamping and scraping the ground are used as means of expression.

Facial expression is not lacking in hoofed mammals, but apparently it does not play as great a role as it does, for example, in primates. Movements of the mouth and the mouth organs are quite common. For example, wide-open mouths in hippos and symbolic biting in swine and peccaries ("squabbling"—Schweinsburg and Sowls 1972) are threats. Tongue flicking occurs in courting males of quite a number of species. Folding the skin of the nose or inflating the nose region is found in certain species, such as gazelles (Walther 1958a, 1966a, 1968a). Eye movements—including a straight look, a look from the corner of the eye, and a popeyed look—do occur in ungulates. However, they have not been thoroughly investigated, and thus virtually nothing is known about their effects on recipients.

Ear movements occur rather frequently in connection with expressive displays in hoofed mammals (Freye and Geissler 1966). Examples of common ear movements are: the laying back of the ears in threat and courtship behavior; the "ear-drop" (similar to the permanent ear attitude of Indian cattle) in courting males of species such as wildebeest and hartebeest; the "pointing" with one ear toward the opponent in threat and dominance displays of certain antelopes; and holding the ears sideways during fights in many bovids. However, it is uncertain whether ear movements are important signals to conspecifics or release responses in them since they are usually combined with other, more striking, postures or gestures of the head, neck, torso, or legs. Thus, the probability is great that the recipients may primarily react to these other behavior patterns.

The same may be said for many tail movements. Striking movements of the tail are combined with flight behavior in quite a number of ungulate species. However, they occur either when the animal is already fleeing or immediately preceding flight. Thus, it is hard to say whether conspecifics become alarmed by these tail movements or by the first animal's running away, its alert posture, or its alarm calls. The communicative role of tail movements is even more dubious in courtship and threat displays. Here, the displaying animal is frequently frontally oriented to the recipient, and the latter cannot see the sender's tail.

According to Tembrock (1959, 1963, 1964, 1965), acoustical communication in hoofed mammals has developed to different degrees. In the swine (and possibly also other groups of ungulates) three trends in differentiating vocalizations seem to be significant in the development of information transmission: transmission of short sounds to long sounds, adding rhythm to the short sounds, and transformation of the frequency range. Except for a relatively few loud, striking sounds such as whistling, roaring, and barking, vocalizations are often soft in hoofed mammals and can only be heard at close range.

Vocalization can be brought about by the combined activities of the larynx and the mouth organs. Some sounds appear to be closely related to belching. Sometimes, special postures of the neck and/or head appear to be necessary to produce certain sounds (for example, the rutting call of red deer). In a number of ungulate species (such as gazelles and some other bovids), sounds uttered through the nose are quite common. In this case, certain cartilaginous structures of the nose (vibrating organs), skin folds and skin bags in the nose region that can be enlarged, and the opening of the nostrils produce these vocalizations. Some noises are made with the teeth, and a few species produce sounds by stamping with their legs.

Hoofed mammals are considered to possess a keen sense of smell. Not only urine and feces (and possibly saliva), but also secretions (pheromones) of skin glands are supposed to be important in intraspecific communication. Skin glands are frequently found in ungulate species. However, it must be emphasized that in the majority of cases the importance of these glands and their secretions in intraspecific communication is at present postulated on the fact that these animals have such glands and a keen sense of smell. Except for notations of an occasional sniffing of glands or secretions, or of the addition of urine, feces, or secretions to an already existing marking site, convincing observations of responses to these scents are meager. Assumptions on repellent effects of secretion marks to potential territorial competitors should be treated with particular caution. The studies of Müller-Schwarze (1967, 1969, 1971) have brought a clearer and more detailed picture of the social functions and effects of certain pheromones in mule deer (*Odocoileus hemionus*). As far as I can see, no statements or only very limited ones can presently be made on the communicative functions of the following glands: mental, crural, circumcaudal, infracaudal, circumanal, proctodeal, prevulval, preputial, inguinal, tibial, parungular, interdigital, and occipital glands. However, all of them may possibly play a role in communication of certain ungulate species. Somewhat better is the situation with respect to skin glands located on the animal's head, such as preorbital (or antorbital), maxillar, frontal, subauricular, and postcornual glands.

In tactile encounters such as nosing, licking, or rubbing, the epiphenomenal mode (gentle or violent, brushing or knocking, with increasing or decreasing pressure, etc.) appears to be of greater importance with respect to the expressive character of such behaviors and their role in communication than are the behavior patterns themselves, but no studies on this subject are available at present. It appears inopportune to deal with other tactile stimuli as they occur in fighting, copulatory behavior, nursing, cleaning the young, etc., since this would inflate our discussion of communicative and expressive behavior at least to a discussion of social behavior, if not to behavior in general.

2. SOME THEORETICAL PROBLEMS OF COMMUNICATION

The Tower of Babel situation is more than just a myth from pre-historic times. It is in full effect in our lives today. I am not thinking so much here of the communication problems resulting from the number of foreign languages, but rather of the many cases of verbal confusion among people who speak the same language. There are several "mechanisms" which contribute to this type of confusion. One of the most common is the following: originally, a given word may have had a more or less definite meaning. Later, the same word is used in a broader and/or more abstract sense and it now also applies to subjects which originally did not belong to it. This broadening of a term may be justifiable and even advantageous. However, the term may easily—too easily—be broadened too much and thus become vague. Like money in times of inflation, it loses its value, and may end up meaning anything and, at the same time, nothing. Consequently, some people feel a need to limit its sense again. Although it seems to be the simplest way to go back to the word's original meaning, they usually do not do so. Instead, they "cut a piece" out of the broadened field, a "piece" which often is not completely synonymous with the original term, but which particularly fits their special interests and intentions, and they now use the word for this special "piece." Thus, the same word now has at least three meanings (possibly more), and confusion arises because some people use it in its original form, others in its broadened, and still others in its secondarily restricted sense.

To illustrate the principle of this "mechanism" by at least one simple example, let us take the well-known word "America." When Martin Waldseemüller (erroneously) coined this term in 1507, it referred to that part of the New World which had been described by Amerigo Vespucci: South America (or, more precisely speaking, certain parts of it). Later, the term was broadened to include both South and North America. Still later, people, when speaking of "America," frequently had only North America in mind, or, even more specifically, the U.S.A.—a political part of North America.

As can be seen from this one example—out of thousands—such things happen in our everyday language. They are even more common in science. Since scientists often feel a need to use special terms for special subjects, they may even cut several "pieces" out of the same broadened term with the result that they finally all use the same word, but each of them means something different.

I once experienced an almost classic case during a discussion between psychologists, philosophers, and ethologists. Among other things, we came to speak of "displacement," and the discussion ended in utter confusion. As it turned out later, all three groups had meant something different when they used the word (in addition to which, we ethologists had minor differences of opinion among ourselves). The ethologists had in mind a behavior which results from an inner conflict of opposite tendencies and is irrelevant to the situation. For example, when aggression and escape tendencies are conflicting in an animal during an agonistic encounter, the animal may neither fight nor flee, but instead groom itself. The psychologists were thinking of a behavior that more or less coincides with a "redirected response," in the terminology of ethologists: an animal's directing its reaction toward a substitute object, as when an angry man does not beat up his opponent but bangs his fist on the table. The philosophers, finally, had spatial displacement in mind; for example, when a person is displaced. At least one of the participants in the discussion found this situation alarming. Indeed, it is.

I would not speak about this linguistic confusion here if it did not play such an enormous role in a discussion of "communication" and "expression" and all the subjects and terms related to these topics: "sender," "recipient," "meaning," "sign," "signal," "symbol," etc. The reader may well encounter the same words used here in another publication, but with more or less different meanings. Or he may sometimes encounter the opposite situation--different terms that mean precisely the same things we have in mind here. In any case, I am not arrogant enough to believe that I am capable of solving all these problems, and it also is at least not the primary purpose of this chapter to add more definitions to the dozens already existing in literature, and/or to investigate whether and to what extent several more or less different interpretations of the terms are justifiable and possible. However, it is germane to point out in which sense certain terms are used in this book, how they particularly apply to ungulate behavior, and also which behaviors of hoofed mammals are considered to fall into the central realm of a given term or category and which ones appear to be more peripheral to it, since the best approach, given this Tower-of-Babel situation, may be to find out in which sense a given term can be used without any doubt and then to proceed from this central realm to cases which appear to be related but are not beyond possible reservations.

As a matter of fact, the area in which the word "communication" has been applied, by many and often very different branches of science and technology, is enormous. Sometimes one may get the impression that the word has been inflated to such an extent that it comprises any stimulus-response situation or at least any kind of social interaction and/or any process in which some kind of "information" (in its likewise enormously inflated sense) is involved. For the type of communication we have in mind here, it appears to be essential (a) that two living and complete animals interact as a sender and a recipient (other more or less synonymous terms used in literature for "sender" are "addressor," "communicator," "transmitter," etc.; more or less synonymous terms for "recipient" are "receiver," "addressee," "communicant," "target," etc.); (b) that the sender is aiming for a more or less definite response of the recipient, and (c) that the recipient's response is not brought about by mechanical means or forces on the sender's part. As Cherry (1957) put it: when somebody tells a man to jump into a pool, this is an act of communication, while pushing him in is not. Furthermore, (d) a perfect case of communication is a mutual and circular process; the sender becomes aware of the recipient's response. I consider this dialogue-type situation to be the central realm of communication, and it appears to be didactically advisable to make it a starting point in our discussions. However, I may emphasize that when speaking of a central realm of communication, I mean it in the sense of a phenotypical prototype. I do not wish to imply that this central realm was the origin from which the more peripheral forms of communication phylogenetically evolved. On the contrary, it was probably the other way around.

Taking these aspects into account, I propose the following operational definition: Communication is a form of social interaction in which a sender addresses a recipient and delivers a message to him by signs, signals, or symbols, aiming for an adequate response. In the case of a dialogue-like situation, the recipient's response is recognized by the sender and it, in turn, influences the sender's behavior. For example, a dominant bull (sender) turns toward (addressing) a subordinate herd member (recipient) and threatens him (message) by presenting his horns (signal). The subordinate withdraws (recipient's response), whereupon the dominant ceases his display (influence of the recipient's response on the sender's behavior).

At first sight, none of this appears too complicated or too difficult to understand. The sad truth is that almost every word of this seemingly simple definition is loaded with problems. Some of them are even so difficult that our contemporary science can hardly answer them (e.g., problems of animal awareness). It also does not make the discussion easier that all the terms in our definition (sender, recipient, message, signal, etc.) are so interrelated that it is impossible to fully understand one of them before one has understood the others. This is like a ring which does not have a beginning or an end. However, a discussion must have a beginning—and, fortunately, also an end. There is no choice other than to cut this ring somewhere. We will do it at its relatively (!) "softest" and easiest section by beginning with the last part.

That the recipient's response is recognized by the sender and influences his behavior is sometimes not mentioned in definitions of communication. This is understandable when we think of the broad field to which this term has been extended. For example, when certain plants secrete chemical compounds (which apparently are considered by some authors to contain some kind of "information") that hinder the growth of other plants, there is, of course, no possibility that the "senders" (or more correctly speaking, the producers) can recognize the reactions of these other plants. Consequently, the production of "information" goes on regardless of whether it is effective, and even regardless of whether there are "recipients." In such and similar cases we may notice with a certain satisfaction that our definition is not applicable; it is precisely these cases which we wish to exclude from our discussion.

However, this part of our definition also cannot be applied to cases in which the senders are animals but are not in sight of the recipients, and/or address not individual partners but a certain class of partners. Such cases definitely occur in hoofed mammals, and they probably should be included in a discussion of communicative behavior. These problems will be investigated later. For the moment, it may be enough to say that such cases belong to the—in a sense outlined above—peripheral realms of communication.

In dialogue-type communication, the recipient's response influences the sender's behavior. Theoretically, one could argue that it is sufficient for the sender to be aware of the recipient's response, that it is not necessary for him to behaviorally react to it. However, practically speaking—and particularly with respect to animals—we can usually only take it from the sender's change in behavior that he has recognized the recipient's response.

The sender recognizes from the recipient's response that the other "has got the message." The most common result is that he stops signaling—at least, that signal which he has used until now (he may possibly continue the communication by other signals). In certain cases, the sender's reaction to the recipient's response also offers an additional possibility to the observer for recognizing what the sender had expected the recipient to do by providing the signal—a very important but somewhat difficult problem in animal communication (p. 26). If the recipient has not reacted, or not reacted in the expected way, to the sender's signal, the latter may continue and reinforce his display, or he may try, by physical means, to force the partner to respond. For example, when a dominant animal threatens a subordinate, and the latter does not react by withdrawal, submission, etc., the sender may now physically attack the subordinate. Less frequently in hoofed mammals, he may eventually stop signaling, and possibly perform a "conflict behavior" (e.g., grooming) if the communication has not worked.

The most important presupposition for the recipient's response is that he "has got the message," i.e., he must have perceived the sender's signal and must have understood it. This "understanding" results from an "agreed-upon code" which sender and recipient have in common, whether it be that their sending and receiving devices are innately and phylogenetically adapted to each other—more or less according to the principles of key stimuli and innate releasing mechanisms (details can be taken from any ethology textbook)—or whether it be that sender and recipient have both learned the same things. This "agreed-upon code" plays a great role in much literature on communication, and it certainly has its important and interesting aspects. We will need to mention some of them when discussing certain special problems of expression or of the communication between animals of different species. However, since the bulk of our discussions concerns the communication between animals of the same species (intraspecific communication), we can largely unburden this text from questions concerning the "agreed-upon code": we can simply take it for granted that a recipient is able to understand the signals of a conspecific sender.

For purposes of our discussion, it appears to be more important that the recipient's response is adequate. Hence the sender's message largely restricts the number of the recipient's possible responses; however, it never limits them to only one. In other words, out of the great number of possible reactions in an animal's species-specific behavioral repertoire, only a very few adequately meet a definite message of the sender; however, there is always at least one alternative. This "degree of freedom" in the recipient's response is significantly different from the principle of causation in classic mechanics and largely also from the stimulus-response principle in physiology.

Perhaps the simplest example of verbal communication in humans is the question-answer situation. "Did you see Mr. X today?" This question considerably limits the number of adequate responses: for example, "perhaps" would be a rather silly answer. But the alternatives "yes" or "no" are absolutely possible, and both adequately meet the question.

An alternative that is always possible in animals such as ungulates is for the recipient to ignore the sender's signal and not react to it. In some cases, this simply means that the communication has failed. The sender may cease signaling, or he may repeat the signal, or use a different signal, or take stronger measures such as physical attack.

On the other hand, there are situations in which no response is a response. For example, when a weak or subordinate animal aggressively displays to a strong and high-ranking herd member, the latter may just ignore the threat. This unshakable attitude of the recipient can have a strong effect upon the subordinate sender. In some cases, he may even turn and flee at full gallop. Above all, no response as being a response seems to be a frequent behavior of females in the courtship rituals of hoofed mammals, and it adequately fits this situation: when the female no longer actively responds (by defense, etc.) to the male's displays, she is ready to tolerate his mounts.

Besides not reacting to the sender's signal, there are mainly two types of alternatives in the responses of ungulate recipients. The first may be said to work along some kind of intensification scale. For example, the recipient's responses to a threat display of a dominant sender may involve assuming a submissive posture (in which again different degrees of intensity are possible) without leaving the place, or withdrawing by walking (at any of a number of different speeds), or fleeing at a full gallop—to name the most common responses which seem to belong to the same major category (inferiority behavior in this case).

The other type of alternative responses works according to the principle of a dichotomy in effects; the alternative responses to the same display are more or less opposite behaviors. Here, much depends on the physical condition and the social situation of the recipient relative to that of the sender. For example, a threat display may have a challenging or intimidating effect upon the recipient, depending on whether he is equal or unequal to the sender. If the sender is considerably stronger or of higher social status than the recipient, the latter usually responds to the sender's threat by submission, withdrawal, or even flight. If he is at least of approximately equal strength or social status, he commonly responds by an equivalent counter-display (most frequently the same as shown by the sender), occasionally even by an immediate attack. These two alternatives—taking the challenge or performing an inferiority behavior—certainly are opposites but both are adequate responses to an aggressive display.

With the discussion of the intensity scale in the recipient's responses and of the dichotomy in effects, we have approached the problem of the influence of circumstantial factors in communication—some authors (e.g., Smith 1977) would say the "context," a term which in my opinion can lead to misunderstandings. Of course, circumstantial factors comprise more aspects than the physical strength and the social status of the participants (e.g., when a standing animal directs a threat display toward a resting herd member, the latter's response may be different depending upon whether this happens at the beginning or at the end of a resting period, etc.), and they concern not only the recipient's response, but also the sender's message. Consequently, some authors have put great emphasis on circumstantial factors in communication. We will return to these when we speak of motivating situations later in this book. On the other hand, at least in hoofed mammals, these situational motivations and with them the circumstantial modifications of messages and responses appear to be restricted to a quite tolerable number of categories and are not too difficult to understand. Moreover, such circumstantial factors do not change the sender's signals and their basic messages, nor do they cause considerably more modifications in the recipient's responses than those which work along the intensity scale or according to the dichotomy principle mentioned above. Thus, when talking here of principal points of communication, there is no need for an extensive consideration of the influence of circumstances beyond the mentioned aspects.

Very important, however, is another, final problem related to the role of the recipient in communicative processes. Up to now, we have talked of a dialogue-like situation in which sender and recipient are in view of each other, and the sender clearly addresses a definite partner. A minor variation is given in the—on the whole, rare—cases in which the sender does not display to one individual recipient but to several of them standing more or less closely together. In such cases, the single recipient has much greater latitude as to whether he relates the sender's signal to himself and reacts to it than in situations in which he is individually and "very personally" addressed.

The role of the recipient in a communication process—his readiness to react to the sender's signal—becomes even more prominent when sender and recipient are not in sight of each other and the recipient can only hear the sender's vocalizations or smell an odor emitted by him, etc. On the sender's part, such signals can still be more or less individually addressed. For example, when in a dense forest, although he does not see the other he can hear or smell him, so that he is aware of the other's presence or approach. However, as compared to a face-to-face situation, this communication is more anonymous, in that the recipient's reaction is not as directly under the sender's control.

Such cases may be considered to be transitions to the completely anonymous "to-whom-it-may-concern" type of communication in which the sender gives (e.g., a vocalization) or leaves (e.g., a scent mark) some kind of message without a partner actually being present, and addresses not an individual, but a certain class of potential recipients. In the broadest sense, this may be just any conspecific. In more specific cases, it may be any conspecific of the opposite sex, or any conspecific of the same sex or status (e.g., any potential rival), etc. It is a matter of mere chance or, at best, of a certain probability, that a recipient will become aware of such a sign; and when he becomes aware of it, he is outside the sender's immediate sphere of influence, and the sender cannot see his reaction. With this pure "to-whom-it-may-concern" type we have reached the peripheral realms of communication. From here it is only a small step, or a more or less gradual transition respectively, to cases which obviously do not belong to communication anymore—at least when we take this term seriously and try to keep it free of undue inflation.

For example, quite a number of hoofed mammals mark objects (grass stems, branches, etc.) with the secretion of skin glands at their heads (preorbital glands, frontal glands, etc.), and this usually is a very special procedure, which we shall discuss later in detail. Provided that such a marked object is later encountered by a conspecific and that he reacts to the mark, one could argue that this secretion is some kind of sign or signal of the "to-whom-it-may-concern" type, and thus one could still speak of an act of communication in such a case. However, some of these animals also have glands near their hooves (interdigital glands), and/or at the "knees" of their forelegs (metacarpal glands), and/or at the posterior region of their bellies (inguinal glands). Secretion of these glands may be deposited when the animal moves through high grass, or when it beds down for a rest. However, this deposition of secretion is not due to any special behavioral act, but is unavoidably linked to the animal's usual maintenance activities (walking, resting, etc.). Thus, one could hardly say that the animal has "given a signal" and "sent a message," even if later a conspecific finds this secretion and can take something from it about the producer's species, sex, age, or physiologic stage. And if, for some reason, someone wished to insist that such a case be considered a form of communication, what is to be made of the next small step—that an animal not possessing such glands simply leaves its tracks on the ground? Again, a conspecific may later more or less accidentally encounter these tracks and find something out about the first animal's species, sex, or state, and may possibly follow them. However, by now probably even the most inveterate defender of a broad conception of "communication" will have some scruples about using this term, and such scruples certainly are not out of place.

The gradual vanishing of the communicative character in the events mentioned above is mainly due to changes in the sender-recipient relationship. In the central realm of communication—the dialogue-type situation—the sender plays a decisive role. In the peripheral realms of communication, the role of the sender becomes more and more moderate until finally one can hardly speak of a "sender" anymore, and the interaction rests more or less completely with the recipient who "reads" something out of the (indications of the) other's presence and/or movements. In a sense, the other *is* no sender, but the recipient *makes* him a "sender"—or better, a source—without the other having given a signal and sent a message. In the animal kingdom, good examples of the latter can be found in predator-prey relationships. The flight of a prey animal may release the predator's pursuit, or certain movements of the predator may make the prey aware of the predator's presence and hunting intentions so that it reacts to them by withdrawal, flight, or hiding. In humans, this can be carried to the extent that the source need not even be a living being or the product of a living being—for example, when we recognize the coming of bad weather from the formation of clouds. The clouds are not senders who address us by signals and deliver a message to us. We "read" information out of their appearance. Of course, one can define "communication" in such a way that it even comprises such cases. The question is whether it makes sense to do so, and whether the term "communication" does not lose its value when broadened to such an extent.

The concept of the sender is so interrelated to that of the recipient that it was necessary when discussing the recipient's situation and responses to mention the sender over and over. In particular, the sender's prominent role in a dialogue-type communication has already been emphasized. It even appears that all the other aspects of communication may simply follow from the concept of the term "sender" if one takes it seriously and literally enough. However, not many authors seem to be inclined to do so. Some of them even try to evade the issue by substituting another, and, with respect to the problems under discussion, vaguer and more neutral word such as "communicator," "transmitter," "source," etc. As always, however, going around a problem does not make it disappear.*

Taken literally, sending is an active process; thus there is no such thing as a passive sender. For example, when an animal merely reacts to another's presence or unavoidable spoor of presence, one cannot speak of a sender, or of a communication either. It is only when the other animal behaviorally emphasizes its presence that it may become a sender and a communication process may develop.

Moreover, there is a difference between a "sender" and a "producer" or a "source." One may perhaps say that a sender is always a producer, but one cannot say that any producer would be a sender. For example, the human body *produces* sweat and its typical odor under certain circumstances. However, although another person may see or smell it, nobody will say that we *send* sweat or its odor to another human. It seems to me that quite a number of authors speak of a "sender" or a "communicator," respectively, when they merely mean a producer.

The essential difference is that the term "producing" lacks any directional implications and does not, at least not necessarily, imply the existence of an addressee (as when the human body produces sweat), whereas the term "sending" postulates a process being addressed and aimed at an—at least potential—recipient. Only in the latter case can one speak of a true communication.

When we insist on the term "sender" as being a substantial part of a conception of communication, and when we take it in the strict sense as suggested above, two further questions arise: the problem of ad-

---

*Cherry (1957), in his frequently cited book on human communication, argues against the use of the term "sender" for other reasons, stressing the point that communication is an act of sharing; he writes (I am quoting from the 1978 edition): "The word communication comes from the Latin *communico* meaning to share. [To the best of my recollection, the Latin infinitive meaning "to share" is *communicare*—FW.] We do not send messages; we always share them. Messages then are not goods or commodities which can be exchanged or sent from one person to another. Thus, if I tell you something, I have not lost it. . . ."

In my opinion, these arguments against the term "sender" miss the point. About 140 years ago, certain philosophers found that one must distinguish between material goods and "goods of the mind" (experience, knowledge, information, etc.) and that these nonmaterial goods are not diminished when shared with others—in contrast to material goods. Thus, when Cherry rightly states that the sender does not lose anything when sending a message, but that now both sender and recipient share it, this proves only that a message does not belong to the class of material goods, not that a message cannot be sent. Moreover, it is quite commonplace to say "I have sent him a message." In short, I think I only follow common usage when I speak of the sender of a message, the sender of a signal, etc., and I do not think that the concept of sending a message is incongruent with that of sharing the (contents of a) message between sender and recipient.

dressing, and the problem of the sender's aiming at a definite response of the recipient.

In a dialoguelike communication, the animal which plays the role of the sender does not simply perform a given display, it performs this display *with respect to the recipient* (Fig. 1), i.e., the sender addresses the recipient. For example, when using a threat display in a face-to-face encounter, the sender does not only signal "I am ready to fight," he signals "I am ready to fight *you*."

Except for a very few special cases, addressing goes hand in hand with the sender's orienting and directing himself toward the recipient in hoofed mammals. One must, however, keep in mind that this "directing" toward the recipient is primarily the directing of a display (threat display, courtship display, dominance display, submissive display, etc.), and thus it does not always imply a frontal orientation of the sender. Frequently, it is a frontal display. On the other hand, broadside displays are quite common in hoofed mammals (Fig. 1a), with the sender assuming a lateral orientation to the recipient. In other cases—such as in female sexuality, in certain submissive postures, and (in animals such as horses that fight by kicking with their hind legs) in certain agonistic displays—the sender may orient himself with his hindquarters toward the recipient. However, it does not make a principal difference whether the sender orients himself frontally, laterally, or with his hindquarters to the recipient; in all these cases, he addresses him and directs his display toward him. Furthermore, one has to take into account that orientation of the head plays an especially important role in these animals when addressing a partner (Fig. 1b). Thus, it happens quite frequently that the sender does not bring his entire body but only his head into a—frontal, lateral, or reverse—orientation toward the addressee according to the *pars pro toto* principle.

The decisive component in this process of addressing is the sender's turn, i.e., the emphasized and often mimically exaggerated change from his "until-now" position into a new orientation relative to the recipient (Fig. 1). This "I-mean-you" component suggests that many displays of hoofed mammals are much more aimed, purposive, and intentionally used than many authors (e.g., Cherry 1957) wish to acknowledge for animals.

Readers with some knowledge in ethology and physiology may perhaps raise the objection that this addressing is nothing but a tropism (taxis). Certainly, one could take into consideration whether the addressing processes have phylogenetically originated from tropisms. On the other hand, addressing as we have it in mind here cannot be satisfactorily explained by tropisms, in my opinion; at least,

Fig. 1a. The alpha bull (left) of a mixed, migratory herd of East African oryx antelope (*Oryx beisa callotis*) has stopped a straggler by assuming a broadside position in front of him (lateral T-position). The subordinate bull (right) responds with a head-low posture. b. The dominant bull turns his head toward the subordinate with intention to high presentation of horns. c. The subordinate turns and withdraws. The dominant ceases displaying and looks after him. (Walther 1978*d*. Serengeti National Park.)

it would have to be a very special kind of "tropism." Two simple arguments may suffice here. First, in addressing, as previously mentioned, the animal often does not orient "itself" to the recipient, but instead orients the *display* toward him. Thus, when the animal uses two different displays toward the same partner in the same encounter, its orientations to the recipient can be very different. For example, a horned ungulate may first use an erect broadside posture (Fig. 1a) and subsequently a horn presentation (Fig. 1b) toward an opponent. In such a case, standing on the same spot, at the same distance, and with the opponent in the same position as before, the sender is laterally oriented to the recipient during the broadside display, but he—or, at least, his head—is frontally oriented toward him in the horn presentation. I hardly see how these changes of the sender's orientation can be explained by the tropism theory.

Second, it is by no means rare in gregarious hoofed mammals that an animal is part of a group, with several conspecifics standing around it at equal distances and at equal angles. Thus, the stimulus situation for a tropism is more or less the same with several group members. However, when displaying, the animal addresses only one of them. Again, this "choice" is hard to explain by a tropism.

As stated above, the addressing with a directional component in it is very frequent in the communication of hoofed mammals, and its communicative character is clear and obvious. However, even when sender and recipient are in view of each other, directing and addressing may diverge in special cases, as when, in an agonistic encounter, the sender for some reason does not attack the opponent but a substitute, frequently an inanimate object. Or, when the approach of a dominant herd member releases aggressive tendencies in a subordinate, the latter may perform a threat display that, since he does not "dare" direct it toward the dominant, is directed sideways "into the air." In such and similar cases, the action is not directed toward the partner concerned, and thus the precision of the addressing process is considerably diminished. On the other hand, one may still speak of a kind of addressing since the display is clearly released by the other's presence and/or behavior, the latter can definitely perceive it, and it is absolutely appropriate for delivering a definite message to him.

The addressing process becomes most problematic in the peripheral realms of communication: for example, when an animal utters a special vocalization (e.g., a rutting call) without any recipient actually being present. However, one may argue that such a signal is still "made" for a (potential) recipient of a given class; i.e., when perceived by a conspecific of a definite sex, and/or age, and/or psycho-physiological condition, it can influence his behavior. As always in the "to-whom-it-may-concern" type, of course, the major part of the communication process is now with the recipient, and the role of the sender's addressing has dwindled to a minimum; however, such a minimum may still be said to be recognizable.

Very important, very interesting, and very difficult are the problems of the sender's aiming at a definite response from the recipient. Frequently, one will hear the opinion that such an aiming would require awareness and conscious intentions on the part of the sender; however, this is not necessarily so. Even when we think only of human communication, we find all shades of transition from a fully conscious to an absolutely unconscious aiming for a recipient's response. The latter may even go so far that it takes place against our conscious will and that we—more or less successfully—try to prevent it. For example, if somebody enters my office who disturbs me during important work and is unwelcome, I can tell him to go away. This may be said to be a conscious aiming for a definite response of the recipient—although it may happen that I put my request into words which I later regret and may try to excuse by the well-known phrase "I did not mean it" which clearly indicates that even this verbal action was not fully under my conscious control. The proportion of unconscious intention is even greater in the case of gestures, as for example, if I raise my arm and shake my fist at the unwelcome intruder. This gesture clearly aims for the other's withdrawal in this situation, but—as anybody with some gift of self-observation will readily confirm—the aggressive raising of the arm, at least, is initiated before any conscious consideration takes place. In a sense, I become aware of my action only after my arm is already raised, and then I may continue the gesture consciously. Even when I do not use such a gesture and I also do not say anything, my facial expression may still indicate so much fury and aggression that it clearly signals that the other had better leave. Except in the very special case of acting, such facial expressions are even more outside our conscious control than gestures of the limbs. Finally, if I were to belong to the very small class of people who have perfectly mastered the difficult art of controlling their gestures and facial expressions (as a matter of fact, I do not), I might keep smiling and try to be polite to the disliked and unwanted visitor, but I could never be sure that my hostile feelings would not break through, eventually, in an unconscious action— perhaps a *lapsus linguae* of the Freudian type. In short, the aiming at a recipient's response is not exclusively a matter of conscious intentions, not even in humans.

Ethologists usually try to go around the question of animal awareness, which includes the problem of conscious intentions in animals. However, this question cannot be permanently silenced by taking an agnostic attitude. Consequently and rightly, at least two outstanding scientists, Griffin (1976) and Hediger (1980), have recently raised it again. Personally, I am convinced that it will be impossible to avoid the problem of animal awareness in a discussion on communication and expression in the long run. However, I think it is neither absolutely necessary nor the right place to discuss it in this book. It may be sufficient to say here that, in my opinion, gestures, vocalizations, etc., which aim at definite responses from the recipient may originally be performed without conscious intentions on the part of the sender in hoofed mammals. However, it is absolutely unlikely that animals of the organizational level and with the learning capacity of ungulates are and remain unaware of what they are doing and, above all, of the effects which their displays have upon the recipients, and that they then may come to use these displays deliberately, or, at least, in the same "half-conscious" way that we may use gestures such as raising the arm and shaking the fist. Leyhausen (1967) came to very similar conclusions in his studies of felid behavior. For the present discussion, however, the conception of conscious intention in the sender's aiming at the recipient's response does not appear to be absolutely necessary and may be left aside by those readers who are unwilling to accept it, since there is enough evidence that this aiming can be brought about without conscious intention.

When we speak of "intention" without raising the question of whether it is conscious, we refer to the fact that certain movements, postures, vocalizations, etc., clearly indicate to a conspecific recipient (as well as to a human observer who is familiar enough with the animal's specific behavioral repertoire) what the sender is going to do next and/or what he is expecting the recipient to do. Consequently, such behaviors are termed "intention movements" in ethology. Apparently, some people think that one can make a conclusion about the sender's intentions only by investigating the recipient's responses, and, of course, the validity of such conclusions may be doubted on theoretical grounds because the recipient's response is no convincing proof that something is going on in the sender. Therefore, it may not be superfluous to emphasize here that the investigation of the recipient's responses is only one way of approaching the problem, and not necessarily the primary or possibly even the best one. Most intention movements are the initial movements of a given action. When a goat presents its horns toward an opponent (threat display), this is the very first movement for butting. Thus, the other and more important way of determining the sender's intention is to investigate which actions are initiated by the movements under discussion. This means we can entirely remain with the sender when determining his intentions—

and the recipient's responses are only an additional confirmation of these findings. More about intention movements will be said in chapter 3.

In the case of intention movements in the outlined sense, the sender's aiming at a definite response of the recipient is often very clear and obvious—and, fortunately, such cases are frequent in communication of hoofed mammals. However, the discussion of such "aiming" problems leads us to more difficult questions which are closely linked to certain problems of signs, signals, and key stimuli. An animal may possess—sometimes very special—physical and/or behavioral structures that more or less automatically trigger certain responses in conspecific partners, but the animal is not "aiming" at a response of the recipient. The difficulties lie (a) in the distinction between this sort of "built-in" triggering of a response and "aiming" at a response, and (b) in the question of whether and to what extent this triggering of a response by a structure "built-in" for the purpose should be considered to belong to communication.

For example, in animals such as ungulates, the adults can obviously recognize a conspecific's sex—be it by smell, by his visual appearance (e.g., in species with a pronounced sexual dimorphism), or by sex-specific behavior patterns (e.g., differences in the male and female urination and/or defecation postures), etc. Such physical or behavioral characteristics can work like signals (and, according to certain theoretical concepts of signs and signals, they also can be considered to be such), and they can release responses in conspecifics. An adult male may recognize another adult male at a distance, let us say, on the basis of color patterns (as, e.g., in Indian blackbuck (*Antilope cervicapra*) where only adult males have a black coat), and then— depending on his own psycho-physiological state and condition—he may stay away and withdraw or he may come closer for a display encounter and/or a fight. Thus, under certain conditions, the other male's coloration may have about the same effect upon the recipient as a threat display, and may be said to be "made" to trigger a response—very comparable to the red belly of a territorial male stickleback in spring, as has been so well investigated by Tinbergen (1951) and his students. Consequently, ethologists (e.g., Lorenz 1935, Eibl-Eibesfeldt 1970) usually unite such physical and behavioral structures with intention movements and other expressive displays within the same major category: the social releasers. Under merely functional aspects, this unification appears to be justifiable. Otherwise, however, I hope at least some of my readers will feel as uncomfortable with it as I do, and I think there are quite good reasons for such a feeling.

In the case of an intention movement functioning in social communication (e.g., when a goat turns and presents its horns toward another goat), the display, of course, is within the framework of the species-specific behavioral inventory; however, it is the animal as a subject which individually and actively addresses the recipient and aims at the individual recipient's response. In other words, the process is individualized and the displaying animal is a sender in the strict sense. However, in such cases as the black color of a male Indian blackbuck or the male's possession of horns in a species with hornless females, etc., the animal is no sender but simply the bearer of such a structure. If such a structure is "made by Mother Nature" to trigger a response in a companion, or when the latter has learned to react in a definite way to such a structure, the bearer as an individual does not aim at anything. In a sense, he cannot avoid releasing a response in a conspecific equipped with a (by phylogenetic evolution, by learning or tradition, etc.) sensitive and correspondingly adapted receiving mechanism in his central nervous system. One may perhaps approximate this situation to that of a policeman or a soldier wearing a given uniform. This also may release responses in certain people in certain situations, not because the man has done or said something, but simply because he is a wearer of that uniform. In principle, the situation is at least not too different when the animal is not or not only the bearer of a physical structure, but the performer of a mere maintenance activity (such as walking, running, eating, urinating, defecating, etc.) which also may have effects upon conspecifics under certain conditions. However, the signal character of such physical or behavioral structures gives the impression of a (possible) side effect, and it is not the animal as a subject and individual which addresses the other and aims at his response. In any case, the communication again now rests primarily with the recipient, as is typical when we leave the central realm of communication and come to its periphery or even its border.

The discussion of such problems would be a true pleasure if this border could be clearly determined. For example, when, under certain circumstances, the mere sight of a male's "uniform" releases aggression in another male, the bearer may be said to be "innocent" of the other's reaction. However, he can behaviorally emphasize his presence and actively expose himself to the other's sight, e.g., by staying in completely open terrain—in the case of a territorial male, for days and weeks—although cover may be available in the surroundings which he may readily use at other times and occasions. In such a case, the animal behaviorally supports the (possible) effects of its physical structure and the role of the bearer approximates that of a sender in a communication of the "to-whom-it-may-concern" type. In short, it seems to be impossible in the present state of our knowledge and conceptions always to make a precise cut between active aiming at a recipient's response (by which the animal becomes a true sender) and the passive release of responses by certain physical structures or unspecialized (maintenance) behaviors (i.e., the cases in which the animal is no sender, but merely the bearer of such structures). For the time being, the relatively best distinction seems to be provided by assigning the former cases to the central realm of communication, and the latter to its periphery in which the communicative character is gradually fading away. We will have to face similar problems in the later discussion on physiognomy and expressive behavior which may perhaps contribute to some further clarification.

In the operational definition of communication suggested above, I spoke of the delivering of a message by signs, signals, or symbols. Admittedly, the formulation "by signs, signals, or symbols" was rather cowardly. There are authors who treat at least "signs" and "signals" as synonymous terms. Others distinguish between "signs" and "signals." Again, others use the term "signs" as a major category with "signals" and "symbols" being its subcategories, etc. One also has distinguished more subcategories of signs, such as "icons" and "indexes." However—as far as I could figure from the literature—here, too, different authors suggest more or less different definitions and interpretations. In short, we are again confronted with the Tower of Babel confusion, and I do not feel qualified to decide who is right and who is wrong. Thus, in a sense, I try to please everybody when speaking of "signs, signals, or symbols," and I hope that most of my readers can accept this formulation without too great an inner resistance.

Regardless of how signs, signals, or symbols are defined or classified in detail, their mention is absolutely necessary in a definition of communication to distinguish it sufficiently from merely mechanical influences (the difference between telling a man to jump into the water or pushing him into it). As compared to mechanical influences upon the partners, the communication by signs, signals, or symbols has one great disadvantage which, however, is more than outweighed by at least three advantages. The disadvantage is that communication by signs, signals, or symbols is not as reliable as mechanical influences. To stay with the example of the man pushed into the water: provided that he stands close enough to the water, and that the push is strong enough, the result is certain. When I tell him to jump or signal him by gestures, he may not become aware of my actions, he may ignore or disobey my order, etc. In short, the effect is not as sure and unavoidable as when I push him. This greater insecurity of the effect is valid for any communication by signs, signals, or symbols, and this is their major disadvantage. The advantages of the communication by signs and signals are (a) that it usually needs considerably less effort on the part of the sender (but often also on the part of the recipient); (b) that—linked with this saving of energy—it can be relatively effortlessly repeated and thus several or even many recipients can be addressed one after the other; and (c) that it enables the sender to influence the partner at a distance. These advantages appear to be so important to social life that communication by signs and signals obviously has been invented in the behavioral repertoires of many and very different animal species.

Furthermore, and again regardless of whether one speaks of signs, signals, symbols, or subcategories of them, they all have one important feature in common: they are indicative and, frequently enough, also anticipating behaviors: i.e., they indicate the sender's momentary psycho-physiological state and/or his readiness for a definite action with respect to the recipient and—in combination with the last point—sometimes also what the recipient is expected to do. We will come back to these aspects in our discussion of expressive behavior. For the moment, we are concerned with the nature of signs, signals, or symbols, which is very difficult to describe adequately. There are formulations, such as: a sign, signal, etc., always "stands for something," is an "incomplete behavior," "refers to something behind it," "besides the impression it conveys to the senses, makes something else come into cognition." All these and similar definitions and interpretations have their merits, but, on the other hand, they appear to be somewhat inadequate formulations at least with respect to signals such as postures, gestures, vocalizations, etc. For example, when an animal or a man is in a state of emotional arousal, this has its physiological aspects, its psychological aspects, and its behavioral aspects. Only the latter occur on the surface of the body (postures, gestures, color changes, vocalizations, etc.), and they are the signals. The division of the process into physiological, psychological, and behavioral aspects and their more or less isolated treatment is probably unavoidable when one takes the limits of our human modes of recognition and of scientific investigation into account. However, it is absolutely an artifact. In reality, the whole process is one unit. Thus, it certainly is no adequate formulation when one says that such signs or signals would "stand for something," "refer to something," "make something else come into cognition"; rather, they *are* the thing, i.e., they are that part of the process which externally appears. This being part of a more complex process apparently has given rise to the formulations mentioned above and may be said to be the grain of truth in them. Furthermore, one may say (although I am by no means convinced that this was what the inventors of such phrases had in mind) that, for example, a fighting action "stands behind" a threat display since the latter is the intention movement for fighting and frequently fighting is the next action to follow after it. Thus, the display gets its relevance from a potential action "behind it."

Likewise, the talk about signals as being "incomplete behaviors" has its right and its wrong points. Many signals are very elaborate displays, and thus they are by no means incomplete. However, they are not executive actions: they "only" indicate the *readiness* for a given action. To stay with the example of a threat display, this can be an absolutely complete behavior in itself but it is no fighting action. It shows that the sender is ready to fight the recipient, but he is not yet fighting him. Insofar as they indicate the sender's readiness for definite executive actions, signs and signals frequently are of an anticipating nature; and since—what apparently has sometimes been overlooked in literature—they often are not only "descriptions of the sender's state" but of his state *with respect to the recipient*, and since, furthermore, there is always only a very limited number of adequate responses to each signal, they may also anticipate the recipient's reaction, and thus, they not only indicate what the sender is going to do next but also what he expects the recipient to do. The latter becomes particularly evident in two cases: (a) when a recipient has ignored or insufficiently reacted to a sender's display (e.g., a threat), the latter may take stronger measures (e.g., attack him) that indicate that the recipient has not done what the displaying sender had expected him to do; and (b) when an animal performs a display that "invites" a definite action of the recipient, e.g., when a female assumes the copulatory posture in front of the male during a mating ritual without being mounted as yet.

Insofar as signs and signals indicate the readiness to perform a given action but are not executive behaviors, one could also say that they are all more or less symbolic—if one takes the terms "symbol" and "symbolic" in a broad sense, which frequently seems to be the case in ethological literature. However, some authors wish to restrict the term "symbol" to cases of substitutive representation, so that the sign is an item on its own and exists independently of the producer, that it represents something without being that thing, as a flag with stars and stripes represents the United States of America. Most of these authors also have the opinion that symbols in this sense are the prerogative of humans. However, there exist phenomena that fulfill the requirements of a definition of symbols in animals such as hoofed mammals—and it certainly is noteworthy that they concern communicative mechanisms that are absolutely primitive in terms of evolution as well as of general aspects of communication.

Perhaps I should mention at this point that a certainly rough but in many regards useful "classification" used by biologists is that of intrinsic and extrinsic signs and signals. Intrinsic signals are bound to the animal's body—a facial expression, movements of the tail, postures of the torso or the neck, etc. Extrinsic signals have a physical existence of their own, apart from their producer. Thus, they come close to being symbols in the strict sense or are even synonymous with symbols. At least with hoofed mammals, such extrinsic signals are predominantly dung piles and secretion marks. These are independent items and they can substitutively represent (the presence of) their producers.

These few examples may suffice here. In this book, problems arising from the use of the term "symbols" are largely avoided. Only the term "symbolic action" is used in a rather special sense which will be discussed in more detail in chapter 3.

Another general problem of communication lies in the relationship between message and signal (or sign, or symbol). We touched on this problem when we stated that a signal indicates the readiness of an animal for a certain action with respect to a recipient and that it aims at an adequate response from the latter. When one takes this readiness in a somewhat general and abstract way, and when one adds the recipient's response for which the signal is aiming, one has the message. To stay with the example of a goat presenting its horns toward another goat, this display concretely indicates the sender's readiness for butting with the horns. Under slightly more abstract terms, we may say that it indicates his readiness for fighting, i.e., it is a threat, and the term "threat" already refers to the message. For the completion of the latter, it is only necessary to add the aiming for the recipient's response, e.g., withdrawal. Thus, "translated" into human language, the message of that signal—the presentation of the horns—is "I am ready to fight you—go away" or "I am ready to fight you—come on," when we consider the dichotomous effects of such threat displays. The major reason why signals and messages cannot simply be treated as being identical in a discussion on behavior of hoofed mammals is that several different signals may deliver the same message. This is often true in animals of the same species, but it becomes even more important when animals of different species are considered. The ibex's rising on the hind legs, the wildebeest's dropping to the "knees," the elk's presentation of antlers, the horse's lifting of one hind leg are certainly different behaviors and different signals, but they are all threats and have the same basic message.

Readers with some knowledge of theoretical problems of communication probably will have noticed the absence of the word "meaning" from both our operational definition and our previous discussion. This term is another horrifying example of how an originally absolutely meaningful (!) word can be ridden to death by verbal confusion, and discussions about the "meaning of meaning" are endless, so that finally certain contemporary authors have suggested that one should discuss problems of communication without "meaning." (The reader is invited to think about this sentence for a moment—there is a nice ambiguity about it.) Since we primarily have in mind the problems of communication in hoofed mammals, not a discussion of all the theoretical problems of communication in general, I have largely tried to avoid this term and its discussion; however, it has occasionally shown up implicitly. When we talked about the adequate response of the recipient, the implication was that the latter's behavior meaningfully meets the sender's message (restriction of the recipient's reactions by the sender's signal). Thus, adequate response and meaningful response are synonymous terms. Furthermore, when the sender is aiming for a definite response of the recipient, the response which he expects or intends to elicit may be said to be the meaning which the sender puts into his message (Cherry 1957). Finally, one may speak of a meaning which the recipient extracts from the sender's message. Normally, this will be the same as what the sender has put into it. However, occasionally—particularly when the sender and recipient belong to different species, or when the recipient is very young (so that not all of his receiving devices have yet matured, or that he has not yet learned the corresponding things)—the recipient may get no meaning out of the sender's signals or extract one that is different from what the sender has put into it. Thus, in principle, one must distinguish the meaning of a message on the part of the sender and that on the part of the recipient. In our discussion, we came close to the latter when mentioning the "agreed-upon code."

3. SOME THEORETICAL PROBLEMS OF EXPRESSION

As we saw from the previous chapter, the discussion of general problems of communication is burdened with quite a number of difficulties and uncertainties. Unfortunately, the situation is at least as bad, if not worse, with respect to expression. Not only is our Tower of Babel situation rampant here too but the basic theoretical problems of expression largely represent an area which has not been treated to any considerable extent. There exist many investigations and correspondingly many books and papers, on special topics, but only a very few approach truly basic problems.

The great theoretical problem of mankind is the psychosomatic problem. On the one hand, there are our wishes, feelings, emotions, our thinking, our memory, our will—in short, the psychological processes, and, on the other hand, there are the movements of our arms, legs, eyes, lips, the contractions and dilatations of our muscles, the nervous impulses coming from the central nervous system and running to the effector organs—in short, the physiological processes. As each of us knows from experience, the physiological and psychological processes work hand in hand. In the same moment in which I decide (psychological process) to raise my left arm, my muscles go to work (physiological process) and do it. But we do not know how we come from the one to the other. In expressive behavior, the connection between physiological and psychological processes is particularly close, and is, perhaps, even more striking than in other behaviors. Thus, one might think that it offers a particularly promising starting point for the investigation of the psychosomatic problem, and that the study of expression would be a central domain of human psychology. However, almost the opposite is true, and publications of psychologists on truly basic problems of expression have been rare during the last decades.

Up to the middle of this century, a few scientists—they often were not psychologists, but physicians, anatomists, zoologists, etc.—at least tried to approach basic problems of expressive behavior, but they did not get very far for several reasons. Perhaps the most important reason was that these authors usually were after a limited and special—with respect to the great field of expression, one may safely say, a too limited and too special—section of expression from the beginning, perhaps the facial expressions of humans, or the facial muscles underlying such expressions, or expression in handwriting (graphology), etc.

Because of this narrowness of focus, general considerations are always brief in these publications, and what is even worse, the authors' thinking is so absorbed by their special topics that they presume to deal with expression in general when they have at best only advanced to some principal points valid for their special field. Perhaps the most instructive example of this kind is Klages's (1936) book *"Grundlegung der Wissenschaft vom Ausdruck"* (Fundamentals of the science of expression). Klages's major interest is in graphology, and when he speaks of "expression" he always has expression in handwriting in the back of his mind, so that he considers other forms of expression more or less only as a framework to graphology. This goes so far that he himself gives examples of expressive behaviors which contradict certain principles he has derived from his graphological studies, apparently without becoming aware of the contradictions. For example, he considers expression exclusively as an epiphenomenon, as is true in handwriting, although he once quite vividly describes the gestures of an enraged man (clenching the fist, raising and shaking it, etc.) that can hardly be said to be mere epiphenomena. Thus, Klages's book perhaps provides us with the fundamentals of a science on graphology (I cannot judge it due to my limited knowledge of this field), but certainly not with those of the science of expression, as its somewhat pompous title promises.

A special word may be said about Darwin's (1872) famous work, *The Expression of the Emotions in Man and Animals*. With respect to the principal problems of expression, this book is probably the most thorough approach among those of older authors, and it has influenced certain modern ethological conceptions of the subject, particularly in that Darwin brought up and pointed out the importance of evolutionary aspects in expressive behavior, and the book introduces and describes a few carefully observed details which will always remain correct. Speaking of actions which "are the direct results of the constitution of the nervous system, and have been from the first independent of the will, and, to a large extent, of habit," Darwin takes over and elaborates Bell's (1844) conception of the relationships of emotions to processes in the autonomic nervous system (as we would say in modern terms). In this connection, he investigates blushing in humans in such a careful way that it is probably the most complete and best account on this subject ever written. However, Darwin rightly feels that this is only a relatively small section of expression. For the rest, he offers two more principles. One is that of antithesis: that certain expressive gestures, postures, etc., simply get their special message and meaning from the fact that they are the opposites of certain other expressive behaviors. This point has turned out to be fruitful and valuable, and we will come back to it later, particularly when describing and discussing concrete cases of submissive displays. On the other hand, it is also clear that the principle of antithesis covers only a relatively small and special section of expressive behavior and that it can only be used and understood when one knows the displays to which those behaviors form the opposite, and which obviously cannot be explained by the principle of antithesis. Consequently, the most original and most important principle of expression suggested by Darwin is that of "serviceable associated habits." In a nutshell, Darwin's thinking goes along the following lines: In certain situations, animals perform certain movements that are useful and adapted to these situations. For example, biting animals draw their ears backwards in a fight and in this way "take care to prevent their ears from being seized by their antagonists." (Leyhausen's studies of cat behavior [1956] in particular have shown that this drawing backwards of the ears follows from an intensive tension of the masticator muscles in a reflexlike action; it is neither a deliberate protection of the ears nor restricted to agonistic interactions—a cat may also show it, for example, when eating tough meat.) According to Darwin, these serviceable behaviors become habits; when the animals have drawn their ears back to protect them frequently enough, they will begin to do so automatically at any time when they fight, just as humans first have to learn certain behaviors that later are performed automatically—dancing, swimming, riding, etc. (This point may be valid for certain learned behaviors, but it certainly is not applicable to instinctive behavior, which Darwin had in mind.). Finally these automatic habits become associated with emotions, such as rage in the case of Darwin's favored example of the ears in biting animals. (Here, Darwin is obviously following the "association theory" that dominated psychology in his day, but, at least as a general explanation, has been abandoned since because of its many inadequacies.)

In the above, I have always added some of the objections which recent scientists would have in parentheses. There are more, but these few may suffice to demonstrate that Darwin's major hypothesis of the serviceable, associated habits is vulnerable in more than one regard, and it is almost ironic how strictly Darwin follows Lamarckian conceptions. Even when one does not take issue with the use of the association hypothesis, since in Darwin's day nothing better was available, it remains rather obscure, in his discussions, (a) from which source "the emotion" comes in his conception, (b) why this emotion and its expression are considered to be basically independent items so that they secondarily need to be brought together by an "association," and (c) how the association is supposed to work in this case since the aforementioned association theory of the psychologists dealt only with associations of perceptions, ideas, memories, etc., in a person's mind, and said nothing about an "association" of an emotion (or any other psychological process) with a behavior. These last points may be taken as examples of the greatest weakness in Darwin's approach toward principal problems of expression: he simply took too many very essential theoretical matters—expression, emotion, association, etc.—so for granted that he did not even try to define, describe, or explain them. Thus, in spite of some incontestable merits, Darwin's work forms as little basis for a general conception of expression as do Klages's books.

A related rather general weakness in the approaches of psychologists is that they usually consider expression only as one tool among many for investigating problems of human personality—their true goal. This approach has led to the inclusion of physiognomy (i.e., more or less permanent features) in the field of expression, and to its often indistinguishable intermixture with expressive behaviors. Of course physiognomy (whose validity with respect to problems of human personality will not be discussed here) has a certain relationship to expressive behavior. For example, a man or an animal that lives in fear for a long period may eventually show permanent features of fear (crouched posture of neck and body, widely opened eyes, downward pulled angles of the mouth, etc.), which in other individuals only occur as temporary movements or postures in the short moments when they actually are in fear. In principle, however, (permanent) physiognomic features and (momentary) expressive behaviors are two different matters, and the expressive behaviors are, and have to be, the primary subject of a discussion on principal problems of expression. Since psychologists, in particular the earlier ones, did not clearly distinguish (if they distinguished at all) between physiognomic features and expressive behavior, or even turned things upside down by making physiognomy the primary subject of their consideration of expression, their approaches toward general problems of expression were condemned to fail from the beginning. In addition, they frequently made methodological mistakes by confusing expression and impression, as Leyhausen (1967) has pointed out extensively. These appear to be the major reasons why the approaches of psychologists toward principal problems of expression did not take us very far and why they were more or less terminated during the last three decades.

That the discussions on expression did not come to a complete standstill and that recently even human psychologists have again begun to show an interest in these problems may be credited largely to the work of ethologists. In particular, early ethologists such as O. Heinroth and C. Whitman took a strong interest in the use of behaviors with respect to taxonomic classification. Thus they sought to find behavior patterns that are relatively frequent, striking, and easy to observe, that with certain modifications occur in more or less all the species within a genus, subfamily, or family (in a taxonomic sense) and that are not easily changed by adaptations to environmental conditions (since closely related species may live under different environmental conditions). They found, or at least believed they had found, such behaviors in the various displays shown by animals, particularly in agonistic and sexual encounters, and these were expressive behaviors. Consequently, ethologists began to think and to theorize about general problems of expression.

I shall say from the beginning that I do not think that ethologists have delivered a masterpiece in their theoretical approaches toward expression. However, three merits cannot be taken away from them: (a) ethologists kept the discussion going at a time when it had come more or less to a standstill in psychology and all the other branches of science; (b) it was ethologists who pointed out the great role of "ritualization" in expressive behaviors, i.e., a number of recognizable changes in these behaviors as compared to nonexpressive behaviors, such as exaggeration of the expressive movements, performance in slow motion, movements "freezing" into postures, rhythmical repetition, etc. (details can be taken from ethology textbooks—e.g., Eibl-Eibesfeldt 1970); (c) the research of ethologists has broadened the comparative background in this field to an almost incredible extent in a relatively short time. This tremendously broadened base of facts certainly is our strongest tool and weapon in all future approaches toward general problems of expression.

With reference to theory, ethologists made a very promising beginning with the concept of intention movements (Heinroth 1910, Daanje 1950), which we will discuss later in detail. However, later, this concept did not receive the attention which it deserved. That is, there is hardly any ethology book which does not mention intention movements, but this mention plus a few usually rather unimpressive examples is more or less it. Instead, the displacement hypothesis (Tinbergen 1940, Kortlandt 1940) began to play a great—and with respect to the general problems of expression, one may safely say an unhappy—role which still influences the ethological literature nowadays.

Whether or not the authors literally state it, the displacement hypothesis is based on the concept of functional circles (*Funktionskreise*—von Uexküll and Kriszat 1934) or major instincts (Tinbergen 1951), respectively. This concept has become established with some additions and modifications, and so we may talk about the functional circles of sexuality, aggression, territoriality, antipredator behavior, parent-offspring relationships, etc. Certainly these functional circles are more than mere products of the human fantasy; they are very useful in bringing a certain order to a multitude of phenomena, and they provide the titles for papers, books, and chapters in books—we will have to come back to them when talking about the classification of communicative and expressive behaviors. However, the concept of functional circles or major instincts involves the great danger of being taken too literally, so that a given movement, gesture, posture, or vocalization may be thought of as strictly belonging to this or that functional circle. Sometimes this is perfectly correct, but at least as frequently it is not, since it is quite common for one and the same behavior to serve two or more functions, and to show up in several different functional circles. To take one example of many: in hoofed mammals, scraping the ground with a foreleg may occur in searching for food, before lying down for a rest, before rolling on the ground, linked with urination and/or defecation, before or during a fight, etc. In short, the same behavior shows up in at least five different functional circles. Ethologists, of course, had become aware of such cases, but they insisted that such a behavior always belonged originally to only one of these functional circles. (In the example above—scraping the ground in hoofed mammals—the reader is kindly invited to make his own choice.) Thus, the question arose: how did the behavior come into the other functional circles? This is precisely the point where the displacement hypothesis came into play. This hypothesis envisioned a model of the underlying physiological mechanisms in that two opposite tendencies, such as aggression and flight in an agonistic encounter, were assumed to be activated simultaneously within the animal, and that these two opposite tendencies block each other so that neither the one nor the other occurs, and that finally the blocked nervous energy may "spark over" in the central nervous system and activate a third behavior, such as grooming, which is not blocked, and thus is eventually performed. This behavior is assumed to be neutral and irrelevant to the momentary situation of the animal; it belongs to another functional circle from which it has been displaced. Thus, the displacement hypothesis tried to give some kind of causal explanation of how a given behavior may come from one functional circle into another. With increasing knowledge, however, especially with respect to physiological processes within the central nervous system, this model became increasingly dubious, so that eventually Hinde (1966) had to state, "for causal analysis, the term [displacement activity] can no longer be used." Nevertheless, many ethologists apparently liked "displacement activity" and kept it as a "descriptive term" (although it certainly is anything but descriptive), and they continued to discover displacement activities. It is so easy: here is the observer, and over there is the animal, and now the animal does something which, in the opinion of the observer (!!), does not make sense in the present situation. Thus, he does not know what it means, but he immediately has an interpretation: this is a displacement activity. One may say that this is an abuse of the displacement hypothesis, and one may grant Tinbergen and his coworkers that this was not what they had in mind. However, they certainly opened the door for this development—"and lead us not into temptation," as the Bible says. In this way, the displacement hypothesis has become a *deus ex machina* in ethology and has given rise to endless lists of displacement movements which do not contribute anything to an understanding of the behaviors. For example, just in agonistic encounters of hoofed mammals, grooming with mouth and hind feet, scraping the ground, stamping, lying down, rolling on the ground, grazing, "alarm calls," turning the head sideward, erect posture, mounting, gland marking, urination, defecation, and other behaviors have been declared to be displacement activities. That these are not direct fighting movements goes without saying. That they are completely irrelevant and neutral in an agonistic encounter can be severely doubted in quite a number of the cases. It also does not help with respect to their classification when one unites them under the same term, because they obviously are rather heterogeneous behaviors. In short, when one declares them to be displacement activities one is no wiser than before.

With respect to the problems of expressive behavior, it is necessary to say first that Tinbergen and his followers were of the opinion that many more or less ritualized displacement activities serve as expressive displays in social communication (at least in ungulates this does not hold true, as will be shown later), and, furthermore, they developed a general conception of expressive behavior which obviously was closely related to the displacement hypothesis. They mainly restricted their discussions to threat displays (occasionally courtship displays were also taken into consideration, but hardly any other expressions), and they postulated that an animal is in a conflict between tendencies to attack and to escape in an agonistic encounter, and that the expressive displays—as far as they do not directly go back to displacement activities—are caused by this inner conflict. An argument frequently heard in such discussions is: if the animal's aggression were not inhibited by escape tendencies, the animal would not threaten but fight. One may name this the "conflict hypothesis" of expression.

Later I shall describe many concrete facts from the behavior of hoofed mammals which contradict this "conflict hypothesis." In the present theoretical discussion, I will only mention that, in this case, exclusion has apparently been mistaken for inhibition. When an animal walks, it cannot gallop at the same time, and vice versa, since walk and gallop are different modes of locomotion which largely exclude each other. This, however, does not mean that an animal would walk only when it is inhibited from galloping. Correspondingly, threat displays and fighting are different and mutually exclusive modes of aggression—as long as an animal shows threat displays, it does not fight, and when it actually fights, it cannot threaten any longer—but this does not mean that an animal would only threaten when fighting is inhibited.

Occasionally, of course, an animal may be in a conflict between aggression and fear in a hostile encounter; however, this is not generally so, and fear—or, more "objectively" speaking, escape—is no constitutive factor of threat displays. There are many situations where the rivals walk straight toward each other, either threatening all the time during the approach, or starting the threat displays as soon as they are close enough. There is nothing in the behavior of the opponents which would justify the assumption of a conflict between aggression and escape tendencies. Moreover, in encounters between unequal opponents, it usually is the *stronger and dominant* animal that performs the aggressive displays while the subordinate often withdraws without any display, and the dominant frequently shows threat displays while pursuing (!) a withdrawing or fleeing subordinate (Fig. 54.). It simply does not make sense that the stronger and dominant partner should be inhibited by escape tendencies in such encounters. More examples of this kind will be described later in this text. Applied generally, the "principle" that in a hostile encounter the animal is in a conflict between aggression and fear simply because it is in a hostile encounter comes unpleasantly close to a dogma, which is out of place in science.

The facts point toward the conclusion that, in principle, each expressive behavior represents only one tendency, e.g., a threat display indicates the readiness for (offensive or defensive) fighting and nothing else. In special cases sometimes two or more tendencies, e.g., aggression* and escape, may be activated simultaneously. Then the threat display, as the expression of fighting intentions, may be combined with an expression indicative of flight tendencies. However, these are special cases and the combination of expressions of aggression with expressions of fear is merely additive: features of the two may occur side by side, but the threats exclusively express the aggressive tendencies and are not brought about by a conflict with escape tendencies. Analyses of such combinations are only possible under the presupposition that each single expressive feature is indicative of only one tendency.

As mentioned several times, we will have to come back to corresponding facts and conclusions over and over later in this book. With respect to the theoretical situation, it is sufficient to say that in spite of the multitude of contradictory facts and contradictory logical conclusions, the "conflict hypothesis" of expression still prevails in ethological literature. Unfortunately, this is also true for the unquestionably most elaborate and comprehensive ethological contribution to the theoretical problems of expression: Leyhausen's (1967) discussion of the biology of expression and impression, a paper which has received inadequate appreciation. Although Leyhausen's contribution is more thorough than anything else produced by ethologists in this area, and although he distances himself from the Tinbergian views in many regards, he still retains the "conflict hypothesis," although in a modified and more subtle form. This becomes especially clear in his definition of expression.

To understand Leyhausen's point of view, we must first take a glimpse at another definition of expressive behavior. Human psychologists had eventually come to a definition which perhaps, for their purposes, was quite acceptable. Leaving aside the various modifications by different authors, this definition may be put into these words: Expressive behaviors are all those externally perceptible, bodily changes of an organism by which it voluntarily or involuntarily demonstrates its psychological condition. As stated above, many ethologists take an agnostic attitude toward psychological processes in animals. Consequently, they did not accept this or similar definitions. More severe is another objection: this definition of expressive behavior stands and falls with the validity and the completeness of the underlying (psychological) mechanisms, and these are by no means

---

* The word "aggression" is not used in the same sense throughout the behavioral literature (Tower of Babel!). Some authors wish to restrict it to offensive fighting or, even more specifically, to a completely unprovoked attack. Other authors use it in a much broader sense, i.e., as a major category that includes both offensive and defensive behaviors. In this book, the term "aggression" is always meant in this broad sense.

beyond any doubt and discussion, even when we stay exclusively with the human situation. Usually the authors base the categories of the underlying psychological processes on their everyday experiences and their spontaneous subjective impressions of them, and they end up with long lists of expressions. For example, Leonhard (1949) mentions sixty-five human feelings and emotions, such as fear, rage, joy, grief, friendliness, hate, disgust, amusement, having fun, etc., which he considers to be reflected by different expressions. However, these underlying feelings and emotions have their own problems and questionable points. For example, relatively often psychological categories which are treated as equal items in such a list, are in truth rather unequal (in the few examples mentioned above, one may doubt whether the "feeling of amusement" is as different from "having fun" as it is from "disgust"), and one can never be sure whether even the longest list of underlying psychological processes is approximately complete.

Leyhausen also based his definition of expression on underlying mechanisms. However, being a "good ethologist," he did not take psychological, but physiological, mainly central-nervous, processes into consideration. In principle, however, this does not make much difference; such a system also stands and falls with the validity and completeness of the underlying—now physiological—processes against which one may raise the same objections as against the psychological ones plus the further objection that in a tremendous number of concrete cases of expressive behaviors the underlying physiological processes are unknown or at best only hypothetical at present. Furthermore, Leyhausen combines this concept of the underlying mechanism with an elaborate form of the "conflict hypothesis." He writes: "Ausdruck sind jene Veränderungen im effektorischen System eines Organismus, welche die jeweils in der Minorität befindlichen Tendenzen hervorrufen" (Expressions are those changes in the effector system of an organism which are brought about by the minority of the tendencies momentarily involved). Thus, Leyhausen—here obviously following Tinbergen's views—also presumes that expression generally is the product of at least two different (physiological) and opposed tendencies. (By the way, he makes a finer distinction with respect to these opposite tendencies than Tinbergen and his followers did. According to Leyhausen, the threat displays of a cat—his favorite example—are brought about by a conflict not between aggression and escape, but between attack and defense, i.e., two forms of the same major category: aggression.) However, one of these tendencies is "in the minority," it is less intensive than the other, and it is this weaker tendency that brings the expressive character of the behavior about by inhibiting to some extent the full performance of the other (stronger) tendency.

This principle may be said to be true, but it is not only true for expressions, but for any coordinated behavior. For example, when I bend my arm, only under certain pathological conditions is this movement brought about exclusively by the flexor muscles, the biceps in this case, resulting in an atactic performance. Under normal physiological conditions a minority of the antagonistic extensor muscles, mainly belonging to the triceps in this case, is involved and checks and controls the action of the biceps, resulting in an ordinary and well-coordinated movement of the arm. When taken in this sense, Leyhausen's statement certainly refers to an important principle of behavioral coordination, but it is no definition of expression since it does not allow the distinction between expressive behavior and other (nonpathological) behaviors.

Among other scientists concerned with animal behavior, Hediger (1954) also tried to give a general definition of expression. Precisely speaking, he did not claim to have found a generally valid definition of expression, but rather intended it only as a guide for practical use in zoological gardens. He considered expression to be "all the variable non-pathological phenomena of the animal which help to an understanding of its situation." Thus, Hediger rightly defines expressive behaviors to be phenomena (in the word's literal and true sense—see below), and he does not base his definition on the physiological or psychological processes "behind them." By the formulation "variable phenomena," furthermore, he rightly excludes more permanent physiognomic phenomena from the discussion. Obviously he also wishes to exclude pathological features—a suggestion which is perhaps not fully justifiable under every aspect, but which certainly is very understandable. All these are positive points in Hediger's definition. Its weakness is the same as in Leyhausen's definition: it does not allow the distinction of expression from other behaviors. For example, when an animal approaches the water and drinks, the walking as well as the drinking behavior are "variable and non-pathological phenomena," and they also "help to an understanding of the animal's situation": it is thirsty. However, neither walking nor drinking are expressive behaviors. In short, Hediger's definition also is too broad.

Being "too broad" seems to be the greatest danger of all general definitions of expression. Probably some ethologists have become more or less aware of this danger, and tried to limit the field. However, they took the wrong way. For example, Schenkel (1947) defined: "Ausdruck ist die Funktion von Strukturen, deren biologischer Sinn es ist, durch Stimmungsübertragung bzw. Reaktionsauslösung an der Steuerung sozialen Zusammenlebens mitzuwirken" (Expression is the function of structures whose biological meaning is to contribute to communication in social life by influencing the mood or by releasing reactions). Eibl-Eibesfeldt (1957) rightly criticized this definition as still too broad because it includes all those behavior patterns which may occasionally have contagious (allelomimetic) effects.

In part, the latter is linked with the problem that expression may be a phenomenon (a special posture, gesture, vocalization, etc.), but it also may be an epiphenomenon. In the latter case, the expression is not a behavior per se; rather, the expressive character is brought about by the special way in which a nonexpressive behavior is performed, e.g., the expression of fatigue in the movements (such as walking) of an animal or a man. Since this may happen with almost any behavior, the suggestion to restrict or at least focus the discussion of expression primarily on phenomena is very understandable.

Taking this aspect into account, Lorenz (1951) and, after him, Eibl-Eibesfeldt (1957) suggested, "nur dann von Ausdruck zu sprechen, wenn ein Verhalten im Dienste der Koordination sozialen Gemeinschaftslebens besondere Differenzierungen bekommen hat, denn diese beweisen, dass die soziale Funktion die wesentliche Leistung der fraglichen Bewegung ist" (to speak of expression only in those cases in which a behavior serving coordination in social life has obtained special differentiations because these [differentiations] prove that the social function is the essential achievement of the movements under discussion).

In short, all these authors tried to restrict the term expression to the social life of animals and they emphasized the social functions of expression. When one is primarily or exclusively interested in the role of expression in communication, as we are here, the limitation of the discussion of expressions to those which are of importance in the social field is absolutely justifiable and advisable. However, one must be aware—and the quoted authors apparently were not—(a) that one now is dealing with only a section of expressive behavior since there are also expressions without any special social functions, as Leyhausen (1967) has pointed out extensively, and (b) that the mention of the function, important as it may be, does not make the definition, since a subject *and* its function are two different matters. First one has to define the subject, then one may add some remarks on its function for a more detailed explanation. (The habit of "defining" a subject in terms of its function is very common in literature, but it is always at least a severe weakness of the definition, if not a downright mistake.) Above all, the restriction of the discussion to the social aspects of expression does not advance us one step because all the objections which were raised against the above-mentioned attempts to define expression in general are again valid in this now-restricted field. For example, all the various fighting movements and techniques are very special and often highly differentiated behaviors that definitely serve important functions in social life and release definite reactions of the partners; however, they are not expressive behaviors. Thus, neither Schenkel's, nor Lorenz's, nor Eibl-Eibesfeldt's definitions allow a distinction of expressive behavior from nonexpressive behavior—which, after all, is the purpose of such a definition. Thus, in spite of certain merits in contributing to the clarification of some special points, these definitions have failed. It certainly does not make things easier that there is not even a special summarizing term, much less a definition, which characterizes the nonexpressive behaviors as opposed to expressive behaviors. Of all the authors mentioned above, only Klages (1936) has at least seen this problem and tried to coin terms for several classes of nonexpressive behaviors. Unfortunately, his "classification" of behaviors is again based on "underlying mechanisms" and the latter are anything but beyond reasonable doubts and objections in this case.

How important the distinction between expressive and nonexpressive behaviors can be may be illustrated by a quite widely spread error in ungulate literature. In many ungulate species, the males stand in a more or less erect posture, with lifted nose and open mouth (Fig. 2), after having sniffed at the urine of a female. (Ungulate males, and sometimes even females, can show this behavior in a few more situations and sometimes also with substances other than urine, but it occurs most commonly after the male's sniffing at the female's urine, and this seems to be the biologically most important situation). The first scientist to describe and discuss this *Flehmen* ("lip-curl"), was Schneider (1930, 1931), and he considered it to be an expressive behavior (1934). Since then, many scientists—including myself in some earlier papers—have taken up this interpretation, so that a mention of *Flehmen* is hardly lacking in any book or paper on expressive behavior of hoofed mammals. However, subsequent research (Backhaus 1960a, Knappe 1964, Estes 1972) has shown that apparently the male "tests" the female's urine by *Flehmen* and can recognize something about her estrous state. Thus, *Flehmen* apparently has as little to do with an expressive display as any other (olfactory) perceptive action.

The little "historical review" above appeared to be necessary to show the dilemma of any present-day discussion on expression. However, there also are more positive aspects to it in that the above discussion may help us to avoid a few approaches which obviously are

Fig. 2. *Flehmen* ("lip-curl") in a male sitatunga (*Tragelaphus spekei*) after sniffing a female's urine. (Walther 1979. Frankfurt Zoo.)

dead-end roads, and, on the other hand, it may provide useful material for an approach toward a reasonably good operational definition. To summarize the most important consequences from the above discussion:

(a) When we are interested in a discussion of expressive behavior, it appears to be a mistake to take the—physiological or psychological—"underlying mechanisms" as a starting point. They certainly are important, but they represent different aspects of the entire process, and they absolutely require treatments and investigations on their own—just as the investigation of the subject of a painting is one matter, and the investigation of the artist's painting technique is another. We have to stick with the phenomena in the strict sense, i.e., the movements, gestures, postures, vocalizations, etc., as they occur at the surface of the body of the intact animal.

(b) We have to distinguish physiognomic, permanent features from expressive behaviors, i.e., momentary movements. Although there may be relationships and transitions between the two, the focus has to be on the expressive behaviors.

(c) There are expressive behaviors which function in communication and others which do not have a special function in social life. Two important conclusions follow from this statement. For one thing, expression in general cannot be defined by its social functions—without mentioning that a definition by function is a vulnerable business anyway. Second, expression and communication are overlapping fields, but they do not coincide. Of course, in many animals, expressive behaviors are used in communication, and in such animals as ungulates, they are even the most important means of intraspecific communication. However, there is also communication without expression as well as expression without communication.

(d) Expression can be a phenomenon, i.e., a special and well-defined display, and expression can be an epiphenomenon. In the latter case, an ordinary maintenance behavior is performed in a somewhat modified way. Because this can happen with almost any activity, a discussion of the expressive epiphenomena includes the danger of inflation of the topic, i.e., it easily may end up as a discussion of behavior in general. Certainly these epiphenomena cannot simply be ignored; however, it appears advisable to focus on the phenomena because they represent expressive behavior in its most pronounced and purest form. A restriction to this point is that at present the distinction between expressive phenomena and epiphenomena can only be carried out in visual behavior (movements, gestures, postures) but is difficult to apply to olfactory and acoustical expressions—mainly due to insufficient theoretical investigation of the latter.

(e) It is imperative to find at least an operational definition that adequately distinguishes expressive from nonexpressive behavior, in order to outline the field under investigation.

In approaching such an operational definition, we can largely use what we have said about signs and signals in the previous chapter, since expressive behaviors belong to them. However, signs and signals comprise, at least, two more categories: the extrinsic signals and the permanent physiognomic features, which are not behaviors, and thus have to be excluded here. On the other hand, all the characteristics of signs and signals are fully valid for expressive behavior. Above all, this is true with respect to the indicative nature of these behaviors as opposed to executive behaviors. When understood in this way, the perhaps somewhat special but by no means unusual use of the terms "indicative" and "executive" may provide the key to the required distinction between expressive and nonexpressive behaviors. Nonexpressive behaviors are executive behaviors which comprise all the maintenance activities (such as feeding, drinking, breathing, urinating, defecating, grooming, resting, and walking) as well as those social behaviors by which the animal fully executes an action (such as fighting, marking, copulating, giving birth, and nursing). Expressive behaviors are indicative behaviors, i.e., movements (including postures as being "frozen movements" and vocalizations as being "acoustical movements") by which the animal does not execute but "only" indicates something. This "something" comprises several major categories which certainly are not without connections and transitions but often can be separately recognized and at least should be distinguished for didactic reasons.

Some expressive behaviors indicate nothing but an animal's momentary psycho-physiological state and condition. These expressive behaviors are neither directed nor addressed toward recipients; consequently, they also occur in the absence of any social partner, when the animal is completely alone. If they have any influence upon another animal, this is brought about either by contagion (allelomimetic behavior), i.e., another animal, which happens to be close by and is in about the same psycho-physiological state as the performer, does the same thing, or by "reading" something from the performer's behavior; that is, it is a reaction for which the performer did not aim at all. These two occasional response mechanisms also occur with almost all the nonexpressive behaviors; for example, when a resting animal arises, another animal resting close by may also arise (contagion), or when an animal has found something edible and eats it, another animal may "read" something from the first animal's eating behavior, approach the place, and seek there for food. Examples of expressive behaviors indicative of the animal's momentary state are the features of exhaustion in walking (and other maintenance activities), vocalizations in different stages of (unspecific) excitement as well as other signs of restlessness, postures of general discomfort (e.g., when exposed to cold or rain), etc. On the whole, these are the expressive behaviors to which the phrasing "descriptions of the animal's state" can be attributed without major restrictions or additions. They are not specialized to serve social functions. Insofar as they occasionally may influence the behavior of others, this influence does not go beyond the possible effect of any maintenance activity.

Other expressive behaviors indicate an animal's readiness to perform a definite behavior. Thus, they are not merely "descriptions of the animal's state" but, in addition, include an important anticipatory component. They do not only reflect the condition which the animal is in right now, but they also and primarily refer to the action that is going to take place next. Above all, we must mention intention movements in this context. With respect to their role in communication, it makes a decided difference whether these intention movements are related to maintenance activities or to social behaviors. Intention movements related to maintenance activities have no greater importance for communication than the maintenance activities themselves and those expressive behaviors which indicate nothing but the animal's momentary psycho-physiological condition. Among them, however, "additional movements" deserve some special attention because, although they still clearly belong to the expressive behaviors related to maintenance activities, they are somewhat on the line toward expressive behaviors with some more significance for communication.

As stated above, intention movements indicate what the animal is going to do next. Thus, when a standing ruminant lifts its foreleg and angles it as in the process of bedding down, but without kneeling down, so that the movement is performed "in the air," this is an intention movement for lying down in these animals, and its relationship to the corresponding executive behavior (i.e., the full bedding-down behavior) is perfectly clear. "Additional" intention movements are those which cannot be understood as being initiating movements of the following action but which nevertheless occur regularly or, at least, frequently when the animal is ready to perform a definite action. They are mainly reflexlike combinations with other movements, such as pulling back the ears when the masticator muscles are tensed, or they are symptoms of processes in the autonomic nervous system, such as the ruffling of the hairs in limited regions of the body (withers, rump patch, etc.), or changes in the muscle tonus (from tense to slack, etc.). In hoofed mammals, good examples are provided by certain species-specific postures or movements of the tail (to be described in detail later in this book) immediately before the animal starts running at a gallop. Of course, these tail movements have nothing to do with the actions of the legs, and the animal certainly can run without performing them, but they are, in certain species, so strongly correlated with the intention for galloping that they reliably indicate what the animal is going to do next.

Intention movements related to social (executive) behaviors indicate an animal's readiness for a definite action toward a partner (recipient). Thus, they not only indicate what the animal is going to do next but what it is going to do *to this partner*. At least in hoofed mammals, the most important expressive behaviors which function in social communication belong to this category.

Both in maintenance activities and perhaps to an even greater extent in social behaviors, at least two types of intention movements can be distinguished. The first type or subcategory is simply the first initiating movement for the corresponding (executive) action. The movement may be "frozen" into a posture, or somewhat exaggerated, or otherwise ritualized, e.g., performed in slow motion, or (more or less rhythmically) repeated, etc.; however, otherwise it is nothing but the first movement for the action in question. For example, when a goat or another horned ungulate threatens an opponent by presenting its horns toward him, this is nothing but the first movement to a butt or blow.

The other subcategory of intention movements is the swing-out movements, which are not immediate initiations of the corresponding executive actions, but rather movements by which the animal prepares for the following executive behavior, and which, consequently, frequently do not go in the direction of the ensuing (executive) action, but more or less opposite to it, and thus away from the recipient. For example, in a hostile interaction between two human opponents, the one may stretch his arm and hand backwards and may even lean the upper part of the body backwards as a swing-out movement for a powerful slap in the other's face. When used as expressive displays, it is the same as with other intention movements, i.e., such swing-out movements can "freeze" into postures, or they can be performed in slow motion, or can be rhythmically repeated, etc. An instructive example from the repertoire of hoofed mammals is the head-turned-away display (which can occur in several forms—as will be discussed later) in which the displaying animal turns its head more or less away from the opponent as a swing-out movement for an emphasized turn toward him. At least in some cases, the lateral orientation of the whole body toward the recipient can be interpreted the same way.

Perhaps the reader may now understand better what I said in the beginning of this discussion: that the old, promising concept of intention movements has been treated somewhat shabbily by classical ethology. In the anything-but-thorough outline above, we have already found three subcategories of intention movements—additional movements, initiating movements (in the strict sense), and swing-out movements—which, to the best of my knowledge, have never been pointed out *expressis verbis* in previous literature on the subject.

As emphasized several times, intention movements serving in social communication indicate what the sender is going to do next with respect to the recipient. Since the recipient can meaningfully respond to the sender's intention in only a limited number of ways—sometimes even in only one way—these intention movements do not only anticipate the sender's action, but they also indicate which response of the recipient is expected by the sender, and thus, in a sense, they also anticipate the recipient's reaction. However, there are some expressive behaviors that anticipate the recipient's reaction in a stronger way. For example, when a male sexually mounts a female, she may assume a special—in some species lordosis-like in other species kyphosis-like—posture of her back under the weight of the male's body. However, in an advanced mating ritual, it may sometimes happen that a female—standing or walking in front of the driving male—assumes such a posture before the male's mounting, usually with the result that he now immediately mounts her. The female anticipates the male's mount by a behavior which represents the *re*-action to the male's mounting, i.e., it is an intention movement not for mounting but for being mounted, and thus the anticipation of the partner's behavior is particularly clear and obvious. Perhaps one could speak of "invitation movements" in such cases. As we will see in later chapters, invitation movements are not restricted to the occasional expression of the female's readiness for copulation; for example, in an agonistic encounter, a combatant may invite the other's attack by assuming a corresponding defensive attitude (Fig. 3), i.e., an intention movement indicating not the readiness to attack, but the readiness to be attacked, etc.

Finally, there are also expressive behaviors which are not intention movements but are as indicative. With respect to ungulates, perhaps the most important category is "symbolic" actions, to which the aforementioned female invitation posture for copulation comes rather close. In contrast to the intention movements, the animal not only uses the initiating movements of an (executive) action, but performs the full action; however, not toward the recipient but toward a substitute object (e.g., butting a tree or the grass or the ground with the horns) or into the air. In the latter case, the action can be absolutely directed toward the recipient, but it does not touch him (e.g., a full blow, as in a fight, but struck at a distance from which it cannot

Fig. 3. The "defender" (left) invites the opponent's attack by leaning his horns toward his own nape (head-low posture) in an agonistic encounter between bulls of South African oryx antelope (*Oryx gazella*). Walther 1980. Etosha National Park, South West Africa.)

possibly touch the opponent). The action toward a substitute object, of course, coincides with that behavior which is commonly termed "redirected response" (Moynihan 1955) in ethology. At least in ungulates, however, such an action is not necessarily a response, but it often is very spontaneous. Perhaps also Chance's (1962) category of "cut-off acts" can be included here. A cut-off act means, in this case, that the animal interrupts the visual contact with an object by turning its head or its entire body away, i.e., it visually screens itself from the sight of the object. In hoofed mammals, such cut-off actions do not seem to be frequent—due to the often enormous visual circle of many of these species—but one could identify a few.

When we consider all aspects of expression discussed in this chapter, it may not be too difficult to accept and understand the following operational definition: expression is indicative behavior; it comprises the behavioral phenomena and epiphenomena that are (a) bodily manifestations of an animal's momentary psychosomatic state, and/or (b) indications of its readiness for definite (executive) actions, and/or (c) "symbolic" performances of certain (executive) actions.

For that section of expressive behavior which serves communication, and thus is of particular interest in this book, it would only be necessary to add the words "with respect to a partner (recipient)" to the definition above. However, since—as pointed out previously—the expressive behaviors indicative of the readiness to perform a definite action are more important in this regard than those that merely indicate the animal's state and condition, and since, furthermore, the phenomena appear to be more important than the epiphenomena, and since, finally, it appears advisable to exclude behaviors with merely contagious effects upon the recipient, we may define it somewhat more explicitly (Walther 1974): expressions which function in social communication are momentary behavioral phenomena (movements, gestures, postures, vocalizations, emissions of scent, etc.) that are indicative of the animal's readiness to perform definite actions toward a definite (usually conspecific) partner. They are addressed to him and are aimed at releasing adequate responses of the recipient (sender's "expectation") above the level of contagious effects—without influencing the partner mechanically (i.e., in contrast to certain executive behaviors) and without the performer's leaving the partner's sphere of action.

After our previous discussions of expression and communication, explanations of this operational definition appear to be superfluous, except perhaps with respect to the phrasing "without the performer's leaving the partner's sphere of action." This formulation is simply meant to exclude reactions of the recipient due to the sender's mov-

ing away—which, of course, also does not influence the partner mechanically, but which can hardly be considered an expressive behavior. Admittedly, things may become somewhat complicated when
we have to apply the formulation "without influencing the partner
mechanically" to tactile behavior. It appears that tactile expressions
generally belong to the epiphenomena—that is, it is not the touching
per se, but its modes (strong–gentle, long–short, etc.), that bring
about the expressive character. Moreover, tactile expression in general, and in hoofed mammals in particular, is at present so poorly
investigated that we will not have much to say about it anyway.

In terms of evolution, the relationship of expressive behavior to key
stimuli is unmistakable. As previously mentioned, however, the term
"key stimuli"—or, synonymously, "sign stimuli" or (social)
"releasers"—is broader in that it also includes bodily badges. Furthermore, ethologists exclusively refer to innate behavior when speaking of (behavioral) key stimuli, whereas "expression" comprises both
innate and learned behaviors. Also, expressive behaviors often appear
more elaborate and refined, with a greater involvement of the individual, and less "mechanical" with respect to their effects upon recipients, than the "classic" key (!) stimuli. In short, the expressive behaviors are, at least, a very special category among the (social) "releasers."

A last word may be said concerning the distinction between message (and meaning), effects, and (social) functions of expressive behaviors in hoofed mammals. These three categories are sometimes
confused in the literature, particularly in discussions of the so-called
ambiguity of expressive displays. During my studies of ungulate behavior, I have come to the view that true ambiguity in the message
and meaning of expressive displays is infrequent. When I catch myself considering the possibility of the ambiguity of a given expression,
I always take it as a serious indication that I have at best not fully
understood this display, or perhaps even misinterpreted it completely.
For example, the message of a threat display is always "I am ready to
fight you." Often, it even includes information on a very specific
fighting technique which the sender intends to use. As previously
mentioned, one can methodologically approach the question of the
message of a given display by investigating its relationship to executive behaviors. In somewhat complicated cases, it may be necessary
to study variations of the same behavior in several closely related
species until our understanding of the basic message is clear. However, the greatest hindrance to recognizing the basic messages of
animal displays seems to be a human factor. At least in our recent
western civilization, we often think in too abstract a way, and thus,

we easily take the second step before the first one in our interpretations. For example, a male Thomson's gazelle may stretch head and neck forward and then abruptly erect them and lift his nose when approaching a female (Fig. 4). Since these gestures can regularly be seen when the male follows the female in a mating ritual, human observers may be inclined to speak of courtship displays with the message and meaning—to put it somewhat anthropomorphically but simply—"I'll make love to you." Under this assumption, of course, it may come as a surprise when one sees such a tommy buck also use these gestures in quite different situations, such as herding females in a territory (which is not directly related to sexual behavior in this species), or even when driving females ahead during migration (Walther 1978a). Consequently, one may come to think of an ambiguity in these expressions. However, when one does not interpret these gestures as courtship displays but as pushing actions with the basic meaning "Girl, go ahead!" then there is no ambiguity in them, and the message and meaning are precisely the same in all the different situations in which they may occur.

Fig. 4a. Male Thomson's gazelle (*Gazella thomsoni*) with head and neck stretched forward follows a female. b. Nose-up posture in close approach. (Walther 1977a.)

Another case in which some people speak of an "ambiguity" may be given when an executive behavior happens to resemble an expressive behavior. For example, in humans, the blinking of one eye may be used as an expressive behavior and as a signal to a partner in certain situations. However, the same or at least a very similar blinking may also occur when a small object, e.g., a tiny insect, has hit the eye. In the latter case, the blinking serves to remove the little object from the eye, and thus, it is an executive behavior whose resemblance to the expressive eye blinking is merely accidental. Corresponding events may also happen in animals. For example, when a bongo (*Taurotragus euryceros*) scratches his own shoulder with his horns, it may sometimes resemble a dominance display (neck-stretch) of this species, and it may occasionally happen that the scratching movement is mistaken for the display by conspecifics (Hamann 1979). We will meet a few more concrete examples of this type in later chapters. Generally speaking, there are many expressive behaviors which more or less resemble quite different executive behaviors without any genuine relationship between the two. Although, of course, such resemblances may occasionally lead to misinterpretations and misunderstandings on the part of the recipient, I do not think that it is justifiable to speak of an ambiguity of the expression or of its message and meaning in such cases. Rather, they are comparable to errors by which we may mistake a stranger for a friend due to some accidental similarities which have nothing to do with any ambiguity in the appearance of our friend. Finally, the message and meaning of a given display may sometimes vary when it occurs in the behavioral repertoires of different species. This goes almost without saying and has nothing to do with an ambiguity of this display either.

In short, the "ambiguity"—when one wishes to use this term—often does not lie in the expressive behaviors but in their functions or in their effects upon the recipients. At times it is advisable to distinguish between effects and functions. By "effects" I mean here the immediate influences which a given expressive display may have upon the recipient. These effects are frequently two and opposites (dichotomy of effects). For example, in the case of a threat display, they may be a challenge or an intimidation depending on circumstances, as discussed above. Sometimes a given expression may have even more than two effects, but their number is small. Methodologically, the effects of a given display can be recognized by the recipient's responses.

The term "function" can be used on very different levels (the Tower of Babel again!). I mean it here with respect to the functional circles and social situations. Thus, the study of the situations in which a given expression occurs provides us with an insight into its social functions. In contrast to effects of a given display, the number of its social functions can be great. For example, the same threat display may serve in territorial establishment and defense, establishment and maintenance of a social hierarchy, coordination of group activities, keeping a group together (rounding up), female defense against (unwanted) sexual advances of a male, competition over food (in captivity), etc.

In short, as a rule of thumb, each expressive behavior usually has one basic message and meaning, two (dichotomus) effects, and multiple social functions in hoofed mammals.

4. TOWARD A CLASSIFICATION OF COMMUNICATIVE ADVERTISEMENTS AND DISPLAYS

As with definition, the classification of communicative and expressive behaviors has problems of its own. One approach frequently used in the literature is a classification according to sensory impressions, largely of the observer (!), resulting in the categories of visual, acoustical, olfactory, and tactile displays. This approach, although clear and simple, is also superficial and unsatisfactory, somewhat resembling a "classification" of plants by the colors of their flowers. Moreover, it breaks up natural and well-integrated behavioral units (although an occasional separation of behavior patterns that belong together can hardly be avoided by any classification system). The same is true of a "classification" of expressive behaviors according to the body regions where they occur, such as expressions of the mouth, the eyes, the arms, the legs, etc. When discussing these phenomena in detail, one often cannot avoid describing first the visual displays, then the acoustical, then the olfactory behaviors. Or one may have to describe the positions of the neck separately from the movements of the legs, etc. However, one should at least not take these as the major categories, but only as subdivisions. Another approach is the classification of displays according to functional circles (*Funktionskreise*—von Uexküll 1934). Thus, one may speak of aggressive displays, sexual displays, alarm signals, etc. This approach certainly agrees better with biological situations than one utilizing the sensory modalities or body regions. However, it too has its problems. At least in ungulates, it happens quite frequently that the same behavior serves several functions, and correspondingly occurs in several different functional circles. Thus a classification according to functional circles can also result in more or less artificial separations between similar or even identical behavior patterns. Much the same is true of a classification based on the involved partners ($\male{:}\male$, $\male{:}\female$, $\female{:}\female$, etc.), as was suggested by Carpenter (1942).

Another approach would be a classification based on phenomenological characteristics of behavior patterns: head-up postures, head-down postures, broadside positions, etc. This approach is definitely a good one, but difficulties arise from the position of a given behavior pattern within the entire behavioral inventory of a species. Since behavioral inventories vary with species, the message and the meaning of phenotypically very similar behaviors can be different and even opposite in different species. For example, in certain bovid species, the opponents routinely drop to their "knees" (carpal joints) during a fight. If such an animal drops to its knees in an agonistic encounter without establishing horn contact with its opponent, this action can be considered as an intention movement for fighting, and thus a threat. However, many other bovid species do not drop to their knees in fighting; when one of them exhibits this behavior during an agonistic encounter it is usually an intention movement for lying down, i.e., a submissive behavior. Thus, the message and meaning of the same behavior pattern (dropping to the knees) in the same situation (agonistic encounter) can be quite different depending on its position, its "bedding," within the entire species-specific behavior inventory. This is a root for misunderstandings in encounters between animals of different species. Occasionally similar problems may arise with respect to certain behavior patterns even within the same species. In short, a classification under merely phenotypical aspects also has inherent problems, particularly when the discussion includes many different species.

Possibly a classification according to phylogenetic origin and evolution of communicative and expressive behaviors would be helpful. However, our present knowledge of this subject is limited and frequently in a state of speculation.

In this book, an attempt is made to combine aspects of several classification systems, in an approach that strives for a classification of behaviors with communicative functions according to their messages and meanings by taking some aspects of functional circles for the outlines and, as much as possible, incorporating phenotypical and phylogenetical aspects but using categories derived from sensory modalities only for the subdivisions.

In our previous discussions of definitions and interpretations of communication and expression, we always took the most pronounced cases, the "central realms," as starting points, branching out from there to talk about more peripheral, transitional, or even questionable cases. In an approach toward a classification of the behaviors under discussion, it appears advisable to go the opposite way. This means we will begin with phenomena which do not belong to communication but are its presuppositions and may lead in the direction of communications of the "to-whom-it-may-concern" type, and from here we will advance to more and more individually addressed communications. The goal of this procedure is to establish some kind of "natural classification" in which the more advanced categories can be understood as elaborations of the more primitive ones and follow from them. Aspects of expression are incorporated ranging from communications in which expressions play no role or only a minor role, to communications that largely consist of expressions of the epiphenomenal type but may also include some expressive phenomena, to communications in which the latter, i.e., distinct expressive displays, are the most important components.

I consider the development of communicative behaviors of hoofed mammals to be based on four major roots: (a) the social attraction among conspecifics; (b) the animal's presence with all its attributes including maintenance activities and their spoor in the environment; (c) the animal's general motivational state; and (d) special activities of particular significance to social life, the three most important of which being sexual advances, fighting, and flight.

When we consider communication to be essentially a dialoguelike process with an active sender as a constitutive element, which follows from our previous discussion, the mere existence and presence of an animal are not sufficient to establish a communicative interaction with a partner. However, existence and presence are the absolutely necessary presuppositions for any communication, and in the concrete case of the living animal, they include: (a) the animal's belonging to a given species with all its bodily (visual, olfactory, acoustical) characteristics; (b) its being either a male or a female, which can also be linked with rather striking differences in appearance (body size, color of the coat, presence or absence of antlers and horns, or their size and shape respectively, etc.); (c) its belonging to a given age class (juvenile, subadult, adult, senile); and (d) its physical features that distinguish it as an individual; also, (e) clues to an individual's physical condition and strength, and thus to its social status; furthermore, (f) maintenance activities (feeding, drinking, resting, moving, grooming, urinating, defecating, etc.); and finally, (g) the spoor (tracks, feces, urine, etc.) left by the maintenance activities in the environment. Since animals of the psycho-physiological organization of hoofed mammals are well equipped visually, acoustically, and olfactorily to perceive the physical appearance of a conspecific and its maintenance activities, as well as the spoor in the environment, a partner may take in quite a lot of socially important "information" from the mere presence of an animal before any special communication process has taken place.

True communication begins when the animal behaviorally *empha-*

sizes its presence and position by (a) spatial or social exposure, which is, of course, a behavior but is accomplished without expression being involved, (b) intensifications of maintenance activities by expressive epiphenomena, and (c) certain vocalizations reflecting the animal's general motivational state (see below).

To partners familiar with the sender, presence and position advertisement may also include individual identification. For example, the whinny of an adult male horse may not only signal "Here is a stallion!" but, at least for group members, it may contain the message: "Here is the stallion Godolphin!"

Finally, certain indications of the individual's social status may also belong to the animal's appearance and are closely related to position advertisement. These features show whether the individual is physically strong (massive body, massive neck, size of horns or antlers, etc.) and thus at least potentially of high social status, or whether it is not so strong and thus of subordinate rank. Generally, territorial individuals are always high-ranking individuals in hoofed mammals. Thus, advertisement of territorial status is only a special case of the advertisement of high rank in the corresponding species. The features indicative of physical strength come into full effect when the animal emphasizes its presence and position by *spatial and/or social exposure*, which is particularly typical of animals of high social status, while subordinates tend much more to use environmental cover and/or to keep among the others in gregarious species. Also, subordinates do not usually perform maintenance activities in any striking fashion and do not readily assume particularly tonic postures, while these are frequent and pronounced in high-ranking individuals. Furthermore, vocalizations can be involved in status advertising. Some of them are more or less intensifications of those used in position advertisement. Others are more specialized, i.e., they are more or less distinct (acoustical) displays. Moreover, postures and gestures indicative of high rank are closely related to dominance displays (see below), and those of low rank show connections to certain submissive displays. In some cases, these relationships are so close that it is difficult to say whether certain features of high rank, such as an erect attitude, gave rise to certain dominance displays, and those of low rank, such as a somewhat slumped attitude, gave rise to certain submissive displays, or whether it was the other way around. If the latter is true (and there are some aspects which speak in favor of this possibility), certain features of high or low social status may be considered as permanent physiognomic residues of dominant or submissive postures and gestures. (Similarly, in humans, repeated wrinkling of the brow in hard thinking may eventually result in the permanent wrinkles of a typical "thinker's brow.")

Although our discussion has up to now been concerned only with presence and position advertisement, I could not avoid mentioning the animal's *internal psycho-physiological state* (frequently referred to as "general motivational state" or "mood" in ethological literature). A living animal without a mood is an artifact, and this mood belongs to its concrete existence and presence as well as its physical characteristics and its maintenance activities. On the other hand, it is justifiable to consider the general motivational state as a factor on its own, since (a) it changes much more readily and often also much more abruptly than all the aforementioned features, and, (b) in contrast to them, it is manifested by expressive epiphenomena and phenomena. The expressive epiphenomena are superimposed on maintenance activities. Even when an animal does nothing but stand, the standing is either relaxed, or it is tense, or it shows features of exhaustion, etc. These epiphenomenal expressions occur in different degrees of intensity according to a scale of increasing internal arousal (excitement). In the "normal" postures and movements of hoofed mammals, expressive epiphenomena of low intensity (e.g., the relatively low muscular tonus characteristic of a relaxed state) are absolutely recognizable to a human observer. However, we do not have much evidence so far that the animals themselves recognize them in conspecifics, because often they do not show special reactions to them. The more tense and/or restless an animal becomes, and thus, the more intensive and striking the external features of its internal arousal are, the greater is the probability that other animals will react to them. The same principles are also true for vocalizations. As Kiley (1974) has pointed out extensively, many vocalizations of hoofed mammals cannot be attributed to specific actions such as aggression, flight, or sexual activities, but instead reflect the animal's general motivational condition, ranging from a relaxed state (where they are comparable with the purring of a cat) to levels of increased general excitement. Such vocalizations as well as visual expressive epiphenomena and even mere maintenance activities can have *contagious (allelomimetic) effects* by which the individuals may synchronize their internal states within a group. Being in the same mood is a very important factor for group cohesiveness.

The gradually increasing levels of the animal's general state finally lead to *excitement activities* indicative of great inner arousal and culminating in such phenomena as, e.g., distress cries. In hoofed mammals, alarm signals frequently develop on the basis of excitement activities.

Maintenance activities can always leave visible and/or olfactory spoor in the environment. As with emphasizing its bodily presence and position, an animal may also emphasize and elaborate the environmental spoor of its activities. We then speak of *marking behavior*. This can be achieved in different ways. The simplest method is the localized accumulation of products of certain maintenance activities, mainly urination and/or defecation, which may result in the establishment of dung piles, for instance. Moreover, many of the animals under discussion can enrich the signs of their presence in the environment beyond the spoor of (moderately modified) maintenance activities by more special marking activities such as scraping the ground with their hooves, goring the ground or beating the vegetation with their horns (object aggression), or the deposition of secretion from special skin glands. Generally, this marking by urine, feces, secretion, etc., belongs to communication of the "to-whom-it-may-concern" type.

Only in a few, not infrequent but very circumscribed, situations can marking behavior be more individually addressed. The most common of these cases is marking in connection with agonistic encounters, i.e., urinating, defecating, or secretion marking right in front of the adversary. In certain species, other activities such as rolling on the ground or somewhat specialized forms of grazing may occur. All these behaviors seem to have something to do with the immediate space around the sender in these situations, and one may perhaps speak of *space-claims*.

Mere position and state advertising ("mere" in that it does not include special features of dominance, agonistic, or sexual tendencies, etc.) may be said to be neutral in the sense that it is left to the recipient whether he will react by approach or withdrawal (provided that he reacts at all). In gregarious animals, the approach tendencies usually preponderate since a conspecific is always attractive to a gregarious animal so long as he does not specifically signal hostile intentions. When this social attraction is effective in both sender and recipient, presence and position advertisements easily merge into a *"calling" for contact*. Group members who have been separated may find each other again by means of reciprocal presence and position advertisements, and, within a herd, the repeated advertisements of the members may contribute to group cohesiveness. Basically, such advertisements are anonymous. However, when the partners know each other, the contact-seeking advertisements may become individualized.

Successful contact seeking often merges into *making contact* which is most commonly established in hoofed mammals in the form of olfactory testing: the animal touches with its nose and sniffs at definite regions of the partner's body. Such bodily contacts can be intensified by several forms of social grooming (e.g., licking the partner) which frequently seem to convey the sender's friendly intentions and to have appeasing effects upon the recipient.

Particularly individualized are contact seeking and contact making in *mother-offspring relationships*. I think it is a tolerable anthropomorphism when one says that there are cases in which e.g., to the young, it is not only "an adult female conspecific" which is calling but it is "my mother."

Except for the behaviors in making bodily contact and for certain modifications of space claims and of signals occurring in mother-offspring relationships, all the advertisements mentioned above are communications of the to-whom-it-may-concern type. Some of them (e.g., spatial or social exposure, marking, etc.) are not expressive behaviors. In others, the expressions involved are mainly epiphenomena. Only certain vocalizations may be said to be expressive phenomena or at least to come close to them. Furthermore, all these signals are merely "descriptive," i.e., they "describe" the sender's species, sex, age, position, state, status, or involvement in a maintenance activity, but they do not include indications of what he is going to do next; at best, they indicate that the sender will continue with his present activity.

With the so-called *alarm signals*, the situation is only slightly different. Usually they are special cases of excitement activities in hoofed mammals. What makes some of them special is their combination with features indicative of the readiness for flight, or, more precisely speaking, for running at a gallop. Thus, they can include some information about a special executive behavior following immediately after them. Otherwise, they show all the features of behaviors of the "to-whom-it-may-concern" type.

The communicative behaviors discussed below are strikingly different in that (a) they occur in much more circumscribed situations, (b) most of them are distinct displays with expressive phenomena (in the strict sense) as their most important components, (c) they are related to rather special executive behaviors, (d) they strongly indicate what the sender is going to do next, (e) they usually are addressed and directed to individual recipients, and—following from (d) and (e)—(f) they include more or less definite "requests" by the sender of what he expects the recipient to do.

The addressing of a display is mainly brought about by the sender's specific *orientation* toward an individual recipient. This addressing orientation can be considered as an elaboration and precision of presence and position advertisement. *Cum grano salis*, it is a special kind of presence and position advertisement. Frequently the orientation is only a component in a distinct expressive display in such cases.

However, in certain cases, the orientation per se is sufficient and can indicate the sender's intentions. Moreover, the sender can signal, by his orientation to the recipient, the direction in which he wants him to move or not to move. The clearest examples of such communications (merely by the sender's orientation relative to the recipient as well as of direction signaling to the latter) are provided by the herding behavior of certain ungulate species.

In physiological terms, the expressive phenomena that we now must consider are indicative not of levels of general arousal but of very special internal motivational states. One may speak of special drives; Lorenz (1963) has emphasized the importance of the "big four": feeding, flight, reproduction, and aggression. However, the roles of these "big four" in the development of expressive displays appear to be very unequal in hoofed mammals. For example, in the galliformes (chickens, pheasants, peacocks), some of the most important courtship displays apparently have evolved from feeding and food enticing (Schenkel 1958). Hardly anything comparable to that can be found in ungulates. Also, features derived from flight behavior only occur as additional components of certain alarm signals and submissive displays. Interestingly enough, even genuine sexual displays are rather infrequent. Thus, with only minor exaggeration, one may say that, in hoofed mammals, the role of the "big four" in the development of expressive displays boils down to one: aggression.

Intraspecific aggression plays a prominent role in the social life of most ungulate species and has given rise to various *threat displays*. These threat displays are predominantly more or less ritualized (i.e., exaggerated, slowed down, "frozen," rhythmically repeated, etc.) intention movements for fighting. Since it is quite commonplace in ungulates for a species to use several different fighting techniques, it often also has developed several threat displays. Some of them may be related to offensive, others to defensive, techniques—and others can be used both ways. Some *offensive threat displays* show a connection with dominance displays, in that frequently features of the two occur in combination. One may speak of threat-dominance displays in such cases. *Defensive threat displays* often are related to submissive displays in ungulates.

Dominance displays are also aggressive displays, and it is interesting to speculate whether they may have evolved from ancestral fighting behaviors in hoofed mammals. However, dominance displays are not as directly related to recent fighting techniques as are threat displays. Most commonly, the sender tries to impress the recipient by emphasizing his size and/or breadth. In doing so, he exposes himself to possible attacks of the opponent ("daring"), and this exposure feature

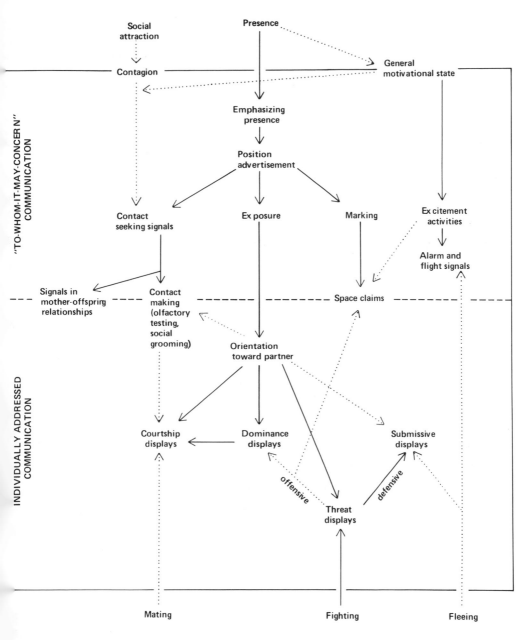

Fig. 5. Categories of advertisements and displays in hoofed mammals and their (presumable) relationships (see text).

resembles certain forms of presence and position advertisement. The strong relationship of dominance displays to the advertisement of high social status has been mentioned above. In short, while the message of a threat display can be put in the words "I am ready to fight you," the message of a dominance display may be said to be: "I am stronger than you!" or—more anthropomorphically but possibly even better: "I am the boss—don't forget it!"

Many male *courtship displays*, especially the more elaborate ones, of hoofed mammals do not seem to be directly related to sexual behaviors in the strict sense, but rather to threat displays or even more frequently to dominance displays. In somewhat simplified form, one may say they are a special kind of dominance display used predominantly, in some species even exclusively, by males in encounters with females.

Submissive displays are the antithesis of dominance and offensive threat displays in hoofed mammals. However, many of them show a strong and direct relationship to defensive threats which can go so far that there are only gradual and minor differences between the two. Sometimes, also, features from excitement activities and/or flight intentions may be involved.

The most important categories of the advertisements and displays described above, as well as some important relationships between them, are schematically summarized in Fig. 5. These categories provide the key for the organization of the following fact material.

5. ADVERTISING PRESENCE, POSITION, STATE, AND STATUS

One of Hediger's (1949) many valuable contributions was to call attention to the importance of position and status advertising in ungulates and other mammals. He spoke of olfactory, acoustical, and visual marking, and within the latter, he distinguished between static-visual and dynamic-visual marking. This conception and terminology gave rise to some criticism (Schenkel 1966a), which was perhaps not completely out of place. As happens frequently in a pioneer situation, Hediger primarily had a special case of marking in mind: the marking of a territory. This of course is an important function of marking behavior, but only one among others. Also, the term "marking" does not appear to be equally adequate for all the behaviors under discussion. Here the term "marking" will be restricted to cases in which the animal deposits marks of its presence in the environment by special or at least somewhat specialized (ritualized) actions, or when it transfers odiferous substances to conspecifics or onto its own body. Thus, what we mean here by "marking" corresponds to Hediger's olfactory marking. Of course, Hediger's visual and acoustical marking fall into the category of presence and position advertisements, but they are not termed "marking behaviors" in this book.

Advertisements of presence (including sex, age class, and sometimes also individual characteristics) and position, and also often of social status (territorial or nonterritorial, high ranking or low ranking) and/or of the general motivational state of the animal (relaxed, alarmed, in migratory mood, etc.), can have attractive or repulsive effects upon the recipients. Some of these advertisements are attractive or repulsive by nature. Frequently, however, their effects depend more on the state and status of the recipient. Even an advertising behavior which basically may be considered to be on the repulsive side, such as spatial or social exposure (see below), can sometimes attract the other when he is of equal status to the sender and aggressive enough to take the challenge. The attractive effects of certain presence and position advertisements make them suitable to serve as contact signals in gregarious species. Thus, there is no clear-cut difference between position advertising and calling for social contact. Furthermore, advertisements of presence, position, state, and status are often closely interrelated. For example, when a white-bearded wildebeest bull (*Connochaetes taurinus albojubatus*) stands alone in his territory and a herd of conspecifics appears at a distance, he may begin to gallop around in his territory in a rocking-horse canter with raised head (Fig. 6) uttering a low-pitched, groaning-croaking call. His standing alone in open terrain as a form of self-exposure works as an advertisement of presence, position, and territorial status. The epiphenominally exaggerated performance of gallop is another advertisement of his position as well as of his very active state. The erect attitude, as a kind of dominance display, indicates his high (territorial) social status. The "ugh"-call, so typical of wildebeest, identifies him as a member of the species and also contributes to position advertisement, and the low pitch of this vocalization identifies him as an adult male. Thus presence, position, state, and status are advertised simultaneously. If one were to "translate" the animal's behavior into human words, the full message would be: "Here is an adult wildebeest bull, and he is strong and territorial and very active!" Moreover, several behaviors (e.g., the visual self-exposure, the striking performance of the gallop, and the described vocalization) advertise the same thing (e.g., the animal's position). On the other hand, the same behavior (e.g., the "ugh"-call) may serve several purposes (e.g., position advertisement as well as species and sex identification). For these reasons, the various aspects of advertisement often cannot be treated separately, and in the following discussion we will frequently have to "jump" from one to another.

One method of advertising presence and position is self-exposure, i.e., Hediger's (1949) static-visual marking, either relative to other conspecifics (social exposure) or to the environment (spatial exposure). The use of self-exposure has at least two important prerequisites. Since it is mainly effective in long-range communication, the animals must possess good visual powers and live in relatively open habitat. In addition, the more gregarious the species is, the more striking exposure by separation from conspecifics becomes. In solitary species, isolation from conspecifics is nothing special; it belongs to the general life habits. These prerequisites are by no means fulfilled in all hoofed mammals. For example, the eyesight of rhinos and tapirs is not very good, and most of these species live solitarily in very dense vegetation. In short, advertising of presence and position by self-exposure is predominantly found in gregarious or at least semi-gregarious Hippomorpha and Ruminantia species living in open terrain (e.g., short-grass plains).

Fig. 6. Territorial wildebeest bull (*Connochaetes taurinus albojubatus*) galloping with raised head (position and status advertisement). (Walther 1979. Serengeti National Park.)

In species that form permanent harem groups (one adult male with several females and their offspring) such as plains zebra (Klingel 1967) and mountain zebra (Klingel 1968), or temporary and/or seasonal harems such as Grant's gazelle (*Gazella granti*) in some areas (Walther 1972*a* and *b*), or even only "pseudoharems" (p. 8), such as white-bearded wildebeest (Estes 1969), Grevy's zebra (Klingel 1969), and Thomson's gazelle, it is the male who, linked with his "shepherd" role, keeps himself separated from the females in social exposure (Fig. 7). This means he frequently stands, moves, grazes, and rests at the periphery of the group, often ten to thirty meters or more from the females. Thus he visually forms a figure of his own, separated from the "crowd," and thus his presence can be recognized by other males at a distance.

In the case of nonterritorial species, such as plains and mountain zebra, the male may remain separated from the females but he moves together with them. In territorial/gregarious species such as brindled wildebeest (*Connochaetes taurinus*—Estes 1969), Thomson's gazelle (Walther 1964*a*, 1968*a*, Estes 1967), and Uganda kob (*Adenota kob thomasi*—Buechner 1961, Leuthold 1966), the territorial males do not participate in the daily movements of the female herds (and not, of course, in those of nonterritorial males), but remain behind as solitary individuals. This separation and social exposure is characteristic of their territorial status (but neither is it the only, nor an absolutely unmistakable, indication of territoriality) and it effectively advertises the position of these males in the open grasslands where these species live.

Fig. 7. Territorial stallion (left) of Grevy's zebra (*Dolichohippus grevyi*) stands separated (social exposure) from a group visiting him in his territory. (Klingel 1969. Photo: H. Klingel. Northern Frontier District, Kenya.)

In visual self-exposure relative to the environment, the animal does not make use of cover (otherwise quite a common strategy); on the contrary, it often stands motionless in completely open terrain, on the rim of a slope, or on the top of a rock, hill, or termite mound (Fig. 8). This standing freely on elevated ground can serve several functions. It may be used for better observation of the surrounding area, and in hot climates this exposed position may also allow the wind to cool the animal's legs. However, it also makes the animal highly visible, and thus emphasizes its presence and position according to the principle of "seeing and being seen." Such elevated exposure is particularly well known in hartebeest (*Alcelaphus buselaphus*) and topi (*Damaliscus lunatus topi*), which frequently stand on termite mounds, but corresponding exposures can be observed in many species.

Social and spatial exposure can be combined. For example, in chamois and in pronghorn the male often separates himself somewhat from a female group during rutting season and stands or rests above them on the slope of a mountain or a hill in an almost "strategic" position where he can keep the females as well as the surroundings under watch. At the same time, it is readily recognizable to potential rivals that there is an adult male at that place and with that group.

Besides spatial and social exposure, an animal can visually emphasize its presence, position, state, and status by the mimic exaggeration of maintenance activities, epiphenomenal expressions, vocalizations, additional (but basically independent) "framing" movements to cer-

Fig. 8. Territorial topi bull (*Damaliscus lunatus topi*) standing on a termite mound (environmental exposure). (Serengeti National Park.)

tain maintenance activities, and special postures. Among the latter, erect attitudes are quite common. For example, within a concentration of wildebeest or topi, one can often recognize territorial males at a distance even when they are standing in a crowd because they carry their heads strikingly higher than females and nonterritorial males (Fig. 9). Such postures indicative of high social status are more or less identical with certain dominance displays.

Mimic exaggeration of maintenance activities is mainly found in locomotor patterns and in urinating and/or defecating. Even without any exaggeration, locomotor patterns become striking when executed unusually slowly or unusually fast. Exaggeration is added by lifting the legs, in hoofed mammals particularly the forelegs, higher than usual and/or by placing them down in a stamping fashion. In this way, the walk becomes a prancing gait, as is quite frequently seen in territorial Uganda kob (Buechner and Schloeth 1965), and a slow gallop (canter) becomes a rocking-horse gallop in which the withers and croup are alternately thrown high up as in territorial wildebeest bulls. Furthermore, the head and neck go up and down somewhat in the rhythm of walking in all ungulates. However, in certain species such as topi and hartebeest, these movements are exaggerated into a striking nodding and headthrowing, particularly in the beginning of a move. (By the way, there are interesting similarities of these nodding movements to certain threat displays.) These nodding movements are

Fig. 9. Even when standing in a crowd, a territorial wilde-beest bull (center) is easily recognized since he carries his head higher than the others. (Serengeti National Park.)

not addressed to conspecifics or aimed at releasing definite reactions from them, since they also occur when such an animal is completely alone. They primarily reflect the general motivational state of the animal and emphasize the performance of a maintenance activity, i.e., walking or the beginning of a walk. (It may be mentioned here that some species such as blesbok [*Damaliscus dorcas phillipsi*] also perform nodding movements when standing for a rest. Apparently this nodding is an expression of sleepiness, and thus it has another motivation than the nodding linked with moving. It is an open question whether there are small differences in the performances of these two types of head nodding.)

Females and adult males urinate differently in most ungulate species. Females squat, while males assume a more or less sawhorse-like posture (Fig. 10). Thus, the "normal" urination postures need only moderate exaggeration to emphasize the sex of the performer. Such modifications are mainly found in males, and they are achieved in two ways which can be combined. In quite a number of ungulate species, urinating males erect the shoulder region and neck, assuming a "proud" stance which may resemble the posture in a dominance display. Not quite so commonly, they step somewhat forward with the forelegs leaving the hind legs at the same spot so that the distance between forelegs and hind legs is increased and the stretching of the back is emphasized (Fig. 11b), in contrast to the female's squatted posture.

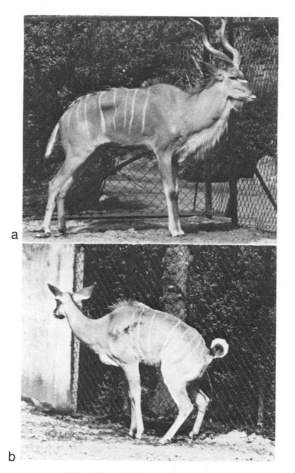

Fig. 10a. Male urination posture
. . . b. . . . and female urination
posture in greater kudu (*Tragelaphus
strepsiceros*). (Walther 1964*b*. Hamburg
Zoo.)

There is no striking difference between sexes in the defecation postures in many ungulate species. However, in some species such as the oryx species and addax antelope, an adult male may squat considerably deeper than females do so that his anus is only a very few centimeters above the ground (Fig. 12). In species such as gazelles and their relatives, pronghorn, and dikdik, in which the adult males urinate and defecate in sequence, the abrupt change from a stretched urination posture to a squatted defecation posture can be very strik-

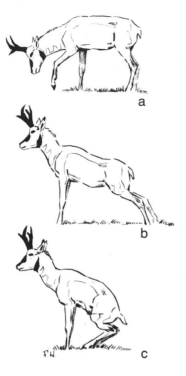

Fig. 11a. Territorial prong-horn buck (*Antilocapra ameri-cana*) scrapes the ground, . . . b. . . . urinates, . . . c. . . . and defecates in a sequence of striking postures. (Walther 1977a.)

ing (Fig. 11). There are some interesting differences in the messages of these exaggerated urination and/or defecation postures in different species. For example, in gazelles, these postures can be somewhat more pronounced in territorial bucks than in nonterritorial males. However, in principle, all adult gazelle males assume them regardless of social status. Thus, it is basically an emphasizing of the (male) sex. In addax and oryx antelopes, which do not urinate and defecate in a sequence, the deep-squatted defecation posture is only used (in addition to the "normal" defacation posture) by males of particularly high social status, often only by the bull with the highest rank at a given location or within a given group—i.e., either a solitary (probably territorial) bull or the alpha bull in a herd. Very typical are Manski's (1979) observations on a group of addax antelope with several adult males and females kept on the pastures of a Texas ranch. Usually only the alpha bull exhibited the squatted defecation posture. The second-ranking bull defecated in this manner in encounters with lower-ranking males, but never when the alpha bull was close by. When one male was kept alone on a pasture, or was the only male among females, then this male showed the deep-squatted defecation posture.

Fig. 12. Dominant bull of East African oryx antelope defecates in deep squatted posture. (Walther 1958a.)

These exaggerated male urination and/or defecation postures are often related to marking behavior, and the same is true for certain other movements which may "frame" urination and/or defecation (such as scraping the ground with forelegs or hind legs), and for special methods of depositing urine and/or feces in the surroundings. Therefore, these behaviors will be discussed in greater detail in the chapter on marking.

Probably certain reflexlike tail movements during maintenance activities also work as presence and position advertisements in some of the species. For example, the blue duiker (*Cephalophus monticola*) almost constantly flips his little tail up and down when moving. Since the underside of this tail is white, this may act like an intermittent flash in the dim forests in which these small creatures live. Another species particularly famous for constant tail movements is Thomson's gazelle and, about seventy years ago, a scientist expressed the opinion that this tail-wagging may be a kind of "conversation" among these animals. If this were true, the tommy—as Thomson's gazelle are usually called in East Africa—would be the greatest talkers of the world, since one may say with little exaggeration that they wag their black tails all the time they are on their feet. They do not do it (or at least it cannot readily be seen) when they are resting. Thus, it may characterize activity as opposed to rest, and signal to conspecifics: "Here is a tommy, and he is up and doing!"

Also, quite a number of vocalizations may occur during simple maintenance activities and apparently reflect low levels of the animal's general motivational state. One may think of the "common grunts" (Kiley 1972) of domestic pigs which occur when the animals are wandering around, standing, and rooting; or of the rhythmical and regular grunts of peccary (Sowls 1974); or of the "long snort" (Klingel 1977) as an expression of well-being in horses, e.g., during eating; or of the previously mentioned groaning-croaking calls ("ugh") of wildebeest, particularly when moving, but also during other maintenance activities.

These and other vocalizations automatically emphasize the animal's presence and advertise its position. Although certain vocalizations of different species may be similar, they are in principle species-specific. Furthermore, the pitch of the sound varies with sex and age; and finally, there are often individual differences, so that even a human can distinguish the cows in a small herd by their voices without being a professional ethologist.

Many ungulate vocalizations are intimately related to increasing levels of excitement (Kiley 1972), and they usually are emulative— that is, they easily evoke responses by the same vocalizations in conspecifics. These two aspects will be discussed in more detail later. However, a few of these vocalizations may be mentioned here because they appear to be more specialized, in that they do not, or at least do not only, reflect different levels of the animal's general mood but are related to relatively specific internal states, and/or are sex specific, and/or are restricted to rather circumscribed situations. They often are relatively loud, some of them even very loud, vocalizations suitable to advertise the animal's presence and position at a considerable distance (e.g., the trumpeting grunts of hippopotamus). Such vocalizations are often said to be typical for species which live in habitats (water, high reed, thickets, dense forests, etc.) where visual displays do not work. This usually is true. For instance, bush pig (*Potamochoerus porcus*) and giant forest pig (*Hylochoerus meinertzhageni*) are two swine species living in densely vegetated habitats, and they vocalize considerably more than warthog, a species living in a much more open habitat (Frädrich 1965). However, it should not be forgotten that quite a number of ungulate species living in dense vegetation are comparatively primitive in terms of evolution, and do not possess great powers of vision. Thus, when acoustical and olfactory means of communication preponderate in such animals, it may not always be a special adaptation to environmental conditions; sometimes it may simply be due to their comparatively primitive evolutionary state. In any case, it should not be concluded from the existence of pronounced acoustical advertisements in forest animals that they are lacking in open plains animals. A few examples may substantiate the statements above.

In the lowland tapir (*Tapirus terrestris*), living solitarily in dense tropical rain forests, Hunsaker and Hahn (1965) describe clicking noises that are considered to be an aid in species identification, and a sliding squeal, mainly uttered by dominant individuals, which also advertises position and apparently has a strong attractive effect upon conspecifics. In captive tapir, von Richter (1966) notes a cough "e'he-e'he"—e as in "leg") that releases response vocalizations and approach in partners. Schenkel and Lang (1969) mention a whistling in Javan rhinoceros (*Rhinoceros sondaicus*) that apparently also serves species identification, while a similar whistle in Indian rhino is uttered by females in heat, and thus advertises a special internal state. Vocalizations typical of females in estrus have been described in other species as well, and males may also utter rather specific vocalizations when sexually approaching females, e.g., a clicking sound (with closed mouth) in greater kudu, a soft "brrrl" (uttered through the nose) in several gazelle species, etc. In gaur (*Bibos gaurus*), extensive roaming and calling by the males mark the onset of the rut (Schaller 1967). When walking alone through the forest, or when approaching or moving around a herd, or in response to the call of another male, a black gaur bull stops at intervals, raises his muzzle and, with opened mouth, produces a clear, resonant "u-u-u-u-u" call. This note may be followed by a second one somewhat lower in tone, by a third still lower, and so forth, so that Schaller (1967) spoke of "the song of the gaur." The loud roar of the red deer (Fig. 13) and the bugling of elk in autumn are particularly well known. Similar vocalizations were exceptionally recorded in female red deer (Raesfeld 1957) and in other seasons, but they generally are typical of adult males in rutting condition. Thus, they advertise the sex and a special psychophysiological state of the performer. Simultaneously, they serve as strong position advertisements, and they are related to the social status of the stag. For this last point, I once had a particularly convincing experience. Four red deer stags were kept together with several females in a very large wooded enclosure. It was during rutting season, but only the strongest stag roared; no rutting call was heard from the three others. However, they started roaring in the evening of the very day when the dominant stag had been removed from the enclosure. As is the case with many visual, acoustical, and olfactory position advertisements which are combined with indications of activated dominance, the roaring of rutting red deer can be heard in a number of more or less different situations. Bützler (1974) lists seven such situations: (a) spontaneous roaring—regardless of whether the stag is alone or together with females (this is particularly frequent after lying down or arising from rest); (b) in response to the sight or the roaring of another stag; (c) before and after a fight; (d) after chasing away subordinate males; (e) after scraping and goring the ground; (f) after herding females; (g) after sexually driving a female and after copulation.

As examples of acoustical advertisements of a male's position, territorial status, or activated dominance (e.g., when herding females or chasing nonterritorial males) in open plains situations, we may mention the whistling of the Uganda kob (Buechner and Schloeth 1965), the black wildebeest's (*Connochaetes gnou*) shrill and strophic blares ("he-itt"—Fig. 14), the strophic "laugh" of the pronghorn (Gregg 1955), and the deep, intermittent roaring (in exhaling) followed by a shrill whistling sound (in inhaling) of Grevy's zebra (Klingel 1972).

When we now consider olfactory advertisement of presence, posi-

Fig. 13. Roaring red deer stag (*Cervus elaphus*). Note the opened preorbital glands. (Bützler 1974. Photo: W. Bützler, Woburn Park, Great Britain.)

Fig. 14. Black wildebeest bull (*Connochaetes gnou*) uttering his shrill blares of position advertisement. (Frankfurt Zoo.)

tion, state, and status, we shall exclude olfactory marking for the time being, and predominantly have in mind behavioral and at least somewhat specialized performances. This considerably restricts the field. For example, certain skin glands, such as the inguinal glands in quite of number of species, are open and produce secretion more or less constantly. Thus, their scent is unavoidably with the animal. Similarly, the vulva of a female in estrus may emit a scent specific of her sex and physiological state, and the famous belly gland of musk deer may produce a strongly smelling secretion during rutting season. In these and similar cases, animals with a keen sense of smell may be able to "diagnose" quite a lot about the producer's species, sex, and state, but one can hardly speak of any behavioral advertisement. These scents simply belong to the morphological or physiological structures of the animals—as the smell of decay belongs to rotten meat. Olfactory advertising may be said to occur when the opening of a skin gland and the emission of its odor depends upon the performance of a maintenance activity. It becomes clearer when the opening of such a gland is linked to the performance of a distinct display, and the more the gland can be opened at will, the more perfect it be-comes (i.e., the less the process of scent emission appears as an automatic, reflexlike consequence of another behavior). An example of skin glands which are opened during a simple maintenance activity are the interdigital glands of many Artiodactyla species. Such glands are located above the two hooves of a foreleg and/or a hind leg and remain more or less closed as long as the two hooves are close to-gether. The glands are opened automatically when the hooves are spread. This regularly happens when the feet are abruptly forced against the ground e.g., during galloping and jumping as simple maintenance activities. It also occurs in stamping or scraping the ground (commonly with one foreleg in ungulates), which are some-what more special behaviors. Finally, the hooves can also be spread and the interdigital glands can be opened when the animal emphati-cally stretches a foreleg, as in foreleg kicks—a quite special courtship behavior of certain species. Similarly, when the preorbital glands of a red deer stag are opened during roaring, this gives the impression of a reflexlike automatism in combination with assuming the typical rutting-call posture with open mouth and head and neck stretched forward and upward (Fig. 13). On the other hand, males of this and certain other cervid and bovid species can open their preorbital glands at will and in combination with a great variety of movements and postures in agonistic and sexual encounters (Fig. 86). In this case, the (presumable) emission of odor can be timed, restricted to special occasions, and even addressed to a particular individual. Thus olfactory advertisement occurs at very different levels of communica-tion, and it functions in species, sex, and individual identification as well as in the signaling of an animal's general state or even its specific condition.

It was not by chance that the examples of olfactory advertising by gland secretion were taken exclusively from ruminants. Tapirs and rhinos possess comparatively few specialized scent glands, and no be-haviors related to such glands have been described. Horses and their relatives have circumanal, circumoral, and perineal glands (Schaffer 1940), but their role in communication is unknown. However, al-though it is certain that horses—like all the animals under discussion—can recognize their partner's sex, species, special physio-logical state (e.g., a mare's estrous condition), and individuality (familiar group member or stranger) by sniffing at specific regions of its body (particularly nose, anal, and genital regions), this has little to do with communication and nothing to do with advertisement. In hippos, the entire skin is rich in mucous glands, but more specialized scent glands are lacking (Haltenorth 1963). In swine, special skin glands, such as mental, preorbital, and carpal glands, sporadically show up in some genera, but nothing is known about their use in communication. By contrast, the dorsal gland of peccary plays a great role in intraspecific communication. Llamas have interdigital glands, and camels possess occipital glands which can be used for marking objects and "self-impregnation" (see below). In short, the situation in Nonruminantia and Tylopoda is only somewhat different from that in odd-toed ungulates. It is in the Ruminantia that special skin glands are frequent and, in at least some cases, have an obvious use in communication.

In addition to secretions from skin glands, urine and feces are the major means of olfactory communication. These types of excrement are, of course, available to all the species under discussion. However, because they are always deposited in the environment and soon become independent of the individual, they are much more important in marking behavior than in advertisements by bodily means. Their smell can only indirectly be transferred to the bodies of their producers, which can also be the case with the secretions of certain glands. Such "self-impregnations" can, of course, strongly reinforce the species or sex-specific odors, and thus they certainly can be considered as means of olfactory advertisements. Here again we find the whole spectrum from more or less accidental events to very aimed and special procedures.

Tapirs frequently defecate when wallowing or bathing (Krieg 1948, Kuelhorn 1955, von Richter 1966); urination also frequently takes place in the water. Likewise, Javan rhinoceros urinate and defecate when wallowing (Schenkel and Lang 1969). In this way, the body may be infected with the smell of urine and feces and thus the species-specific and sex-specific smell may be reinforced and secondarily transmitted to trails, vegetation, etc. However, this self-impregnation and/or olfactory impregnation of the environment is not much more than an accidental byproduct of elimination during wallowing or bathing. Also, when a dromedary rubs the back of his head on his hump and thus transfers the strongly smelling secretion of his occipital gland to this body region, the self-impregnation is still more or less the byproduct of a quite usual maintenance activity (rubbing as a comfort behavior, in this case). Slight changes toward a more aimed self-impregnation may be seen, e.g., in the European bison (*Bison bonasus*) when wallowing in his own urine (Hediger 1949), or in moose, where males paw pits during the rut and urinate and then lie down in these pits (Kakies 1936). Similarly, in bontebok (*Damaliscus dorcas dorcas*—David 1973) and blesbok (Lynch 1974), territorial males often bed down right on top of their dung piles. From such cases, there is a continuous transition to cases of self-marking in which special behaviors are involved to reinforce the body odor and thus the olfactory advertising. For example, peccary may spray secretion of their dorsal gland up in the air in certain situations (Sowls 1974). This of course then drops down on the animal's back. Stags of certain deer species, e.g., fallow deer (*Dama dama*), in rutting condition, spray urine on their bellies by quivering movements of the penis. A male chamois may slowly and emphatically shake his body when urinating during rutting season, thereby infecting both the place where he is standing and the hair of his belly, with urine and its smell (Krämer 1969). In goats and their relatives such as ibex (*Capra ibex*), the males spray urine, and probably also sperm, into the hair (beard) of their throat region during the rut. A similar procedure is found in Gray's waterbuck (*Onotragus megaceros*) where a male arches his back, lowers his head almost to the ground, and then squirts urine between the forelegs into the long hair of his throat and lower jaw. In the Bactrian camel, the self-impregnation with urine is an even more complicated procedure. According to Wemmer and Murtaugh (1980), males in peak rutting condition frequently assume a more exaggerated hind-leg stance than in usual urination and defecation and indulge in bouts of rhythmical tail-flapping while urinating and defecating. Typically, the tail is held momentarily between the hind legs, saturated with urine and audibly flapped upward against the rump and the posterior surface of the rear hump. Feces are not voided when the tail is down. Thus, the self-impregnation is exclusively with urine. Furthermore, there seems to be a self-impregnation with saliva in camels. Their saliva is normally viscous and relatively clear, but excited animals, and particularly males during the rut, work this into a white fluffy foam by repeated tooth gnashing. Head-shaking distributes this foam onto the face and neck (Wemmer and Murtaugh 1980).

A combination of the use of urine and secretion for self-impregnation is found in some of the deer of the Telemetacarpalia group, e.g., white-tailed deer (*Odocoileus virginianus*), mule deer (Müller-Schwarze 1971), and reindeer (Espmark 1964). Besides "normal" urination, individuals of all ages rub their hocks together while urinating in a somewhat squatted posture (Fig. 15). In this manner, the smell of the urine is mixed with that of the tarsal gland, which is located in the center of a hair tuft on the inner side of the tarsal joint. After rub-urination, the tarsal hair tufts are soaked with urine which is then licked off by the animals with the exception of males in rutting condition. On them, scent material accumulates on the entire hind foot (Müller-Schwarze 1974). The odorous substances from the tarsal

Fig. 15. Posture during rub-urination in mule deer (*Odocoileus hemionus*). (Walther 1977*a*.)

tufts of male black-tailed deer (*Odocoileus hemionus columbianus*) belong to the few mammalian pheromones that have been chemically analyzed (Müller-Schwarze 1967, 1969), and whose effects upon conspecifics have been experimentally tested (Müller-Schwarze 1971). Gas chromatograms show differences related to sex, age, and individuals, and the conspecifics apparently can recognize these differences when sniffing the hocks of the producer. Rub-urinating and the mixture of urine and secretion smell, respectively, serve as distress signals in fawns and have an attractive effect on the mother and other females, but in adult stags they advertise a highly dominant status and may release flight or withdrawal in subordinates. It is quite interesting that urinating on the hocks also occurs in moose (another cervid of the Telemetacarpalia group); however, moose do not rub their hind legs together, and they do not possess tarsal glands (Geist 1963, 1966).

A very aimed self-impregnation with the secretion of preorbital glands is reported in the Arctic musk ox, which places one foreleg forward and rubs his preorbital gland on it (Pedersen 1958, Tener 1965, Gray 1973) in the same fashion as certain other ruminants mark inanimate objects. One may literally speak of self-marking in this case. Hartebeest rub their faces on their shoulders and flanks, and some authors (e.g., Dowsett 1966) consider this also to be a self-marking with preorbital gland secretion. However, since it usually takes place after hartebeest have intensely gored in muddy ground, I am not sure whether they are actually marking their flanks with preorbital gland secretion or only smearing themselves with mud.

6. MARKING BEHAVIOR AND MARKS

As was pointed out in the previous chapters, marking is simply a special way of emphasizing presence and advertising position, state, or status. The animal deposits signs of its presence on environmental objects. These marks have an existence of their own and a certain independence of the producer; they are extrinsic signals. The other methods of position, state, and status advertisement gradually merge into marking behavior in this limited sense. The transition is particularly evident in quite a number of cases of self-impregnation. For example, when a musk ox deposits preorbital gland secretion on its own foreleg, as just described, the foreleg seems to be treated like an external object. Also, when a dromedary rubs the occipital gland at its withers, impregnating them with odorous secretion, this is not principally different from the behavior by which the animal deposits secretion of the same gland on environmental objects.

Another transition from olfactory advertisement and self-impregnation to the marking of inanimate objects may be seen in marking of conspecifics. The use of dung for this purpose by hoofed mammals is unknown to me; urine is only infrequently and indirectly used. A good example of the latter is provided by Gray's waterbuck: a male of this species sprays urine into the long hair of his throat and chin region. He sometimes then approaches a female and rubs his wet chin and throat on her croup, head, or withers. Considerably more frequent in ungulates is marking the partner by gland secretion; however, the number of species that do so is still relatively small as compared to the great number of species that possess such glands. Particularly well known is the marking of partners in peccary. Two peccary stand in reverse-parallel (head-to-tail) position, and rub their chins and cheeks at each other's dorsal gland (Fig. 16). Since they frequently do so with different partners, it may be assumed that they create a mutual group smell in this way that allows them to distinguish group members from strangers. The situation in peccary appears to be somewhat exceptional among hoofed mammals in that the dorsal gland is used in marking the partners. More commonly, such marking is executed with glands of the head. In larger and lesser Malayan mouse deer (*Tragulus napu* and *Tragulus javanicus*), the male marks the female during the mating ritual with his interramal glands (Davis 1965, Cadigan 1972, Ralls et al. 1975, Robin 1979) by placing, rubbing, or pressing his chin on her back (Fig. 17a). In other Ruminantia species, the partners are marked with the secretion from preorbital glands (or maxillary glands in duikers). In Maxwell's duiker (*Cephalophus maxwelli*), male and female press their glands together and mark each other alternately (Aeschlimann 1963, Ralls 1969), and in banded duiker (*Cephalophus zebra*), mothers were observed marking their young (Frädrich 1964). Male gerenuk (*Litocranius walleri*—Backhaus 1958, Walther 1958a, Leuthold 1972) and dibatag (*Ammodorcas clarkei*—Walther 1963) mark the female's lower neck, anterior chest, or croup with their preorbital glands. Furthermore, when animals lick each other, they possibly may infect each other with the smell of their saliva. Particularly in mother-offspring relationships, it has been suggested by Gubernick (1981) that the mothers "label" their own young in this way.

Little is known with respect to the functions of this partner marking. In some cases, particularly when mothers "label" their young with their saliva, or when duiker mothers mark their fawns by secretion from their maxillary glands, one may presume that this marking is helpful in identification of their offspring. Some scientists are inclined to presume a repellent effect upon other males when a female has been marked by a male. There is no concrete proof that this is the case, but if it should be true, the repellent effect certainly would

Fig. 16. Collared peccary (*Tayassu tajacu*) in reciprocal rubbing of the head at the other's dorsal gland region. (Sowls 1974.)

a

b

Fig. 17a. Male of lesser Malayan mouse deer (*Tragulus javanicus*) marks the female with his inter-ramal (intermandibular) glands. (Robin 1979. Photo: N. P. Robin. Zurich Zoo.) b. Wildebeest bull rubs his preorbital gland region at the opponent's rump during a territorial encounter. (Walther 1979. Serengeti National Park.)

not be greater than that of a wedding ring in humans. Also, it should be mentioned that marking the partner is not necessarily restricted to friendly interactions. In certain species, e.g., Maxwell's duiker (Ralls 1974), the rivals also mark each other during agonistic encounters.

Secretion marking by ungulates of inaminate objects is far more frequent than marking of partners. However, it must be emphasized that not all the species that possess such glands mark with them. This varies even within a subfamily or genus. For example, all the gazelle species have preorbital glands, but only some of them—such as Thomson's gazelle, goitered gazelle (*Gazella subgutturosa*), and red-fronted gazelle (*Gazella rufifrons*)—mark objects with them, whereas others—such as Grant's gazelle, Sömmering's gazelle (*Gazella soemmeringi*), and dorcas gazelle—do not (Walther 1968*a*, 1977*a*). In all the gazelle species that do mark both males and females possess preorbital glands, although those of females are usually smaller; however, only the males mark objects with them. The same is true for a great number of other bovids and cervids. However, e.g., in klipspringer, dikdik, bontebok (David 1973), and blesbok, the females also mark occasionally.

As stated above, the glands used for object marking are most commonly located on the head. These include subauricular glands in pronghorn, frontal glands in roe deer (von Schumacher-Marienfrid 1939), fields of sudoriferous glands of above-average development in the skin of the forehead in black-tailed deer (Quay and Müller-Schwarze 1970), postcornual (supraoccipital) glands in chamois and mountain goat, interramal (intermandibular) glands in mouse deer, occipital glands in dromedary, maxillary glands in duikers, and, above all, preorbital (antorbital) glands in numerous bovid and cervid species. Glands used for aimed object marking that are not located on the head are relatively rare in hoofed mammals. I have already mentioned the dorsal gland in peccary with which the members of a group mark each other. However, they also mark high grass, reed, brushes, etc., by backing into these objects and stripping off secretion from the dorsal gland. Pawing the ground with the forelegs frequently accompanies this scent gland rubbing in peccary (Schweinsburg and Sowls 1972). A similar use of a dorsal gland may be presumed in the yellow-backed duiker (*Cephalophus sylvicultor*). Unique among ungulates is the use of glands of the anal region (proctodeal gland) in the primitive lesser Malayan mouse deer (Robin 1979). The male flips his tail up, slowly sits down like a dog, and presses the anal region with arhythmical movements against the ground. In addition to this anal gland marking, lesser Malayan mouse deer also mark with their interramal glands by rubbing their lower jaws horizontally over the objects. Interestingly, eating sometimes occurs in connection with this object marking: the animals take marked or unmarked objects (twigs, small branches, etc.) in their mouths, hastily chew them, and swallow or spit them out (Robin 1979).

Preorbital gland marking may be described by the example of blackbuck (Hediger 1949, Walther 1966a—Fig. 18). The male frequently, although not necessarily, first sniffs at the object to be marked (most commonly a twig of a shrub or tree, a thorn, a grass stem, etc.) and touches it with his nose. Occasionally he also may briefly lick or nibble at it. He turns his head so that one cheek more or less points toward the ground, brings it near the object, and opens the preorbital gland wide. He carefully brings the tip of the grass stem into the open gland, and deposits some secretion on it during quivering movements of the margins of the gland. After marking, he may again briefly lick the object. More frequently, he licks his upper lip and performs slight snapping movements with the mouth and/or nodding movements with the head.

In its major points, the procedure is much the same in all the bovid and cervid species that mark objects with their preorbital organs.

Fig. 18. Male Indian blackbuck (*Antilope cervicapra*) marks the tip of a branch with his preorbital gland. (Walther 1977*a*.)

Even duikers, which use their maxillar glands, or pronghorn, which use their subauricular glands, behave very similarly. On the other hand, of course, there are some variations in the different species. For example, in species such as klipspringer, where the preorbital gland is permanently open and/or does not have movable margins, the described process of opening the gland as well as the quivering movements of its margin is lacking. In wildebeest, the marking movements often are not aimed at a single twig or grass stem; rather, the animal wipes the secretion onto the vegetation. More or less ritualized rubbing or butting of the object on which the secretion is deposited with forehead, horns, or antlers may precede the gland marking or follow it. In cervids, this is even rather frequent. Axis stags (*Axis axis*) often rise on their hind feet when marking trees or bushes, and apparently try to deposit the secretion as high up as possible. A particularly interesting variation of preorbital gland marking has been described in oribi (*Ourebia oribi*) by Gosling (1972). These little antelopes live in areas where the grass is often considerably taller than they are. An oribi male may first bite off a grass stem, bring it down to body height in this way, and then mark the stump. In some of the species, e.g., dikdik, the secretion on the marked object is blackish brown and quite visible, particularly when it takes the size and form of a small pearl due to multiple marking; however, it is almost odorless to humans. By contrast, the subauricular secretion of pronghorn, for example, is invisible but leaves a strong, musky odor on the vegetation.

Territorial animals mark their territories, but gland marking does not necessarily imply that the species or the individual is territorial.

For example, many cervids, such as axis deer, white-tailed deer, and red deer, mark with their preorbital glands. However, territoriality is absent in these species as in the majority of cervids. Even within a species where some of the males become territorial, object marking is not restricted to the territorial individuals. Thus the mark per se indicates only the presence or past occurrence of a male, not necessarily his territorial status. It is the concentration of marks by the same individual within a comparatively very limited area, that makes marking indicative of territoriality (Walther 1964a, 1978b).

It is tempting to assume that the secretion marks, particularly within territories, have an intimidating or repellent effect on potential competitors. Occasionally one can observe such reactions; however, on the whole, they are rare. In many species of the territorial/ gregarious type, nonterritorial males as a matter of course enter well-marked territories without paying any attention to the marks. They may be of somewhat greater importance to the immediate territorial neighbors for recognizing the position of the boundary, but they seem above all to be important for the orientation of the owner of the territory himself. The most commonly observed reaction of an animal to another's secretion mark—insofar as it pays attention to it—is to sniff the marked object; sometimes the newcomer will mark it too, or mark another one close by. Thus, the first animal leaves an indication of its presence and the newcomer adds his own "visiting card."

Saliva is another secretion available to all ungulates, but it is not used for environmental marking in most of the species. However, Beuerle (1975) describes a marking by saliva in wild boar (Sus scrofa). During the rutting season, males produce a "foam" of saliva around their mouths by continually clapping with their lower jaws. They deposit flecks of this foam as high as possible on thin tree trunks, branches, etc., as well as on females when sexually driving them.

Dung and urine are available to all hoofed mammals; thus marking with these types of excrement is more widespread among them than marking with secretions from special glands, although it by no means occurs in all the species under discussion. For example, cervids usually do not use feces as a special means of marking, and urine too plays a comparatively minor role in their environmental marking. In certain swine species—e.g., giant forest hog—localized dung patches have been noticed (Dönhoff 1942), but other species—e.g., warthog—defecate at random (Frädrich 1967). As with secretion marking, marking with excrement is often linked with territorial behavior; however, it is by no means restricted to it. Clear observations of its repellent effects upon potential rivals are as rare as they are in secretion marking.

Not many ungulate species known to me mark exclusively with urine, while there are some species in which apparently only dung plays a role. (In self-impregnation and marking the partner, it is almost the opposite, as previously discussed). In a number of species, both urine and feces are used for marking, quite frequently in combination. Since urination and defecation are normal physiological processes, one can think of these processes and their products as having a communicative importance only when other conspecifics clearly react to them and/or when an animal deposits urine and feces in definite places (resulting in dung piles in the case of defecation) and/or when urination and/or defecation are performed in a special way or are combined with other striking behaviors that emphasize the significance of these procedures.

Among the criteria for the communicative function of urine and/or feces, the reaction of conspecifics is probably the most common but also the most problematic. Frequently, an animal may only sniff the excrement and—not quite as often—deposit its own urine or dung at the same place. That animals with a keen sense of smell will sniff an odorous substance when they happen to encounter it is not surprising and is by no means restricted to urine and feces. Also, the tendency to deposit the droppings where there are some already is very common in hoofed mammals. The excrements need not necessarily even be from animals of the same species. There is unmistakable evidence that many ungulate species are able visually to recognize urination and defecation postures in conspecifics. Thus even when the other approaches the urinating or defecating animal and urinates or defecates close by, it is more or less a case of "contagion," and thus—at best—only at the borderline of a true communication process. In short, there are numerous cases in which animals react to excrement or to another's urination and defecation postures, but these reactions are frequently rather unspecific and thus do not provide particularly convincing proof of communication. Of course, it is often equally hard to prove that no communicative process has taken place. It frequently remains a "maybe-or-maybe-not" matter.

The situation becomes somewhat clearer when the reaction is restricted to one sex or to animals of a special social status. For example, as Feist and McCullough (1976) found in feral horses, a stallion detecting the urination or defecation of a mare of his harem band approaches, smells her droppings, steps over them, urinates or defecates on them, turns, and smells again. But the authors did not see mares respond to excrement of other horses. In all-male bands, dominant stallions eliminate on top of the eliminations of subordinate males, and when the lowest-ranking group member defecates first, the rest or part of the group may follow in order of dominance. Thus, the restriction of reactions to the stallion of a harem as well as the dominance sequence in the members of a bachelor group indicate at least that specific social factors are involved, i.e., that sniffing the feces is not simply a curiosity behavior and that elimination on top of the other's feces is not merely due to contagion.

It is likely that horses can recognize the dung of group members and that stallions can learn something about a mare's estrous state when sniffing her urine and subsequently performing *Flehmen* (lip-curl). Trumler (1958) claimed that a stallion alters the smell of a mare's droppings when marking them, thus hiding the female's estrous state from other stallions. However, Klingel (1974) did not find evidence for this interpretation in his studies on plains zebra. A zebra stallion with a harem does not mark all the feces and urine of an estrous mare, and even when other stallions come across such unmarked droppings, they do not approach the mare but respect the presence of the harem stallion. Although all equine species may defe-cate and/or urinate onto feces and/or urine of their conspecifics or on their own droppings, the latter habit becomes particularly striking in the territorial stallions of Grevy's zebra and wild ass, who establish enormous piles in the course of time which may cover several square meters and be up to 40 cm. high (Klingel 1974).

Generally, localization of urination and/or defecation to definite spots, resulting in the establishment of dung piles, may be said to be quite good proof that excrement plays a role in presence and position advertising. To establish large dung piles, of course, an animal must stay in a relatively limited area for some time. This is easily achieved in territorial species. In many of them—e.g., kongoni (*Alcelaphus buselaphus cokei*—Gosling 1974), dikdik, topi, and gazelle species—dung piles are found either in the approximate center of the territory (close to the owner's preferred resting place) or along the boundary (linked with agonistic encounters), whereas in square-lipped rhinoceros, the twenty to thirty dung piles of a territorial bull are scattered throughout the territory (Owen-Smith 1974). Sometimes several individuals use the same dung pile, making it larger than one animal alone could do. This may happen with boundary dung piles of owners of neighboring territories, or when a whole group perma-nently stays in a territory as, e.g., in vicuna (Franklin 1974). In short, dung piles are very common in territorial ungulates, and when ter-ritorial and nonterritorial males occur beside each other in a species, frequently only the territorial individuals establish and use dung piles while the bachelors defecate at random. On the other hand, there are exceptions to this general rule. For example, pronghorn bucks are territorial and even mark with urine and feces but they do not establish noteworthy dung piles. In nonterritorial species, dung piles are infrequent but do sometimes occur, as in nilgai (*Boselaphus tragocamelus*) where several males and females use the same pile (Fall 1972). Even in certain territorial species, dung piles (as well as urination sites) are not necessarily restricted to the territorial grounds but may occasionally also be found outside the territories, e.g., on heavily frequented trails. Hence, although the connection between territorial behavior and marking by dung piles appears to be even stronger than that between territorial behavior and secretion marking, it is not so strict that one could say, The animal establishes dung piles and thus is territorial; or, It does not establish dung piles and thus is not territorial.

When urine and/or feces serve a special function besides the normal elimination of physiological waste products in a species, the process of their deposition is usually behaviorally emphasized. This can be achieved by a specialization of the performance of urinating and/or defecating. Tapirs—predominantly the males—(von Richter 1966)—and rhinoceroses (Schenkel and Lang 1969) can urinate in both a "normal" and a "ritualized" way. Apparently the latter is always linked with a certain degree of excitement (von Richter 1966); at any rate, the animal is not completely relaxed. Sometimes even the (mild) state of "arousal" caused by placing the urine at a special marking site may be sufficient. Even when urinating in the "normal" way, the urine is splashed backwards by a rhino bull at an angle of about 45°. However, in ritualized urination (Fig. 19), he splashes his urine backwards horizontally in the form of a fine spray in three to five spasmodic bursts (Owen-Smith 1974). Rhino cows may also show ritualized urination, but less frequently than bulls (Schenkel and Lang 1969). Well known is the habit of male hippopotamus of vividly and vehemently wagging the short tail while defecating. Since, when defecating outside the water, a hippo bull is usually oriented with his hindquarters toward a shrub, reed, etc., the dung is distributed and flung high up in the vegetation, and such defecation places mark the trails from the water to the terrestrial feeding areas in hippos (Frädrich 1967).

In our discussion of the visual emphasizing of sex-specific peculiarities of urinating and/or defecating in gazelles and certain other bovid species and in pronghorn, we mentioned the strikingly exaggerated postures of the males. Of course, by stretching the hind legs extremely far backwards during urination, such a male lowers his belly and penis as close to the ground as is possible for an ungulate without lying down. Lang (1956) describes the marking of small

Fig. 19. Square-lipped rhinoceros bull (*Ceratotherium simum*) sprays his urine backward. (Owen-Smith 1975. Photo: R. N. Owen-Smith— Umfolozi-Corridor-Hluhluwe game reserve, South Africa.)

bushes with urine by okapi bulls during which the animals even almost lie down. In extremely crouched defecating postures, the anus is only a few centimeters off the ground. Thus, these urination and defecation postures are not only specialized and visually striking, but they also enable the animal to place the excrement more accurately than in the "normal" postures. When urination and defecation are executed in a sequence, it is possible in this way to deposit urine and dung at precisely the same spot. In mouse deer and water chevrotain (*Hyemoschus aquaticus*) where the males also lower their bellies toward the ground in urination, it is presumed that secretion of the preputial gland may run down together with the urine (Dubost 1965, 1975, Robin 1979).

Another way to emphasize the process of urination and/or defecation—frequently combined with spray-urination or the special postures mentioned above as well as with the establishment of dung piles—is "framing" the elimination act by other behaviors, among which scraping the ground is particularly common. Tapirs scrape alternately with their hind feet before and after urinating and defecating. According to von Richter (1966), they hardly touch the dung pile in doing so. By contrast, black rhino (*Diceros bicornis*) and territorial white rhino bulls powerfully kick backward with their hind legs so that the dung is broken up and scattered over the heap (Schenkel and Lang 1969, Owen-Smith 1975). In white rhino, a bull may also dig his anterior horn deeply in the dung heap after sniffing it. In connection with urination, Schenkel and Lang (1969) describe a "complex bull's ritual" in black rhino: the bull sniffs at a shrub, assumes the attack posture, and snorts as in an attack. He swings his head alternately to the right and the left so that snout and nose rub over the shrub. He intensifies this swinging until the brush is smashed by horns and head. He steps forward over the plant with stiff hind legs, spraying urine over it in several dashes. He then steps backward over the brush, scraping and kicking backward with the hind legs at each step. In white rhino, wiping the anterior horn over a low bush or the ground as well as dragging the hind legs stiffly over the marking site belong to the urination ritual (Owen-Smith 1974).

In even-toed ungulates, stamping-like movements with the hind legs (alternately lifting the hind legs) before defecating have been reported in lesser Malayan mouse deer (Robin 1979), and the little steenbok (*Raphicerus campestris*) may sometimes scrape with one or both hind feet after defecation, partly covering the droppings with soil. Otherwise, steenbok scrape with their forefeet. Generally, in most even-toed ungulates—insofar as they scrape the ground in connection with elimination (there are species which do not, or which only exceptionally paw the ground, such as greater and lesser kudu, sitatunga, nyala, bongo)—as well as in the horse-related animals, the most remarkable difference from tapirs and rhinos is that they scrape the ground with their forelegs and that this pawing usually precedes urination and/or defecation; scraping after elimination is exceptional. Pilters (1954) and Franklin (1974) describe a "defecation ritual" in vicuna. A territorial male and the females of his harem use localized dung piles. They regularly first sniff at the dung, stamp alternately with both forelegs in it, scrape, make a quarter turn, position their bodies over the pile with their hindquarters lowered, and defecate and/or urinate. The scraping can be lacking, and when a territorial male is involved in an agonistic encounter with neighbors or strangers, he does not necessarily even defecate or urinate; however, stamping and turning are obligatory. According to Pilters (1954) the other llama forms—wild and domesticated—do not show this ritual. Its special point is the prevailing role of stamping; in other Artiodactyla the leg movements can be described as scraping or pawing but hardly as stamping. The "push-scraping" (*Stemmscharren*—Beuerle 1975) of wild boar may come closest to stamping. This behavior is sometimes (but not necessarily) combined with the male's urination during rutting season. The boar makes a few small steps with the forelegs, lowers the head, and pushes the forelegs alternately against the ground. Another behavior of the same species may be related to this push-scraping. When a boar comes across a place where a female has urinated during rutting season, he sniffs at this spot, roots somewhat and takes her urine in, steps over the spot and splashes his urine over it, nodding with his head and abruptly lifting a foreleg—in a fashion somewhat resembling the foreleg kick in the mating ritual of certain bovid species.

In pronghorn, gazelles, and their relatives as well as in certain dwarf antelopes (e.g., dikdik), in which the males urinate and defecate in a sequence, scraping the ground often although not regularly precedes this sequence (Fig. 11a), predominantly in owners of territories. (In dikdik, females may also do so—Dittrich and Boer 1980). They do not alternately scrape with both forelegs but make several strokes with one foreleg and then several strokes with the other. Since all these animals have interdigital glands on their forefeet, one may presume that secretion scent is added to that of urine and dung. Also, visible tracks are often left by this scraping. In steenbok, the situation deviates somewhat from the usual in that males *and* females scrape, and they do it not only before they urinate and defecate but also in between and after. Scraping the ground also occurs in some antelopes which do not urinate and defecate in a sequence, and in which only the dung seems to be used as a means of marking, such as hartebeest, topi, oryx, and addax. In these cases, of course, scraping does not precede urination but only defecation. In bovid species where neither dung nor urine plays a role as a means of marking, such as wild goats (*Capra*), sheep (*Ovis*), bushbuck, and greater and lesser kudu, scraping in combination with elimination is usually lacking. An exception to this general rule may be seen in cattle, where scraping the ground is frequently accompanied by defecating relatively small portions of dung. However, cattle do not establish dung piles and usually do not take much notice of droppings (Schloeth 1958). On the whole, scraping the ground appears to be more related to preparing a wallowing site in oxen (McHugh 1958, Schloeth 1961a). Scraping in combination with elimination is also lacking in the majority of the deer species; however, quite a number of cervids, e.g., red deer and roe deer (Fig. 20), show scraping combined with object aggression (Müller-Using and Schloeth 1967). It is an interesting fact that roe deer possess interdigital glands only on their hind feet. Thus, interdigital gland secretion cannot be deposited by their scraping and pawing with the forelegs.

Scraping the ground may also occur in connection with wallowing (and also in connection with feeding, or prior to lying down for rest, but these are cases which are not of interest in a discussion on communicative behavior). Wallowing in mud, sand, or dust occurs in a

Fig. 20. Combination of scraping the ground and object marking with frontal gland in roe deer (*Capreolus capreolus*).

number of hoofed mammals but by no means in all of them. It generally is present in the odd-toed ungulates and in Nonruminantia and Tylopoda, and it sporadically occurs in a few Ruminantia species such as red deer and elk, oxen (Fig. 21), and wildebeests; however, most of the cervid and bovid species do not wallow. In a few of these latter species, however, there are behaviors which could be considered as derivations of wallowing. For example, during rutting season an adult male mountain goat may sit down on his hindquarters like a dog (Fig. 22) and paw quickly and vigorously with a foreleg, throwing snow, sand, and dirt at his belly, hind legs, and flanks (Geist 1965). The males dig rutting pits in this way, and can be distinguished from females at a distance by their dirty "trousers" during this season. Although they may rest in their rutting pits, they do not wallow in them. Generally, well-frequented wallowing places are rather striking locations, and it may be presumed that scraping the ground adds more marks to these places—be it the tracks of scraping or the scent of interdigital glands. For example, in wildebeest, a territorial bull has a "stamping ground" of bare soil in his territory where he most frequently defecates, stands and lies, paws, kneels, horns the ground, and wallows, and these "stamping grounds" are also attractive to the (nonterritorial) cows and calves as standing, resting, and rolling places (Estes 1969). We will return to further peculiarities of pawing the ground when discussing space-claim displays.

Fig. 21. Yak bull (*Poëphagus mutus*) rolling on the ground. (Walther 1979. Munich Zoo.)

Next to sniffing at excrement, scraping the ground is the most commonly performed action to occur in combination with urination and defecation, as stated above. However, there are other "framing" actions, as can be taken from previous descriptions of certain "rituals," such as the complex bull's ritual in black rhino; in quite a number of species, gland marking frequently precedes or follows urination and/or defecation as, e.g. in territorial blesbok bulls (Lynch 1974). Such "framing" actions often work two ways: they make the whole performance visually more striking, and at least some of them are suitable for leaving visual and/or olfactory marks in the environment. The same may be said of object aggression, which shows connections to urination or defecation in only a relatively few species; e.g., in bontebok, territorial males may kneel down and horn in patches of dung (David 1973). More often it is related to secretion marking (particularly with glands on the head); frequently it occurs completely on its own. Certainly these object aggressions are special forms of fighting behavior, and I will come back to them when speaking of space-claims and threat displays. On the other hand, they are clearly connected with advertising presence, position, state, and status as well as with environmental marking. Object aggression means that the animal attacks inanimate objects such as trees, branches, bushes, grass, rocks, and ground, and, in captivity, fences and feeders. It comes close to what has been termed "redirected aggression" in ethology, but is not quite identical with it: in "redirected aggression," the object being attacked (a) can also be another animal,

Fig. 22. Male mountain goat (*Oreamnos americanus*) pawing a rutting pit. (Geist 1965.)

and (b) is used as a substitute for an opponent who originally released the aggression. The former is not applicable, and the latter is only a special case of "object aggression," in the sense that is meant here.

One could almost say that instances of object aggression occur in all hoofed mammals. However, in the case of swine and peccary, for example, they are difficult to distinguish from rubbing the head on objects, rooting, and the like. As for giraffe, camels, and llamas, there are only a very few reports of object aggression in captive animals (Pilters, 1954, 1956, Backhaus 1960*a*), and no proof that it has any function in social communication. The clearest examples are provided by animals that possess horns or antlers (Fig. 23)—i.e., the bovids and cervids—but it must be emphasized from the outset that object aggression is by no means restricted to territorial species or individuals. Sometimes, as in sheep of all ages and sexes (Geist 1971), horning shrubs, grass bunches, or small trees may simply be done to remove an uncomfortable lump of hair or other irritant from between the horns, and in this case, of course, the "object aggression" has nothing to do with marking. In cervids, acts of object aggression are often presumed to aid in getting rid of the velvet after the antlers have grown. That this is an insufficient explanation for all object aggression in cervids is very evident from the fact that stags continue to attack objects long after their antlers are free of velvet. From the human point of view, one may say this is unfortunate, since they can do quite a bit of damage to forest cultures in this way. Moreover, pronghorn as well as most of the bovid species show intensive object aggression although their horns are never surrounded by velvet. Almost all the movements used in a fight with a living opponent can also occur in cases of object aggression. Quite often the animals also rub their foreheads between the horns or the antlers on the object. Particularly in goring the ground or grass, the animals often do not push or butt straight forward but sideways. In some species such as Grant's gazelle, this has been ritualized into a more or less rhythmical "weaving" alternately from right to left and back. This weaving action can last for minutes or even up to a quarter of an hour and is a rather striking performance. On the whole, object aggressions can be considered visual displays under certain aspects. However, particularly when animals fight branches or trees in a forest, as deer frequently do, the performance can also be heard at a distance. Since many of the species under discussion have special skin glands on their heads, the possibility that they may wipe off secretion from these glands during object aggression cannot be rejected, although not much hard evidence has been found for this presumption up to now. Finally, object aggression often leaves visible marks in the environment, particularly when executed in muddy soil as is frequent in certain species. For example, in the territories as well as the home ranges of bachelors in red hartebeest (*Alcelaphus buselaphus caama*), there are always a number of hollowed-out and denuded patches caused by ground-horning (Kok 1975). Occasionally, object aggression may also be seen in females, but it is considerably more common in males. When territorial and nonterritorial males occur in the same species, object aggression is more frequent in the owners of territories, and when the animals of a given species routinely drop to their "knees" in fighting, they also do so in object aggression.

The motivations of object aggression appear to be manifold. Generally, one may say that the animal is in a more or less intensive state of aggressive arousal. As previously mentioned, object aggression in cervids may aid in getting rid of the velvet on the antlers. This and some other cases seem to be close to comfort behavior. On other occasions, it gives the impression of an aggressive game. Sometimes it can be said to be or at least come close to a threat display. Sometimes it is clearly combined with and connected to secretion marking. However, quite frequently it is also performed spontaneously, i.e., without any combination and connection to other behaviors and without any recognizable situational "reason."

This last point is something which object aggression has in common with marking behavior, but there are more relationships. In the aforementioned "complex bull's ritual" of black rhino, object aggres-

Fig. 23. Greater kudu bull goring muddy ground with his horns. (Etosha National Park.)

sion as well as spray-urination belong to the performance. Also, in several bovid species, and here particularly in encounters between territorial neighbors, object aggression may occur in close temporal proximity to urination and/or defecation. Even more striking are the relationships to secretion marking. For example, territorial pronghorn bucks may alternately butt with their "prongs" and mark with their subauricular glands the same object. Topi rather regularly take a grass stem between their horns and perform gentle butting movements before they mark it with their preorbital glands. Several bovid species sometimes execute nodding movements with their heads while marking with their preorbital glands (i.e., while the tip of the grass stem is introduced into the gland), and these nodding movements resemble mild butting. Moreover, the movements in which certain species, such as chamois and mountain goat, mark with their postcornual glands more or less completely correspond to those in playful, gentle fighting. A young blesbok I raised years ago (Walther 1966a, 1969) performed the first aggressive movements of its life (boxing with the forehead) not half an hour after the first marking movements (with preorbital glands) toward the same object. Thus, aggressive and marking behavior occurred and apparently matured on the same day (the sixteenth day after birth) and within the same hour, which may be taken as a clue to the close relationship between the two behaviors. Possibly the relationship of object aggression to scent marking goes rather deep under phylogenetic aspects. Bubenik (1971) has proposed an interesting hypothesis according to which the antlers of cervids may have evolved from glandular organs. If this hypothesis were correct (and if it could possibly be extended to the horns of bovids, for which no corresponding investigations are available at present), it would explain a lot.

The cases in which the object aggression comes closest to a threat display are those which best fit the concept of redirected responses (Moynihan 1955). These types of object aggression are usually released by and performed in the presence of an opponent or potential opponent, and they also include aggression toward living objects, i.e., usually subordinate conspecifics that did not release the performer's aggression but happened to be around when it was released by a rival in the vicinity ("*Radfahrer-Reaktion*" —Grzimek 1949). The latter— aggression toward living substitutes—is found in all hoofed mammals. In accordance with the "conflict hypothesis," ethologists commonly interpret the redirected aggression (against other animals as well as against inanimate objects) as resulting from a simultaneous arousal of conflicting tendencies to attack and to escape. At least in hoofed mammals, however, the situations in which such redirected aggression occur are often rather complex and—provided that the animal is in some inner conflict, which is not always certain—it is frequently not flight that counterbalances aggression. For example, in Thomson's gazelle, a buck may be alone in his comparatively small territory when a nonterritorial male or several bachelors show up in the vicinity, but without entering the territory. In this situation, the territorial buck usually remains inside his territory, but he frequently begins to gore the grass and the ground with his horns. Or—to give an example of redirected aggression toward other animals—when an impala male (*Aepyceros melampus*) is rounding up a herd of females and another adult male appears at a distance, the buck with the herd may start chasing immature males ("yearlings") which were among the females and which he previously had ignored. In both events, aggressive tendencies are released by the presence of a potential competitor. However, they conflict not with flight but, in the case of the tommy buck, with the strong tendency of a territorial male to stay in his territory, and in the case of the impala buck, with the tendency to stay with the females and to keep them together in a tight bunch. In both cases, the males advertise not only their presence and position but also their very aggressive state, and under this aspect, these acts of redirected aggression may be considered threats. As compared to other (and—at least to the human observer—sometimes less striking) threat displays, however, they are considerably less effective; they do not as easily release withdrawal or flight, and even absolutely subordinate addressees often simply watch the sender's display, or ignore it completely, in the case of bovids. Possibly it is different in cervids, since Geist (pers. comm.) has observed that in mule deer the sound caused by beating the trees or bushes with the antlers may release flight in immature males during the rut, and Bergerud (1974) found that thrashing trees was more frequent in large than in young caribou stags. On the whole, redirected aggression seems to represent an intermediate stage between addressed and unaddressed behavior as well as between advertisement of presence and position, marking behavior, and threat displays.

In some swine species (Frädrich 1967) but particularly in quite a number of cervid species object aggression, frequently combined with other marking activities, may result in the establishment of "signposts." For example, in white-tailed deer in certain areas (Hirth 1977), a buck may thrash from side to side with his antlers near the base of a shrub and/or push and rub his antlers and forehead up and down the trunk of a sapling and/or pull at branches with his mouth. At the same time he may also paw the ground with his forefeet beside or under the tree or bush and urinate there—sometimes the "normal" way, sometimes by rub-urination. Thus, broken branches and a depression in the ground—visual signs—as well as the smell of urine and probably also that of secretion of sudoriferous glands in the skin of the forehead may make such a "signpost" striking to conspecifics. In sambar (*Rusa unicolor*) and axis deer, a somewhat modified behavior is found (Brander 1923, Schaller 1967) which—in matchless anthropomorphism—has been termed "preaching" by certain authors and which has been previously mentioned in a somewhat different context. In these species, a stag rears up on his hind legs under low-hanging branches of a tree. He shakes his head back and forth, thrashing the leaves with his antlers and depositing secretion from his preorbital glands on them, at the same time, treading with his hind legs to remain upright. Prior to and after "preaching," he may paw the ground so that marks of his activity are left not only on the tree but also in the form of bare patches on the ground below it. Less striking but basically along the same lines are the marks which red deer stags leave on tree trunks, working them with the basis of their antlers and rubbing their foreheads and cheeks on them (Schloeth 1961b). Elk stags behave the same way, and female elk may remove long strips of bark from trees with their teeth, and rub chin and cheeks at these denuded spots (Graf 1956). In short, some kind of marking activity, more or less related to object aggression toward trees, bushes, etc., and with it the establishment of "signposts," is present in almost every cervid. "Signpost trees" have also been noticed in certain swine species (Frädrich 1967), and horning trees until the bark hangs in shreds has been observed in certain bovids such as European and American bison (Hediger 1949, McHugh 1958). In some cervids and bovids, stamping grounds and wallows appear to complement the "signpost trees" functionally, and again object aggression is involved. For example, according to Schaller (1967), barasingha stags (*Rucervus duvauceli*) in rutting condition dig out wallows by jabbing either their brow tines or the tips of their antlers into the sod and then jerking their heads up vigorously. These actions, as well as churning the sod with sharp hooves, create a muddy depression in which the stags lie down, sometimes continuing to dig with their antlers during wallowing.

It is certain that other males take notice of such signposts, wallows, and stamping grounds—usually by adding marks of their activities to those of the previous performer(s). Whether females are attracted by signposts is not as certain. Some authors presume so, but others have not found much evidence for it. On the whole, it may be best to end the discussion on extrinsic signals and marking behavior in hoofed mammals with the remark that, at present, conclusions on their significance for communication are often much more speculative and uncertain than some authors would apparently like to admit. Of course, when one has seen, for example, how in a captive situation a new animal, when brought into an enclosure with conspecifics, frequently first explores and sniffs the signposts, dung piles, marking sites, etc., before it engages in contacts with the other animals, although they may approach, bother, and even attack it, one may attribute quite an importance to the olfactory marks. The question is whether this importance lies in communication. On the other hand, when one has seen how frequently and carelessly nonterritorial males enter a well-marked territory in many ungulate species in the wild, one may severely doubt whether the dung piles, secretion marks, etc., have much communicative significance. Consequently, several contemporary field workers have come, independently of each other, to the opinion that such extrinsic marks may be more important for the orientation of the animals in the environment, and not least for the producers themselves, than for communication among the conspecifics.

7. SPACE CLAIMS

In agonistic encounters of hoofed mammals, certain behavior patterns may show up which are not direct aggressive activities but which are strongly related to marking behaviors, and some of them possibly also to excitement activities. On the other hand, in all of them is at least an undertone of aggression. They are released by and occur in the immediate presence of an opponent. However, they are directed not toward the opponent but toward the ground or vegetation, and—as with all marking behaviors—they are not restricted to hostile interactions but may also (and even frequently) occur in other situations and in the absence of any potential opponent. As always when the interpretation of a behavior becomes difficult, they have frequently been declared in ethological literature to be displacement activities. However, it is generally recognized as a characteristic of displacement movements that they are irrelevant to the situation. This is not true of the behaviors we have in mind here, for they meaningfully fit into an agonistic situation. When using them in a hostile encounter, the animal may be claiming occupancy of a place, either literally, in the case of a territorial animal, or more symbolically and only very temporarily, in the case of a nonterritorial animal. Intimidating or challenging effects on recipients are recognizable but are often considerably less pronounced than in threat and dominance displays. One can imagine that these behaviors perhaps may have a somewhat reassuring effect on the performer and, above all, may signal to the opponent: "This is my place—you'd better stay away!" This view is supported by the usual absence of these displays in situations where threat and dominance displays may be used but where a space claim would not agree with the requirements of the situation, such as in coordination of group activities, mother-infant relationships, and courtship (but they may occur in herding behavior, which is often related to space). Therefore, I will speak of space-claim displays.

Space-claim displays in hoofed mammals predominantly include urination and/or defecation, marking with skin glands (especially of the head region), object aggression, pawing the ground or—much more rarely—stamping, and in some species also wallowing and grazing, in agonistic encounters. Thus, not only are many of these behaviors related to object marking, they are simply the same activities as described in the previous chapter on marking behavior. As compared to the usual marking activities, the special point of space claims is not so much a modification of these behaviors but their occurrence in a specific situation and, above all, their being addressed toward an individual recipient, since otherwise marking behaviors are predominantly advertisements of the "to-whom-it-may-concern" type.

Urination and/or defecation—in certain species, both in sequence—frequently occur in connection with agonistic encounters in ungulates. Sometimes the urination and/or defecation stances appear somewhat more exaggerated than usual in such "demonstrative" eliminations in front of the opponent, but basically they are the same as normally shown by the species. In the case of a territorial male, marking in an agonistic encounter may serve to emphasize his special social status and the precise position of the territorial boundary to the opponent as well as to himself. This means the owner can, if necessary, retreat to the marked area in the course of the encounter, as this is his territory, into which the hostile neighbor will not readily follow. In certain species, a "defecation encounter" may even occur in lieu of a fight between territorial neighbors. For example, in kongoni (Gosling 1974), one or both bulls nose the ground, paw, kneel down and rub the forehead on the ground, stand up and defecate—the latter apparently being the culmination point of the ritual. Sometimes a fight still ensues, but about as often they begin to graze after defecation and slowly move away from each other. If the animal is not territorial, it may create a fixed starting point for the combat by marking with urine and/or feces—comparable to the "corner" in the boxing ring. Fighting horse stallions often provide a good example for this last point. Each of them regularly and often repeatedly defecates at a prescribed spot before the beginning of the fight, and then returns to the same spot and defecates again during pauses in a lengthy combat.

More or less the same principles as in urination and defecation can also be applied to gland marking in connection with agonistic encounters; in the case of unequal opponents, the dominant usually marks frequently whereas the subordinate marks much more rarely if at all. The resemblances and relationships of marking with glands on the animal's head to aggressive movements have been pointed out previously. Moreover, the males of some species open their preorbital glands wide during threat displays. Thus, it does not seem too far-fetched to presume a connection between gland marking and aggressive behavior in these animals, which makes the frequent occurrence of gland marking in agonistic encounters quite understandable. In cases of object aggression, of course, this connection is even closer since they may be considered to be fighting behaviors used for marking.

Wallowing (rolling on the ground) in connection with agonistic encounters is much less frequent than urination and/or defecation, gland marking, and object aggression. Wallowing is generally restricted to comparatively few ungulate species, and most of them use it infrequently during agonistic encounters. An exception is the American bison, where rolling on the ground often occurs during aggressive interactions of bulls (McHugh 1958, Lott 1974). However, in wildebeest, for example, it is so infrequently seen in agonistic encounters that it may be said to be the exception rather than the rule.

A special performance which also could be considered a type of space-claim display occurs in hippopotamus. Adult hippos sometimes rise up out of the water and then loudly splash down into it, or they may eject air under the water, producing a fountain effect (Frädrich 1967).

Widespread and frequently observed is scraping the ground with a foreleg in connection with agonistic encounters (Fig. 24). One could speak of three roots of this behavior in hoofed mammals, but possibly all three arise from one. The aforementioned wallowing of bison during hostile encounters is regularly initiated by pawing (and/or horning) the ground, frequently resulting in the excavation of a wallow (Lott 1974). Thus, when bison paw in an agonistic encounter without wallowing afterwards, it may be considered to be a kind of "abbreviation" of the whole procedure. Domestic cattle show the same pawing (Fig. 25a) in agonistic encounters, although they do not wallow (Schloeth 1959, 1961a). However, their scraping frequently initiates a sequence of behaviors in which the animal drops down to its "knees" (carpal joints), gores the ground with its horns, and rubs head and throat on vegetation (Fig. 25b). Under phylogenetic aspects this behavior seems to be a diminished form of rolling on the ground, and thus one still may say that the pawing of domestic cattle is a derivate of wallowing. By contrast, the pawing of cattle does not appear to be genuinely related to defecating although pawing and defecating may simultaneously occur in their agonistic encounters. However, this defecation (in which the feces are more watery than usual) is apparently due to the great arousal in the autonomic nervous system of the animal in an excitement situation, and thus its combination with scraping appears to be more or less coincidental in cattle (Schloeth 1959). It must be mentioned that in all oxen, pawing of the ground appears different from that of most other hoofed mammals (Fig. 26), in that the hooves scrape the ground over a longer distance in oxen and the

Fig. 24. Topi bull pawing the ground (before defecation) in an agonistic encounter with his territorial
neighbor. The latter stands in erect posture.
(Serengeti National Park.)

movement of the foreleg is often continued until the hoof hits the
performer's body (Fig. 25a) with an audible noise.

In many other ungulates, a more genuine connection of scraping
with a foreleg to urination and/or defecation is obvious, since scraping can also precede elimination in situations other than agonistic
encounters, as previously discussed. Apparently it is more frequent in
agonistic encounters than in other situations, more frequent in territorial than in nonterritorial individuals, and usually only performed
by males. Interestingly, there seems to be a "trend" toward a separation of scraping the ground from urination and/or defecation in some
species. For example, when gazelle males scrape the ground during
agonistic interactions, this is usually followed by the urination-
defecation sequence typical of these animals. Cases in which they do
not urinate and defecate after pawing in such situations do occur but
are very exceptional. By contrast, in agonistic encounters of species
such as East African oryx antelope (*Oryx beisa*), scraping the ground
is not followed by defecation in about 50 percent of the cases. Some
features of such a "trend" for separation are also recognizable in
scraping preceding wallowing, since scraping may occasionally occur
in agonistic encounters without wallowing ensuing.

These observations that there exists a certain independence between pawing the ground and wallowing or elimination in bovids become especially interesting when one compares them to the situation
in certain cervids, such as roe deer. Roe deer do not wallow, nor are

Fig. 25a. Pawing the ground in Camargue cattle
(*Bos primigenius taurus*). Note that the hoof of the
scraping leg hits the bull's chest. b. Rubbing head
and throat on vegetation (Schloeth 1961a. Photos: R.
Schloeth—Camargue, France.)

they known to scrape the ground in connection with urination or
defecation. Moreover, they lack interdigital glands on their forelegs.
Nevertheless, male roe deer are famous for their frequent pawing
(Fig. 20), often combined with object aggression and marking with
the frontal glands (Henning 1962, Müller-Using and Schloeth 1967).

Fig. 26. Marco Polo ram (*Ovis ammon poli*)
scraping the ground. The foreleg is not moved much
further backward than shown in this picture. Compare to the scraping in cattle in Fig. 25a. (Kronberg
Zoo, Germany.)

Pawing the ground and object aggression of roe deer occur not only
in territorial marking, but also and especially in agonistic encounters
(space-claim displays).

Two points are particularly noteworthy. For one thing, there is obviously a strong connection between pawing the ground with a
foreleg and thrashing vegetation with the antlers, in roe deer and in
certain other cervid species. For another, female cervids usually fight
by kicking and beating with their forelegs, and the males also do so
after shedding their antlers and while the latter are in velvet. When
taken together, these aspects suggest that pawing the ground may
simply be another form of object aggression in these animals. The
question arises whether this is not generally so. This would mean that
pawing the ground in general could be interpreted primarily as a kind
of object aggression that had become secondarily combined with wallowing or with urination and/or defecation in certain ungulate species. If this presumption is correct, the frequency of its occurrence in
the agonistic encounters of so many ungulate species and also the
aforementioned cases of separation from wallowing or urination
and/or defecation in certain species become comprehensible. One
may raise the objection that the situation in bovids is different, since
these animals do not shed their horns and do not fight with their
forelegs (Walther 1979). On the other hand, one may argue that there

is strong paleontological evidence that the bovids have evolved from ancestors that had no horns (Thenius 1969) and, thus, these ancestors were in the same situation as cervids after shedding their antlers, or as horses, llama, etc., which all use their forelegs in fighting. Consequently, it is possible that these hornless ancestors of recent bovids also used their forelegs in fighting, that pawing the ground was a form of object aggression in them, and that recent bovids have kept this ancestral form of object aggression as a display although they no longer fight with their forelegs. Such cases of "survival" of ancestral behaviors are by no means unusual in hoofed mammals, and we will refer to them again later when talking about threat and dominance displays.

A last behavior possibly belonging to the category of space claims is grazing in agonistic encounters, in which a mechanism similar to that of a transitional action (Lind 1959) seems to be involved. The head of an ungulate is close to the ground in a number of aggressive displays, such as head-low posture, low presentation of horns, downward-blow, etc., as well as in actual fighting in many species. Such a lowered-head position, of course, is also a proper position for grazing, and an aggressive lowering of the head may sometimes induce grazing. In certain situations and/or species this behavior appears to be limited to subordinate animals, whereas in others there is no indication that inferiority is involved. Unfortunately, the relationship and significance of grazing in agonistic encounters have not been realized until recently (Estes 1969), apparently because earlier observers always assumed that grazing could not belong to the agonistic interaction and that the encounter was over when both combatants started grazing. So, at present, somewhat detailed studies on agonistic grazing are available in relatively few species, although this behavior is probably widely spread in ungulates.

In species such as Grant's gazelle and oryx antelope, grazing in connection with agonistic encounters occurs relatively often on the part of inferior opponents. They frequently respond by grazing when approached by a dominant. Occasionally, however, a dominant combatant or both opponents may graze. When both rivals graze at the end of an encounter, they may move away from each other while doing so. This "ambiguity" is probably due to agonistic grazing's being a transitional action from the lowered head posture that may occur during fighting but also in submission. On the whole, one may say that grazing in agonistic encounters frequently, although not necessarily, indicates subordinate status in these and some other species.

The situation is clearly different in Thomson's gazelle. Here, agonistic grazing is primarily a behavior of territorial bucks, and both opponents generally perform it simultaneously. I speak of a "grazing ritual" (Walther 1968a, 1977a,b, 1978c) in this case, because there are very pronounced and predictable position changes between owners of neighboring territories. Grazing almost uninterruptedly, the opponents go from a frontal position to a parallel or reverse-parallel position to a reverse position (hindquarters to hindquarters). Three changes in position are the minimum. There can be many variations and repetitions in such a grazing ritual, and it may last from a few minutes up to half an hour. It rarely precedes a fight. Incomplete attempts are frequent during pauses in fights. Especially when grazing in frontal position, the rivals can easily change from grazing back to fighting. The complete, pronounced ritual, however, is seen only following or in place of a fight. When used at the end of an agonistic encounter, the grazing ritual allows an exit without either combatant's "losing face," the battle, or territorial status. Thus, agonistic grazing is closely related to fighting in Thomson's gazelle, is most commonly shown by territorial peers (i.e., nothing speaks for a behavior of inferiority), and appears to belong to that category of behavior that is concerned with space relations (taking place right on the boundary or, at least, in the boundary zone of neighboring territories).

In wildebeest (Estes 1969), one territorial bull may approach another and may intrude deep into his territory, grazing all the while (a situation which was never observed in Grant's and Thomson's gazelles). When they approach each other, the owner of the territory often threatens the intruder by sideward angling of his horns. The intruder keeps his present grazing attitude; that is, he behaves like a subordinate male Grant's gazelle. On the other hand, the owner of the territory may also start grazing, and both animals may go through changes in position similar to those of territorial male Thomson's gazelle (except that this occurs inside the territory belonging to one of the wildebeest bulls and not at the territorial boundary as in tommy). They may even circle around each other in grazing, something gazelle bucks do not do. Furthermore, in wildebeest, grazing apparently is not followed as easily and as readily by fighting (or vice versa) as in Thomson's gazelle. In short, agonistic grazing of wildebeest offers an even more complicated picture than that of the two gazelle species; however, it also is restricted to territorial individuals in wildebeest (Estes 1969) as well as in bontebok (David 1973), kongoni (Gosling 1974) and topi (Fig. 27). Thus, it could have something to do with space relations also in these species.

Possibly the key to a general interpretation may be seen in the relationship of agonistic grazing to fighting in general, and to horn fighting in particular. Biting and snapping as threat and fighting be-

Fig. 27. Parallel grazing in a border encounter of territorial topi bulls. (Serengeti National Park.)

Fig. 28. Greater kudu female threatens a subadult male by symbolic butting with her forehead. Simultaneously, she performs snapping movements with her mouth. (Walther 1964*b*. Frankfurt Zoo.)

haviors are found in quite a number of even-toed ungulates. One may presume that snapping was also a fighting technique of the ancestors of recent Artiodactyla. It even still occurs in hornless or antlerless females of certain bovid and cervid species. Interestingly enough, symbolic snapping (with the mouth directed toward the ground) was observed in combination with butting the opponent with the forehead in greater kudu (Fig. 28) and sitatunga females (Walther 1964b). Thus, one could imagine that, in some species of the recent horned ungulates, biting could become activated simultaneously with horn or forehead butting in agonistic interactions and (since the head is lowered according to the head-low posture or the low or medial presentation of horns) that this may turn into grazing (biting the grass). In other words, the agonistic grazing of horned and antlered ungulates is possibly derived from an ancestral form of redirected aggression. Since the recent deer and bovids mainly fight with their antlers and horns, agonistic grazing may contain only a mild undertone of aggression in these animals. This may appear to be a rather bold speculation, but it is in absolute agreement with our knowledge of the paleontology of these animals and with the behavior that has been observed in the recent species. Also, it would explain not only the occurrence of grazing in agonistic encounters but also the species-specific variations of agonistic grazing. It is likely that such a common ancestral behavior has become differentiated in a variety of ways in the different recent species during phylogenetic evolution, and, in connection with these variations, it is understandable that such a mild form of aggressiveness can sometimes occur in a dominant animal and sometimes in an inferior one, depending on the species and/or the situation. More comparative data are required to substantiate these assumptions.

8. EXCITEMENT ACTIVITIES; ALARM AND FLIGHT SIGNALS

The term "excitement activities" refers to movements and vocalizations indicating that an animal is in an unspecific state of agitation. The animal is more restless than usual—in humans, one would speak of "nervousness"—but there are as yet no indications that the arousal will result in a specific action such as aggression, flight, courtship, etc. Correspondingly, such excitement activities occur in several heterogeneous situations, some of them even in many different situations—when an animal watches a predator or another "dangerous" object (a man, a car, etc.) at a distance; when it is forced to cross unfavorable terrain; when it is separated from a familiar group, mate, or locality; when it is involved in an agonistic encounter; when it is expecting food or is prevented from getting food in captivity; when it is kept in a stall and is waiting for the door to the outside enclosure to be opened; when it happens to find the dead body of a conspecific, etc.—and they do not contribute to the solution of these situations. Excitement activities in the described sense are often termed "displacement activities" (Tinbergen 1949). I hesitate to use this term not only because of certain theoretical reservations, but also because it does not cover the whole range under discussion—in part it is much broader; in part it is more limited.

When one wishes to relate such excitement activities to an inner conflict between opposite tendencies—which is by no means certain in quite a number of cases—this conflict boils down to the rather general formula: "Should I now do something or shouldn't I?" It certainly is not always a conflict between aggression and flight—not even always in agonistic encounters. Sometimes frustration may play a role, but is not necessarily involved. Very generally speaking, excitement activities seen to serve to get rid of some dammed-up nervous energies, and thus they may subjectively bring a certain relief to the performer. They do not have much influence on partners, except occasional contagion. In this latter regard, however, they may be quite important.

Some excitement activities are nothing but, or at least come close to, maintenance activities. Thus they are not different from behaviors which usually occur during an animal's 'round-the-clock activity.

116

However, in certain exciting situations, they occur more frequently than under "normal" conditions. Common examples from the behavioral repertoires of hoofed mammals are several forms of self-grooming (e.g., scratching the neck with a hind leg, grooming the shoulder with the mouth, etc.), shaking (ears, head, or entire body), tail wagging, walking up and down, the volte (stepping around in a narrow circle), stationary vertical jumps, tripping in place, in some species also stamping as if bothered by flies, etc. Other excitement activities apparently are symptoms of an arousal within the autonomic nervous system. Examples are the ruffling of hair of rump patches or manes on nape, withers, croup, or along the entire back, raising the crest—i.e., the long hair on the forehead of certain species such as dikdik and some duikers, "explosive" discharges of certain skin glands, spontaneous erections of the penis (in nonsexual situations) in the males of certain species (such as Uganda kob— Buechner and Schloeth 1965), urination and/or defecation in exciting situations, and at least some tail movements, such as the vertical erection of the tail in certain species. Such reflexlike behaviors also show up as additional components of distinct displays (e.g., courtship and threat displays). However, since they are primarily symptoms of certain levels of autonomic-nervous arousal (in a particular body region), many of them always occur when the corresponding level of excitement is reached. This can happen in combination with several different displays and/or in several different situations. For example, certain bovid and cervid species ruffle the hair of the rump patch when urinating and/or defecating, but also when alarmed by the presence of a predator. Also, there are great differences in the different species. For example, warthog almost always defecate in the beginning of a flight (Frädrich 1965), whereas ibex hardly ever do so in such a situation.

Vocalizations play a particularly great role among excitement activities. This is easy to understand, since any excitement results in an increased metabolic rate and with it a faster and noisier breathing. It needs only minor specializations to transform such respiratory murmurs into snorts, grunts, whistles, etc. As Kiley (1972) has pointed out, many vocalizations are typical of different levels of excitement (Fig. 29); they regularly occur in combination with other excitement activities (such as listed above); and they indicate an increase in what has loosely been called "arousal" or "general motivational state." She described quite a number of grunts (e.g., in swine, the "common grunt," staccato grunt, long grunt, repeated grunt), squeals, screams, snorts, "mm," "menenh" calls, etc., for various species of hoofed mammals, although each species possesses only a relatively limited

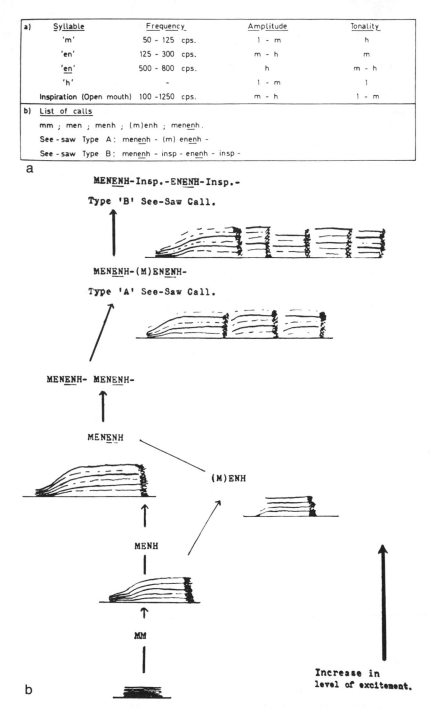

a) Syllable	Frequency	Amplitude	Tonality
'm'	50 – 125 cps.	l – m	h
'en'	125 – 300 cps.	m – h	m
'e̲n̲'	500 – 800 cps.	h	m – h
'h'	–	l – m	l
Inspiration (Open mouth)	100 –1250 cps.	m – h	l – m

b) List of calls

mm ; men ; menh ; (m)enh ; mene̲n̲h.

See - saw Type A: mene̲n̲h - (m) ene̲n̲h -

See - saw Type B: mene̲n̲h - insp - ene̲n̲h - insp -

a

MEN̲E̲NH-Insp.-EN̲E̲NH-Insp.-

Type 'B' See-Saw Call.

MEN̲E̲NH-(M)EN̲E̲NH-

Type 'A' See-Saw Call.

MEN̲E̲NH- MEN̲E̲NH-

MEN̲E̲NH

(M)ENH

MENH

MM

Increase in
level of excitement.

b

Fig. 29a. Syllables of cattle calls and the way they combine to form the calls. l = low, m = medium, h = high. b. Interrelationships of the calls in cattle. Note that amplitude, frequency, length, and/or repetition increase with excitement. (From Kiley 1972.)

number of such vocalizations. For example, Kiley identified fourteen calls of domestic pigs, six of cattle, and six of horses. However, it must be emphasized that these calls are not discrete vocal displays, but rather occur as part of a continuum of sound. The changes work along an intensification scale, with a gradual increase in length, amplitude, pitch, repetition, and tonality. Calls at the bottom of the continuum are short, low in pitch and amplitude, and accompanied by little activity. Higher up the continuum, the calls become longer, more often repeated, louder, and of higher pitch. They are accompanied by an increase in locomotion, and the performance of more different activities more often. Thus, functionally, these vocalizations convey information concerning one dimension of the general motivational state of the animal (Kiley 1972).

The emulative effects of such vocalizations and their role in transmission of mood will be discussed in another context. Here, only three points need be stressed: (a) As stated above, the type of vocalization given depends on the level of excitement of the animal rather than on a specific situation (Kiley 1972). This means that the same vocalization may occur in several very different situations provided that the level of excitement is the same in all of them—which is generally characteristic of excitement activities. (b) The effects of such vocalizations—particularly of those of low-level excitement—upon conspecifics are usually rather unspecific and often not very striking. (c) Despite the general occurrence of the various vocalizations in many situations, some calls are more characteristic of a certain situation, although they also occur in others (Kiley 1972).

The latter is more or less expected since the animal is likely to be at a similar level of excitement each time it encounters the same situation. This may now be the point where ritualization can take place, i.e., one could imagine that a given, originally rather unspecific, vocalization may become more or less restricted to a special situation during the course of phylogenetic evolution, and that it may eventually become so typical of this situation that it works as a special signal and releases more or less definite responses in conspecifics. Kiley refers here to the famous example of the *"chant de coeur"* of the male pig (Signoret et al. 1960), which releases a kind of immobilization reaction in an estral sow so that she stands stiff and motionless for his mount. On the other hand, Kiley emphasizes that such ritualizations of vocalizations are rather the exception than the rule in ungulates. I think that this last point may be an overstatement. Rather, it seems to me possible or even likely that, e.g., the not very small number of vocalizations typical of aggressive or sexual arousal in hoofed mammals and perhaps also the so-called play calls—rather specific vocalizations uttered by juveniles of certain species during running games—may have evolved on the basis of expressions of general excitement. Of course, such a development is particularly likely in vocalizations that reflect a relatively high level of general excitement. Interestingly enough, there are two types of vocalizations in hoofed mammals which—in terms of evolution—strikingly give the impression of behaviors "on their way" from mere expressions of high excitement to becoming special displays: the distress cries and the alarm calls. With respect to the latter, one may even go further and generally extend the suggested conception of displays *in statu nascendi* to all the so-called alarm and flight signals, i.e., not only acoustical but also visual and olfactory forms.

Distress cries should be distinguished from alarm calls, perhaps not so much with respect to their effects upon conspecifics and their functions, but with respect to their motivation and the vocalization itself: a distress call is absolutely different from an alarm call. There are several forms of vocalizations indicating that an animal is in great fear, in pain, or other severe discomfort, ranging from soft groaning and mourning to full and loud cries. I have the latter predominantly in mind when talking here of distress cries. They usually are long calls uttered with an open mouth; they are loud and relatively similar in many of the species under discussion. For example, in swine and their relatives, there are the well-known screams; in bovids and cervids, distress cries usually sound like a roaring or bleating "aaaaa" (*a* as in "ha re") or "uuuuu" (*u* as in "murder"). They are motivated by great pain or mortal fear, and apparently fear is often a considerably more important factor than pain. For instance, some of my captive dorcas gazelle would give loud and persistent cries when being captured for veterinary treatment, but were silent during the treatment itself although it was sometimes likely to be painful. Similarly, gazelle fawns in the wild cry loudly when chased (but not yet bitten) by jackals, and subordinate oryx antelopes may cry out when heavily chased (but not beaten or wounded) by very dominant conspecifics. Distress cries can also be heard in the moment when a sick or wounded animal is dying. Perhaps also the famous "scare call" (Geist 1966*a*) of moose, a short, harsh, and very loud roar, is not too dissimilar from a distress cry. It is uttered by moose standing belly-deep in snow and being harassed by predators.

Phenotypically, all these distress cries still appear to be high-intensity forms of vocalizations belonging to the acoustical continuum linked to increasing levels of general arousal. However, their motivation is not a general excitement, but specifically the fear of being captured and/or of dying. Of course, mortal fear can arise on different occasions, and thus distress cries are not limited to one situation. On the other hand, the number of situations in which fear may reach such a high level is comparatively small. Consequently, distress cries may be said to be *relatively* situation-specific. Since they belong to the loudest sounds that can be heard from ungulates, it is not surprising that they can release rather strong reactions in conspecifics and often also in animals of other species. In African buffalo (*Syncerus caffer*), whole herds could be attracted with tape-recorded distress cries of calves (Sinclair 1974); in plains zebra, the screaming of a foal may alarm the whole parental harem group (Klingel 1967). However, in most ungulates, only the mothers of crying young react in a truly specific way. The other animals only become more or less alarmed.

Distress cries of young chased by predators release the mother's defense, provided that the predator is not too big and dangerous. In the latter case, the mother may try to distract the predator by placing herself between the predator and her young or may even only watch from a distance—of course with all signs of great excitement. The mother's defense of the young against smaller predators sometimes ceases when the young is killed and is no longer crying (Walther 1969*b*).

The same "being on the way" from expressions of excitement to more specialized signals seems to be largely true for alarm calls in hoofed mammals, although there are differences in comparison to distress cries. For one, the situational motivations are different. Alarm calls are most frequently given while the animal is still watching the predator, i.e., before flight or in its very beginning and when the animal is not in immediate danger of being captured. In psychological terms, they often appear more related to high levels of curiosity than to fear. Secondly, there is great species-specific variety in forms and volumes of alarm calls, while distress cries usually are very loud and rather uniform within broad taxonomic units of hoofed mammals (such as swine, bovids, etc.). Furthermore, although the level of excitement certainly is quite high in alarm calls and flight signals, it does not appear as high as in the distress calls, and, on the whole, they seem to be more similar to expressions of general excitement than distress calls.

In some ungulate species, the alarm calls are emitted through the mouth, as in the loud, doglike barking of many cervids and certain antelopes such as bushbuck, kudu, and eland antelope. Axis deer (Fuchs 1976) and Manchurian sika deer (*Sika nippon dybowskii*) utter loud, shrill screams. Other alarm calls are emitted through the nose (Fig. 30). They too can be very loud, as for example, the whistling of

Fig. 30. Expanding the nose region in uttering the alarm call (through the nose) in a female dorcas gazelle (*Gazella dorcas*). (Walther 1966*a*. Kronberg Zoo.)

ibex, chamois, and Bohor reedbuck (*Redunca redunca*); or they can be of medium volume, like the short, explosive snorts in pronghorn (Einarsen 1948), horses and zebras (Klingel 1972), wildebeest, topi, and goats, and the longer snorts in rhinoceroses (Schenkel and Lang 1969); or they can be rather soft, like the "quaking" alarm calls of some gazelle species. Especially in Thomson's gazelle, the alarm call, "quiff" (*i* as in "hill"), is so soft that a human cannot hear it beyond a distance of about thirty meters, and the conspecifics apparently cannot hear it at a much longer distance. In some species, nose calls are apparently vibration sounds the timber of which may vary considerably with distance.

When one considers the alarm and flight signals of hoofed mammals as being "on their way" from mere expressions of high excitement to becoming special displays, one has to add that apparently none of them has yet completely reached its final state in these animals, and also that the degree of perfection in this change from unspecific excitement activities to specific alarm signals varies with species as well as with respect to the single behavior patterns. It follows, then, that all these behaviors also occur more or less frequently in situations which have nothing to do with alarm, and merely express a rather high level of excitement. Apparently this fact has often not been fully realized due to a human factor. Since all hoofed mammals are more or less shy toward man in the wild, the human observer frequently releases flight. Consequently, when studying the behavior of a species, he usually sees these excitement activities first when they precede flight, and terms them "alarm signals." When he later observes the same or similar behaviors in situations which have nothing to do with flight, he does not realize that his terminology may be inadequate, that these behaviors are not primarily flight or alarm signals; instead, he asks himself how these "alarm signals" may come to occur in—in his opinion—inadequate situations. When he has read enough ethology books, he will also have an interpretation: these are "displacement alarms." However, it is much more likely that these behavior patterns are not alarm signals by nature and origin, nor do they exclusively convey and release alarm; consequently, their occurrence in different situations has nothing to do with displacement behavior, but simply indicates that the animal has reached the same level of excitement. Since alarm is one of their striking and common functions, it is not completely out of place to use the term "alarm signals"—as I do here—since it is at least short, but one has to be well aware of the relativity of this terminology.

At least in certain situations, every fast-running or leaping animal—not necessarily even a conspecific—may attract the attention of the others and release alarm or flight reactions in them. This "running away" can be made more conspicuous by striking locomotor patterns (such as stotting), special movements or postures of the tail, ruffling the hair of the (in many species, white) rump patch, emitting scents from certain skin glands, and certain vocalizations preceding flight. In some species, the animals also emphatically hit the ground with their feet in a few high bounds so that the beginning of a flight is audible, as e.g., Schaller (1967, 1977) reports from Punjab urial (*Ovis orientalis punjabiensis*), axis deer, and gaur.

Relatively few olfactory alarm signals have been described in hoofed mammals. For example, in black-tailed deer, metatarsal scent (the metatarsal gland is located on the outside of the hind leg and is not identical with the tarsal gland, previously mentioned in another context) is discharged in fear-inducing situations (Müller-Schwarze 1971), and in springbuck, an emission of scent from the dorsal gland is likely during stotting (or "pronking," as a modified form of stotting is often termed in springbuck—Bigalke 1972). Also, pronghorn discharge an odor from their ischiadic gland, but no effects on conspecifics are known (Müller-Schwarze 1980). Other olfactory alarm signals appear possible in hoofed mammals; however, at present, their purposes are speculative.

Among alarm-releasing locomotor patterns, stotting (Fig. 31) has

Fig. 31. Stotting of a subadult Thomson's gazelle. (Walther 1969b.)

attracted particular attention in literature but has often been inadequately interpreted. This special, striking kind of jumping, usually not used for clearing obstacles, often results in a chain of leaps, during which the animal bounces up and down with all four legs rather stiffly stretched. Stotting is common in gazelles and their relatives, but is also found, e.g., in pronghorn and in certain cervids such as fallow deer and mule deer. It is not an antipredator "strategy" to get a further look over the surroundings as sometimes has been assumed (Steinhardt 1924, Cronwright-Schreiner 1925, Pitcher 1979) since e.g., pronking springbuck lower their heads toward the ground during the leaps (which certainly would be a most stupid thing to do if the leap's purpose were to get a better look at the surroundings). Nor does stotting necessarily have alarm effects. For example, stotting frequently occurs in running games of juvenile or subadult animals, during which the adults remain completely relaxed and undisturbed, while other juveniles may join the stotting game (contagion). On the other hand, when a gazelle fawn which has been lying out (see ch. 10) leaves its resting place stotting, it has a strong alarm effect upon the mother—but usually only upon the mother, even when a whole herd of other conspecifics is around. When used in flight, stotting also occurs when the animal is completely alone. On the other hand, all the members of a herd may stot simultaneously in certain situations. When running hard, the animals do not stot, but they frequently begin and end a run by stotting. Thus, in the case of flight, stotting is frequently performed at the beginning of a run (provided the pursuer is not too close), but it is also performed frequently at the end of a run (when the enemy has ceased pursuit). With this and other information (Walther 1964a, 1969b, 1981) on stotting in mind, it is somewhat obscure to me how one can arrive at such conclusions as that stotting may be an "altruistic" behavior linked to "kinship" (Wilson 1975). At present, we can only say that it apparently corresponds to a high—but not the highest—level of running excitation, which does not even necessarily mean flight; that it occurs when the running excitation is rising or falling; that it is highly contagious in certain situations but not in others; and that it is considerably more frequent in young animals than in adults.

Ruffling of rump patch hairs (springbuck also ruffle the white hair in the pouch of the croup, which has a dorsal gland inside) is combined with flight (and also stotting) or may precede flight in species having a rump patch. The same is true for certain tail movements of some species. A relatively common movement is the vertical erection of the tail, found in various ungulate species such as black rhino, warthog (Fig. 32a), mountain gazelle (*Gazella gazella*), dibatag, goats, and white-tailed deer. It certainly is noteworthy that taxonomically distant species (e.g., warthog and dibatag) behave more alike than certain more closely related species (e.g., mountain gazelle and Grant's gazelle—the latter species does not erect its tail during flight, but rather tightly presses it to the hindquarters). In some species, such as nilgai, only juvenile animals erect the tail during flight (or stotting), while adult animals commonly do not. During running, and thus also during flight, greater and lesser kudu, bushbuck, and their relatives curl the tail up so that its tip almost touches its root (Fig. 32b). In these as well as in some other species, such as white-tailed deer, it may be of importance to the signal character of those tail movements that they expose the white underside of the tail when it is erected or curled.

Of course, there are also other tail and body movements linked with flight, or, more precisely speaking, with running generally. For example, South African oryx antelope (*Oryx gazella*) wave their tails high before taking off, and giraffe curve their tails and press them laterally to their hindquarters at the beginning of a gallop. In young giraffe, this is almost obligatory; in adult giraffe, it is at least frequent. Some species, such as impala (Schenkel 1966b) and warthog (Frädrich 1965), jerk their heads upward before taking off, and caribou may perform an "excitation jump" with their forelegs (Pruitt 1960). Certain other species such as Thomson's gazelle and Kirk's dikdik often shake their flanks before flight. This last case is a quite good example of how one can be misled when one interprets a behavior which is present in a number of species but one knows it from only one of them. Thomson's gazelle have a broad black band at the flank. Thus, it has been presumed that shaking the flank serves to make this black band more conspicuous as an important alarm signal for conspecifics (Brooks 1961). But—as just mentioned—dikdik also shake their flanks before taking off, but dikdik do not possess such a band. On the

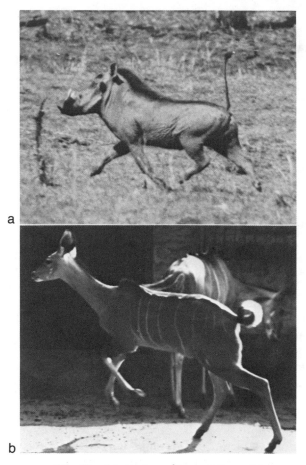

Fig. 32a. Vertical erection of the tail in
fleeing warthog (*Phacochoerus aethiopicus*).
(Serengeti National Park.) b. Tail-curl in a
galloping greater kudu female during a running play. (Walther 1964*b*. Frankfurt Zoo.)

whole, with respect to the obviously very strong tendency of many
contemporary scientists to base all animal behavior either on feeding
or antipredator "strategies," and consequently to detect flight and
alarm signals everywhere, it can hardly be overemphasized or repeated too often that all these behaviors also occur in situations other
than flight where they do not release alarm in conspecifics and sometimes do not even attract their attention.

When watching a potential danger, all hoofed mammals assume a
more or less pronounced stance of alertness. Commonly they tense

their muscles and stand in erect postures, motionless as statues, re-sembling the male urination posture of some species and/or the erect postures in certain dominance displays (i.e., another case in which an executive behavior may happen to resemble an expressive display—p. 57). In species with a relatively long and movable neck, the animal stiffly erects it to a maximum height ("long-neck posture"—Fig. 33b). Frequently the animals also utter "alarm calls" in this posture, and in some species they sometimes may stamp with one leg.

This stamping has problems of its own. Possibly, tripping in place, which, as has been mentioned, is a common excitement activity in ungulates, has given rise to the development of stamping under evo-lutionary aspects. However, only in a relatively few species has the stamping with all four legs become somewhat ritualized. For exam-ple, lesser Malayan mouse deer "drum" with fore- and hind legs in a sequence with intermittent pauses and seven beats per second at maximum (Robin 1979). This drumming, in which the stamping of the legs apparently is used to produce an acoustical signal, has also

Fig. 33a. Female greater kudu standing relaxed. b. In the "long-neck" posture of alertness.

been described in the larger Malayan mouse deer, although apparently with a somewhat different rhythmicity. Here, Ralls *et al.* (1975) interpret it as an exaggerated and ritualized form of the intention movements of fleeing. However, Robin (1979) lists quite a number of releasing situations for animals in captivity (being placed in a new cage, meeting with a new partner, on the part of the dominant in encounters among males, on the part of the male when the female has not been cooperative in copulation, etc.) that rather indicate a relation to more general excitements than specifically to flight. The stamping of vicuna in connection with defection has been mentioned. In many bovid and cervid species, tripping is often restricted to a short lifting of a foreleg. This movement obviously is unritualized and it occasionally occurs during intensive watching in almost any species. Ritualization to an exaggerated stamping with one foreleg is relatively rare. I know it mainly from sheep, such as Afghan urial (*Ovis orientalis cycloceros*), which lift the angled foreleg as high as possible, and vertically force it down with an audible sound (Walther 1961a). It was predominantly seen in mothers of neonates when watching a potential danger (Fig. 34)—a situation in which an alarming function was possible but not absolutely clear. (I always had the impression that aggressive tendencies were involved.) Very similar events are reported from mothers in mouflon sheep (*Ovis orientalis*

Fig. 34. Female Afghan urial (*Ovis orientalis cycloceros*—mother of the lamb to the right) stamping with a foreleg in response to my approach. (Walther 1961a. Kronberg Zoo.)

musimon — Goethe and Goethe 1939). In bighorn sheep (*Ovis canadensis*), Geist (1971) also noted stamping with a foreleg as a rather uncommon behavior in excited, captive specimens, and a few times in rams confronting a coyote. In short, this stamping may sometimes have an alarming effect, but it is infrequently found in ungulates, and even in species in which it is present, it is often infrequently used.

Of course, when, for example, an animal is watching a predator in the long-neck posture of alertness and utters "alarm calls," and when the conspecifics react by becoming alert, the communication of the alarm appears to be quite significant. On the other hand, all the "alarm" postures, movements, calls, etc., also occur in other (exciting) situations, as well as when the animal is completely alone. Even when they occur in the presence of conspecifics, there are no indications that they are being addressed to definite partners, perhaps with the exception of their use in mother-offspring relationships. Thus, generally, the "alarm and flight signals" may be said to be communications of the "to-whom-it-may-concern" type; however, even in this category, there are other signals, such as certain position advertisements, which are often aimed at potential recipients in a clearer way.

9. BEHAVIORAL CONTAGION; CONTACT SEEKING AND CONTACT MAKING; ALLOGROOMING

"Contagion," contact seeking, contact making, and allogrooming are of course different behaviors but they have two things in common. First, all four function to establish group cohesiveness and positive social relations among group members. Second, contact seeking, contact making and allogrooming often follow each other in a sequence. Thus, it appears justifiable to treat these behaviors together in one chapter.

When a group of people have to listen to a boring talk, and one of them starts yawning, the others will soon yawn too. Yawning is particularly well known to be contagious in humans, but the same is true for a variety of other behaviors, not only in humans but also in animals. Scientists often speak not of "contagion" but of "allelomimetic behavior" or "social facilitation." These more or less synonymous terms may sound somewhat more scientific than "contagion" but they are no better, and they cannot conceal the fact that the process of contagion in general, and its underlying physiological mechanisms in particular, are not well understood at present. All we can say is that when an animal is (presumably) very ready to perform a given behavior due to its internal or external situation, apparently the visual, acoustical, or olfactory perception of the performance of that behavior by another animal provides enough stimulation to bring it "above the threshold" in the first animal.

There are a few factors which may facilitate this behavioral contagion. For example, young animals are often particularly prone to it. It works predominantly when the other animal is nearby, and it is more prominent and frequent in gregarious animals. This may be because solitary animals simply do not have much occasion for contagion, or possibly because their corresponding central nervous receiving mechanisms are not as sensitive as in gregarious animals, or are even lacking. Furthermore, it sometimes seems that contagion works particularly readily in expressive behaviors, although it is by no means restricted to them.

130

As a matter of fact, almost any maintenance activity, such as self-grooming (Fig. 35a), walking, bedding down or arising from rest, feeding, urination, or defecation can, at least occasionally, have contagious effects. The same is true for more special executive behaviors such as fighting and sexual mounting. For example, in all-male groups of hoofed mammals, it sometimes happens that several pairs will begin to fight simultaneously for no other "reason" than that one pair has started fighting close by (Fig. 35b). The contagious effects of maintenance activities and special executive behaviors are probably rather important for the social life of some species. They may essentially contribute to synchronization of the activities of the individuals within a herd, and thus also to group cohesiveness. On the other hand, contagion is absolutely a side effect of maintenance activities and other executive behaviors. For example, when an animal grooms itself, this grooming is neither addressed to a partner, nor does it aim

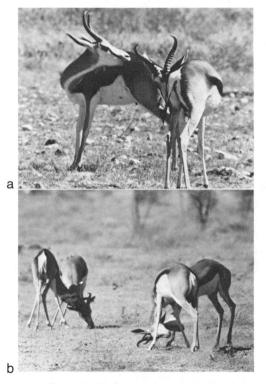

Fig. 35. Behavioral contagion in springbuck (*Antidorcas marsupialis*) a. in grooming, b. in sparring. (Etosha National Park.)

at any response on the latter's part; thus, when a neighbor of the grooming animal then begins to groom himself, it has as little to do with communication as the contagious effects of yawning upon the human listeners of a boring lecture.

It is perhaps not out of place to mention here a possible source of error to which, in my opinion, Leyhausen (1967) has fallen a victim. Contagion is not the same thing as a response by means of the same behavior, as when an animal threatens an opponent and the latter responds with the same threat display. At least in hoofed mammals, such threats are always addressed and usually also directed to an individual partner, and they clearly aim at definite responses. This situation has little to do with contagion. Rather, it is comparable to a dispute between human partners in which one says, "Go away!" and the other responds, "No, *you* go away!"

When discussing the advertising of presence, position, and general state, we mentioned that these advertisements may have repellent or attractive effects upon recipients. This alternative depends only in part on the sender's signals; the situation of the recipient is at least as important. Moreover, the most favorable factor for attractive effects seems to be that sender and recipient belong to a gregarious species. Gregariousness means that social relationships are not restricted to those between sex partners or between mother and offspring, but that conspecifics generally are attracted to each other—a behavioral "mechanism" that appears to be lacking or at least poorly developed in solitary species. It is not of interest to our present discussion whether it is possible to trace this social attraction back to adaptations to environmental features, feeding style, antipredator strategies, or whatever. We can treat it here as given *a priori*. Thus, in gregarious animals, it needs a relatively special situation on the part of the recipient and/or quite special features in the sender's presence, status, and position advertisements to bring about a repellent effect. Otherwise, the readiness to be attracted by a conspecific's presence and position advertising greatly preponderates in recipients of gregarious species, and the same readiness for social contact on the sender's part easily turns his presence and position advertisement into a calling for companionship: "I am here—where are you?"

Perhaps the closest connection between presence and position advertisement and social attraction is found in the visual field. This is especially true in open plains areas, where the figure of an animal (of the size of an ungulate) is often the single striking sight in the vast and uniform surroundings. In addition, body markings (black stripes or bands, white rump patches, etc.) and sometimes tail movements (as the perpetual tail wagging of certain gazelle species) may play a role in making an animal readily recognizable to conspecifics. Like landmarks, the striking figure of an animal on the open plains attracts the attention of other animals, which often turn toward it and approach it (Walther 1972b). In this way, conspecifics join to form groups and, eventually, the large herds so typical of many ungulate species (bison, wildebeest, springbuck, gazelles, reindeer, etc.) on the open plains.

Because of their annual and circadian rhythms, all the animals in such herds are approximately in the same mood, and this provides the best opportunity for behavioral contagion, which contributes to coordination of activities among herd members. This synchronization of group activities is of special importance during moves and migrations. Obviously, a moving conspecific easily causes others to follow. Besides the contagious effects of walking, one may think here of a modification of the infantile following reaction. In this regard, it is certainly important that in gregarious hoofed mammals herds commonly march in file, with one animal behind another, at least during moves of some length. This means that the animal behind always has the preceding animal's rump in front of him. Presumably, rump patches and tail movements again play an additional role in releasing this following reaction.

Vocalizations used in contact calling are also related to signals advertising the animal's presence and position. In some cases, they are more or less identical with the latter. On the other hand, the tendency to develop special contact signals is even greater in acoustical than in visual and olfactory advertisements. Probably linked with this "specialization" toward contact seeking signals, such calls are often heard more frequently from females and young animals than from adult males. Since these vocalizations are highly emulative in the animals under discussion, they easily evoke the same or similar vocalizations in conspecifics, they sometimes are transitions between contagion and the aforementioned responding by the same behavior, and the calling for social contact becomes a "question-answer" communication in which sender and recipient reciprocally signal their positions until they finally join each other. Moreover, as Kiley (1972) could demonstrate in experiments with domestic swine, cattle, and horses, the partners may synchronize their general motivational states in the course of exchange of vocal signals. For example, when two animals are in different moods, the one being more excited than the other, the more excited animal may utter vocalizations characteristic of its high excitement level, and the other animal may first respond with vocalizations which correspond to its own low level of excitement. However, if the first animal continues with high excitement vocalizations, the other animal may eventually respond with vocalization of the same high excitement level (Fig. 36). Thus, it is not only reciprocal position advertisement and a calling for social contact, but also a transmission of one animal's mood to the other, i.e., it is possible to change the general motivational state of the respondent in this way. This change is not only expressed by the vocalizations; the respondent also begins to show other signs of a greater excitement, such as an increase in locomotion.

Contact sounds are frequently repeated, sometimes in a rhythmical manner, and they often are relatively short and soft. Grunting sounds in swine (Snethlage 1957, Kiley 1972), cattle (Schloeth 1961b, Kiley 1972), red deer (Darling 1937, Burckhardt 1958a), fallow deer (Gilbert 1968), and axis deer (Schaller 1967), roaring and growling in camels, and bleating in llamas (Pilters 1954, 1956) may be mentioned as a few examples. Nonvocal noises, such as the clicking from the feet of moving reindeer or eland antelope, possibly serve a similar function. In large herds of gregarious ungulates, the vocal contact sounds are not addressed to definite partners. With their emulative effects upon conspecifics and their great role in the transmission of certain levels of general motivational states from one animal to the other, such vocalizations may generate and sustain a particular mood throughout the herd when mutually uttered and repeated by the members. Perhaps the most spectacular example of this is provided by migratory herds of wildebeest, which almost constantly give croaking calls, so that the herds are enveloped in "clouds" of familiar sound.

The loudness of vocalizations, of course, depends somewhat on differences in the physical structure of the sound-producing organs in different species, and generally increases with excitement. To be separated from the others is a situation which can easily create excitement in a gregarious animal, and the excitement increases if no contact is established. Correspondingly, the contact calls may become louder and louder. The greater the need for social contact in a given species, and/or the stronger the bonds among the group mates, the easier and the more frequently even a brief and/or spatially relatively small separation of an individual from the group may result in a quite considerable inner arousal.

In this way, separation from the group becomes the most typical and most frequent releasing situation for such vocalizations. Thus they often are more situation-specific than many other expressions of the animal's general motivational state; however, never to such an extent that they would not, at least occasionally, occur in highly exciting situations other than separation from the group. Good examples of loud, frequent, and relatively specialized contact calls may be

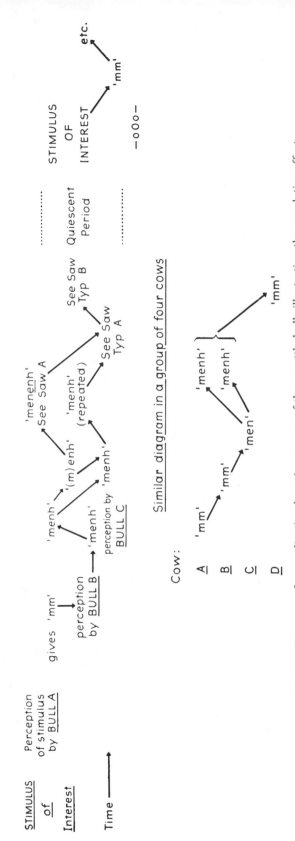

Fig. 36. Diagram of a vocalization bout in a group of three cattle bulls illustrating the emulative effect and change in the vocalizations. (From Kiley 1972.)

seen in certain vocalizations of Hippomorpha such as the well-known whinny of the horse, the bray of the ass, the Grevy's zebra's intermittent roar succeeded by an "ee" sound (*ee* as in *"bee"*) during inhalation, or the plains zebra's three-syllable barking "ha, haha, hahaha."

As previously mentioned, position advertisements and contact calls usually include species, sex, and age class identification. Moreover, at least some of them are also individually different. In this way, position advertisements and contact-seeking signals may lose their anonymous character and serve in individual recognition, particularly among members of relatively small and stable groups. For example, in the harems of plains zebra, the stallion vocalizes when searching for his mares. The same is true of the mares searching for their stallion, stallion and mares searching for the foals, and foals searching for their mothers. They take no interest in strange zebra, with the exception of the stallion of a harem, who may establish vocal (and other—see below) contact with the stallions of neighboring harem groups (Klingel 1967).

Of course, recognition of the partner's sex, state, etc., as well as of his individuality is not restricted to visual and acoustical means. Olfaction also plays an important role. In these situations, however, the sense of smell is not commonly used at a distance in hoofed animals. Usually the sniffing animal literally or nearly touches the partner with its nose. Thus, olfactory and tactile contact are established simultaneously. Certain regions of the partner's body are particularly important for olfactory recognition. The other's nose (Fig. 37) and mouth as well as his anus and genitals are sniffed and touched by nose in almost all the ungulate species, and frequently both partners test each other at the same body region reciprocally and simultaneously. Sniffing the partner's ears and eyes, his withers and/or shoulder region are not quite as common but still frequent enough. Furthermore, certain skin glands such as preorbital glands, maxillary glands, dorsal glands, tarsal glands, etc., are preferred regions of the partner's body in olfactory testing. Also, striking structures, such as hair tufts on the forehead (e.g., in dikdik or duikers), and sometimes the horns, are tested somewhat more frequently than other body regions. Of course, sniffing other body regions is not completely absent, but is rare in comparison to those that have been mentioned.

It should be emphasized that this sniffing serves to recognize the partner's sex, age, specific physiological state, or individuality—and "recognition" is not the same as "communication." However, it is a basis from which communicative processes, either friendly or agonistic, may develop.

Allogrooming (social grooming, grooming the partner) may be

Fig. 37. Nose-to-nose contact in
greeting between male and female in
lesser kudu (*Tragelaphus imberbis*).
(Walther 1958*a*. Hanover Zoo.)

considered to be closer to true communication than mere sniffing,
and it frequently follows olfactory testing. One may even say that in
hoofed mammals there is hardly any allogrooming without sniffing
preceding it. As with testing, the partners frequently groom each
other reciprocally and simultaneously. In contrast to self-grooming,
the hind legs are not used for allogrooming. Ungulates touch the
partner exclusively with their mouths. They—more or less
gently—bite and chew with their teeth (particularly typical of horses
and their relatives), nibble with their lips, and—most commonly and
widely spread—they lick with their tongues. Swine may also "massage" the partner with their snout disks.

The partner's body regions preferred in allogrooming are largely
the same as in olfactory testing. In addition, his forehead, neck, and
back are frequently groomed. In the literature, it has sometimes been
said that allogrooming serves to clean those regions of the partner's
body which may easily become dirty and which he cannot easily
reach himself. There are cases in which this seems to be true. However, there are at least as many cases in hoofed mammals for which
this interpretation appears to be inadequate or, at best, only half-true.
For example, legs, chest, and belly are frequently dirtied (the latter
two when the animal is resting), and chest and belly are two body
regions which many ungulates cannot easily reach and clean themselves. However, they are hardly touched in allogrooming among

adult animals in the majority of the species under discussion. (Exceptions are the swine, which may groom the entire belly of the recumbent partner. Also, in other species, the mothers' licking of their young, particularly of the neonates, is somewhat different.) By contrast, the head, neck, and shoulder region are comparatively less exposed to dirt. Moreover, the majority of the species (except those with an extremely massive body and short neck and legs, such as rhinos or hippos) can reach and clean all these regions at least by scratching with a hind leg. Species with a somewhat movable neck can also reach the shoulders with their mouths, and almost all the species lick the mouth and nose region with their tongues. Species with a very long tongue, such as okapi, can even reach other head regions, including their eyes, with their own tongue. Nevertheless, the partner's nose and mouth region as well as his neck and shoulders are frequently licked in allogrooming.

In these and other cases, the interpretation of allogrooming as a behavior which primarily serves to clean dirty regions of the partner's body which he cannot reach himself does not fit. It appears more likely that its primary purpose is to establish social contacts. In other words, allogrooming can be a kind of tactile communication. The message and meaning of social grooming may vary somewhat depending on the body regions touched and on situational circumstances. For example, when a male licks the female's genitals, he may signal sexual intentions and the female may become sexually stimulated in this way. Or, in a quantitative study on social relationships among Camargue cattle (*Bos primigenius taurus*), Schloeth (1961a) found that subordinate males lick faces, necks, and shoulders (no body region posterior to the shoulder) of dominant bulls much more often than dominants lick subordinates. Apparently social grooming is some kind of appeasement behavior in this and similar cases. Also, among males and females, allogrooming is often not restricted to the male's licking the female's genitals or rump; both partners may also lick each other's faces, necks, and shoulders, as has been observed in greater and lesser kudu (Fig. 38), sitatunga (Walther 1964b), gaur (Schaller 1967), red deer (Bützler 1974), barasingha (Schaller 1967), roe deer (Kurt 1968), muntjac (Barnette 1977), etc. Generally, the communication of friendly intentions frequently seems to be the function of social grooming, and this may also include cases in which a strong cleaning component is involved, as when two horses or zebras stand in more or less reverse-parallel position and groom each other's back and croup. Furthermore, in quite a number of cases the recipient remains absolutely still when being groomed, and/or he assumes a posture or position which makes allogrooming easier. Or he

Fig. 38. Gentle grooming of the partner's face in lesser kudu.
(Walther 1964*b*. Munich Zoo.)

may actively invite allogrooming by presenting a particular body region to the partner. (Fig. 39. Interestingly enough, such invitation
postures often are more or less identical with certain threat displays.)
Observing such scenes, one can hardly avoid the impression that
often an animal "likes and enjoys" being groomed. Consequently,
one may presume allogrooming to be particularly frequent among
individuals who are familiar with each other and "on good terms,"
whereas hostilities may exclude it. Generally this is true, but not
without exceptions. In a few species, such as kongoni, intense grooming of the other's cheek and neck may initiate agonistic encounters
among males. This occurs not only in playful sparring among
bachelors, but also in serious interactions between territorial bulls.
One may think of a connection between grooming and (ancestral)
biting in such cases. Playful sparring particularly of the "horning"
type, i.e., when the partners slowly and gently rub their horns against
each other, also appears to be a form of bodily contact related to
allogrooming and may alternate with it in certain species such as
Camargue cattle (Schloeth 1961*a*). Finally, there are parallels and
connections of social grooming to marking the opponent with skin
glands, as, for example, when a wildebeest bull rubs his preorbital
region at the opponent's flank or hindquarters (Fig. 17b) in a territorial encounter (Estes 1969). When allogrooming is strongly related to
marking behavior, its message and meaning are different in that it is
not so much an appeasement behavior (as in the subordinate's licking
the dominant in Camargue cattle) as it is a form of dominance be-

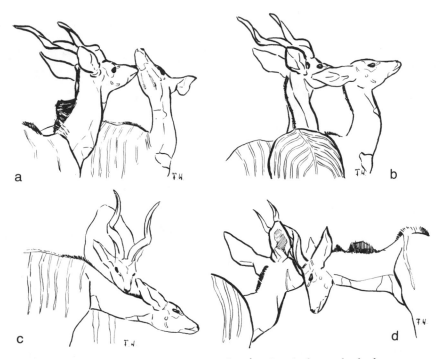

Fig. 39. Invitations for social grooming in lesser kudu by a. nose-up posture, b. erect posture, c. stretching head and neck forward-downward, d. presenting forehead and horns. (Walther 1964b.)

havior. For example, in peccary (whose marking behavior has been described before), it often is the dominant who rubs the submissive animal without having the rubbing reciprocated (Schweinsburg 1969).

Allogrooming (as well as some other forms of bodily contact) is not of equal importance in all the ungulate species. There are species, e.g., gazelles, blackbuck, oryx, addax, and giraffe, in which allogrooming among partners other than mother and offspring is infrequent in the wild (it may sometimes be different under captive conditions), whereas other species, such as animals of the cattle subfamily (Bovinae), are "great lickers." Again in others, such as many cervids, licking the partner is particularly prevalent in sexual interactions, where the male licks not only the female's genitals but also her entire back prior to mounting.

In part, such differences can be related to the mobility of the tongue. Some species can stretch the tongue much further out of their mouths and/or also use it during other occasions, e.g., in feeding, much more than others. In part, it seems to have something to do with whether a species belongs to the "contact type" or the "distance type." These two types were described by Hediger (1954), and they are by no means restricted to ungulates but can also be observed in carnivores, rodents, birds, etc. Animals of the contact type often rest in bodily contact and generally "like" being touched—when domesticated or when kept in captivity also by humans. Animals of the distance type usually keep a certain minimum distance from each other even when they come relatively close together as, e.g., in resting, and their need for being touched is much less pronounced. In captivity, they sometimes may even avoid being touched by their human keepers with whom they otherwise can become quite familiar. It must be emphasized that contact type and distance type have little, if any, relationship with gregariousness. There are highly gregarious ungulate species, such as reindeer, which belong to the distance type, and there are solitary species, such as tapirs, which belong to the contact type. On the whole, the distance type seems to be more common among hoofed mammals; the majority of the numerous bovid species fall into this category. On the other hand, the contact type is not absent; the equids, the swine, the peccaries, and the hippos are "contact animals" in this sense.

There are no relationships between contact type or distance type and sniffing the partner. These olfactory tests occur in all the species under discussion. However, there may be a relationship between these two types and the frequency of licking the partner. There is certainly such an influence in certain other forms of bodily contact: rubbing against the partner or standing (Fig. 40) or—more frequently—lying in touch with him. Rubbing with the head, usually the cheek or chin, or with the shoulder or the entire flank on the other's head, neck, or flank may still be considered to be related to allogrooming, although the performer may be groomed as much as the "recipient" in this case. In accordance with this view, rubbing a partner is mainly restricted to ungulate species such as swine, peccary, rhinos, horses, zebras, etc., which wallow and/or commonly rub their bodies against trees, rocks, termite mounds, and other environmental objects. However, not all species that at least seasonally rub on inanimate objects rub on partners. For example, ibex may quite intensively rub their flanks on rocks and the like during moulting, but they infrequently rub on each other. Finally, resting in bodily contact is *the* criterion for an animal's belonging to the contact type. It is found in all the ungulate species listed above as typical examples of contact animals. At present, we can only guess at the communicative significance of this form of being in touch. It may convey to the partners some feeling of friendly companionship and a certain "social

Fig. 40. Standing in reverse-parallel position with head on the partner's back in East African plains zebra (*Equus quagga boehmi*). This form of body contact is frequently found in equids and may easily lead to social grooming. (Serengeti National Park.)

security," and may also play a role in temperature regulation in certain cases which, of course, are outside the realm of a discussion on communication.

Olfactory testing as well as allogrooming can be one-sided or reciprocal. When strangers, or animals which had been together in the past but later were separated, meet each other, the reciprocal sniffing of the partner's nose, anus, genitals, etc., is in some cases so obligatory and "stereotyped," and often also occurs in such a predictable sequence, that some authors have spoken of "greeting rituals." The impression of a ceremonial character in such a meeting is enhanced by certain predictable changes in the position of the partners relative to each other. Such positions and position changes are, of course, often determined by the body regions to be tested. For example, the partners may first stand in more or less frontal orientation when establishing nose-to-nose contact (Fig. 37), and then they may move into a reverse-parallel (head-to-tail) position for sniffing each other's anus and genitals (Fig. 41b). However, sometimes there are very typical positions which involve more subtle components. For example, partners who are both somewhat shy and insecure may move into a reverse-parallel position without having established any bodily contact before, and then both may turn their heads and necks backward until their noses meet for a naso-nasal contact (Fig. 41a). In species

a   b

Fig. 41a. Naso-nasal contact from reverse-parallel position in plains zebra. b. Naso-anal and naso-genital contact. (Schloeth 1956.)

in which allogrooming plays a role, the reciprocal licking of particular body regions may follow the olfactory tests as a further component of greeting. Finally, certain ritualized aggressive behaviors and/or sexual behaviors can be incorporated in the greeting rituals. These behaviors will be discussed in the chapter on threats, dominance, and courtship displays. Klingel's (1967) description of the meeting between plains zebra stallions follows. It may give the reader an impression of the complexity of such greeting rituals.

The most typical case is when two owners of neighboring harem groups meet. The two stallions approach, stretch their heads forward and sniff each other's noses while standing parallel or oriented frontally and showing a special facial expression, the so-called greeting face (Antonius 1939), by drawing the corners of their mouths upward in a jerking movement and usually directing their ears forward (Fig. 42). They may also open their mouths somewhat and perform "chewing" (probably one should better say ritualized biting) movements into the air. This is followed by reciprocal sniffing of the other's genitals in reverse-parallel position. Then, each of them presses his forehead against the other's flank and vigorously rubs up and down. They again establish nose-to-nose contact followed by a "parting jump." In the full "parting jump," a stallion jumps up with his forelegs. However, he frequently performs only an intention movement by kicking into the air with one foreleg and/or throwing his head upward and backward. Thereafter, the stallions depart. The same behaviors also occur among members of all-male groups (although these stallions are together more or less permanently), but here the sequencing is not as fixed. Also there are some further vari-

Fig. 42. "Greeting face" in East African plains zebra. (Klingel 1967. Photo: H. Klingel. Ngorongoro Crater, Tanzania.)

ations. For example, at the end of greeting, one of the partners frequently places his head on the other's back—as the dominant may do with the subordinate after an agonistic encounter (Backhaus 1960b). This behavior does not occur in the greeting rituals of harem stallions. When the partners are clearly unequal from the beginning, as when an adult stallion meets a subadult, the greeting does not proceed beyond the naso-nasal contact. The young stallion shows the facial expression of submission (p. 206) at this point and turns away (Klingel 1967).

When we come to threats and related displays, the reader will easily recognize how many aggressive "elements" are involved in these greeting rituals of plains zebra. Also, in many other ungulates, meeting frequently includes threat and dominance displays or submissive behaviors on the subordinate's part. Conversely, hostile interactions may be initiated by reciprocal olfactory testing in certain species.

Looking back at the points discussed in this chapter, we may say that such an elaborate ritual as was just described for zebra stallions is doubtless an act of communication in the most literal sense. However, certain "elements" of aggression and/or sexual behavior are usually involved in such well-pronounced greeting rituals. This is probably not by chance since contact seeking and contact making behaviors per se seem to belong more to the peripheral realms of communication. Allogrooming is still relatively close to a communication in the strict sense. It clearly is an interaction between two individuals, the behavior is aimed at and directed toward the partner, and at least in some of the cases, the sender seems to deliver a message to the recipient (friendly intentions, appeasement, etc.). On the other hand, there are cases of allogrooming in which it remains uncertain what the sender's message may be, and/or in which allogrooming seems to be a mere executive behavior (cleaning) without much communicative function, and/or in which the "benefit" is only on the part of the performer who uses the "recipient" more or less as substitute for an inanimate object (e.g., when rubbing his flank against him). Making contact in olfactory testing is also an aimed and directed interaction between individuals. However, it is doubtful whether the initiator is truly delivering a message to the other. Olfactory testing primarily serves in recognizing something—a female's estrous state; whether an individual belongs to the same group; the identity of a group member—and, as stated above, such a recognition may become the basis for a communicative interaction, but it is no communication in itself. In contact seeking, the directional component is often missing—simply because contact seeking usually occurs when contact is lost and the other's position is uncertain. It can still be aimed at a definite individual, as when members of a stable group search for each other. More commonly, however, contact seeking is a rather anonymous matter. The sender seeks contact with conspecifics in general, or with any conspecific of the opposite sex, etc. Thus, it frequently is a communication of the "to-whom-it-may-concern" type. In contagion, finally, there is no aiming at a partner at all. Insofar as one still wishes to speak of some kind of communication, this is a side effect of basically noncommunicative behaviors.

10. SIGNALS IN MOTHER–OFFSPRING RELATIONS

Communication between mother and offspring adds few principally new aspects to our discussion of advertising presence and position, contact seeking, contact making, and alarm signals. Most of the means of communication used in mother-offspring relations are only special cases or modifications of the above advertisements and signals. Any difference is not so much in the signals per se but in the individualization of the communication process brought about by the strong bond between the two partners involved and by the reciprocal recognition of individual characteristics in the other's appearance, vocalizations, and odors. For example, a mother may utter a vocalization which is nothing but the usual species-specific position advertisement. However, after her offspring has learned to recognize her voice and to distinguish it from that of other conspecifics, it automatically relates this vocalization to itself and reacts to it. The same is also true for the mother with respect to signals given by her young.

The presence of individual features in odors and vocalizations of ungulates and their recognition by partners is not a theoretical assumption but has been proven in at least a few species, and is very likely in many further species which have not yet been investigated in this regard. For example, Lent (1975) found individual differences in audiospectral analyses of bleats by caribou calves (Fig. 43), and Espmark (1971) could demonstrate individual recognition of the infant's voice by playing back tape-recorded vocalizations of reindeer calves to their mothers. Furthermore, individual recognition of the mother's voice has been described in species such as Dall's sheep (*Ovis dalli*—Murie 1944), bison (Marjoribanks-Egerton 1962), Camargue cattle (Schloeth 1958), musk ox (Lent 1974), and others.

Also quite interesting with respect to problems of individual recognition between parent and offspring were a few little experiments with a blesbok calf I raised years ago (Walther 1969a). The calf recognized me (the "mother") olfactorily at the latest by the age of two days. It took milk only from me and rejected being nursed by

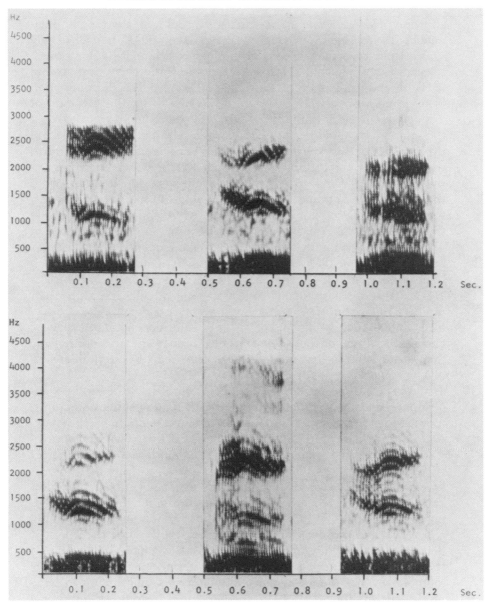

Fig. 43. Six bleats of caribou calves (*Rangifer tarandus*). Three of these were successive bleats of the same individual. They are scattered randomly. The reader is invited to identify them. (The center one on top and the two side ones in the lower row.) (Lent 1975. Photo: P. C. Lent.)

strangers. However, when my worn shirt, socks, or anything impregnated with my smell was wrapped around the bottle, the calf readily took it from any stranger, even from a person whom it had previously rejected when he had first offered the bottle without my shirt around it. Thus, the recognition of an individual odor and its discrimination from others was very obvious. During its first week, this calf did not distinguish my voice from that of other persons when they called to it the same way as I did. However, at least by the age of four weeks (no experiments of this type were conducted between the first and fourth week), the calf had learned to recognize my voice and reacted exclusively to my calls and not to those of strangers. On the other hand, the young blesbok could not reliably distinguish me from other persons in a visual way, not even at the age of four months. Apparently there are differences in different species. For example, according to Tschanz (1962), mouflon lambs can visually recognize their mothers at the age of three days, and blackbuck fawns acoustically distinguish their mothers after the second day of their lives (Benz 1973). Thus, as a general rule, young ungulates learn to individually recognize their mothers by imprinting-like processes within a few days—be it olfactorily and/or acoustically and/or visually, and, depending on species, apparently in one of these sensory fields sooner and/or more reliably than in the others—and consequently, they react to the mother's individual signals.

More species-specific differences seem to occur in the mothers' individual recognition of their young. At least under captive conditions, mothers of certain species nurse strange young quite readily; they do not seem to make much distinction between their own and strange young, whereas in certain other species, the mothers absolutely reject sucking attempts by strange young. In species in which the mothers know their young individually, olfactory cues appear to be the most general means of recognition. In contrast to the relatively slow bonding of the young to its mother, the mother's attachment to her young is a very rapid process which takes place shortly after the infant is born. Therefore, there may be a period of a few days (depending on the species) during which the young cannot yet distinguish its mother, and the whole "responsibility" for avoiding mixups in large herds falls on the mother. In species such as goats (Klopfer and Gamble 1966), it has been presumed that the mothers become olfactorily imprinted to their young when sniffing and licking them after they are born. However, according to more recent studies (Gubernick 1981), it appears more likely that the mothers "label" their neonates with their saliva when licking them after birth: they impregnate the young with their own smell, and later recognize them on this basis.

That mothers of certain duikers mark their young with maxillary gland secretion has already been mentioned in another context. Generally, licking may contribute to the establishment and maintenance of the bond between mother and offspring in many ungulate species. It may also convey certain messages. However, little is known as to the identity of these messages.

To better understand the bonds and the role of the signals between mother and young, it appears necessary to describe at least briefly a few general aspects of mother-offspring relationships in hoofed mammals—although, of course, these descriptions somewhat exceed the realm of a discussion on communication. With apparently only a very few exceptions (e.g., possibly moose, according to Stringham 1974), the mother-offspring relations of ungulates differ according to two alternative categories in the behavior of the young, particularly during the first weeks of the young's life when the bond between mother and offspring is especially strong. (Later, the young of several mothers form "kindergartens" in certain species, and the bond to their age-mates becomes at least as important as that with their mothers.) These young either are "followers," or they belong to the "lying-out" type (Walther 1966a). In the "followers," roughly speaking, the young follows the mother (Fig. 44) wherever she goes and is together with her most of the time. Since the young do not yet take much solid food and since they rest more often and longer than adults, the grazing mother may sometimes move away from her offspring. However, such a temporary and more or less accidental separation is always initiated by the mother in species with young of the "follower" type. By contrast, a young of the "lying-out" type actively turns and moves away from its mother (Fig. 45) after it has been with her for a relatively short time (thirty minutes to one hour or so) during which it has been nursed and intensively cleaned by her, and it seeks a place where it beds down and stays for hours until the mother calls it again for the next nursing. The mother usually only approaches but does not enter the place where the young is lying out, and she never rests side by side with the young (except during the first twelve hours following birth at maximum)—very much in contrast to the "followers" (Fig. 46). The length of the lying-out period seems to vary with species (Lent 1974). It is in full effect at least during the first two weeks (reports on considerably shorter periods are erroneous, in my opinion; i.e., this is not lying-out behavior), and later it gradually wanes; the periods during which such a young is together with its mother become extended, and the periods in which it is lying out are correspondingly progressively reduced.

"Followers" in this sense are the horses and their relatives, appar-

Fig. 44. Chamois fawn (*Rupicapra rupicapra*) following its mother. (Walther 1977*a*.)

ently also the rhinos (Schenkel and Lang 1969), and the camels and llamas (Pilters 1956). Also, I am inclined to consider the swine and their relatives as "followers," although here the young stay in a den or "nest" for the first four to five days (Frädrich 1967). However, the mother is together with the young for long periods during this time, and thus the young do not actively separate from her, which is the most important criterion of lying-out behavior. Furthermore, young giraffe seem to be "followers." Among the cervids, only reindeer (Espmark 1971) and caribou can be said for sure to belong to the follower type. Among the bovids, wildebeests are pronounced followers; furthermore, all the sheep and apparently also the wild goats (Walther 1961*a*), the chamois, mountain goat, aoudad, and the majority of wild oxen (Walther 1979). Lying-out behavior is found in the majority of deer species, in pronghorn, and in many of the bovids such as the gazelles and their relatives, greater and lesser kudu, bushbuck, waterbuck and their relatives, dwarf antelopes, duikers, etc.

The following reaction, of course, dominates the life of the "followers," but it is not lacking in the young of the "lying-out" type; the latter follow their mothers during the short periods when they are together with them. Apparently, the reaction to follow an object which is close by, bigger than the young, and moving and vocalizing, is innate in these animals. When repeatedly following the same object (the mother, under normal conditions) within the first day or days of its life, the young becomes individually imprinted to this object. Thus, the young ungulate does not learn to follow, but it learns *whom* to follow, and it learns to recognize several different features of the object followed, such as individual odor, voice, etc.

a

b

Fig. 45a. Grant's gazelle fawn (*Gazella granti*)
turns and moves away from its mother and . . . b. . . .
seeks a place where it beds down and stays for the
next hours. (Walther 1979. Serengeti National Park.)

"Maternal calls," such as growling and bleating in camel (Pilters
1954, 1956), bleating in fallow deer (Tembrock 1968) and axis deer
(Schaller 1967), guttural grunting in cattle (Schloeth 1958, 1961a),
grunts in swine (Frädrich 1967), soft twittering whistles in dikdik (Dittrich and Böer 1980), and many others, have been described. However, it usually has not been investigated whether these truly are discrete and special calls, or only slightly modified forms of vocalizations
commonly used as contact signals among conspecifics. The latter is
certainly true in species which I have had occasion to investigate in
this regard, such as blackbuck and dorcas gazelle.

The young may also contact its mother vocally, and there is often a
"question-answer" vocalization between mother and offspring.
Sounds made by the young are usually higher in pitch than the calls
of adult animals, but they usually are nothing more than the infantile
forms of adult vocal contact sounds. The mother reacts to the call of
her young by calling back and/or approaching it. When moving in
front of the young, she may stop and wait for it. Some reactions of
mothers to distress calls of their young have been previously described. In wild boar and warthog, mothers lying together with their
offspring in a "nest" immediately change their position when a young
begins to squeak loudly (Frädrich 1967).

Fig. 46a. In the follower type—here, black wildebeest—mother and young often rest together side by side. b. In the lying-out type—here, white-tailed deer (*Odocoileus virginianus*)—the young rests separated from its mother, often close to (vertical) environmental objects such as a tree, a bush (or several bushes), or a rock. (Stuttgart Zoo; Welder Wildlife Refuge, Texas.)

As stated above, it is certain that mothers can individually recognize the voices of their offspring at least in some of the species. However, in contrast to the rapid development of the olfactory individual recognition immediately after birth, it often seems to take the mothers a longer time to distinguish their own infants' vocalizations from those of strange young. Thus, when the offspring are still very young, the mothers often react more generally to the call of "a neonate" (Lent 1974).

Of course, contact calling and individual recognition of the partner's voice become particularly important when mother and offspring have been separated from each other. In species in which the young lie out, such separation is a normal biological situation, whereas one may assume that, in young of the "follower" type, a separation from the mother is always accidental or due to a more or less severe external disturbance. Frequently it is so. However, even here, deliberate separations are possible under special circumstances. An especially impressive example of this kind, which at the same time beautifully demonstrates the importance of contact calling and acoustical individual recognition on occasion of the reunion, is provided by Klingel's (1974) studies on the behavior of Grevy's zebra.

In Grevy's zebra, as well as in some other African game animals (e.g., South African oryx antelope—Walther 1980), the mothers apparently do not take their young with them when visiting water-holes. When during the dry season only distant water-holes are available, the Grevy's mares sometimes leave their young foals in the early morning and do not return before evening. They do not make their young stay behind by an act of communication. The young foals commonly doze for a few minutes after nursing. The mares take advantage of this situation and move away. When they can make it to a distance of 100 to 200 meters without the young becoming aware of the mothers' departure, the foals do not follow the mares upon waking up. They form a "kindergarten," remain at the place, and wait until their mothers come back. When the mares return from the water-hole, they begin to vocalize while still at a distance. The foals answer the mothers' calls; however, sometimes not only a mare's own foal but several others may respond to her calling. The mares now continue walking ahead toward the foals which, on their part, advance toward the mares in a tight bunch. Nevertheless, each mare directly moves toward her own foal and threatens strange foals approaching her, i.e., she clearly distinguishes her foal from the others without any olfactory testing but obviously on the basis of acoustical individual recognition.

Visual signs may serve the same or similar purposes as the mother's vocalizations. For example, Pruitt (1960) describes how a mother caribou can lure her neonate calf by head-bobbing (Fig. 47). Also, I could make my tame blesbok calf approach me by silent bowing movements, similar to those that adult blesboks frequently perform with head and neck when they start moving. Apparently, in such and similar cases, the effects of the vocal and visual "calling" act cumulatively when displayed simultaneously or alternately. With the strong reaction to follow a moving object and the imprinted individual bond to the mother, it is not surprising that frequently the mother's mere walking is sufficient to get the young going. Since generally the following reaction is released more promptly the faster the releasing object moves (Walther 1969a), the mother's running at a gallop is a particularly strong stimulus. This is provided that the young is on its feet. For example, when a mother begins to run while her young is lying out, it does not follow her. Since, in the case of flight, the mother may utter high-excitement vocalizations when or immediately before taking off, the young may also learn the meaning of alarm calls on such occasions (if it does not innately respond to them).

Communication between mother and young begins immediately after birth—in some cases even during birth, since the first vocal contacts, according to the "question-answer" principle, sometimes occur when the young's body is only half out of the mother's vulva. Apparently the neonate's vocalizations can be quite important for stimulating maternal care. For example, Alexander (1960) noted that merino ewes frequently desert stillborn lambs, and in goats (van der Hammen and Schenk 1963) and caribou (Lent 1966) unusual behaviors of mothers were observed when their young remained silent after birth.

With respect to the mothers' behavior toward their neonates at birth, Hediger (1954) distinguished an active and a passive type.

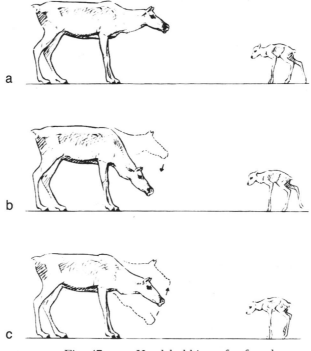

Fig. 47a.–c. Head bobbing of a female caribou to her neonate calf. (W. D. Berry in Pruitt 1960.)

Mothers of the active type lick their young intensively; mothers of the passive type do not lick their young. Although mothers in such groups as swine, camels, and llamas belong to the passive type, the majority of the ungulate mothers are of the active type. This licking of the neonate immediately after birth somewhat differs from social grooming among adult animals. It is not restricted to a few definite body regions; the mother may lick more or less the entire body of the neonate, including its belly and legs, although a certain preference for the head and the anal region is often recognizable. (Later the mother more or less restricts her licking to the anal and genital region, and still later she prefers to lick the young's head, neck, and shoulder region as with an adult partner.) Apparently the licking of the neonate serves a variety of functions. Among others, the mother may receive olfactory and gustatory stimuli which appear to be important in strengthening the bond with the infant. The possibility of some kind of olfactory "labeling" of the young by the mother's saliva has already been mentioned (Gubernick 1981). Interestingly, *Flehmen* has even been observed in mothers of a few species, such as musk ox (Lent 1974) and horses (Fraser 1968), after licking their neonates for the first time. Another function of the mother's licking of the neonate may be to stimulate its blood circulation, and thus to aid the young's first attempts to stand (although very intense licking may hinder it). When observing neonate gazelle fawns, I sometimes had the impression that the young were "following" the mother's tongue message and were "pulled up" onto their feet—as if by an invisible string—while the mothers were intensively licking their foreheads.

In quite a number of ungulate species, mothers can tactually stimulate their offspring by means other than licking, particularly when the licking proved ineffective and the neonate did not respond to it by rising. Domestic cattle (Naaktgeboren and Vandendriesche 1962) as well as bison (Fraser 1968) and musk ox (Lent 1974) do so by prodding the neonate with the head. Kongoni mothers were observed (Gosling 1969) placing the nose under the calf to lift it up. Perhaps even more frequently, an ungulate mother may kick or scrape her fawn with her foreleg to make it stand for the first time. Such events have occasionally been recorded in roe deer (Bubenik 1965), fallow deer (Gilbert 1974), blesbok (Lynch 1974), and Dall's sheep (Pitzman 1970), among others. Furthermore, the mother's vocalizations may also have stimulating effects in this situation.

Perhaps I may here remind the reader of a point which we touched on in the theoretical discussions on communicative and expressive behaviors. Some scientists are of the opinion that animals such as hoofed mammals can express nothing but their psycho-physiological (emotional) state and are unable to address the recipient, or to directly aim for a definite response from the latter. Additional evidence to the contrary will be found in later chapters; for the moment, suffice it to say that tactile stimulation by the mother of the neonate, particularly the prodding with her head or kicking and scraping the infant with her hooves, etc., when it does not arise after birth, is hardly congruous to this view.

Nursing, of course, is a very important interaction between mother and offspring. It also requires some communication between the partners. Not necessarily, but very frequently, nursing is initiated by vocalizations of the mother and/or the offspring. The "calling out" of lying-out young by the mothers (Fig. 48) has been described in a variety of species, including greater kudu (Walther 1964b), several gazelle species (Walther 1968a), musk deer (Lerov 1954), white-tailed deer (Faatz 1976), pronghorn (Prenzlow 1964), Uganda kob (Leuthold 1967), and dikdik (Hendrichs and Hendrichs 1971). In "follower" species, initiation of nursing by vocalizations of mothers was noted, e.g., in ibex and markhor goat (Capra falconeri—Walther 1961a), bighorn sheep (Geist 1971), and warthog (Frädrich 1965). Infant vocalizations preceding or associated with nursing and in part in response to the mother's vocalizations are mentioned in llamas (Pilters 1956), swine (Hafez and Signoret 1969), markhor (Walther 1961a), Barbary sheep (Ammotragus lervia—Haas 1959), caribou (Lent 1966), and many others.

Relatively rarely will an ungulate mother invite the young's suckling by tactile stimulation, such as by pushing her resting infant with her head, horns, or forefeet. A few events of this kind have been reported, e.g., in roe deer (Kurt 1968), bison (Marjoribanks-Egerton 1962), reindeer (Espmark 1971), and musk ox (Lent 1974). On the other hand, it is quite commonplace for the mother to direct her neonate's searching activities toward her udder and to guide her young into the typical reverse-parallel position for nursing (Fig. 49) by her nosing and licking of its anal region after it has approached her.

In a number of ungulate species, the mother may stiffen her legs and assume a more or less erect posture during nursing. When she assumes this attitude before nursing, it may sometimes work as a visual nursing invitation. This erect stance resembles the posture of intense watching, and this resemblance may possibly account for the "disturbance nursing" (Walker 1950, Schloeth 1958, Walther 1964b) that occurs in several or even many ungulate species when a predator or a human shows up at a distance. In this situation, the mothers watch for the potential danger, and their young approach them and are nursed. In some species, e.g., reindeer (Espmark 1971), the mother may make it easier for the neonate to reach her udder by somewhat bending and straddling her hind legs, thus assuming a posture similar to the (female) urination stance. However, truly striking and very specialized udder presentation postures, by which the mothers invite the suckling of their offspring, are found in relatively few ungulate species. For example, in muntjac (Dubost 1971) and all the mouse deer species (Davis 1965, Cadigan 1972, Dubost 1975, Ralls et al. 1975, Robin 1979), the mother lifts one hind leg—like a male dog when urinating—and stands on three legs during nursing, and in tapirs (von Richter 1966) and swine (Frädrich 1967), the mother lies down on her side for nursing small young and may lift her upper hind leg. In swine, furthermore, the mother utters a series of grunts in the beginning of nursing which also seem to invite suckling in the piglets (Frädrich 1967). However, in most ungulates, mothers do not vocalize after nursing has started. Soft vocalizations can be heard from the young of many species during suckling but nothing is known of their function in communication.

As long as the offspring are very young, nursing is usually initiated by the mothers. When the infants grow somewhat older, they frequently initiate the nursing. Other than by vocalizations, young ungulates commonly stimulate their mothers for nursing by nudging their bellies and/or flanks with their muzzles (in addition to the usual nuzzling and pushing of the mother's udder region during suckling). In tapir and swine species, the mother lies down for nursing in response to the violent nosing of her side and belly by her older offspring. In other species, the young may sometimes approach the resting mother and prod her with snout or forehead to induce her to rise and to nurse. In some species, the young also have a special technique for stopping the walking mother for nursing by placing themselves laterally in front of the mother, immediately in front of her forelegs. This has been reported of Camargue cattle (Schloeth 1958), Marco Polo sheep (*Ovis ammon poli*—Walther 1961a), bighorn sheep (Geist 1971), greater kudu and sitatunga (Walther 1964b), and sika deer (*Saik nippon*—Kiddie 1962). With increasing age of the offspring, the milk-soliciting behavior can take rather vehement forms. The young may butt its mother's flank with its forehead, or may mount her, or kick with its foreleg (like a male in courtship) in certain species. These are not infantile behaviors but more or less aggressive behaviors which in some species can even result in the mother's fleeing from her own young (Walther 1978c).

The nursing of neonates is usually terminated by the young. Later, it is frequently terminated by the mothers. In many cases, the mother

b

d

f

a

c

e

simply steps forward and walks off. However, at least in certain species and in certain situations, the mother may also use threat displays to terminate the nursing or to reject suckling attempts by her older offspring.

When a dangerous object appears suddenly and/or approaches, very young ungulates in quite a number of species may "freeze" (prone response). This means they lie down flat with head and neck stretched stiffly forward (at least in some of the species, head and neck are held a few centimeters above the ground) and remain motionless. This prone response is not the same as lying-out behavior. Of course, a lying-out young can assume the prone posture when, e.g., a predator or human comes close. However, the young do not rest in prone posture all the time when lying out. Moreover, the prone response apparently is not restricted to young of the lying-out type but may also occur in at least some of the "followers" at a very young age. As stated above, this "freezing" usually is a response to the sudden occurrence of a potential danger, including somewhat unusual and relatively loud sounds. However, in certain species and in certain situations, the prone response apparently can be induced by signals from the mothers. When the fleeing mother's high bounding motions stimulate the prone response, as was observed in white-tailed deer (Downing and McGinnes 1969), caribou (Lent 1966), and mule deer (Linsdale and Tomich 1953), this may be said to be a reaction to the sudden and relatively loud sounds of these bounds. The most aimed and deliberate actions are the mother's pushing or pressing the infant down with her muzzle, head, or forelegs in alarming situations, as has been described, e.g., in elk (Altmann 1963), red deer, and roe deer (Bubenik 1965). It is not quite clear at present whether sometimes the mother's alarm calls may induce the prone response of the young. It is said to be the case in pronghorn (Autenrieth and Fichter 1975) and mule deer (Seton 1929), and I also noted a few instances in Grant's gazelle from which one could get this impression. However, it certainly is not a general rule that alarm calls, including those of the mother, regularly induce "freezing" in the young.

Fig. 48. "Calling out" the lying-out young in Thomson's gazelle. a. A tommy fawn is lying out (arrow). The mother appears at a distance. b. The mother calls, and the fawn rises. Note that the fawn has not yet seen the mother, but merely reacts to her call. c. The fawn spots the approaching mother. d. It runs toward her at a gallop. e. The mother olfactorily tests the arriving fawn. (If it were not her young, she would start butting it at this moment.) f. Nursing. (Walther 1979. Serengeti National Park.)

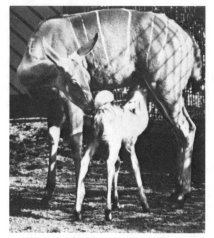

Fig. 49. Greater kudu female nursing and licking the anal region of her calf in reverse-parallel position. (Walther 1964*b*. Frankfurt Zoo.)

Olfactory testing when mother and offspring meet after a separation, and social grooming between the two, are in principal the same as in adult partners when they are familiar enough with each other. However, in mother-offspring relationships, olfactory testing and, to an even greater extent, allogrooming often remain one-sided for quite a while: it is predominantly the mother who sniffs and licks her young, and it may be days or weeks until the young reciprocates. Furthermore, there are some differences between mothers of young of the lying-out type, who intensely lick the anal and genital regions of their offspring on the occasion of each nursing, and mothers of young of the "follower" type who lick their young much less frequently and intensively. However, these and more behavioral peculiarities do not primarily appear to be related to communication.

To sum up: Although individual bonds other than those between mother and offspring definitely occur in at least some of the ungulate species, the affiliation of mother and young is the single individual bonding that is present in all the species. Moreover, it is one of the strongest, if not the strongest, of all bonds between individuals that is recognizable in hoofed mammals. Of course, this bond is very important under biological aspects (reproduction, etc.). All these points justify one's paying attention to mother-offspring relationships in a discussion on communication. On the other hand, as stated from the beginning, the majority of the signals and communicative behaviors used in mother-offspring relationships of hoofed mammals are the same or only somewhat modified forms of behaviors used among adult conspecifics. A number of them, such as position and state advertisements, contact seeking signals, alarm calls, etc., are even more or less the same as in communications of the "to-whom-it-may-concern" type. Thus, their individualized function in mother-offspring relations often is not brought about by the signals per se but simply is a consequence of the individual bond between mother and young.

11. ORIENTATIONS RELATIVE TO THE PARTNER

In general, the sender's orientation toward the recipient and the latter's orientation relative to the sender are of minor importance in all communications of the "to-whom-it-may-concern" type. When anonymous means of communication (position advertisements, contact calls, alarm signals, etc.) are used in individualized relationships, such as that between mother and offspring, the sender's orientation may contribute to focusing the signal in the direction of the recipient—for example, when a mother stands frontally oriented toward her young when uttering a contact call at a distance. However, even in such cases, the sender's orientation only facilitates the perception of the signal; it is not a true component of the communication process. When making bodily contact in olfactory and tactile testing or allogrooming, the partners sometimes simply have to assume a definite orientation toward each other. For example, when both partners simultaneously sniff each other's anal region, they necessarily must move into a reverse-parallel position. In other cases, however, olfactory testing or allogrooming permits a great variety of orientations. For example, in naso-nasal contact the partners may be frontally oriented toward each other, or in parallel position, or in a rectangular position, or at an angle that is somewhere between a frontal and a parallel position, etc. In short, the orientations in olfactory testing and social grooming primarily depend on the partner's body region to be sniffed or groomed, and they otherwise are relatively irrelevant.

By contrast, in most of the individually addressed communications other than contact seeking, olfactory testing, and allogrooming, the sender's orientation relative to the recipient is a significant factor, and the recipient's orientation with respect to the sender is often also quite important; that is, these orientations may come close to, or even directly work like, specific signals and expressions. Perhaps one may distinguish (a) the "signal value" of an orientation per se, (b) the "signal value" of a turn—the change from one given orientation to another, and (c) the component character of an orientation in specific (threat, courtship, etc.) displays—the orientation being the "carrier" of an expressive behavior.

In the following discussion, we will focus on the "signal values" of certain orientations per se. The importance of the sender's turn, i.e., the change from an until-now position into a new orientation relative to the recipient, for addressing an individual partner has already been stressed, and we will encounter it so frequently in the later discussions on threat displays, dominance displays, etc., that it may not be necessary to treat it here as a special topic. Likewise, the role of orientation as a component in expressive displays will become evident in the discussions of these displays, or it will immediately follow from the descriptions of the "signal values" of the orientations.

Among the many orientations which a sender can assume with respect to a recipient, the frontal, lateral, and reverse orientations may be said to be the three basic forms. The others can be understood as being transitions between them. Let us presume the recipient always stands with his head directed toward the sender. The sender orients with his head toward him (head-on position) in frontal orientation, he stands broadside in front of the recipient (lateral T-position) in lateral orientation, and with his hindquarters toward him in reverse orientation (Fig. 50). Frequently the sender orients his whole body toward the recipient according to these three basic orientations. About as frequently, however, he only orients his head in the corresponding direction while his body remains in a different position, e.g., the body may be in frontal orientation in all three cases. Then, as far as the "signal value" and the effect upon the recipient are concerned, the orientation of the sender's head substitutes for and represents that of the whole body.

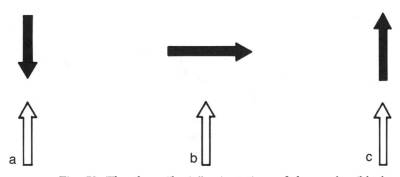

Fig. 50. The three "basic" orientations of the sender (black arrow) and the positions resulting from them with the recipient (white arrow) in frontal orientation. a. Frontal orientation of the sender—head-on position. b. Broadside orientation of the sender—lateral T-position. c. Reverse (hindquarters) orientation of the sender—tandem-position with sender in front.

When the sender assumes a frontal orientation toward the recipient (Fig. 50a), he directs his most important weapons (teeth, tusks, horns, antlers, neck, forelegs) toward him. Consequently, the frontal orientation often is the initial position for fighting and may express the sender's readiness for aggression. His hostile intentions become clearer when the frontal orientation is combined with more specific threat displays. However, quite frequently the frontal orientation per se is sufficient to intimidate (Fig. 51) or challenge the opponent. Consequently, gregarious ungulates often avoid meeting each other in head-on position during maintenance activities such as resting (Fig. 52), standing, or grazing, and when they do meet head-on without hostile intentions, they often try to appease the other by licking his face, etc. The avoidance of the challenging effect of the frontal orientation is also the reason why insecure partners sometimes move into a reverse-parallel position and then turn their heads around for naso-nasal testing or licking (Fig. 41a).

The reverse orientation toward the partner (Fig. 50c) is the opposite of the frontal orientation, and so is its message and meaning. In agonistic encounters, it is typical of the flight or withdrawal of the subordinate. Thus, the reverse orientation is suitable to diminish the dominant's aggressiveness—the other has already accepted his role as an inferior, and there is no "reason" for further aggression—or to release the dominant's pursuit which can be a chase at full gallop.

Fig. 51. Adult springbuck (center) interferes ("takes offense") in a fight between two subadult males by approaching them in frontal orientation. (Walther 1981. Etosha National Park.)

Fig. 52. Hoofed mammals often avoid frontal orientation during maintenance activities. This may result in a "star-formation." Here, two subadult males of Defassa waterbuck (*Kobus defassa*) rest together in a 180° star-formation. (Serengeti National Park.)

However, more frequently it is a pursuit march, i.e., he follows walking behind the withdrawing subordinate. The release of the following reaction by the reverse orientation, furthermore, plays an important role in mother-offspring relationships with the mother walking in front of the young (Fig. 44). It is also recognizable among moving adults where the file formation of the herds may result from it. Finally, there can also be a sexual component in the reverse orientation since it is the usual position of the female toward the male during mounting and copulation, and females of many species stand or walk in front of the driving male during the courtship ritual. However, the female's orientation during mating as well as that of animals in moving herds are not without connections to the reverse orientation of the subordinate in agonistic encounters. In most of the species under discussion, the female is inferior in strength and size to the male, and in the herds it is the weaker, younger, and/or subordinate animals which commonly move in front of the stronger and more dominant ones. On the whole, then, the reverse orientation is frequently typical of inferiority, the female's readiness for sexual behavior, and for situations in which the sender wants to release the other's following reaction. Thus, it generally indicates peaceful intentions. Perhaps the most remarkable exception to this general rule is in animals such as horses, where the reverse orientation may be used for kicking with the hind legs in a fight.

Literally or implicitly, the lateral orientation (Fig. 50b) has often been said to result from a conflict between aggression (frontal orientation) and escape tendencies (reverse orientation) in ethological literature (e.g., Fraser 1957, Ewer 1968). Since lateral displays occur in a great variety of vertebrate species and since I do not know the behavior of all of them, I cannot say whether this interpretation is generally wrong. But I can say that this "conflict explanation" of the broadside orientation is, at best, applicable in a few special and, on the whole, relatively infrequent cases in hoofed mammals. Thus, it certainly cannot be accepted as a general explanation. There are some ungulate species, such as the mountain goat (Geist 1965), giraffe, and Barbary sheep, which customarily fight from a broadside position. Here, assuming the broadside position is the initiation of a fight; it is purely aggressive and has nothing to do with escape. On the basis of certain facts, Geist (1966b) has suggested that fighting from a broadside position may be a phylogenetically old form of aggression in hoofed mammals. Under this assumption, it is even possible to consider the broadside position as being an ancestral relic in recent species which no longer fight from it.

However, even when one does not accept Geist's hypothesis, there is enough evidence that the lateral orientation cannot generally be understood as resulting from a conflict between aggression and fear in ungulates, not even in those species which do not fight from it but only use it as a display. Above all, an animal blocks the other's path by assuming a broadside position in front of him. This blocking of the other's path is not a theoretical assumption or postulation but can actually be observed in many cases, including species which move into a head-on position for fighting.

As previously mentioned, a young may stop its mother for suckling in this way in certain species. More frequently, the lateral T-position occurs in agonistic encounters among adults, particularly in encounters of a dominant with a subordinate (Fig. 1a). In these cases, it is always the dominant who blocks the other's path and forces him to stop, withdraw, or at least deviate from his original course. Thus, it is the dominant who assumes the lateral orientation in such encounters, and he often approaches the subordinate from quite a distance and/or passes him and walks around him in order to display the broadside position in front of him. For example, when a kongoni bachelor has happened to enter a territory, has been threatened by the owner and is now already withdrawing, the territorial bull may confront the subordinate once more, run after him, pass him, and assume a lateral stance in front of him. These facts are incompatible with the "hypothesis" of a constitutive role of flight tendencies in the lateral orientation. If the broadside position were caused by conflicting desires to fight and to escape, one would expect its occurrence on the part of the subordinates in encounters between unequal opponents. However, the subordinates do not show it. Moreover, when standing in lateral position in front of the opponent, the sender is more exposed to possible attacks against his unprotected and vulnerable flank than in any other orientation. This is more than a mere theoretical possibility, since such flank attacks can actually, although infrequently, occur in such situations (Fig. 130b). Thus, there is a certain "daring" in assumption of the lateral position which certainly does not speak in favor of the involvement of fear. In psychological terms, the broadside position needs much self-confidence on the part of the sender.

In species that fight from a lateral position, assuming a broadside orientation is a clear threat. Also, in the far more numerous species that only assume it as a display in agonistic encounters, the effects upon the recipients are the same or at least similar to those of threats. On the other hand, the lateral orientation cannot be directly related to fighting behavior when the animals do not fight from it. It seems that the sender is asserting a certain dominance over the recipient without, however, indicating immediate fighting intentions. Thus, the broadside position is suitable to intimidate or challenge the recipient but not as severely as the frontal orientation. With this, of course, the lateral orientation plays a great role in dominance displays as we shall discuss later. In short, the lateral orientation cannot generally be understood as a "compromise" between frontal and reverse orientation in hoofed mammals. We must consider it on its own merits, as equivalent to the frontal and the reverse orientations.

When the recipient is not frontally oriented toward the sender, it only somewhat modifies the messages and meanings of the sender's orientation. First, let us look at the reverse orientation of the recipient (Fig. 53). We have considered the reverse orientation as being indicative of peaceful intentions, inferiority, female sexuality, and releasing the following response. Thus, when the recipient stands or moves in reverse orientation in front of the sender (tandem position—Fig. 53a), he has accepted and obeyed the latter's aggressive intentions expressed by his frontal orientation. Consequently, the tandem position is typical of a chase, a pursuit march (Fig. 54), and for pushing ahead the animal in front during a move. The relatively greatest changes with respect to message and meaning of the sender's frontal orientation may be seen in those cases in which the sender is a male and the recipient is a female. One may argue that now the sender's, i.e., the male's orientation is not indicative of ag-

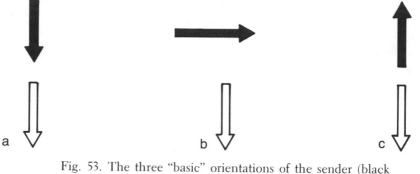

Fig. 53. The three "basic" orientations of the sender (black arrow) and the positions resulting from them with the recipient (white arrow) in reverse orientation. a. Frontal orientation of the sender—tandem position with the sender behind. b. Broadside orientation of the sender—lateral T-position behind the recipient. c. Reverse orientation of the sender—hindquarters-to-hindquarters position.

gressive but of sexual intentions. However, (a) a male can also sexually approach a female when she is standing or moving in any other position relative to him and thus, the expression of sexual intentions is not necessarily restricted to the male's orientation toward the female's hindquarters; (b) aggressive components are frequently involved in a male's courtship displays (p. 259); and (c) the mating march—the female walking in front of the driving male—is nothing but a moderately ritualized version of the agonistic pursuit march. Thus, even in the mating ritual, the change of meaning of the male's frontal orientation is not as great as one may presume at first sight. On the whole, the tandem position somewhat relaxes the situation as compared to the head-on position, but it does not truly change the message and the meaning of the sender's frontal orientation.

The relaxation of the situation is even greater when the sender stands in lateral orientation behind the recipient in reverse orientation (Fig. 53b). When we think of the broadside position as a means to block the recipient's path, to stop him, to make him withdraw or to deviate from his course, one may even presume that the sender's lateral position has lost its meaning in such a case. Quite in accordance with this view, the broadside position behind a recipient in reverse orientation often occurs only more or less by chance and is infrequently used as means of communication. In the comparatively few cases in which it apparently has a "signal value," the message and meaning of the sender's lateral orientation are unchanged. His broadside posture now signals to the recipient not to turn around and not to return when he is moving away. For example, a very dominant

Fig. 54a. Pursuit march in East African oryx (after display encounter). The subordinate recipient (right) withdraws with head-low attitude. The dominant bull (sender) follows with intention to high presentation of horns. b. Chase (after a fight) with symbolic downward-blow on the part of the pursuer. (Walther 1979. Serengeti National Park.)

or territorial male may have had an agonistic encounter with a subordinate male, and the latter eventually turns and moves off. Then, the dominant male—sometimes after a pursuit march—may stand and assume a lateral position behind the withdrawing opponent: "Do not come again!" (Fig. 55).

The sender's reverse orientation toward a recipient in reverse orientation (Fig. 53c) is indicative of peaceful intentions on both sides. It often may even be more than the mere affirmation of peaceful intentions. When resting or standing in reciprocal hindquarters position (a special case of "star formation"—Walther 1958a), the visual ranges of the partners complete each other (Fig. 52). Thus, they can better observe the surroundings. One could even think of a mutual defense position in strong animals such as rhinos.

We come to situations in which the recipient stands with his flank

Fig. 55. East African oryx bull in broadside position behind the withdrawing subordinate.

toward the sender (Fig. 56). When the sender assumes a frontal orientation toward the recipient's flank (sagittal T-position—Fig. 56a), this may indicate his readiness for a flank attack (Fig. 28). The recipient frequently reacts by speedily moving ahead and away. Thus, the aggressive character of the sender's frontal orientation is in full effect. Sometimes, the recipient may turn into a broadside position in response to a sender's frontal orientation. This usually happens only when he is at least equal or even superior in strength and/or social status to the sender. Thus, he responds to the latter's threat by an intention for blocking his path, i.e., a claim of dominance—a possible and absolutely adequate reaction by a strong and high-ranking individual to a challenge.

With the sender's reverse orientation toward the recipient's flank (Fig. 56c), it is the same as with all reverse orientations, i.e., it indicates absence of aggressive intentions—as always, provided that we are not dealing with one of the relatively few species which fight with their hind legs.

Particularly interesting is the situation when the sender assumes a

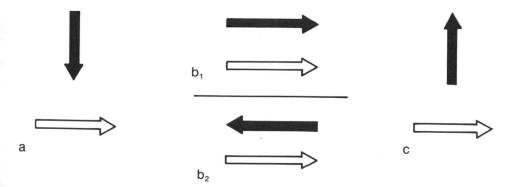

Fig. 56. The three "basic" orientations of the sender (black arrow) and the positions resulting from them with the recipient (white arrow) in lateral orientation. a. Sender in frontal orientation—sagittal T-position. b. Sender in broadside orientation—b_1 = parallel position; b_2 = reverse-parallel position. c. Sender in reverse orientation—reverse-sagittal T-position.

lateral orientation toward the flank of the recipient (Fig. 56b). Of course, he does not directly block the other's path in this case but he prevents him from turning and moving in his, the sender's, direction. This is nothing but a modification of blocking the path. Thus, the basic message and meaning of the lateral orientation is retained. However, two positions of sender and recipient are possible in mutual lateral orientation, a parallel (Fig. 56b_1) and a reverse-parallel (head-to-tail—Fig. 56b_2) position, and their messages and meanings somewhat differ from each other.

In both cases, the recipient may respond to the sender's claim of dominance (expressed by his broadside posture) by withdrawal, and in both cases, it is most natural for the recipient simply to walk ahead, because he is oriented in this direction anyway, and this direction is not blocked. However, when the recipient walks ahead from an encounter in parallel position, he moves into a reverse orientation in front of the sender which may easily draw the latter's pursuit since the sender also has only to walk ahead for this purpose. Furthermore, when standing in parallel position as well as in a pursuit march, there is always the possibility that now the sender may move ahead or speed up, pass the recipient, and circle into a lateral T-position in front of him. Having stopped the recipient in this way, the sender may even turn frontally toward him with the intention of fighting. A subordinate recipient can only prevent this by moving faster. Thus, when both partners are in parallel position, the sender's lateral orientation apparently does not only prevent the recipient from turning and moving in his, the sender's, direction but it is also suitable to make the recipient move ahead, when he is standing, or to speed him up, when he is moving. On the whole, an intensification of the agonistic character of the encounter (i.e., a transition into a pursuit march, or into a lateral T-position, possibly followed by a head-on confrontation or even a fight) may easily follow from the parallel position of the combatants.

In an encounter in reverse-parallel position, a subordinate recipient can also withdraw by simply walking ahead but this brings him into a reverse position behind the sender, i.e., the latter has to turn 180° for a pursuit. Of course, this happens, but far less readily and frequently than from a parallel position. Thus, the sender's lateral orientation in reverse-parallel position lacks the "pushing" component included in a parallel position, and it indicates that the sender has not much intention of pursuing the recipient in the case of the latter's withdrawal. Consequently, withdrawal is very easy for a subordinate recipient from an encounter in reverse-parallel position—he can unobstructedly walk ahead—and he can be relatively sure that the sender will not pursue him. Thus, the sender dominates the recipient by his lateral orientation in reverse-parallel position but he also builds a "golden bridge" for the other so that he can withdraw "without losing face." It may be mentioned at this point that this "golden bridge principle" is frequently found in somewhat elaborate dominance displays.

Up to now, we have discussed the parallel and the reverse-parallel positions under the assumption that each is brought about by a corresponding move of the sender. However, it can also happen that the sender assumes a lateral orientation in front of the recipient (lateral T-position) and the recipient responds by turning into a broadside position toward the sender, thus reciprocating the broadside display. This happens only in encounters among peers. Now both of them simultaneously signal to each other not to turn toward the other and not to move into the direction blocked by the other, and it makes good sense that such cases are particularly frequent among territorial neighbors in boundary encounters. (The reader may also be reminded of the lateral orientation in grazing rituals.) When peers assume the parallel position, this sometimes leads to a display march side by side (Fig. 57) in some species and in certain situations, the combatants may even gallop side by side.

As stated from the beginning, we will restrict our discussion mainly to frontal, lateral, and reverse orientations since transitions or combinations can easily be interpreted when one has understood the roles

Fig. 57. Parallel march in an agonistic encounter
of elk bulls (*Cervus canadensis*). (Geist 1966a.)

of these three "basic" orientations. However, a few such variations
may be mentioned here because they are particularly frequent.

Sometimes the sender stands in lateral orientation sideways in front
of the recipient so that, at most, his head is directly in front of the
other (frontal right-angle position—Fig. 58a). Obviously this is the
combination of frontal head-on orientation, sagittal T-position, and
lateral T-position. As compared to the head-on position and the sagittal T-position, the aggressive component of the sender's frontal orientation is somewhat diminished, and so is the stopping effect of his
broadside orientation as compared to the lateral T-position in front of
the other. The advantage of the frontal right-angle position seems to
be that it leaves the option open to the sender whether to move into a
head-on position (or a sagittal T-position, respectively) or into a full
lateral T-position—both can be accomplished by only one to three
steps—depending on the recipient's next move. In many cases, this
right-angle position serves to stop the other from walking ahead and
to make him move in a semicircle away from the sender. Thus, it
predominantly occurs in situations similar to those in which the lateral T-position is used.

Another combination of orientations is frequently seen in pursuit
and mating marches. The driving sender does not exactly follow in
line behind the other but is somewhat "transposed" to the side (Fig.
58b). It seems that the "pushing" effect of the sender's frontal orientation toward the recipient's hindquarters is combined and reinforced
by a tendency to move into a parallel position, and thus the latter's

Fig. 58a. Frontal right angle position (sender: black arrow). b. Lateral transposition of the sender (black arrow) in tandem position.

"speeding-up" effect is added to the "moving-off" effect of the frontal orientation.

A special word may be necessary concerning combinations of the orientation of the head with that of the body (Fig. 59). As previously noted, the orientation of the head can represent the orientation of the body and can largely substitute for it. However, this does not mean that the body orientation is always completely meaningless in such cases and that it cannot sometimes somewhat modify the message and the meaning of the head's orientation.

When the sender's body is in frontal orientation relative to the recipient and his head is turned into a lateral position of about 45° (Fig. 59a) or even 90° (Fig. 59b), the message and meaning of the (head's) lateral orientation, i.e., blocking the path and a claim of dominance, is added to the message of the (body's) frontal orientation, i.e., the readiness for aggression. These two messages are by no means contradictory, particularly since such a turn of the head can also be used as a swing-out movement for a turn into a frontal orientation (Fig. 110b,c) and even a frontal attack (which can sometimes also be true for the broadside position of the whole body). Also, when the head is turned more than 90°, this can still be an emphasized lateral display and/or a swing-out movement for a turn frontally toward the opponent (Fig. 67a). However, the more closely the head-turn approximates 180° (Fig. 59c), the more likely it indicates a tendency for withdrawal when performed in front of a frontally oriented opponent in an agonistic encounter. Since the body is still in frontal orientation, it is justifiable (although not always beyond any possible doubt) to presume that the animal is in an inner conflict between aggression and escape in this case. However, with respect to the wide spread "conflict hypothesis" of expressive behavior, it can hardly be overemphasized that this is only a special case of head turning and that it is certainly a mistake to interpret any turn of the head away from the opponent as indicative of flight tendencies. That sideward inclina-

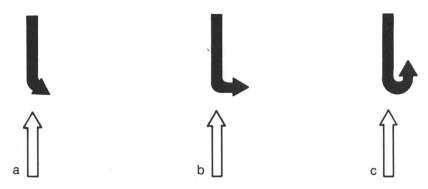

Fig. 59. Head turns of the sender (black arrow) standing in frontal orientation in front of the recipient (white arrow). a. 45°-turn of the head. b. 90°-turn of the head. c. 180°-turn of the head.

tions of the head up to 45° and even 90° usually do not have anything to do with escape tendencies becomes most evident when such head-turns occur on the part of the *pursuer* during a pursuit march (Fig. 60). Even the greatest adherents of the "conflict hypothesis" will have to admit that the involvement of flight tendencies is absolutely un-likely in the behavior of a dominant when he is pursuing a withdraw-ing subordinate.

Sideward turns of the head at angles of less than 45° up to about 90° can also occur when the sender is in lateral orientation toward the recipient (Fig. 61). These head-turns can be directed toward the re-

Fig. 60. After a display encounter of Grant's gazelle (see Fig. 118), one of the opponents (right) has given up and withdraws. The domi-nant follows him in a pursuit march. Note that the pursuer (!) turns his head away (45°). (Walther 1979. Serengeti National Park.)

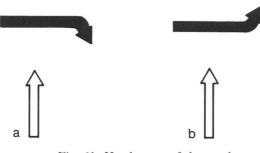

Fig. 61. Head turns of the sender (black arrow) standing in lateral T-position. a. Head turn toward the recipient. b. Head turn away from the recipient.

cipient (Fig. 61a) or away from him (Fig. 61b). When the sender is blocking the recipient's path in lateral T-position and then turns his head frontally toward him (Fig. 1b), this indicates that it is not good enough for him that the other has now stopped moving ahead; he wants him to turn and to withdraw. More difficult to interpret is the head-turn away from the opponent. Perhaps one detail may contribute to a better understanding: the sender always watches the recipient at least from the corner of his eye when turning his head away. When he loses him from sight, he immediately readjusts his position. With this in mind, two interpretation are possible that are not mutually exclusive. The turn of the head away from the recipient can be used to emphasize and to exaggerate the lateral orientation of the body (Fig. 109), and/or it can be a (more or less ritualized) swing-out movement for a vehement turn toward the opponent (Fig. 62). Of course, adherents of the "conflict hypothesis" again will immediately speak of the involvement of flight tendencies when the animal turns its head away from a lateral position. I will not go so far as to say that this is absolutely impossible in all the cases where such a head-turn may occur, but I can safely say that it is very unlikely in the majority of the cases in hoofed mammals. The reader need only be reminded that, in encounters between unequal opponents, it always is the dominant who shows this behavior and that he frequently approaches the subordinate from a considerable distance to assume a broadside position with head turned away in front of him.

The most common and most important combinations, however, are those in which a definite orientation of the sender toward the recipient is combined with a special expressive display. For example, a frontal orientation may be combined with the presentation of horns

a

b

Fig. 62a. Erect broadside posture of a South African oryx bull with head-turned-away at 45° as a swing-out movement for . . . b. . . . a vehement turn toward the addressee. (Etosha National Park.)

or antlers. As a matter of fact, all the threats, dominance displays, courtship displays, etc., usually include an orientation component. When describing these displays later, I will not always point out the orientation components and their contribution to the effects of the displays in detail since their relevance should be clear after the above discussion.

As important as the orientation, as the "carrier" of an expression, may be in such cases, it must be repeated that the sender's orientation per se, i.e., without any display, can have a "signal value." This has been stated frequently in literature but it usually has not been investigated and/or demonstrated in much detail. Likewise, another fact has often not been stated literally—perhaps because it was so self-evident to many field workers that they did not consider it necessary to mention it. By quite a number of his orientations relative to the recipient, the sender can signal the direction in which he wants the other to go. This is another fact which clearly contradicts the opinion that an animal, such as an ungulate, can only signal its psycho-physiological state, and thus the sender cannot directly communicate to the recipient what he wants him to do. In other words, although the recipient can get a meaning out of the sender's message, the sender cannot put a meaning into it. This opinion does not hold up, because definite directional responses of the recipients are correlated to certain orientations of the senders, and the senders use their orientations to maneuver the recipients into definite directions in certain situations. Although the above discussion was primarily meant to be an introduction to the different forms of the senders' orientations, and therefore was not focused on their effects upon recipients, it simply was impossible not to mention them. The reader need only be reminded that the sender's frontal head-on position makes the (subordinate) recipient turn and withdraw in the opposite direction, that the sender's frontal orientation toward the recipient's hindquarters makes him move ahead, that the sender may lead the other in a definite direction by assuming a reverse orientation in front of the recipient, that he makes him turn to the side by assuming a frontal right-angle position, etc.

Such direction signaling by the sender's orientation can occur in most of the cases of individually addressed communication and, thus, in a great variety of situations. It often is particularly striking and important in those actions which have loosely been termed "herding" and which we will discuss in detail in a later chapter.

12. THREAT DISPLAYS

Threat displays indicate a readiness to fight ("I am going to fight you!"). This immediate relationship to fighting (Fig. 63) distinguishes them from dominance displays. However, there are some transitional cases that may be termed "threat-dominance displays," in which features of both dominance and threat displays are combined. Within the threat displays, one may distinguish between "symbolic" actions, in which an animal performs the same movements as in fighting but without touching the opponent, and more or less ritualized intention movements, where the performance is restricted to the very initial movements of a fighting action. Most ritualized are those threat displays where intention movements are "frozen" into postures. Since there are offensive and defensive fighting techniques, there are correspondingly offensive and defensive threat displays (Fig. 63b), besides others that can be used both ways.

Whether threat and dominance displays (as well as space claim displays) challenge or intimidate the opponent primarily depends on whether he is equal or inferior to the sender, but it also depends somewhat on the situation. For example, when during a momentary stop in a migration, one animal threatens another, the recipient will often simply "obey" the threat and move ahead without any counterdisplay, even when he is of equal strength to the sender, simply because the latter's threat aims for something (moving away in this case) which the recipient was going to perform anyway.

In a considerable number of encounters, the threat remains one-sided, i.e., only one of the partners involved shows a threat display (Fig. 99). In a relatively few such cases, the other animal may respond with an immediate attack or simply ignore the sender's threat. Usually, however, the recipient will withdraw, or show submissive behavior, or even flee in a one-sided threat encounter. Also, very closely related to one-sided encounters are interactions in which the recipient responds by a defensive threat to the sender's offensive display (Fig. 63b). In such a case, the recipient's counterdisplay is not equivalent to that of the challenger. He does not signal his readiness for an attack—as his opponent does—but only his readiness for defense in the case of the other's attack. This frequently indicates inferiority and even submission.

Since threat displays occur in the same situations that can lead to

Fig. 63. Most threat displays are intention movements for definite fighting techniques in hoofed mammals. a. An oryx bull attacks by a downward blow (right) which is parried by the defender's head-low posture (left). b. The intention movements to these fighting techniques are "frozen" into postures—an offensive threat (right) and a defensive threat (left). (Walther 1980. Etosha National Park.)

overt aggression, they can substitute for and save fighting in one-sided encounters. Especially in encounters between peers, however, the recipient may respond to the sender's threat by an equivalent counterdisplay, most commonly the same as shown by the sender (Fig. 67b). When a species possesses several threat displays, as is quite common in ungulates, they may be performed one after the other. It can certainly happen that one of the opponents will eventually give in and withdraw after such a reciprocal threat encounter. However, the probability that it will end in a fight is great in hoofed mammals. The aggressiveness of both rivals obviously is heightened by the reciprocal displays, finally culminating in overt fighting. Long-lasting reciprocal threats can affect the following fight in two ways. Sometimes they apparently "consume" most of the aggressive "energies," and then the fight is brief—often consisting of only one clash. Other times, long-lasting reciprocal threat encounters may initiate particularly vehement and long-lasting fights. Either way, fights are not prevented in such cases. However, each opponent has been made aware of the other's hostile intentions by the previous displays, and both are well prepared to fight. Thus, a surprise attack, the most dangerous form of aggression, is effectively avoided by these reciprocal threats.

The statements above, especially the thesis relating to the intimidating and challenging effects of threat displays, may be substantiated by the example of a quantitative analysis of the outcomes of one-sided and reciprocal threat encounters in Thomson's gazelle (Table 1). The data were collected during a two-year study in Serengeti National Park, Tanzania (Walther 1978c). The term "horn threats" refers here predominantly to high and medial presentations of the horns. "Fight" means any form of horn contact. "Other forms of aggression" include mainly air-cushion fights and grazing rituals, but also some rarer cases of continued aggressiveness such as (one-sided or reciprocal) object aggression. "Withdrawal, flight, or submission of one of the opponents" are listed according to the relative frequency in which they occur in response to the sender's threat in this species. In one-sided encounters it is of course always the (non-threatening) addressee who withdraws, flees, or shows submissive behavior. "Ending in other ways" refers to those cases in which the recipients do not react to the threats, and/or the senders or both animals involved continue with clearly new and different activities such as herding females, running plays, or relaxed standing.

The one-sided encounters ended with withdrawal, flight, or submissive behavior on the part of the recipient in 84.0 percent of the 1,680 observed cases, clearly demonstrating the intimidating effect of the threats. On the other hand, the reciprocal encounters (both opponents displaying, usually with the same form of threat) led to fights

TABLE 1:

Intimidating and Challenging Effects of Threat Displays
in Agonistic Encounters of Thomson's Gazelle

	One-sided horn threats	Reciprocal horn threats
N observed cases	1,680	738
%ending		
with fight	1.5	70.7
with other forms of aggression	4.0	11.3
with withdrawal, flight, or submission of one of the opponents	84.0	13.3
in other ways	10.5	4.7

in 70.7 percent of the 738 observed cases (which included several reciprocal encounters between unequal opponents; the proportion of
fights following the displays is even greater in encounters among
peers). These statistics of reciprocal encounters clearly demonstrate
the challenging effect of threat displays. While the intimidating effect
of threat displays has been acknowledged frequently and readily in
ethological literature, the challenging effect has rarely been pointed
out *expressis verbis*. However, it definitely exists; it is by no means
rare; and it should be distinguished from the intimidating effect, since
it does not make sense to speak about intimidation when the threats
lead to fighting and obviously neither of the opponents has become
intimidated.

Threats as well as fighting may serve a multitude of social functions
in hoofed mammals. The most important, many of which occur in a
single species, are: establishment of territories and later ratification of
the boundaries among the territorial neighbors; expulsion of potential
competitors (usually nonterritorial males) from the territories; main-
taining and enlarging individual distance (especially in grazing);
coordination of group activities (especially when a group changes
from one activity to another, e.g., from resting to moving); "voting"
to determine marching direction and order (in the beginning of a
move); pushing during movement (i.e., keeping the migration going);
establishment of a social hierarchy; ascertaining dominance over
group members; eviction of undesired individuals from the group;

exclusion of newcomers attempting to join the group (insofar as the groups are closed societies); herding (in all its various forms); "taking offense" at activities of other animals (e.g., interference in a fight); female's defense against unwelcome sexual approaches of a male; soliciting milk (young : mother) and defense against it (mother : young); and—although in only a few ungulate species—maternal defense of the young against other conspecifics.

Furthermore, in quite a number of species, the tendency to dominate the other is so strong that aggressive displays often occur when strangers meet (which happens particularly frequently at places such as water-holes, salt licks, and wallows, where animals easily congregate). This means that when two conspecifics meet, they first have to determine who is dominant over the other. Apparently these more or less ritualized aggressions at chance encounters gave rise to at least some of the so-called greeting rituals of which the greeting of zebra stallions was mentioned as an example. Also, in mating rituals, threat and dominance displays are used by males in quite a number of species, while in other species the males show special courtship displays which, however, often also appear to be related to aggressive behaviors. In short, there is hardly any realm of the social life of hoofed mammals in which aggressive displays are not involved.

Among "symbolic" fighting actions, we should first mention two forms of the so-called redirected aggression: aggression against an inanimate object and aggression against an animal other than the one which released the performer's aggressiveness. Because of its close relationship to marking behavior and space-claims, redirected aggression has been dealt with in the corresponding chapters (6 and 7). Thus, it will suffice here to remind the reader that redirected aggression seems to represent an intermediate stage between addressed and unaddressed behavior as well as between threat displays and dynamic visual marking or advertising presence, position, state, and status, respectively. Also, its intimidating or challenging effects upon the recipients often are not as great as those of other threat displays, and only redirected aggression against conspecifics is present in all the ungulate species; evidence for aggression against inanimate objects is lacking or, at least, questionable in animals such as hippo, peccary, giraffe, camel, and llama.

Other "symbolic" actions are clearly directed to definite partners in the majority of the cases, and they usually have strong effects upon the recipients. Perhaps the simplest form of these addressed symbolic threat actions is assumption of the proper orientation for fighting with respect to the opponent. In most cases, this is the sender's frontal orientation and/or his frontal approach, which frequently includes an aggressive component. However, provided that the frontal orientation or approach is not combined with other, clearly aggressive displays (presentations of horns or antlers, biting intentions, etc.) it may sometimes become difficult to distinguish them from mere investigation of the partner, or from dominance displays. The distinction from the latter becomes especially problematic when the frontal approach is emphasized by behaviors such as stiff-legged walking, or the erection of hair—be it the hair of the entire body or only of special body regions such as neck, withers, or forehead in certain species. Such additional behaviors—certainly the erection of the hair, but possibly also certain movements or postures of the tail and the ears—are epiphenomenal expressions of an excitation of the autonomic nervous system. Thus they do not only indicate aggressive tendencies, but also occur in other situations when the animal's general nervous excitement has reached a higher than usual level. For example, in Kirk's dikdik (Tinley 1969), the male's crest (on the forehead) is raised not only in agonistic encounters but also in courtship and when the animal is alarmed or uncertain due to the presence of a potential danger (predator, man, etc.). In short, a frontal orientation or a (walking) approach toward a partner often has a threat character, but its proper recognition and diagnosis may sometimes pose problems in specific cases.

Distinguishing between threats and dominance displays is easier in the lateral orientation. When the combatants belong to a species which does not commonly fight from a broadside position, the lateral orientation toward the recipient must be considered a dominance display. If the species habitually fights from a broadside position, assuming a lateral orientation toward the opponent clearly indicates immediate fighting intentions and thus is a threat behavior. There are few ungulate species which fight from a lateral position. Reverse-parallel position with tails raised has been observed in encounters between peers in the larger Malayan mouse deer (Ralls et al. 1975) in which each opponent first sniffs the other's anal area and tail, and then tries to bite the other's neck and shoulders (sometimes after marking these body regions of the opponent by interramal gland secretion) or to slash the adversary's belly with the elongated canines. Lateral fighting is also common in certain swine species such as bush pig (Frädrich 1967) and wild boar, which fight by pushing with their shoulders as well as lifting the opponent's body with powerful upward thrusts of the lowered head. Correspondingly, the rivals assume a parallel or reverse-parallel broadside position when threatening each other with lowered heads, the bristles along the back erected and the tails somewhat lifted. Giraffe also commonly fight from a reverse-parallel or—more frequently—a parallel position (Fig. 64). Thus, assuming a broadside orientation may be considered as a threat display here. In horned ungulates, fighting from a lateral position is rare. The most striking exception known is the mountain goat (Geist 1965), where fighting males direct heavy horn blows toward the other's flank while standing in a reverse-parallel position (Fig. 65a). Assuming the broadside position as a threat display, a male mountain goat stiffly stretches his legs, hunches his back and ruffles up the long hair on withers and croup. Neck and head are lowered (Fig. 65b) as in a horn presentation posture, but the head is more or less turned away from the rival (as a swing-out movement for the sideward blow with the horns).

Chasing occurs in its most serious form after one of two combatants has been completely defeated in a fight (Fig. 54b). This is a purely executive behavior. However, there are cases in which chasing approaches a "symbolic" performance. Without any previous fight, one animal may run after the other as if the latter had been previously defeated (Fig. 66). In a sense, this chasing anticipates victory, and thus can be included in "symbolic actions." Typically, it is most frequently used by animals of high social status, such as territorial males, toward hopelessly inferior partners, especially immature males

Fig. 64. Masai giraffe (*Giraffa camelopardalis tippelskirchi*) fighting from a parallel position. (Serengeti National Park.)

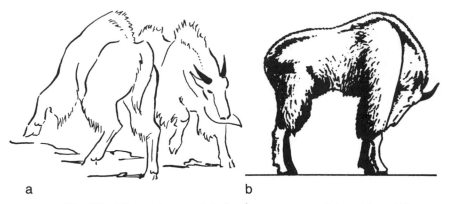

a   b

Fig. 65a. Mountain goat fighting in reverse-parallel position. (After a sketch in Geist 1966*b*.) b. Lateral threat posture of a male mountain goat—the reader is in the position of the adversary. (Geist 1965.)

Fig. 66. Territorial Grant's gazelle buck (right) chases an adolescent male without displaying any fighting intentions and without a previous fight (symbolic chase). The young male (left) assumes a submissive attitude in fleeing. (Walther 1968*a*. Serengeti National Park.)

and females. In quite a number of ungulate species, the males show no intention of actually attacking (e.g., symbolic butting movements or presentations of horns or antlers) during these symbolic chases, but they may utter certain vocalizations, such as a roaring in impala (Schenkel 1966b), which almost always causes an inferior addressee to flee as fast as he can.

Related to the symbolic chase is the feint attack, in which one animal approaches the other in a rush. This action is usually combined with other species-specific intention movements for attacking (e.g., lowered horns or antlers, open mouth, head and neck stretched forward, etc.), but the aggressor stops just before touching the opponent (if the other did not flee). Feint attacks occur at least occasionally in all ungulate species. Particularly noted for their frequent feint attacks are the rhinoceroses. A rhino first usually approaches an opponent in a slow, stiff-legged walk with raised head, and then starts the rush from a distance of a few meters, snorting and lowering his head. The animal usually stops the attack in front of the adversary, just before contact is made, throwing the lowered head upward in a symbolic horn blow that corresponds to the fighting behavior of rhinos (Schenkel and Lang 1969, Owen-Smith 1974).

When both opponents simultaneously perform feint attacks and continue with offensive and defensive maneuvers as in a true fight but without touching each other, one may speak of an "air-cushion fight," in which there seems to be an invisible cushion between the opponents (Fig. 67b). Such air-cushion fights can occur before, after, or—as intermezzos—during true fighting, but they also may sometimes substitute completely for overt fighting. They are frequent among juvenile animals but by no means restricted to them, nor are they necessarily indicative of playful interactions. For example, they can also be observed in absolutely serious encounters between territorial males. Air-cushion fights are probably not lacking in any ungulate species but there are differences as to frequency. For example, they are very common in topi and gazelle species but rather rare in oryx antelopes.

Air-cushion fights as well as feint attacks and other symbolic actions can be combined with all the vocalizations during the fights of certain species: snorting, which can be intensified to bleating and bellowing in rhinos (Schenkel and Lang 1969), loud roaring in hippo, loud growling in warthog (Frädrich 1967) and peccary (Schweinsburg and Sowls 1972), growling, gargling, and roaring in tylopods (Pilters 1954, 1956), a guttural "cry" in Camargue cattle (Schloeth 1961a), a number of usually relatively soft growling sounds in certain bovid and cervid species, etc. These acoustical expressions of aggressiveness usually are more or less specialized forms of vocalizations of high-level excitement.

Other sounds which may be said to be acoustical threats are produced with the teeth in some of the ungulate species. Squabbling, tooth clicking, and tooth chattering, which in severe threat encounters can be intensified to a staccato snapping of the jaws, have

Fig. 67. Boundary encounter between two territorial topi bulls. a. Reciprocal head-turned-away displays (90° and almost 180°) as swing-out movements for a sudden turn and rush toward the opponent. b. Air-cushion fight. (Serengeti National Park.)

been described in peccary (Schweinsburg and Sowls 1972), and similar sounds have been recorded in wild boar (Snethlage 1957). Water chevrotain (Dubost 1975) and mouse deer display a noisy "tooth whetting" (Robin 1979) brought about by a fast side-to-side chewing of the lower jaw (Ralls et al. 1975), sometimes combined with a kind of growling. Interestingly, the "tooth whetting" of mouse deer is heard not only in agonistic encounters but also on other occasions when these animals are in a state of high excitement (Robin 1979). Thus, a connection to excitement behavior is recognizable in these sounds produced by the teeth as in vocal threats. On the other hand, tooth clicking, tooth chattering, etc., seem to be closely related to biting, i.e., an unmistakably aggressive behavior, since all the species mentioned above do bite in agonistic interactions. The grinding of teeth, brought about by exaggerated sideways movements of the lower jaw in camels (Gauthier-Pilters 1959) and in several cervid species (Schneider 1930) during threat displays or when attacking, is probably also related to biting behavior.

Biting (i.e., not an intention movement but the full performance) as a threat behavior takes the form of symbolic snapping (i.e., snapping in the direction of the opponent without touching him) in hoofed mammals. It is very pronounced in llamas and camels (Pilters 1956) when the snapping aggressor (loudly roaring in camels) throws his head and neck forward in the direction of the addressee's head, throat, nape, forelegs, or hind legs. A noisy jaw clapping is also known from peccary (Krieg 1948), babirusa (*Babyrousa babyrussa*— Mohr 1960), and wild boar (Beuerle 1975). In hippo and peccary (Frädrich 1967), the opening of the mouth may be exaggerated to a performance similar to yawning (Fig. 68). In peccary, this usually is a defensive action of a subordinate animal, often accompanied by an explosive "woof" (Sowls 1974). According to Verheyen (1954), there are two phases of this "teeth presentation" in hippo. First, the animal, with head held in horizontal position, opens the mouth halfway, the lower jaw remaining under the water surface in a swimming hippo. This form is found in animals of all ages and sexes. Only in adult bulls is the performance continued by opening the mouth at maximum, raising the head high out of the water, and moving it in a semicircle. This threat-"yawning" cannot always be differentiated from true yawning in hippo.

Furthermore, symbolic biting or snapping, frequently combined with a fast forward stretching of neck and head, is also found in horses and their relatives (Klingel 1977), certain cervids (Müller-Using and Schloeth 1967), certain bovids, and also in mouse deer, where an animal, first standing in an erect posture, rushes, with head and neck stretched forward, ears laid back and mouth opened, toward the opponent (Robin 1979). Such bite-threats can definitely occur as offensive behaviors on the part of the superior opponent. On the other hand, more or less rhythmically repeated symbolic snapping is often

Waither

Fig. 68. Threatening with wide-open mouth in hippo (*Hippopotamus amphibius*). (Walther 1977*a*.)

typical of inferior animals. For example, in horses, a special form of symbolic snapping frequently is a response of foals and subadults when threatened by adult animals (Zeeb 1959, Tyler 1972). Similarly, in some cervids and bovids, it may occur on the part of a female when charged by a male. Thus, the symbolic snapping appears to be a defensive display, sometimes approaching a submissive behavior in these cases.

In cervids, actual as well as symbolic and offensive as well as defensive snapping apparently are not present in all species. For example, it has been reported for sambar, barasingha (Schaller 1967), brow-antlered deer (*Cervus eldi thamin*—Blakeslee et al. 1979), and muntjac (Barette 1977), and I have seen it frequently in red deer, axis and fallow deer, but never in white-tailed deer or roe deer. Possibly these may be behavioral differences between Plesiometacarpalia and Telemetacarpalia, the two major taxonomic groups within the Cervidae. Likewise, in bovids, symbolic as well as actual snapping is found only in some species. It predominantly occurs in bovids with small horns, such as klipspringer and duikers (*Cephalophus*), and in the hornless females of certain species, such as the spiral-horned antelopes (*Tragelaphus*) and waterbucks (*Kobus*). In sitatunga, it was also observed in young males who as yet had no horns, or only very small horns. On the other hand, symbolic snapping also occurs in at least two bovid species with well-developed horns. One is the eland antelope, where cows (whose horns are about as long as those of the males) occasionally show symbolic snapping, predominantly as a defensive-submissive response to the approach of a bull. The other species is the springbuck, where a ritualized form of symbolic snapping seems to be a sort of threat in encounters among males (Walther 1981). Snapping as a fighting technique is unknown in these two species; only the symbolic form has been observed.

Symbolic (and actual) pushing with mouth shut is apparently related to snapping. In lesser Malayan mouse deer (Robin 1979), it is practically the same performance as described above for the bite-threat, except the mouth is closed. In this species, the mouth push is usually directed toward the other's flank. Likewise, wild boar (Beuerle 1975) may push with their snout disk in the direction of the opponent's flank or cheek. In Tylopoda, Cervidae, Giraffidae, and a number of Bovidae, the movement is a short but relatively violent horizontal push forward with the head, often with ears laid back. As with symbolic snapping, this pushing with mouth shut is especially frequent in female bovids without horns. In the genus *Tragelaphus*, the spiral-horned antelopes, it is the most common form of defense of a female against an approaching or driving bull (Fig. 69) at the beginning of the mating ritual (Walther 1958*a*, 1964*b*). Sometimes pushing with the mouth shut may be combined with stretching the whole neck forward in the direction of the opponent, as is the case in snapping. This is possibly the origin of the head-and-neck-stretched-forward posture, a common dominance and/or courtship display of males in a number of ungulate species.

In connection with symbolic mouth and head movements, we may mention the spitting of stomach contents in llama species (genus *Lama*). Standing with neck and head stretched upward and forward (Fig. 70b), the llama growls and regurgitates stomach contents up

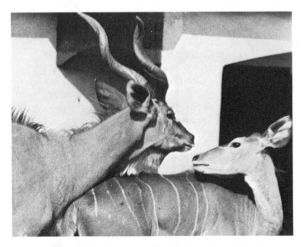

Fig. 69. Greater kudu female defends against the bull's sexual approach by symbolic pushing with mouth shut. (Walther 1964*b*. Hamburg Zoo.)

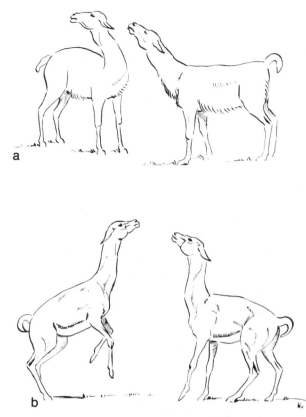

Fig. 70a. Turning away (left) and head-and-neck-stretched-forward-up-ward posture (right) as an intention movement to spit in domestic llama (*Lama guanicoë glama*). (After a sketch in Pilters 1956.) b. Erect posture as intention movement for aggressive rising on the hind legs in guanaco (*Lama guanicoë*). (Walther 1977*a*.)

into its mouth. When the performer only indicates his readiness for spitting, he swallows down the stomach contents after a few ruminating movements. This intention movement often has the same effect upon the recipient as true spitting. The llama only spits when the adversary is close enough to hit, aiming at the other's head and eyes. The recipient often turns his head sideways; if he is subordinate to the sender, he may also spit sideways, i.e., into the air. After spitting, the spitting llama as well as the recipient frequently opens the mouth slowly, pulls up its angles, and moves the lower jaw to and fro. Finally, the underlip hangs deep and loose. Pilters (1954, 1956) who discovered and described this grimace, interprets it as an expression of "loathing."

Species that practice neck-fighting (pressing down or lifting up the opponent with the neck) may show corresponding symbolic neck movements—forward stretching alternating with lowering and steeply erecting and winding the neck (Fig. 71). Such movements are especially striking in females of sitatunga (Walther 1964b) and bongo (Hamann 1979), and, to a lesser extent, in greater kudu (Walther 1958, 1964b). Postures derived from neck-fighting are obviously more common than symbolic movements.

In fighting, certain ungulate species rise on their hind feet. Then the animal either throws its body on the opponent (swine, camels, llamas, also female nilgai—Fig. 72), or bites from above (horses and their relatives, wild boar, the llama species, which may direct their biting toward the opponent's throat—Fig. 73a), or beats the opponent with its forelegs (the equids and especially the cervids—Fig. 73b), or "dives down" into a horn clash (many caprine species). The symbolic form, performed at a distance from which the animal cannot reach the adversary, is a rising on the hind legs, frequently combined with other symbolic actions or intention movements according to the species-specific fighting techniques, such as spitting or snapping in llamas, symbolic flailing with the forelegs in deer (always with ears laid back), and presentations of horns in goat and sheep species.

There are some interesting details related to this rising on the hind legs as a fighting technique as well as a means of threat. For example, in horses and their relatives, it is most typical of stallions (Fig. 74b).

Fig. 71. Undirected snapping and neck-winding of a female sitatunga in response to the male's sexual advance. (Walther 1964b.)

Fig. 72. Throwing the body on the opponent (right) and parrying this attack by a nose-up posture (left) in a fight of nilgai females (*Boselaphus tragocamelus*). It is likely that this defense technique gave rise to the nose-up display in at least some of the ungulate species which practice it. (Walther 1966*a*.)

In deer species, it is very common in the antlerless females and in the stags during the time when they have shed their antlers and as long as their antlers are in velvet (Fig. 73b). After the stags have gotten rid of the velvet, rising on the hind legs becomes rare, although it may happen even then occasionally; other threats—related to the now fully grown antlers—are more frequently used instead. In sheep, rising on the hind legs is lacking or at least not well pronounced in the small European and Asiatic sheep, such as mouflon and urial (*Ovis orientalis*), but it is very striking and common in the American wild sheep (Geist 1971) and in the big Asiatic sheep such as argali (*Ovis ammon ammon*) and Marco Polo sheep (Walther 1961*a*). All the goats rise on their hind legs; however, there are some differences in the details of the performance as compared to sheep (insofar as they show this behavior—see above). The sheep (Fig. 75b) stretch their forelegs rather stiffly toward the ground, and the head may be somewhat tilted but, on the whole, it is directed forward. The goats (Fig. 75a) typically angle their forelegs toward the body and they frequently turn their heads, with presented horns, sideways toward the rival (Fig. 75b). (In an actual clash, the attack may also often be directed sideways, i.e., the rivals are in a more lateral position in the beginning, and then

Fig. 73a. An aggressive jump with biting intentions (right) is countered by a nose-up posture (left)
in guanaco. b. Rising on the hind legs and (symbolic)
flailing with the forelegs in red deer. (Walther 1961b.)

turn frontally toward each other when going down into the clash
from the bipedal stance.)

Up to now, we have discussed situations where the animal assumes
a bipedal stance and rears noticeably, approximating a vertical
posture. Much more widespread in ungulates is the aggressive jump.
As with all the other behaviors previously mentioned, this jump can
be used both as an actual fighting technique and as a symbolic action,
i.e., a threat (*Drohsprung*—Walther 1961a). It is a more or less pro-

Fig. 74a. Intention movement for a (stiff-legged) aggressive kick with the foreleg in Damara plains zebra (*Equus quagga antiquorum*). b. A stallion interferes in the "greeting" of two others by rising on the hind legs and symbolic beating with the forelegs (Etosha National Park.)

nounced jump with the forelegs by which the anterior part of the body is thrown forward in the direction of the addressee. It occurs at least occasionally in all ungulate species, and in some it is even relatively frequent. In species which exhibit a full rising on the hind legs (goats, sheep, deer, horses, etc.), there are all kinds of transitions between the aggressive jump and the bipedal stance. Phylogenetically the latter has probably evolved from the aggressive jump. (It may be mentioned that some authors—e.g., Geist 1971 and Schaller 1977— speak of a "threat jump" or even simply a "jump" when they mean the full rising on the hind legs in sheep and goats.) Most commonly,

a   b

Fig. 75a. Male markhor goat (*Capra falconeri*) rising on the hind legs (note the angled forelegs) as a
threat toward an opponent at a distance (not visible
in the photo). b. Afghan urial ram (remaining on all
four legs) and a subadult male markhor (note the
sideward-turn of the head) are engaged in a sparring
match. A Marco Polo ram (background) "takes offense" and interferes by symbolic rising on the hind
legs with stiffly stretched forelegs. (Walther 1961*a*.
Kronberg Zoo.)

the symbolic aggressive jump is frontally oriented toward the opponent. However, in a few species, it can be performed in broadside
orientation, e.g., when the displaying animal stands in lateral
T-position in front of the addressee. Such cases, in which an original
threat display obviously merges into a dominance display, are frequent and typical in agonistic encounters of tsessebe bulls (*Damaliscus lunatus lunatus*—Joubert 1972), but it seems that the so-called
parting jump in the greeting ritual of zebra stallions is also a ritualized
aggressive jump in lateral orientation.

Some ungulate species (especially wildebeest, hartebeest, blesbok,
topi and its relatives, nilgai, oryx, addax, roan and sable antelope)
tend to drop on their carpal joints during fighting. Again, this can
occur as a symbolic action when the animal is still some distance
from the rival (Fig. 76). In this case, the "kneeling" posture is often,
although not necessarily, combined with goring the ground (as an
object aggression), or it may pass into grazing (as a transitional

Fig. 76. Symbolic dropping to the "knees" (left) and passing into graz-ing (as a transitional activity) in an encounter among territorial topi bulls. (Serengeti National Park.)

action—Lind 1959). Although this dropping down to the "knees" ap-pears to be the opposite of the aggressive jump, the two behaviors can successively be combined. For example, when two topi bulls ap-proach each other in an agonistic encounter, one or both of them may perform an aggressive jump and directly drop from it on their "knees" (Fig. 77).

Kicking with the hind feet as an agonistic behavior is common in horses and their relatives, and it plays a role in the tylopods and oc-casionally in certain cervids, such as the moose (Geist 1963). Other-wise it is rare in hoofed mammals, and so is the corresponding sym-bolic performance. In the equids, kicking with the hind legs is more, although not exclusively, a defensive behavior, e.g., it is typical of a withdrawing animal against the pursuer. It ranges from a slight lifting of one hind leg to a full kicking with one or both hind hooves in the direction of the adversary (Fig. 78). Horses, particularly mares, may also approach the opponent with the hindquarters going in front, associated with tripping movements of the hind legs or slightly lifting a hind leg as an intention movement for striking.

Kicking or beating with the forelegs is common in fighting equids and cervids. Correspondingly, there are also symbolic performances in these animals. In all the other ungulates, the use of the forelegs in agonistic encounters is exceptional or lacking. The horned ungulates in particular do not use their forelegs in agonistic encounters, with the exception of sheep, where a ritualized kick with a foreleg is a frequent behavior of dominant rams. This foreleg kick in agonistic

Fig. 77a. Reciprocal aggressive jump and . . . b. . . . dropping down
to the "knees" from it in an agonistic encounter of topi bulls. (Walther
1979. Serengeti National Park.)

encounters of sheep appears to be closely related to the foreleg kick as
a courtship display, and will be discussed in a later chapter. Whether
in the primitive mouse deer the feet are used in fighting is a matter of
some controversy. Some people say that fighting mouse deer strike
with their hooves, but neither Ralls et al. (1975) nor Robin (1979)
could confirm this behavior in their studies on larger and lesser
Malayan mouse deer. In horses and deer, striking out with the
forelegs in fighting as well as in a symbolic performance can be combined with rising on the hind feet (Fig. 73b) but can also be executed
when standing on three legs. In the latter case, the symbolic kick of
zebra stallions resembles a big, vehement, stiff-legged step (Fig. 74a)
with its force in the upward movement of the leg.

Symbolic butting (a pronounced nodding movement of the head in
the direction of the addressee) as well as head-throwing (in which the
head is thrown up and down in more or less rhythmical repetition—

Fig. 78. Kicking with the hind legs as a defense in fighting Grevy's stallions. (After a photo in Klingel 1974.)

comparable to an emphatic affirmation in humans) are particularly frequent in okapi (Fig. 79b) and in cervid and bovid species—animals which have horns or antlers. However, these behaviors also occur in hornless females of some species, and head-nodding as well as head-throwing is a common threat display in horses and their relatives. Thus, the possession of horns or antlers is not a necessary prerequisite for the occurrence of this behavior. Nevertheless, it probably developed from butting in all cases, since all these animals can butt or push the opponent with their foreheads—with or without horns.

A somewhat special form of head-throwing occurs in rhinoceroses (Schenkel and Lang 1969), and all the swine (Frädrich 1967) but also in certain ruminants such as okapi (Grzimek 1958, Walther 1960b—Fig. 79a) and giraffe (Fig. 80b). In all these species, head and neck are thrown upward from a lowered head posture. This is usually a rather vehement movement, but in warthog (Frädrich 1967), for example, it is slow and exaggerated. All these species fight with corresponding upward blows of their heads.

The nod-threat (Lott 1974) of bison may also be mentioned in this context. The two bulls stand frontally at close range with their heads swung to one side (the same or the opposite) and then held fairly high. At intervals, both rivals abruptly swing their heads down and up again in a matched movement. If the animals start fighting, the contact is initiated while the heads are low (Lott 1974).

In at least some species, head-shaking (like that of humans in ne-

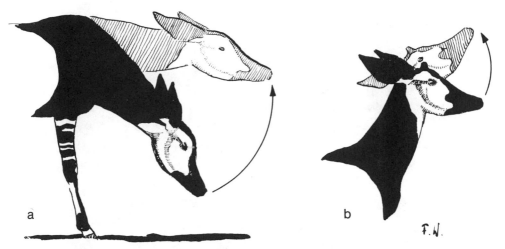

Fig. 79a. "Larger" head-throwing in (a female) okapi (*Okapia johnstoni*). b. "Smaller" head-throwing in (a male) okapi. (Walther 1960*b*.)

gation) can be considered as a symbolic form of twisting the head (and the horns) to the left and the right in fighting. It occurs in rather similar forms in almost all bovids and cervids; however, there are considerable differences as to the frequency of the movement and how pronounced it is. For example, in gazelles and their relatives, head-shaking and head-throwing are rare, but both movements are common in wildebeest, hartebeest, and topi. In bison (Lott 1974), a certain form of head-swinging, from one side to the other, may possibly be related to the head-shaking of other species. It sometimes occurs when a retreating animal backs away from the opponent.

Other behavior patterns used as fighting techniques in bovids and cervids that may also occasionally occur as symbolic threat movements are downward and sideways blows. In the symbolic downward blow, the animal brings its head and horns down from an upright position. Some, apparently species-specific, differences can be observed. For example, oryx antelope usually perform the symbolic downward blow in slow motion and their horns remain in an upward-forward position, whereas blackbuck males bring their heads down in a fast and violent movement so that their foreheads almost or literally touch the ground and their horns finally point horizontally forward, toward the opponent. Occasionally, the head and the horns may be kept at the lowest point of this movement for several seconds (low presentation of horns). In the sideways blow, the head and horns are rapidly moved sideways from either a medial or a lowered posi-

a

b

Fig. 80. Swing-out movements for (lateral) blows with head and "horns" as threat displays in giraffe. a. Neck horizontally stretched forward and held vertically with nose toward the ground (approximating the posture of a medial horn presentation in bovids). b. Head-low posture from which head and neck are thrown upward and sideways. (Serengeti National Park.)

tion. Symbolic downward and sideways blows occur with some frequency only in relatively few species, and the same is true for the horn-sweep, which is a combination of the symbolic downward blow and the sideways blow and resembles "weaving," i.e., an object aggression, but is shorter and more violent.

The threat displays described so far were mostly symbolic actions, i.e., full fighting movements which take on the characteristics of expressive behaviors in that they do not touch the opponent. Only a few of them show features of further ritualization, such as slow-motion performance, (rhythmical) repetition, or exaggeration. By contrast, the threat displays which we are going to discuss below are intention movements, and many of them are strongly ritualized in that the movements are "frozen" into postures that are held for several seconds, sometimes even for several minutes. Generally, these threat postures and intention movements go back to the same fighting techniques as the symbolic actions, and sometimes there may be transitions between the two—for example, the aforementioned symbolic butting could possibly also be classifed as an intention movement. The important point about the aggressive intention movements is that the animal does not perform the entire fighting action but only its initiation.

Vocalizations are not common in connection with these displays but when there are any, they are usually rather soft growling sounds or, in some species, grinding of teeth. When animals have skin glands that can be opened at will—the preorbital glands of males of certain bovid and cervid species are especially important in this regard—they often are widely opened (Fig. 86). Ruffling the (long) hair of certain body regions, e.g., neck, withers, and the mane along the back in certain species, is also often combined with threat postures.

In odd-toed ungulates and some of the primitive artiodactyls, certain facial expressions obviously are, or have originated from, intention movements for biting. According to von Richter (1966), a threatening tapir opens the angles of his mouth so that the canines become visible. With increasing display intensity, the tapir purses the lips until both sets of teeth are visible. Simultaneously the mouth is slowly opened (Fig. 81). If the recipient has not yet withdrawn, the challenger utters a sound, like "wrooff" ("attack call"), and now bites him. The ears are more or less drawn back during the threat; at least they do not stand upright. Malayan tapir (*Tapirus indicus*) also stretch head and neck forward and somewhat tilt the head so that the lower jaw is turned toward the recipient (von Richter 1966).

This "bite-threat" of tapir resembles certain facial expressions in horses, zebras, and asses. First, there is a definite bite-threat which is

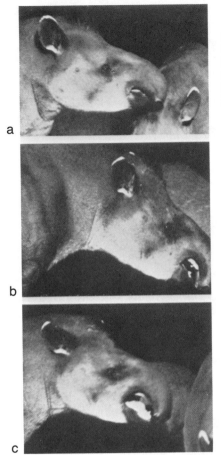

Fig. 81. Bite-threat in South American lowland tapir (*Tapirus terrestris*). a.–c. Increasing intensity of the display. (von Richter 1966. Photos: W. von Richter. Munich Zoo.)

more or less the same in all the equids but may occur in several degrees of intensity. When threatening lightly, the ears are somewhat laid back, the mouth is still shut, and head and neck are somewhat stretched forward. At higher intensities, the ears are straight back, the mouth is still closed (Fig. 82a) or partly opened, the neck is either stiffly stretched forward or the head is lowered to different angles. It can be lowered so much that the underlip almost touches the ground (Fig. 82c). In swaying the lowered head from side to side, the sender "squints" upward at the addressee. The tail is somewhat lifted at its base in horses; in Grevy's zebra it is raised high (Klingel 1977). In the highest-intensity form of the bite-threat, the mouth is opened wide and the lips are retracted, exposing the teeth (Fig. 82b). These forms of bite-threat may occur in any more or less severe agonistic

Fig. 82a. Neck-stretch and light intensity bite-threat with closed mouth in a domestic horse (*Equus przewalskii caballus*). b. Bite-threat of maximum intensity of a Przewalski's wild horse (*Equus przewalskii*). c. Head-low posture as a threat of a stallion of Przewalski's wild horse in herding mares.

encounter on the part of the challenger, and in both opponents before a fight among peers. They also are typical behaviors of the stallion when herding mares or other group members.

Two other facial expressions, the estrous face of the mare
(*Rossigkeitsgesicht*—Antonius 1937, Trumler 1959) and the so-called
submissive expression (*Unterlegenheitsgebärde*—Zeeb 1959) should
be mentioned in this context. In zebras and asses, but not in horses,
the estrous mare, when approached and contacted by the stallion,
shows an "estrous face" (Fig. 83, 122). She more or less widely opens
her mouth and pulls back its corners, and usually performs
"chewing-like" movements, but without closing the mouth. She may
drool. Her ears are folded back. The attitudes of head and neck range
from a "normal" posture to a head-and-neck-stretched-forward
posture and a lowered-head posture. When turning her head back
toward the stallion behind her, a mare may occasionally perform
symbolic snapping movements.

A similar facial expression is seen in young horses when they are
threatened by dominant conspecifics. Zeeb (1959), who was the first
author to describe this behavior, interpreted it as an expression of
submission, pointed out certain differences to the estrous face (in
opening the mouth and in the position of the ears), and was inclined
to consider it as having evolved from allogrooming. However, the
only argument in support of this last point is that the animal may
sometimes groom the dominant partner (provided that he does not

Fig. 83. Estrous face of a Boehm's zebra mare
turning her head toward the stallion behind her—a
situation in which the estrous face may easily merge
into symbolic snapping. (Kronberg Zoo.)

behave aggressively) after having shown the submissive face (Tyler 1972). This argument seems to be vulnerable: (a) the allogrooming may be induced by the submissive face in this situation according to the mechanism of a transitional action (Lind 1959); (b) grooming the dominant by the subordinate is an appeasement behavior in many ungulate species, i.e., it can easily follow after a submissive display without any genuine behavioral connection to the latter; (c) "allogrooming" in more or less agonistic interactions sometimes does not appear to be far away from a ritualized biting.

I have seen both the estrous face and the submissive face frequently and at close range in plains zebra where the submissive face is not restricted to foals but may even show up in adult stallions, although always only on the part of the subordinate in an encounter with a dominant (Fig. 84). Of course, there can be a difference in the orientation. The mare is usually facing away from the courting or copulating stallion behind her (Fig. 122), whereas in a social encounter the subordinate is often more or less frontally oriented toward the dominant. However, in the facial expression itself, there is at best a minor difference. The position of the ears is somewhat more variable in the submissive face, but the performer definitely can also pull his ears back like a mare in estrus, and the differences in opening the mouth seem to be simply a matter of intensity, i.e., in a low-intensity performance, the subordinate does not open his mouth as widely, but in a submissive face of high intensity the mouth is opened

Fig. 84. "Submissive face" of a subordinate East African plains zebra (center) displayed toward a dominant. (Klingel 1972. Photo: H. Klingel, Ngorongoro Crater, Tanzania.)

and its corners are pulled back as much as in a mare's estrous face. Also, Klingel (1972, 1977), with his outstanding comparative background on equid behavior, emphasizes the similarities more than the differences of the two facial expressions.

In short, I think that the submissive face and estrous face are nothing more than two modifications of the same behavior, which seems to be a ritualization of defensive biting. Since such defensive threats usually occur on the part of the subordinate in encounters with dominant partners, this facial expression has more and more assumed the meaning of submissive behavior—as is the case with quite a number of submissive displays in hoofed mammals. The mare more or less is in the situation of a subordinate in a sexual encounter with a stallion.

A ritualization of allogrooming is more likely in another facial expression of the equids, although even here the ritualization of an original biting behavior does not appear to be impossible. This is the so-called greeting face (Antonius 1940, Trumler 1959, Klingel 1967, 1968, 1972, Tyler 1972) that can be observed when two adult partners, e.g., two stallions or a stallion and a mare, meet and establish naso-nasal contact. According to Klingel (1977), in all equid species investigated, the greeting animals extend their heads, usually direct their ears forward, and draw the corners of their mouths up in a jerking movement (Fig. 42), except for horses, where this last movement rarely occurs (Tyler 1972). Plains zebra often open their mouths and make chewing movements with bared teeth; mountain zebra and donkey chew with their lips closed; Grevy's zebra and (domestic) horse do not move their jaws (Klingel 1972).

Although biting and symbolic snapping play a role in agonistic encounters of nonruminants, the more primitive group of the even-toed ungulates, only relatively few intention movements have been "frozen" into postures here. One which comes to mind is the opening of the mouth in hippo (although this may be closer to a symbolic action) during which the animal is said to belch malodorous intestinal gas in the direction of the opponent (Frädrich 1967). Another is a nose-up posture with the cheek turned toward the opponent in peccary which Schweinsburg and Sowls (1972) interpret as an intention movement for biting with the side of the mouth.

In ruminants, the pulling back of the corner of the mouth (*Mundwinkelziehen*—Robin 1979) in lesser Malayan mouse deer may be mentioned as a facial expression probably related to biting (Fig. 85). According to Robin (1979), the animal folds the ears back and opens the lips in the corner region of the mouth; otherwise the mouth remains almost closed. The canines and premolars become visually exposed. This behavior occurs as a response to a social moles-

Fig. 85. Pulling back the corner of the mouth in lesser Malayan mouse deer. (Robin 1979. Photo: N. P. Robin. Zurich Zoo.)

tation on the part of the molested animal. Thus, there are several resemblances to the bite-threat of tapirs as well as to estrous face, submissive face, and greeting face in the equids. In musk deer and Chinese water deer, the two "antlerless cervids," the males possess long upper canines and use them in fighting. It is presumed (Antonius 1939, Müller-Using and Schloeth 1967) that the so-called canine threats, i.e., certain facial expressions (retracting the lips, grinding of teeth by chewing-like jaw movements) of higher cervid species without strikingly prolonged canines, such as axis deer (Fuchs 1976), red deer (Fig. 86), elk and sika deer (Schneider 1930, 1931), are phylogenetically linked to the use of long canines in aggressive interactions of primitive cervid ancestors. Otherwise, facial expressions (other than symbolic snapping) directly related to biting or the use of teeth are rare in Artiodactyla; however, quite a number of head and neck postures appear to be related to (original) biting behavior (see below).

In the head-low posture (*Kopf-tief-Halten* or *Kopf-tief-Drohen* — Walther 1958*a*, 1966*a*, 1979), neck and head are stretched downward and forward in one line (Fig. 1a,b). The nose is close to the ground in

Fig. 86. Facial expression of "canine threat" (also note the wide open preorbital gland) in a subadult stag of Isubra maral (*Cervus elaphus xanthopygus*) displaying to the author. (Kronberg Zoo.)

an attitude similar to that of grazing, and sometimes the animal may switch to grazing as a transitional action. (Unfortunately, some authors speak of a "head-low" posture when they mean a low or medial presentation of horns.) The head-low posture is a widely distributed threat display in hoofed mammals, and apparently meaning and origin vary with species. Sometimes the head-low posture may even be somewhat ambivalent by nature within the same species. For example, in sable antelope, the head-low posture usually is a defensive threat (Huth 1980), but Estes (1974b) found it to be also used by dominant bulls in herding females in the giant sable antelope (*Hippotragus niger variani*).

In rhinoceros, the head-low posture is the "frozen" intention movement for throwing the head upward in fighting or symbolic head-throwing. In wild boar, which commonly fight in reverse-parallel position, the head-low (Fig. 87), frequently combined with a "woof" vocalization (Beuerle 1975), is an intention movement for

Fig. 87. Head-low posture in broadside orientation in wild boar (*Sus scrofa*). (Beuerle 1975. Photo:
W. Beuerle. Schwarzwildrevier Breitenbuch, Germany.)

placing the head under the adversary's body and lifting the opponent
with the back of the muzzle, or for an upward-blow with the tusks.
Male guanaco (Fig. 88) and vicuna frequently approach a rival in
head-low posture (Pilters 1956) which probably evolved from biting
the opponent's forelegs (a common fighting technique in tylopods)
and/or from a special form of neck-fighting (getting under the opponent's body which can also be combined with biting) in these species.
In giraffe and okapi (Figs. 80b, 79a), the head-low is a swing-out
movement for a heavy upward-sideways blow with the head (and the
"horns"). In pronghorn, where I saw it most frequently in territorial
males herding females (Fig. 89), the head-low obviously indicates
readiness to use the prongs. It functionally corresponds to a low or
medial presentation of horns in bovids, which tuck the chin in toward
the throat so that the tips of their horns point forward-upward. However, in pronghorn, the chin is not tucked, apparently because of the
position of the prongs relative to the skull axis. The prongs "lean"
more forward than the horns of most bovids. Thus, the prongs point
forward when a male pronghorn holds his head downward-forward,
whereas a bovid or a cervid (in which the horns or antlers usually
stick straight upward or, in some species, even "tilt" backward) has to
tuck in his chin for the same effect.
    While in the species mentioned so far the head-low posture is
mainly an offensive threat, it seems to be a more defensive threat in

Fig. 88. Head-low posture in male guanaco approaching an opponent. (After a photo in Pilters 1956.)

Fig. 89. Head-low posture of a territorial pronghorn buck in herding females. (Yellowstone National Park.)

other species. This is clearly the case in moose (Geist 1963) where the head-low is combined with raising the hair on neck, withers, and rump, with ears held down (inside toward the opponent—in a less intense threat, they are laid back), and the prenostril region expanded. Sometimes the moose may utter a very loud roar in this posture. This display is frequently used in defense against conspecifics as well as against predators (Geist 1963) and may be followed by a rush attack ending with the moose striking at the opponent with its forelegs.

In bovids, the offensive or defensive character of the head-low threat varies with the species-specific fighting techniques. For example, chamois may attack by upward blows with head and horns toward the opponent's body. Then the head-low posture is the intention movement for such an upward blow, and thus an offensive threat (Fig. 90). In many other bovid species, however, the fighters interlock their horns and then push forward against each other. The head-low posture is also an intention movement for this type of fighting, which can be offensive or defensive. Correspondingly, the head-low threat can be used both ways. Finally, there are bovids such as urial (Schaller and Mirza 1974), oryx, addax, and waterbuck, in which the head-low posture is usually a defensive threat (although it can occasionally be used in a more offensive way also in these animals).

The horns are directed upward and backward in the head-low posture, and thus they screen the animal's lowered neck and are in an ideal position to parry the opponent's butt or downward blow, particularly in species with long horns, such as oryx antelope and their relatives (Fig. 1a,b). When used in response to an offensive threat display (e.g., high presentation of horns) of the challenger, the head-

Fig. 90. Head-low posture in a chamois male (captive specimen with tubes over his horns) when "encircling" me as an opponent (assimilation tendency!). (Walther 1961a. Kronberg Zoo.)

low posture often expresses some kind of inferiority, and then it may merge into a submissive posture that is similar to or almost identical with it. On the other hand, a strong adult male may sometimes assume the defensive head-low posture in front of a rival who is only equal or perhaps even somewhat inferior in strength, inviting the other's attack (Fig. 3). This is understandable, since the fighter can tuck his chin in toward the throat and bring his horns forward from the head-low posture; thus a strong combatant can come back with an immediate, powerful counterattack.

The head-and-neck-stretched-forward posture (briefly: the neck-stretch) is common in courting ungulate males, but may also be seen in agonistic encounters. As a threat display, it occurs sporadically over a range of different species. It also has somewhat different origins and meanings. In the equids, it is combined with the bite-threat in its different forms and intensities. Likewise, in some cervids, such as axis deer (Fuchs 1976) and red deer, and here, particularly in females, the neck-stretch, with ears laid back and muzzle pointing directly at the recipient, is obviously an intention movement for biting. However, the same posture also occurs as a threat in female caribou (Pruitt 1960), which are not known to bite the opponent (Fig. 91). Possibly, the latter is a case of a threat display being "on its way" to becoming a dominance display.

In wild boar (Beuerle 1975), a neck-stretch posture is the typical defense stance of a subordinate (Fig. 92), who directs its snout disk toward the cheek of the challenger displaying in lateral T-position in front of him, in an apparent attempt to prevent the dominant animal from frontally turning toward him. Likewise, in some bovid species, such as oryx antelope (Fig. 101), the neck-stretch appears to be related to defensive fighting techniques which serve to avoid being hit by certain attacking maneuvers (such as downward blow or stab-over-the-shoulder) of the aggressor. Similarly, in white rhinoceros, a subordinate male, a cow, or an adolescent animal may respond to a territorial bull's challenge by standing its ground, uttering loud roars and snarls with head thrust forward, ears laid back, and tail curled upward. Owen-Smith (1974) interprets this "snarl-threat" as a defensive behavior. In white-tailed deer, the neck-stretch display, with the stag stretching his neck forward, staring at the opponent, and laying his ears flat along the back of his neck (Hirth 1977), has been termed "hard look" by certain authors (Thomas et al. 1965). This term, "hard look," is not only anthropomorphic but probably also misleading since the display corresponds to the lowest level of aggressiveness (Hirth 1977) in this and related species, and it can also be used by subordinate animals. Geist (pers. comm.) is even convinced that it is primar-

Fig. 91. Neck-stretch in a female caribou approaching an opponent. (W. D. Berry in Pruitt 1960.)

Fig. 92. Neck-stretch in an agonistic encounter of wild boar. (Beuerle 1975. Photo: W. Beuerle. Schwarzwildrevier Breitenbuch, Germany.)

ily used by subordinates in encounters with dominant stags. In short, the look may not be intended to be as "hard" as the term suggests, and the display may also be more on the defensive side.

In species that practice neck-fighting, such as giraffe (Backhaus 1960a) and nilgai (Walther 1958a), the neck-stretch posture can be considered as an intention movement for a sideways and/or upward stroke with the neck (in giraffe—Fig. 93a), or for placing the neck over the opponent's nape and pressing him down (in nilgai—Fig. 94).

Fig. 93a. The head-and-neck-stretched-forward posture (animal in front—the head can be held more horizontally than in this picture) is an intention movement to a sideward-blow (animal behind) in giraffe. b. Nose-up posture in a pause during a fight of giraffe bulls. (Serengeti National Park.)

Here, this posture is a display between peers, or is used by dominant animals toward subordinates. These aspects, as well as the frequent combination with a broadside position, bring the neck-stretch close to a dominance display, particularly in nilgai.

Also closely related to neck-fighting appear the head-and-neck-forward/upward posture and the nose-up posture. In the head-and-

a

b

Fig. 94a. Neck-stretch combined with broadside display in nilgai bulls. b. Neck-fighting in nilgai between an adult (right) and an adolescent male. (Walther 1979. King Ranch, Texas, and Munich Zoo.)

neck-forward/upward posture (Fig. 95b), the animal stretches head and neck forward and upward in a straight line; it is precisely the opposite of the head-low posture. In a pronounced nose-up posture, the neck and head are stretched upward, the nose pointing skyward (Figs. 73a, 93b). It is unknown to me whether these two postures play any considerable role in odd-toed ungulates; in even-toed ungulates they are restricted to species with a relatively long neck, and not all species possessing a long neck show these postures. In llama and its relatives, the ears lie back, the tail is raised in a sickle-like manner, and both postures show a relation to pushing with mouth shut and/or

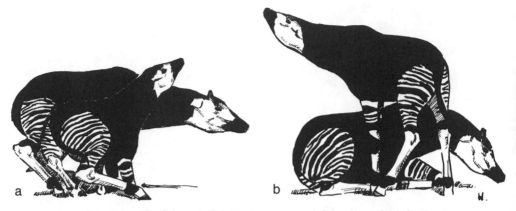

Fig. 95a. Playful neck-fight between an adult and a subadult okapi bull. The "dominant" young bull is "pressing down" the adult bull to a "kneeling" position. (The adult bull, father of the young male, consequently acted the role of the subordinate, the subadult male that of the dominant in this play—detailed description in Walther 1960*b*.) b. Head-and-neck-stretched-forward/upward display of the young bull after his "victory." The adult male lies in submissive posture. (After photos in Walther 1960*b*.)

spitting. Pilters (1954, 1956) even considers pushing with mouth shut to be the direct origin of at least the head-and-neck-stretched-forward/upward posture. However, in giraffe and okapi, it is more likely to be the swing-out movement for placing the neck over the opponent's nape or back, and I think that this is also possible in the tylopods. In any case, the head-and-neck-stretched-forward/upward posture is an offensive threat used by a superior combatant or in encounters among peers in these animals.

In tylopods and in (hornless) nilgai females (Walther 1961*b*, 1966*a*), the nose-up posture was observed as a fighting technique to parry an aggressor's jump attack (throwing the anterior part of his body on the opponent) and to push him back with the chest and the erected neck (Fig. 72). Thus it is a special kind of neck-fighting and basically a defensive maneuver; however, it allows the defender to counterattack immediately, and sometimes a dominant animal even seems to invite a subordinate's jump attack by assuming the nose-up posture. These features also determine the character of the corresponding threat display, which Pilters (1954, 1956) very adequately interprets as the expression of strong resistance in tylopods. In giraffe, the nose-up posture (also shown in parallel position to the rival) may possibly be more offensive in nature (Fig. 93b) relative to the particular fighting technique of this species (sideways strokes of neck and head against the adversary's neck, shoulder, body, or hindquarters), but a defensive component in this threat is at least not impossible because fighting giraffe may very suddenly assume this posture to avoid being hit on the neck by the opponent's sideways blow (which then goes into the air).

In the erect posture, the animal erects its neck—vertically in species with a very movable neck, in others at least as high as the anatomical structure of the neck region allows—with head and nose pointing forward or forward-upward (lifted nose). Pilters (1954, 1956) interprets this posture in the llama species as the utmost readiness for defense. However, I have frequently seen it preceding the jump attack in guanaco (Fig. 70b), and thus I consider it to be more offensive in nature. Of course, "utmost readiness for defense" can be said to be the point where defense verges on offensive action. Generally speaking, the erect posture can be offensively or defensively used in certain species and/or cases but, on the whole, it is more on the offensive side. In Marco Polo sheep (Walther 1961a), the erect posture precedes an aggressive rising on the hind feet. The same is true for many cervid species (Müller-Using and Schloeth 1967) but here, the "head-high threat" (Geist 1966), with ears laid back, may also precede an attack by striking with the forelegs, e.g., in moose, mule deer, elk (Geist 1966a), white-tailed deer (Hirth 1977), axis deer (Fuchs 1976), barasingha (Schaller 1967)—in the latter two species, the muzzle can also be stretched upward—red deer, and others. Typically, the primitive muntjac, which neither rear nor flail with their forelegs, do not have a "head-high threat" (Dubost 1971, Barette 1977). The situation in horses and their relatives is very similar to that of the cervids. They also rise on their hind legs and beat and kick with the forelegs in fighting. Consequently, their erect stance with more or less lifted nose can also be considered as a "frozen" intention movement for these fighting techniques. There also is another head and neck posture in horses (not reported from other equids) which resembles the postures of horn presentation in bovids (see below), i.e., the head is carried above or at least equal to body level and the chin is tucked in toward the throat. It seems that this posture is also related to rising on the hind legs in horses since stallions frequently show it during the levade.

In general, I am inclined to interpret all the erect postures as having originated from intention movements for "going up" with the anterior part of the body in ungulates. Of course, this does not exclude certain species-specific connections to neck-fighting, pushing with mouth shut, biting, and, above all, kicking and flailing with the forelegs, since all these behaviors may occur combined with rising on the hind legs or at least jumping up with the forelegs.

The similarity of the erect posture to the head-and-neck-stretched-forward/upward and the nose-up posture has occasionally led to one being mistaken for the other, or, in earlier literature, to no clear distinction between them being made. (I readily admit to being among the "sinners.") Despite the doubtless close relationships and the transitional stages between these postures, however, one should, as far as possible, try to distinguish them in the interest of a better analysis.

In species with horns or antlers, i.e., all the Bovidae and Cervidae, the presentation of horns (*Hörnerpräsentieren*—Walther 1958a) or antlers is a frequent and very important form of threat. In addition to that of pronghorn bucks (Kitchen 1974), which is not very different from the normal posture (Fig. 96) due to the particular position of these weapons on the skull of this species, the horn presentation can occur in four forms: low, medial, and high presentation, and sideward-angling of horns or antlers. In a pronounced low presentation (Fig. 97), the horns are held parallel to and near or even on the ground, with the tips pointing toward the opponent, e.g., in bison during a rush (Lott 1974), and in caribou (Pruitt 1960) before an attack. As a posture (i.e., not only as a momentary phase in a movement such as a downward blow or a horn sweep), this pronounced form is rare. However, when it occurs, it is a very severe threat. In a more common but less pronounced form the head is not held so low, but is still clearly below body level, and the chin is tucked in toward

Fig. 96. The presentation of the "prongs" in a pronghorn buck (here, toward a female in herding) is not very different from the "normal" posture in this species. (Walther 1979. National Bison Range, Montana.)

Fig. 97. Low presentation of horns (in this case, used as a swing-out movement preceding the rising on the hind legs) of a Siberian ibex (*Capra ibex sibirica*) addressed to me (assimilation tendency!). (Walther 1961*a*. Kronberg Zoo.)

the throat so that the horns point forward/upward. This posture is sometimes similar to the head-low posture, and the two may graduate into one another.

In the medial presentation (Fig. 98a), the neck is held forward at body level, the chin is tucked in toward the throat so that the nose points approximately vertically to the ground, and the horns or antlers subsequently point upward or somewhat forward. This kind of presentation is the commonest, and is probably used by all the bovid and cervid species. As a matter of fact, I could not name any species in which it is lacking.

In the high presentation of horns (Fig. 98b), the neck is held erect so that head and horns are carried distinctly above body level, and the chin is more or less tucked toward the throat. The horns, which tower above the head, point upward. The high presentation of horns or antlers occasionally occurs in many bovid and cervid species. As a frequent and pronounced display, however, it is found in relatively few, the most important of which are the gazelles, particularly the smaller gazelle species, such as Thomson's gazelle, mountain gazelle, dorcas gazelle, and, furthermore, some of the waterbuck species, oryx, sable and roan antelope (Huth 1970, Joubert 1970). In the gazelle species under discussion, it is a very common, serious, and offensive threat, used predominantly by adult males. It is somewhat hard to decide whether this high presentation of horns is a pure threat (swing-out movement for a downward blow) or a combination of a threat (horn presentation) with a dominance display (erect posture) in such cases. According to Huth (1970), the high presentation of sable antelope does not have the same highly offensive char-

Fig. 98a. Medial presentation of horns in South African oryx. b. High presentation of horns. (Etosha National Park.)

acter as in the gazelles, but may possibly be more on the defensive side in this species.

Sideward-angling of horns or antlers in broadside position as well as the broadside position itself is a threat display in those comparatively few ruminant species which fight from a lateral (parallel or reverse-parallel) position. However, the combination of broadside position and sideward-angling of horns also occurs in a number of species in which the rivals fight in frontal orientation to each other. In these cases, a dominance display (broadside position) and a threat display (angling of horns toward the opponent) are combined (Fig. 99). As with the high presentation of horns, such a sideward-angling of horns or antlers is occasionally found in almost all bovid and cervid species; however, I have only observed it to be a frequent and elaborate display, always combined with an erect posture, in a relatively few species, such as Grant's gazelle, oryx antelope, waterbuck, roan antelope, and wildebeest. In medial and high presentation as well as in sideward-angling of horns, one ear is often emphatically turned ("pointing") in the addressee's direction. In the horn presentations, it is usually directed forward; in sideward-angling of horns it points sideward toward the opponent.

Obviously related to the sideward-angling of horns is the "symbolic stab-over-the-shoulder," (Walther 1980) which has been found only in South African oryx (Fig. 100), after a corresponding fighting technique had been described by Huth (1980) in this and other oryx species. In the fighting action, the performer is in more or less parallel position to the opponent, and he—in the most elaborate case—starts out from a lowered head posture, swings neck and head upward, sideways, and backward, turning his nose away from the opponent so that his horns stab from above, over his own shoulder, in the direction of the rival (Fig. 101) who parries this stab either with horns held upright in head-low posture or stretches his head and neck forward so that the aggressor's stab goes into the air. Simultaneously with the performance of the stab-over-the-shoulder, the aggressor rams the opponent with his shoulder and often drops down to his "knees," as oryx frequently do in fighting.

Several points are quite remarkable in the threat display derived from this fighting action. The shoulder ramming is only somewhat indicated in the display by a slight leaning of the body in the recipient's direction. The tendency to drop to the "knees" as well as the initial lowering of the head does not show up at all; rather, the performer stands as erect as possible for an oryx, with lifted nose and his head turned away from the opponent so that the tips of his horns point sideward-backward and even somewhat downward in the direc-

Fig. 99. Sideward angling of horns from a reverse-parallel position in South African oryx. Note the "pointing" ear of the sender.

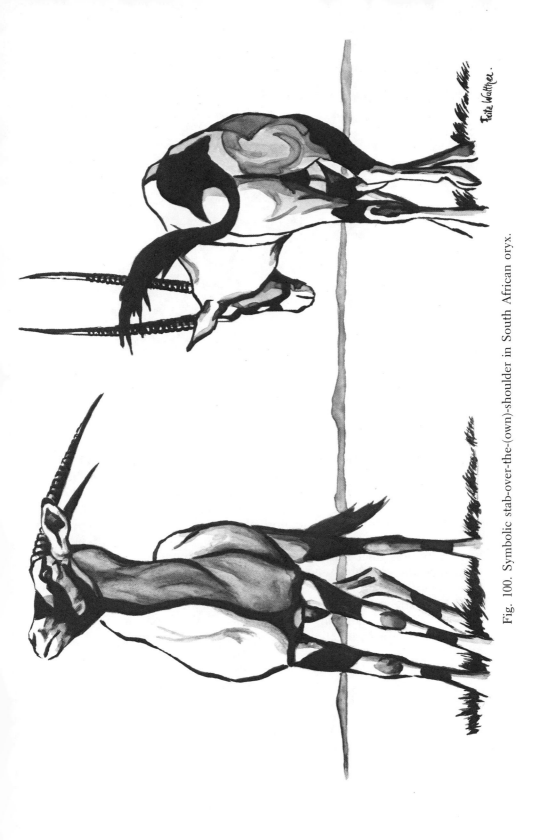

Fig. 100. Symbolic stab-over-the-(own)-shoulder in South African oryx.

Fig. 101. Stab-over-the-(own)-shoulder as a fighting technique in South African oryx (here, subadult bulls). The defender stretches head and neck forward so that the attacker's stab goes into the air. (Walther 1980. Etosha National Park.)

tion of the addressee (Fig. 100). Thus, in contrast to most threat postures of hoofed mammals, it is not the very first movement of the fighting action but, in a sense, its culmination point, which is "frozen" into a posture. It almost has to be so in this case, since the initial lowering of the head could hardly be distinguished from the usual head-low posture or the initiation of a sideward push or swing, respectively, and thus, it would not strikingly enough indicate the sender's readiness to use this special fighting technique. The symbolic stab-over-the-shoulder seems to be a severe threat in South African oryx, performed only by strong and high-ranking animals. As with sideward-angling of horns (which often precedes or follows it in the oryx—Walther 1980), this threat display shows certain features that may indicate a connection or transition to certain dominance displays.

Although all these forms of presentation and angling of horns or antlers obviously refer to the potential use of these weapons, the question arises whether the horns themselves play an important role in these displays. Observations by Hediger (1946) of certain cervid species and by Geist (1971) of bighorn sheep support the view that the conspecific recipients pay attention to the presence or absence as well as to the size of horns and antlers in the senders. However, in other species, there is evidence to the contrary. In a captive, dehorned oryx bull, the postures of "horn" presentation and angling had strongly intimidating effects on conspecifics (Walther 1958a), and later I had occasion to observe the same in a captive, dehorned male of dorcas gazelle and in free-ranging males of Grant's and Thomson's gazelle whose horns were broken off near the base. Also, Geist (1966a) mentions that in moose the posture of medial presentation was clearly recognized as a threat by the recipients when the sender's antlers were shed. Thus, the role of horns or antlers in these displays should be considered with caution. At least in certain species, the recipients may react more, and perhaps even primarily, to the corresponding postures of the head and neck and pay little attention to the challenger's horns in threat encounters. (That they can possibly recognize the other's sex and/or age class from the presence, size, and shape of the horns is a different matter.)

With the exception of sideward-angling of horns or antlers, the sender is usually frontally oriented toward an addressee in all the threats described above. Sometimes the animal will turn not its whole body but only its head and neck in the opponent's direction. The recipient also often stands frontally to the sender. In principle, however, the addressee's position does not matter, i.e., his flank or hindquarters can also face the sender. This last orientation is regularly found in pursuit marches (Fig. 54a), where the inferior animal walks away in a "normal" or a submissive attitude while the superior one follows with a threat or a dominance display.

Occasionally, all the threat displays under discussion can be combined with the sender's broadside position. For example, the sender may block the opponent's path in lateral T-position and may show a high presentation of horns (without turning his head and horns in the addressee's direction). Such cases must be distinguished from the combination of threats with behaviors of inferiority, e.g., when a subordinate opponent withdraws and continues to threaten forward (into the air) while the pursuing dominant marches behind him.

It must be emphasized that these latter cases are additive, mosaic-like combinations of threat displays with inferiority behavior, i.e., withdrawal or turning away. The inferiority tendencies are represented by the orientation or the retreat, respectively, whereas the simultaneously displayed threat behaviors (e.g., symbolic butting, presentation of horns, etc.) represent the aggressive tendencies. The animal may be said to be in an inner conflict in such cases. However, the threat displays themselves cannot be explained as a result of an inner conflict between aggression and escape tendencies.

The immediate relationship of the threat displays to the species-

a

b

c

Fig. 102. Sequence of aggressive displays in a one-sided agonistic encounter of two adult bulls of South African oryx. a. A subordinate bull (left) passes a dominant bull (right) in the opposite direction at close range. The dominant assumes an erect posture. b. The dominant bull in full erect display in reverse-parallel position. c. The subordinate (right) tries to pass behind the dominant bull (left). The latter circles correspondingly in keeping the broadside position. His erect stance

d

e

f

merges into a head-turned-away display. d. In continued circling, the sideward turn of the sender's head merges into a symbolic stab-over-the-(own)-shoulder (left). e. The dominant's symbolic stab-over-the-shoulder merges into sideward angling of the horns. The subordinate (right) responds by lowering his head and waving his tail. f. The dominant turns frontally toward the subordinate. The latter flees at a gallop. (Walther 1980. Etosha National Park.)

specific fighting techniques also largely explains the similarities or the differences of message and meaning of certain displays in different species. When the fighting techniques are similar in two or more species, then the corresponding threat displays also have the same message and meaning. However, when the fighting techniques are different, a phenotypically similar display may have a rather different, sometimes an almost opposite message and meaning. To say it by means of an example discussed above: the head-low posture is a defensive threat, approximating a submissive behavior, in all the species—e.g., oryx, roan antelope—that attack by downward-blows or similar fighting movements, but the message and meaning of the head-low posture simply must be different in a species, such as chamois, that attacks by upward blows from below.

Finally, I wish to remind the reader that many species possess several aggressive displays. While it was necessary here to discuss them individually, this form of presentation should not mislead the reader into concluding that only one display will be shown in an agonistic encounter. Frequently it is so, particularly when the recipient immediately reacts by withdrawal or flight. However, when he does not react, or at least not promptly, or when his reaction to the first display is inadequate, the sender may resort to several other displays in a more or less stable sequence that reflects his increasing aggressiveness (Fig. 102). When threat and dominance displays are used in such a sequence, the dominance displays always occur before the threat displays.

13. DOMINANCE DISPLAYS

Dominance displays ("*Imponierverhalten*" in German literature, "display threats" in Lent 1965, "bravado displays" in Geist 1966*a*, "present threats" in Geist 1971) are close to threat displays in several regards, and transitions between the two (threat-dominance displays) are not infrequent. There are also quite a number of cases in which the distinction between them is somewhat problematic. Nevertheless, it is important that threat displays and dominance displays be distinguished from each other whenever possible. In contrast to threat displays, dominance displays do not indicate an immediate readiness to fight. An animal usually demonstrates its height and/or breadth and may sometimes also use some other striking postures or movements, but none of these is directly related to (recent) fighting techniques of the species. Weapons may also be presented but not in a position suitable for fighting. Thus, dominance displays indicate a claim of superiority over the addressee but without fighting intentions.

On the other hand, dominance displays have the same effects— intimidation or challenge—on the recipient as threat displays, and they occur in the same situations in which offensive threat displays may occur. Typically, they are infrequent in females and juveniles (which often play a subordinate role in ungulate societies) and are often lacking in the agonistic situations predominantly or exclusively found in those sex or age classes, such as soliciting milk and defense against it, playful encounters, females' defense against sexual approaches, etc. In encounters between unequal opponents, dominance displays are very typical of the stronger, older, or higher-ranking (also territorial) combatant. They are rarely, if at all, used by the inferior opponent, whereas defensive threat displays are quite common on the latter's part. When an encounter cannot be settled by dominance displays (a situation especially frequent in reciprocal encounters among peers), the opponents may change from dominance displays, frequently over a transitional phase characterized by threat-dominance displays, to threat displays, which may result in fighting. Thus the rivals rarely advance immediately from reciprocal dominance displays to fighting, whereas such a direct change is very common from reciprocal threat displays, i.e., threat displays are usually interposed between dominance displays and fighting. The reciprocal dominance displays in such cases obviously contribute to the prolongation of the opening phase before a fight ensues. Protracted reciprocal dominance displays may also be more likely to end an encounter without overt fighting than threat displays—be it that one of the opponents gives in and withdraws, or that both opponents cease the interaction. When the encounter remains one-sided, the (inferior) recipient usually withdraws in response to the dominance display of the (superior) sender.

Before we continue the discussion of dominance displays, it may be well to substantiate the statements above by at least one instructive example from the behavior of Grant's gazelle (Walther 1977a). This species has several well pronounced threat displays (the following quantitative presentation refers mainly to medial and high presentation of horns in frontal position), at least one very elaborate dominance display (head-flagging in erect posture and broadside position—p. 250) that can be distinguished beyond any possible doubt from threat displays, and clearly intermediate form, i.e., a threat-dominance display (broadside position and circling with horns angled sideways toward the opponent)—in addition to a few more agonistic displays which we will not discuss here.

The incidences of reciprocal encounters (one-sided encounters are not included) that are continued by other aggressive displays (one or two of the aforementioned displays and/or parallel walk, horn-sweep, object aggression, etc.), by fighting, by withdrawal or submission of one of the opponents, and by cessation of aggression by both opponents (including cases where both began grazing or one or both switched to herding females, etc.) were investigated (Table 2). Cessation of aggression by both opponents was relatively rare after the reciprocal displays. It was rarest after threats. Continuation with other aggressive displays was common after dominance displays and threat-dominance displays but relatively rare after threat displays. Reciprocal encounters were most frequently settled (one of the opponents gave in and withdrew) after head-flagging, a dominance display, and least frequently after horn threats. Sideward-angling of horns, as a threat-dominance display, was intermediate. Perhaps the most conclusive figures are provided by the frequency of fights immediately following the displays under discussion. Fights followed only 2.6 percent of the reciprocal dominance displays, 24.2 percent of the threat-dominance displays, and 77.5 percent of the reciprocal pure threat displays. These figures clearly demonstrate that the threat displays are significantly more closely related to overt fighting than the dominance displays and that the distinction between them is therefore justifiable.

TABLE 2:

Outcomes of Reciprocal Agonistic Encounters after Certain Threat and Dominance Displays in Grant's Gazelle

	Dominance Displays[a]	Threat-Dominance Displays[b]	Threat Displays[c]
N Observed Cases:	153	149	89
% followed by: other threat or dominance displays	60.8	53.7	11.2
fight	2.6	24.2	77.5
withdrawal, flight, or submission of one of the opponents	28.8	19.5	10.1
ceasing aggression, both opponents	7.8	2.6	1.2

[a] Reciprocal head-flagging in broadside position
[b] Reciprocal sideward-angling of horns in broadside position
[c] Reciprocal presentation of horns in frontal position

It should be noted that an animal exposes itself to a possible attack ("daring") by the rival much more during dominance displays than during threat displays, particularly defensive threat displays. This strong component of self-exposure in dominance displays connects them to presence and position advertisements. Dominance displays, then, can be regarded as individually addressed position advertisements intensified by expressive components. These "expressive components" frequently link them to offensive threat displays and to certain fighting behaviors.

We previously spoke of the threat-dominance displays, in which the combination of a dominance and a threat display is very obvious. However, there are more subtle connections. Generally, whether an aggressive display should be regarded as a threat or a dominance display depends not on the posture or movement per se, but on its relationship to the recent fighting behavior of a given species. It is sometimes possible to classify the same posture as a threat display in one species and a dominance display in another. For instance, in mountain goat, which fight from a broadside position, assuming a lateral position to the opponent is an intention movement for fighting and thus a threat display. However, when a broadside display appears in the agonistic encounters of Grant's gazelle, which fight only from a frontal position, the broadside position must be classified as a dominance display. As a matter of fact, I can hardly think of any dominance display of a given ungulate species which does not occur as a threat display and/or a fighting technique in another ungulate species. The suspicion arises that all the dominance displays of hoofed mammals originated via threat displays from fighting behaviors which were lost and replaced by other, "modern" fighting behaviors during phylogenetic evolution. In support of this view, dominance displays are numerous in advanced ungulate species but much rarer or even lacking in more primitive species. For example, according to von Richter (1966), tapirs do not have any dominance displays at all.

The relationship between threat and dominance displays and the possible evolution of the latter is relatively easy to understand in even-toed ungulates. Paleontologists (e.g., Thenius and Hofer 1960) generally agree· that the recent even-toed ungulates have evolved from forms that did not possess special organs for fighting. There are some recent Artiodactyla, such as llamas and camels, that still lack special armament and use their teeth, neck, body, and legs in fighting. Others, like the swine and the hippos, have specialized, already existing organs (the teeth) for use as weapons. Still others, mainly the Cervidae and Bovidae, have developed special "new" organs (antlers and horns) for intraspecific aggression. However, these species have also evolved from hornless or antlerless ancestors (*Archaeomeryx optatus* or related prehistorical ungulates).

It is certainly correct to presume that these "unarmed" ancestors had their fights and threat displays, but they could not use horns or antlers, since they had none. It is not out of place to assume that their fighting techniques were similar if not identical to those shown by recent "unarmed" artiodactyls (e.g., mouse deer, llama, camel). With the development of horns and antlers as special means of intraspecific aggression and with the corresponding development of phylogenetically "new" fighting methods and threat displays, ancestral fighting techniques have been superseded in the bovids and cervids. Of course, this has varied among the species according to differences in advancement (size, mass, shape, permanent or temporary usefulness as weapons) of horns and antlers (Walther 1961b, 1966a). Although these ancestral fighting techniques have more or less disappeared, the corresponding expressive displays—the original threats—have apparently remained in some species. But, even though these ritualized intention movements originated in fighting techniques, they now have no connection with the recent fighting behavior of these species. Because of this separation, these dominance displays are "milder" forms of challenge or intimidation compared to the "new" forms of threat, which refer directly to actual fighting behavior. When, in a species, both "modern" threats and displays derived from ancestral aggressive behavior coexist, a more subtle gradation in the forms of challenge and intimidation becomes possible. This certainly is advantageous to social communication and makes the "survival" of these phylogenetically old displays understandable.

We will come back to this hypothesis in the discussion on courtship displays. For the moment, the reader need only be aware of the possible relationships between threat and dominance displays, and understand why certain postures or movements are considered threat displays in some species and dominance displays in others and why dominance displays are more frequently found in the more advanced ungulate species than in the more primitive forms.

One of the two most important types of dominance displays is most intimately related to the broadside position, previously discussed as a means of blocking another's path (lateral T-position) and as an initiation of fighting from a lateral position—two aspects that are not mutually exclusive. Apparently both gave rise to the broadside attitude as a dominance display. Of course, the broadside position per se is not an expressive display in the strict sense but simply a form of orientation. Thus, one can speak of a true broadside *display* only when further behavioral features are added to the lateral orientation. This can be achieved in many different ways. For example, in warthog (Frädrich 1967), a number of deer species (Müller-Using and Schloeth 1967), mountain goat (Geist 1965), markhor goat, bushbuck, and nyala, the animal may ruffle up the mane on its neck and/or back. In bushbuck (Waser 1975) and nyala (Anderson 1980), the displaying males also erect their tails over the rump and the white hairs on their undersides are fanned out. Such ruffling of the hair can also be combined with frontally oriented threat displays, but it is more conspicuous to the recipient when the sender is in broadside position. In gaur (Antonius 1939), Camargue cattle (Schloeth 1961a), and greater kudu (Fig. 103), the displaying bull humps his back by placing his hind feet more forward under the belly than usual. A male may also stretch head and neck forward, as in bongo (Hamann 1979) and nilgai (Fig. 94a), or forward-downward, as in greater kudu and gaur, in combination with the lateral attitude. In quite a number of species, such as white-tailed deer (Hirth 1977), tsessebe (Joubert 1972), blackbuck, Grant's gazelle, and lesser kudu, the broadside position may be combined with an erect posture of the neck or even with a nose-up posture. In markhor goat, the chin may be tucked in toward

Fig. 103. Humping the back by placing the hind feet further forward under the belly than usual, in the broadside display of greater kudu.

the throat (Fig. 104), corresponding to the posture in medial presentation of horns—a special form of a threat-dominance display. Also, in axis deer (Schaller 1967) and mule deer (Cowan and Geist 1961), the latter displaying a crouched posture with a strong *erector pili* effect, the head and neck are held on body level with the nose pointing toward the ground.

In chamois (Walther 1961a, Krämer 1969), the broadside display per se, with erected neck, ruffled hair at the croup, and straddled hind legs, is clear; however, a chamois very frequently withdraws, walking laterally, from the opponent in this posture. Thus, its character as a dominance display is not quite clear. Possibly one could think of the—in ungulates very exceptional—case that an escape tendency might be involved in a dominance display (conflict hypothesis!). On the other hand, this interpretation is certainly not the only possibility. Chamois typically attack by means of a vehement rush over quite a distance. When the sender displays in lateral position in front of the opponent, the distance is too short for such an attack. Thus, the "withdrawal" in broadside posture may be indicative of the tendency

Fig. 104. Broadside display (hunch) of a markhor goat with chin tucked in toward the throat and slight sideward angling of the horns addressed to me. (Kronberg Zoo.)

to increase the distance to the opponent for a rush attack. If this interpretation is correct, one could consider the chamois' "withdrawal" in broadside posture as a threat-dominance display.

Finally, the combination of the broadside position with postures of the head and neck may vary with the intensity of the display in certain species. This is demonstrated, e.g., by the threat-dominance display of nilgai antelope. Laterally displaying nilgai bulls move their forelegs slowly and stiffly, with their hind legs slightly bent, back somewhat humped (squatting posture), ears dropped, and tail usually clumped tightly between the hind legs (occasionally it is switched upward to a vertical posture). However, the head and neck posture may vary. In the arched-neck form of this display (Fall 1972), the neck is stretched forward but curved somewhat downward so that the nose points downward-forward. When the bull ceases walking, the neck may be brought down to a head-low posture, and the hind feet may be drawn forward under the body as in greater kudu (see above). In the most common form of this display (Fig. 94a), head and neck are stretched forward in one line (Antonius 1939, Walther 1958a). In maximum intensity, the straight-neck display merges into a head-and-neck-stretched-forward/upward posture (Walther 1965a).

An exaggeration of the broadside position by a sideward-turn (usually of about 45°) of the head away from the opponent is very frequent in oryx antelope (Fig. 109), red deer, and many other species. This movement is sometimes related to sideward-angling the horns, e.g., in wildebeest, roan and oryx antelope. In the South African oryx antelope, the head-turn also regularly precedes the symbolic stab-over-the-shoulder, which was discussed as a threat display due to its close relationship to a recent fighting technique of this species. However, a strong dominance display component seems to be involved, since—although the stab-over-the-shoulder is used in fights—an oryx usually does not attack from the symbolic performance of the stab-over-the-shoulder in broadside position, but rather turns first into a frontal position toward the opponent, displaying medial presentation of horns, before it starts fighting.

The importance of the sender's broadside orientation in all these displays is clearly demonstrated when the recipient moves, as is frequent when he is subordinate to the sender, and tries to withdraw by passing behind the dominant. In this case, the dominant sender turns on the spot, always keeping his flank toward the recipient (Fig. 102a–c) until the latter has passed him and is now clearly walking away. Sometimes he may eventually even stand in lateral position with head-turned-away (!) behind the withdrawing opponent.

When both rivals show a broadside display, they are automatically brought into a parallel or (more often) a reverse-parallel position. In many species, they then begin to circle (Fig. 105a,b), always keeping their flanks toward each other. As the encounter becomes more severe, they may change from circling in reverse-parallel position to frontal orientation (Fig. 105c) and may eventually fight (Fig. 105d) one another frontally (provided they do not belong to a species that fights from a lateral position). Circling can also be seen in one-sided encounters. This means the displaying animal moves around the (nondisplaying) recipient. Apparently this "encircling" has a strongly intimidating effect.

Some Suidae species, such as wild boar, fight in lateral position, and pressing and jostling with the shoulder or the whole side of the body against the opponent's flank plays a role in these fights. Such fighting techniques do not require any special armament, and thus could also have occurred in the "unarmed" ancestors of more highly evolved, recent ungulate species. On the other hand, wild boar also use their specialized tusks when fighting in lateral position to each other. In short, one could conclude that assuming a broadside position is closely related to recent fighting, and thus should be considered a threat display in this species.

However, things are somewhat more complicated. Since wild boar fight with their tusks by throwing the head upward from a head-low posture (Beuerle 1975), lowering the head is an intention movement for very severe fighting in this species. Consequently, when the lateral orientation is combined with a head-low posture in wild boar (Fig. 87), this still can be interpreted as a threat display or at least a

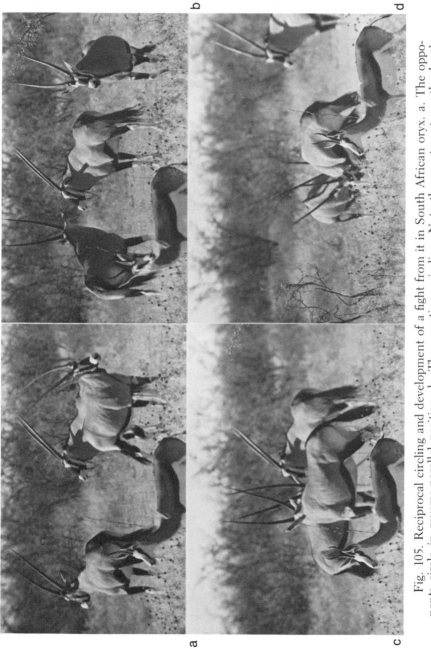

Fig. 105. Reciprocal circling and development of a fight from it in South African oryx. a. The opponents circle in reverse-parallel position. b. They continue circling. Note the erect posture, the head-turned-away attitude, and the "pointing" with one ear (particularly pronounced in the animal to the left. A third oryx bull, standing in the central background, and a springbuck in the foreground, are not involved in the encounter.). c. The opponents turn into a frontal position from reciprocal circling in reverse-parallel position. d. They start fighting. (Etosha National Park.)

threat-dominance display (in lateral T-position). Particularly in encounters between a dominant and a subordinate male, however, the dominant typically moves into a lateral position in front of the subordinate (Fig. 106) with his head held as high up as possible (Beuerle 1975). He cannot fight with his tusks by upward-blows from this erect posture; hence, Beuerle (1975) probably rightly classifies the broadside posture in combination with erect head as a dominance display in wild boar. In particularly vehement encounters, the displaying boar may jump up with his forelegs from the erect posture. As previously mentioned the subordinate stretches head and neck forward in the direction of the dominant's cheek (Fig. 107). In these postures and positions, the combatants may circle at the spot (Fig. 108) until the subordinate finds an opportunity to flee. When both rivals are equally strong, they may walk with erect heads and somewhat flexed hind legs in a parallel march (Beuerle 1975).

In some other Suidae species, such as bush pig and warthog, which—in contrast to wild boar—commonly fight in frontal position (Frädrich 1965, 1967), assuming a broadside position relative to the recipient is certainly a dominance display. Displaying warthogs (Frädrich 1967) circle the opponent, with ruffled mane and a stiff-legged gait, until they come into a frontal position from which fighting may develop. Male bush pig assume a broadside position (parallel, reverse-parallel, or lateral T-position) toward the partner,

Fig. 106. A dominant male (left) moves into a lateral position in front of a subordinate in an encounter between wild boar. (Beuerle 1975. Photo: W. Beuerle. Schwarzwildrevier Breitenbuch, Germany.)

Fig. 107. The subordinate (right) stretches head and neck forward in the direction of the dominant's cheek in an agonistic encounter of wild boar. (Beuerle 1975. Photo: W. Beuerle. Schwarzwildrevier Breitenbuch, Germany.)

turn the head somewhat toward him, and erect the short but dazzling white mane along the back. The ruffling of hair is particularly striking in peccary. It begins at the neck and continues over the entire posterior part of the body. The gland on the back becomes visible, and the animal appears essentially bigger in this way (Frädrich 1967).

The broadside position is also present in at least some of the tylopods, such as vicuna (Pilters 1954, 1956), and in the Giraffidae. However, at least in the latter it is more a threat display because of its close relationship to the recent fighting behavior of these animals. A few Bovidae fight in parallel or reverse-parallel position, but the majority of the species do not. The same is true for Cervidae. Thus, when broadside displays are found in such bovids and cervids, they are dominance displays in the outlined sense. Some of these species have been mentioned above, but there are many more. As a matter of fact, the broadside position is such a common dominance display in bovids and cervids that a list of species which do not show it would be much shorter than a list of species which possess it.

In the head-turned-away display, the head can be turned sideward at an angle ranging from less than 45° to over 90° in some cases. Sometimes it appears desirable to distinguish between the 45°- and the 90°-turn because it seems possible that there may be some difference in their messages and meanings, and the frequency of occurrence can vary with species. For example, the 45°-turn is frequent

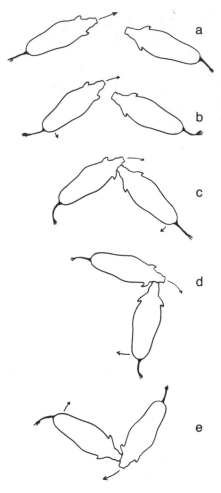

Fig. 108. Display en-
counter between a dominant
and a subordinate male of
wild boar. (From Beuerle
1975.) a. The dominant male
(left) moves into a lateral
position in front of the subordinate. b. The subordinate
assumes a neck-stretch attitude (see Figs. 106, 107) with
his snout-disk directed toward
the dominant's cheek. c.
Keeping his erect posture (see
Fig. 106), the dominant leans
his cheek firmly against the
subordinate's snout-disk.
d.–e. Circling on the spot.

and the 90°-turn is comparatively rare in oryx antelope and mountain
gazelle, while the opposite is true for Uganda kob and impala. Furthermore, the 45°-turn generally has a tendency to be continued by
sideward-angling of horns. This tendency is much less pronounced in
the 90°-turn, so that the 45°-turn is possibly a more offensive form
and more closely related to threat behavior than the 90°-turn of the
head. In short, there are some differences.

On the other hand, the two forms of head-turning (45° and 90°)
certainly are related to each other and transitional cases are possible.
Also, both can be combined with other species-specific dominance
displays, such as the erect posture in topi and oryx, or with the

neck-stretch in nilgai, and occasionally with threat displays such as the presentation of horns.

In some cases and/or species, it even seems primarily to depend on the sender's orientation relative to the recipient whether the 45°- or the 90°-head-turn is used for essentially the same message. For example, a South African oryx antelope usually displays by turning the head away at an angle of 45° when standing in broadside position to the opponent: the head-turn emphasizes the body's lateral orientation (Fig. 109). However, when frontally approaching the addressee, the sender often turns his head at an angle of 90° in this species (Fig. 110), and the head-turn substitutes for a broadside display of the entire body. Of course, this last example demonstrates once more how misleading it is to assume an involvement of escape tendencies in such a sideward-turn of the head: the displaying oryx actually approaches the recipient while turning the head sideways.

As a rule of thumb, in hoofed mammals, a 45°-turn of the head

Fig. 109. 45°-head-turned-away display of a dominant South African oryx bull in erect posture and lateral T-position. The subordinate (right) responds by a head-forward posture. Compare this posture of the subordinate to the defense against a stab-over-the-shoulder during a fight in Fig. 101. (Walther 1980. Etosha National Park.)

a

b

c

d

away from the recipient does not indicate flight tendencies but is a dominance or threat display, or part of one (provided that it is a true posture, held for at least a few seconds, and not merely a transitional phase in a continuous movement of the head). A 90°-head-turn too is a dominance display in the overwhelming majority of cases. It is only the 180° head-turn that indicates escape tendencies relatively often, and even then by no means in all cases.

A very special kind of head-turning is the cheek-patch display (Kitchen 1974) of pronghorn, usually used by dominant males when approaching subordinates. Since this display regularly occurs in sexual encounters of bucks with females during rutting season, it will be discussed in more detail in connection with courtship displays.

One common principle in dominance displays is to make the animal appear as long and broad as possible. This is verified by broadside displays and related behavior patterns. Another widespread principle is to make the animal appear as tall as possible. This is mainly achieved by the erect, nose-up, and head-and-neck-forward/upward postures. Because these three are closely related and their differences were pointed out in the discussion of threat displays, I will lump them together here as "erect displays."

Since most ungulate males rise on their hind feet in sexual mounting, one could consider the erect postures to be intention movements for sexual mounting. Also, in agonistic encounters, a combatant sometimes mounts the rival from an erect posture. On the other hand, some species, e.g., greater and lesser kudu, show erect postures as dominance displays but do not mount in erect postures. (The males of these species lower their heads and necks toward the female's back in mounting.) Hence, their erect postures obviously are not related to sexual mounting. Furthermore, in certain highly advanced cervid species, such as red deer, Manchurian sika (Schneider 1930), and barasingha (Schaller 1967), an erect posture with almost vertical nose, retracted upper lip, and gnashing teeth may correspond to the attitude adopted by related but more primitive species (musk deer, Chinese water deer) when attacking an opponent with their long upper canines (Antonius 1939). Thus, one can also think of a development parallel to that of the broadside displays and infer that

Fig. 110a. A South African oryx bull (right) dominates a cow (with a broken horn) by frontal approach and sideward turn of his head. His erect head-turned-away display becomes a 90°-turn of the head due to his frontal orientation. b. Finally, he stands in front of the cow. c. He turns his head frontally toward her, performing a (slow) symbolic forward-downward blow. She responds with head-low posture, head throwing, and tail waving. She starts moving, passing the bull in reverse-parallel orientation. d. The cow withdraws; the bull looks after her. (Walther 1980. Etosha National Park.)

the erect postures in agonistic encounters are phylogenetic relics of ancestral fighting behaviors.

Finally, it is possible that sexual mounting—of the ungulate type—is itself related to and originated from aggressive jumping at and throwing the body on the partner. In this connection, it may be mentioned that all the Tylopoda—that is, the camels and llamas— copulate lying down. Thus their copulatory posture has nothing to do with rising on the hind legs. However, a male tylopod frequently jumps at and throws his body on the female to force her to the ground for copulation—a behavior that is similar or even identical to that shown in fights between rivals. It is this aggressive jump, not the copulatory posture, of tylopods that corresponds to the mounting be- havior of other ungulates. It is possible that tylopods, which appear to be behaviorally primitive artiodactyls in more than one regard, may have maintained a general feature of ancestral behavior in this case. In short, it seems that the erect postures of hoofed mammals gener- ally have some connection with rearing up with the forelegs. Al- though an origin of the erect dominance attitudes from sexual mounting cannot be decisively excluded at present, the odds appear to be in favor of an origin from (ancestral) fighting techniques.

Other cases in which an ungulate may assume an erect posture occur in females of certain species when nursing their young, in males of certain species when urinating, and generally in animals when watching out in alert posture. Some authors seem to think of possible connections between the above and the erect attitudes in dominance displays. For example, Schenkel and Lang (1969) speak of a corresponding case of "*Imponierhaltung*" (= dominance posture) in black rhinoceros which is shown before an attack (or feint attack) when the animal is standing frontally or half-frontally oriented toward the adversary, and which may be combined with a long snort (Fig. 111). I have seen this behavior several times; however, I had not the impression of a special dominance display but simply of an intense and alert watching. Generally, the similarities of erect dominance displays and erect attitudes in alert stances seem to be brought about by the considerable tension of similar muscles in both cases but with- out genuine relationship between the two behaviors. Another rela- tively superficial connection is based on the rivals' looking intensely at each other at the very beginning of an agonistic encounter. For example, in white rhino (Owen-Smith 1975), two bulls may stare at each other with raised heads at close range (the visual powers of rhinoceroses are comparatively poor). Also, in nilgai antelope, Fall (1972) spoke of a "head-erect display" which probably is no display but simply the observation of a potential opponent some distance away.

Fig. 111. Dominance display (?—see text) of a black rhinoceros (*Diceros bicornis*). (From Schenkel and Lang 1969.)

Certainly the erect dominance displays cannot have evolved from an erect stance in nursing, since they are most prominent in males. Nor can they be understood as derivations from erect male urination posture since there are species that show erect attitudes in dominance displays but usually do not when urinating. Moreover, erect dominance displays occur not only in males but also, although less frequently, in females of certain species, and the females do not assume an erect stance during urination. A mutual factor is possible in erect dominance displays and erect male urination postures, although not in the sense that the one would have evolved from the other. This third mutual factor may be seen in the relationship of both behaviors to presence and position advertisement.

Since a connection between erect displays and recent fighting techniques is obviously present in the horses and their relatives (rising on hind legs, kicking with forelegs), in tylopods (jumping at the other, throat biting, neck fighting), in Giraffidae (neck fighting in several forms), and in Cervidae (rising on hind legs and beating with forelegs), erect postures as true dominance displays occur mainly in certain Bovidae species which do not practice such fighting techniques. However, a kind of dominance component cannot be ruled out in the erect displays of zebra (e.g., in the greeting ritual), guanaco, camel, giraffe, okapi, many deer species, and even the little mouse deer (Robin 1979). The same may be true of a horse stallion's posture with the chin toward the throat. Also, in giraffe, when the opponents stand in parallel position in a pause during a fight, the combatant who is to win the fight, always erects his neck higher than

Fig. 112. In fighting giraffe, the prospective winner erects his neck steeper than the prospective loser in pauses during the fight. (Serengeti National Park.)

the prospective loser (Fig. 112). Such and similar features may be taken as indications of said dominance display components in erect postures that otherwise are basically threat displays. Likewise the facial expression of certain cervid species, the "canine display," which often is combined with erect postures (Fig. 113), can be considered such a dominance display component (provided that the theory of its derivation from ancestral biting or slashing behavior is correct) since male cervids usually do not bite from the erect posture.

In the discussion of the situation in bovids, where erect postures clearly are dominance displays, some problems arise from the major role of the neck in these postures. In species with a relatively long, movable neck, its erection is an essential component in these displays and makes their recognition very easy. However, in species with a relatively short, massive neck, which cannot be erected to any great extent, it may sometimes become doubtful whether one can speak about an erect posture and, if so, whether it can be directly compared to the displays of long-necked species.

In the wild oxen, for example, the anatomical structure of the neck largely inhibits the performance of pronounced erect displays. Raising the head in these animals usually results in a nose-forward posture which can also be said to be a more or less special form of the neck-stretch. Erect postures as clear dominance displays, often combined with a more or less pronounced lifting of the nose, have been

Fig. 113. Manchurian sika stag (*Sika nippon dubowskii*) with nose-up posture and grinding of teeth approaching an opponent. (After a photo in Schneider 1930.)

observed in impala (Schenkel 1966*b*), kongoni (Gosling 1974), red hartebeest (Kok 1975), lelwel hartebeest (*Alcelaphus buselaphus lelwel*—Backhaus 1959), tsessebe (Joubert 1972), greater kudu, lesser kudu, and many others. I do not hesitate to include the "head-up" displays of some species with less movable necks, such as brindled wildebeest (Fig. 114—Talbot and Talbot 1963, Estes 1969) and black wildebeest (von Richter 1971).

An exception within the bovids is certain sheep species in which the erect postures are related to rising on the hind legs as a recent fighting technique, which brings them more to the side of threat displays. On the other hand, such experienced observers as Schaller and Mirza (1974) and Geist (1971) do not hesitate to declare the erect postures of urial and bighorn sheep (Fig. 115) to be "present threats"

Fig. 114. Erect stance with head-turned-away and stamping (left) in an encounter between territorial wildebeest bulls.

Fig. 115. Erect posture of bighorn rams (*Ovis canadensis*) after a horn clash.

(= dominance displays), particularly because the combatants often assume an erect stance *after* the horn clash.

In many species under discussion, the erect displays occur in frontal orientation toward an addressee as well as in combination with the broadside position. Tsessebe bulls displaying broadside in erect posture with lifted nose in front of an opponent (Fig. 116) sometimes jump up into the air with their forelegs (Joubert 1972). This example is of special interest, since one might doubt that erect postures are intention movements for rising on the hind feet in such a case, arguing that this interpretation is unlikely when the erect posture is displayed in a lateral orientation toward the recipient. Regardless of whether it is logical in human terms, jumping up with the forefeet from an erect posture while in broadside position is a fact.

Of the many species-specific modifications that may occur in the erect postures, I will now discuss only one in detail. This is the extremely elaborate dominance display of Grant's gazelle (Fig. 117), which offers several special and particularly interesting aspects. Standing in broadside position with vertically erected or even somewhat backward leaning neck, the displaying buck turns his lifted head and nose sideways *toward* the addressee by a vehement movement (*hohes Kopf-Zuwenden*—Walther 1965*b*), and then forward again. This "head-flagging" may be repeated several times. The tail is often more or less horizontally stretched and may swing sideways during this display. It does not necessarily "point" toward the recipient, and I never had the impression that the tail movement plays an essential

Fig. 116. Territorial tsessebe bull (*Damaliscus lunatus lunatus*) displaying in erect posture with lifted nose in lateral T-position. (Joubert 1972. Photo: S.C.J. Joubert. Kruger National Park, South Africa.)

Fig. 117. Reciprocal head-flagging in Grant's gazelle. (Females are grazing between the two displaying bucks.) (Serengeti National Park.)

role in this display, as has been suggested in literature (Geist 1978). On the other hand, the tension of the neck muscles (Estes 1967) and/or the "flashing" of the white throat patch (Walther 1965*b*) may possibly have an additional effect. However, I think that the term "neck-intimidation display" suggested by Estes (1967) conceals the fact that the head movement toward the rival is its most important component.

The head-flagging is commonly initiated by turning the head at an angle of 45°, in rare cases even 90°, away from the opponent as a swing-out movement (Fig. 118a). Initially I was inclined to see nothing but a modified form of the widespread head-turned-away display in the head-flagging of Grant's gazelle (Walther 1965b). However, later, intensive studies of this species as well as comparative studies of a variety of others, particularly mountain gazelle (Grau and Walther 1976), in which the head-turned-away (without "flagging") is a very common and pronounced display, convinced me that this interpretation is not or is only partly correct. It is only the swing-out movement, the initiating 45°-turn of the head into the opposite direction, that corresponds to the head-turned-away displays of other species, whereas the head-turn toward the recipient cannot be understood as a modification of this behavior.

a   b

Fig. 118a. Left: Erect posture with swing-out movement (head-turned-away at 45°) for the head-turn toward the opponent in a display encounter between Grant's gazelle bucks. Right: Full head-flagging. (Walther 1968a. b. Head-flagging (left) incorrectly oriented due to the opponent's very sudden cessation of displays and his retreat in an unexpected direction. (Serengeti National Park.)

In contrast to the head-turned-away display, which in many cases and species, including Grant's gazelle, may also occur when the animal is moving, the displaying animal always stops walking and stands for head-flagging. Most commonly, the releasing situation comes when the sender is at the point of passing the addressee or when the latter is passing or has just passed the sender. Although sender and recipient can be in various positions relative to each other in this moment, a reverse-parallel position is more frequent than all the others in one-sided display encounters and is almost obligatory in reciprocal encounters. Provided that the partners in such encounters are not peers, the subordinate recipient withdraws sooner or later, walking in a direction opposite to that in which the sender is oriented due to the reverse-parallel position of the combatants. This obviously is the response for which the sender's display is aiming. The dominant, still oriented in the opposite direction with his body, then usually looks after the withdrawing opponent for a moment, which can also be observed in numerous other species which do not show the head-flagging display (Fig. 142b). It appears to be this turn of the head in looking after the withdrawing opponent that gave rise to the ritualization of the head-flagging display in Grant's gazelle. Because of its highly stereotyped nature (Walther 1965b), "failures" occasionally occur when the sender's position relative to the recipient is inadequate (i.e., not reverse-parallel) for the head-flagging (Fig. 118b)—comparable to "failures" in orientation of the inciting behavior of female mallards (Lorenz 1963).

Provided that the derivation of the Grant's gazelle's head-flagging from looking after the withdrawing recipient from a reverse-parallel position is correct, and I am rather confident that it is, one can draw some interesting comparisons from it. For one thing, the sender anticipates and demands the recipient's withdrawal in the direction opposite to his own and, by his head movement, signals to the addressee the direction in which he wants the latter to move. There is an almost perfect analogy in the contemptuous sideward-swing of the head with which one human signals another whom he considers inferior to go away. Furthermore, it is apparently an ending rather than the usual initiating movement of an action that has become ritualized (looking after the withdrawing opponent at the end of the encounter). Finally, the movement per se appears to be largely the same as in the symbolic stab-over-the-shoulder in the South African oryx antelope, but the orientation is the opposite: in Grant's gazelle, the head is turned toward the recipient; in the oryx it is turned away.

Interestingly enough, this symbolic stab-over-the-shoulder has only been observed in the South African oryx (Oryx gazella), not in the closely related East African oryx (Oryx beisa). (The corresponding fighting technique is present in both species.) This difference is probably linked to a slight difference in the preceding erect displays of the two species (or subspecies according to other classification systems). The South African oryx lifts the head at least to horizontal level and frequently even somewhat higher before the symbolic stab—as

Grant's gazelle do before head-flagging. The East African oryx lifts the head at maximum to horizontal level but usually not quite as high, and frequently continues by tucking the chin in toward the throat and turning the head with presented horns toward the opponent from a broadside position. It is a nice example of how a display of obviously mutual origin may begin to diverge in closely related species.

Broadside and erect displays certainly are the most common forms of dominance displays in hoofed mammals. However, there are other behaviors which can be so classified. Some of them—such as certain vocalizations, the emission of scent from the opened preorbital glands, and, above all, the widespread slow, exaggerated, and stiff-legged prancing gait of displaying animals—were previously discussed when we talked about threats and space-claims. However, one could also justify considering them to be dominance displays or components of them, particularly when the prancing gait is performed simultaneously by both rivals, resulting in a lengthy display march side by side, which is quite common in red deer (Bützler 1974), elk (Geist 1966a), fallow deer, moose (Müller-Using and Schloeth 1967), blackbuck (Mungall 1978), and others. Likewise, the bucking and cavorting that frequently occurs in agonistic encounters of territorial bulls of wildebeest (Estes 1969), blesbok (Lynch 1974), and bontebok (David 1973) may not be too far removed from a dominance display. Also, the "hunch" of wild goat (*Capra aegagrus*), blue sheep (*Pseudois nayaur*), takin (*Budorcas taxicolor*) and Nilgiri tahr (*Hemitragus hylocrius*—Schaller 1977), in which the animal hunches its back, bunches the legs under the body, and arches its neck down with its nose almost touching the ground, is apparently at least very close to a dominance display. Perhaps one could interpret the hunch as a gathering of power preparing a stretching movement of the body, and/or an upward throwing of head and neck, and/or a sudden turn into a frontal orientation. However, if such connections to fighting actions once existed, they are now lost, since—except for mountain goat—these animals do not fight from the hunch posture. As a further example, one could mention a display in impala (Schenkel 1966b) in which the male may lift his tail with the white hair spread, stretch his head and neck forward, and utter roaring vocalizations ("roaring display") in standing, walking, and galloping while chasing females, yearlings, bachelors, or rivals. There is also the protruding of a "gular bag" from the mouth of camels (Pilters 1956) combined with "blo-blo-blo" vocalizations and production of saliva while in a very erect posture (Gauthier-Pilters 1959) which may merge into rubbing the head at the hump and/or beating with the tail during urination.

In sheep, the neck-stretch (Fig. 119) and the foreleg kick can be used in agonistic encounters (Walther 1961a, Geist 1968, 1971). Typically, these behaviors commonly occur on the part of a dominant ram in an encounter with a subordinate or in reciprocal encounters among peers. The kick may hit the opponent between the hind legs, on the thigh, chest, side, or other body regions, but frequently it does not touch him. Geist (1971), who did a very intensive study of these behaviors in sheep, considers them to be primarily courtship behaviors; therefore, they will be discussed in detail more in the following chapter. It may be mentioned, however, that certain species rotate the head about its long axis during the neck-stretch so that one cheek is turned toward the ground. In bighorn sheep, this behavior was termed the "twist" by Geist (1971), and he considers it a horn display of the frontally approaching ram. (The horns expand laterally in sheep rams). However, the occurrence of a similar twist of the head, e.g., in the hornless females of greater kudu (Fig. 120) somewhat contradicts Geist's interpretation. At least, it cannot be generally applied to all the species that show this behavior. The twist may also be related to biting behavior (as a phylogenetic relic) since, in many mammalian species, turning the head about its long axis is frequently combined with biting. It fits the picture that urial rams (Schaller and Mirza 1974) occasionally approach the opponent with

Fig. 119. Marco Polo ram in rush-attack with head and neck stretched forward, treating me as an opponent during rutting season (assimilation tendency!). (Walther 1961a. Kronberg Zoo.)

Fig. 120. Neck-stretch and head-twist of a greater kudu female when approaching a subadult male freshly introduced to the group. (Walther 1964*b*. Frankfurt Zoo.)

mouth open and forcefully poke him with the tip of the muzzle in the rump, thigh, or side—a behavior resembling the application of a bite.

Since dominance displays and certain other agonistic behavior patterns (such as offensive threats, symbolic chases, pursuit marches, and mounting) are frequently shown by dominant animals, and since similar (even identical in some species) behavior patterns occur in males of certain species in the mating rituals, the question may be raised whether these behaviors are basically sexual in nature and whether a superior male may be treating an inferior as if he were an estrous female. In a study of the behavior of American mountain sheep, Geist (1971) has strongly argued in favor of this view. In studies of the behavior of oryx (Walther 1958*a*), several *Tragelaphus* species (Walther 1964*b*), and several gazelle species (Walther 1968*a*, 1978*c*), however, I came to an almost opposite conclusion. I fully agree with Geist that in a number of ungulate species an adult male treats inferior conspecifics more or less alike, regardless of sex (insofar as they are of interest to him—in many species, adult males pay no attention to the young, and in some species they also are not interested in females unless the latter are in estrus). Since females are smaller and lighter than males in the majority of the species under discussion, and, in bovids and cervids, usually have smaller horns or antlers, they naturally are inferior partners to (adult) males. Thus the males treat the females as inferiors in their encounters with them, including in mating, just as they treat younger or weaker males as subordinates in agonistic encounters. Although the addressee frequently accepts the inferior role when challenged by a dominant partner, there are cases in which he or she instead reacts with defensive counterdisplays or even fights back. This behavior is easily understood as a recipient's reaction to a basically aggressive behavior of a challenger (i.e., when the latter has treated the addressee—or the estrous female in a sexual encounter—as an inferior opponent). However, it is difficult to understand why an addressee, male or female, should react by submission or defense to a basically sexual behavior, i.e., being treated like a female. (It is unlikely that these animals share the "male bias" of certain humans.) We will come back to this problem when discussing submissive displays.

14. COURTSHIP DISPLAYS

To avoid misunderstandings, it should be emphasized from the beginning that this chapter is not intended to give a full account of all sexual activities. A number of these, such as mounting and copulation, are executive behaviors and do not belong to a discussion of communicative and expressive signals. Others which in part are also executive behaviors have been mentioned in previous chapters. Thus, little discussion will be given to how the sex partners find each other and come together, how they familiarize with each other, and how the males tend or drive or chase the females. Also, herding behavior will be excluded, as far as possible, from the discussion but will be presented later as a topic of its own. Primarily left here are behaviors which (a) occur after the sex partners have found each other and after the male is positive that the female is in mating condition but before the final sexual act has taken place, and which (b) obviously work as signals to the sex partners. Within this outlined realm, the discussion will head toward and focus on expressive displays which, as we will soon learn, are largely a male domain in hoofed mammals.

On the other hand, there are some other sexual behaviors which we cannot ignore completely because certain "trends" are recognizable in them that seem to be more or less important for the understanding of the development of courtship displays. One of these "trends" is the approach toward the sex partner and sniffing or touching of its genital region. This approach is usually made by the male and often accompanied by rather situation-specific vocalizations, which vary depending on the species from loud to very soft. The effects of these vocalizations upon the recipients, too, vary greatly in importance, but they are present in virtually all ungulate species.

There is also a very broad range as regards touching and/or licking by one or both sex partners, from species in which it is frequent and intensive to species where, except for copulation itself, the partners hardly touch each other during a mating ritual. Furthermore, there are behaviors which apparently are linked to a considerable and relatively specific arousal within the autonomic nervous system, such as urinary behavior and the erection of hair on special body regions. (Not all ungulate species which can erect their hair in certain situations do so during courtship.) It is commonplace in hoofed mammals for a female, when sexually driven by a male, to urinate and for the male to sniff her urine and perform *Flehmen*. However, in a few species, such as tapir and Indian rhino, the role of urination goes much beyond that. The female splashes urine in great quantities during the mating ritual; the male urinates considerably more copiously than usual. Some tactile, olfactory, and acoustical stimuli can release reflexlike reactions in the partner of the opposite sex, provided, of course, that he or she is in the corresponding physiological condition. Such reactions are not restricted to the aforementioned urination or to the erection of the penis in the male; for example, in relatively primitive species the male's scent, vocalizations, and/or tactile contacts may release a kind of "immobilization reflex" in the female.

Another "trend" of postures, gestures, and vocalizations in the mating rituals of hoofed mammals is linked to the male's mounting of the female; for example, the posture he assumes when placing his chin on the female's back as an initiation of mounting (which, however, is by no means found in all the species under discussion) and certain intention movements for it.

A last "trend" is linked to aggression. In an apparently still relatively primitive type of courtship, male and female actually fight each other. In a few species, the intensity of such fighting actions is only slightly diminished as compared to that in encounters between opponents of the same sex. More frequently the fighting techniques are the same as in combats with rivals, but the intensity is considerably diminished. A similar intensity scale can be found in the male's sexual pursuit of the female. The range goes from a full-gallop chase to a walking pursuit (mating march). The latter is nothing but a slightly modified form of the pursuit march as it occurs in agonistic encounters.

Physical aggression toward the sex partner is progressively replaced by expressive displays in advanced forms of hoofed mammals, such as cervids and bovids. Theoretically such displays could have originated from approach tendencies and sexual behaviors as well as from aggression. In fact, however, most of them are related to aggressive behavior, and even those which primarily appear to be ritualizations of sexual behaviors or approach tendencies usually have at least an aggressive undertone. Threat displays, as used in hostile interactions between male opponents, can also be used by males in the mating rituals; however, this tends to be rather an exception than a rule. More often the males show dominance displays in either the same form as used in agonistic encounters among males or in slightly modified forms. Finally, the males of some species have "courtship displays" in the strict sense which are infrequently, if at all, used in encounters with other males.

In the mating rituals, these displays apparently serve three major functions: (a) to solicit urine from the female that the male can sniff and, in most of the species under discussion, test it by *Flehmen* (the soliciting and testing of the female's urine often occurs so independently of other sexual behavior that one could argue whether it should be considered as part of the mating ritual; however, the male's displays in soliciting the female's urination response are commonly the same as in true courtship), (b) to "persuade" (Tinbergen 1953) the female to tolerate the male's close approach which may be said to be the major function of these displays in ungulates, and (c) possibly to synchronize the internal sexual state of the partners.

Even courtship displays in the strict sense (i.e., those displays which are not used toward other males) can also occur in herding the females by the male (which in at least some of the species is not necessarily and immediately connected to sexual behavior), in "pushing" female conspecifics ahead during migration, in "voting" over the marching direction when a herd begins to move, in coordinating group activities, etc. Thus, the term "courtship displays" should not be taken in a strictly literal way but only as an abbreviation. While it refers to one function which may be said to be very important, this is not the single function. Precisely speaking, these displays are used predominantly by males, predominantly during encounters with females. Although they are typical for sexual encounters, they are not restricted to them.

In all the situations, the courtship displays basically affect the females as threats do males and, although the courtship displays are phenotypically different from (recent) threat and dominance displays, there are unmistakable connections between them and agonistic behaviors. The most elaborate courtship displays in the more highly evolved groups of hoofed mammals can be described as special kinds of dominance displays that probably originated from ancestral fighting behavior. The corresponding hypothesis (discussed in the chapter on dominance displays) states that, especially in the bovids, ancestral fighting techniques were largely replaced by the "modern" horn fight during evolution, whereas expressive displays (intention movements) related to ancestral fighting techniques were retained. Such displays owe their aggressive nature to their origins; however, since they do not have an immediate connection to the recent fighting techniques of the species, they are milder forms of aggression than the threat displays (which refer to the recent fighting techniques). These expressive displays only mildly intimidate or challenge the partner—enough to diminish his aggressiveness or his avoidance tendencies released by the other's close approach, but not enough to release true flight, severe defense, or even a counterattack. Thus, they are tailor made for mating rituals of the ungulate type where the male approaches the female and establishes some kind of dominance over her. Indeed, male dominance is apparently a prerequisite for successful mating in many of these animals. If, either because the male is too young or for some other reason, the female turns out to be superior, this may mean the end of the mating activity.

The reactions of the females fully correspond to the basically aggressive character of the males' displays in the mating rituals. Most commonly, the females respond by withdrawal; however, in some species or in certain situations the female may instead respond by flight at a gallop, by defensive threats and submissive behaviors (head-low postures are particularly frequent), by appeasing behavior (e.g., grooming the male), and, in rare cases, by fighting and/or offensive threats or dominance displays equivalent to those of the male.

It is noteworthy that there are few true courtship behaviors or other genuine sexual displays of the females in hoofed mammals. The exceptions include the mare's estrous face in certain equids which, however, seems to be closely related to a threat behavior (as previously discussed); certain vocalizations indicative of the female's mating condition, predominantly found in more primitive ungulate species and possibly representing only a high level of general excitement; the female's urination in response to the male's approach and/or driving actions, which, however, also occurs in anestrous females (in addition to which urination is not a specific sexual behavior); and some behaviors directly related to copulation, such as lifting the tail, standing for the male's mount, leaning into the male's mount, etc. Otherwise, most behaviors shown by ungulate females during courtship are either male sexual behaviors, such as the female's mounting of the male (rather infrequent in the majority of nondomestic ungulates), or behaviors of inferiority such as submission, flight, and withdrawal. Aggressive behaviors on the part of the female are generally defensive reactions against the "violation" of her individual distance (Hediger 1941) by the approaching male. Occasionally, aggressively toned behaviors of the female may also serve to invite and stimulate a sexually inactive male to further interactions. Geist (1971), in his description of the "courtship" of an estrous ewe in Stone's sheep (Ovis dalli stonei), gives an instructive example of the latter.

So far the discussion has been somewhat general and abstract. The following is meant to provide a number of concrete examples of these generalizations. At the same time, I will try to give the reader a "feeling" for the previously mentioned "trends" in the mating rituals of hoofed mammals. We will begin with comparatively primitive rituals and progressively discuss more advanced behaviors, largely following the taxonomic classification system. Since, on the whole, the courtship of odd-toed ungulates appears less elaborate than that of even-toed ungulates, the situation in odd-toed ungulates will be presented first.

In Malayan tapir, as a representative of the most primitive group of (recent) odd-toed ungulates, according to von Richter (1966), the male's courtship includes loud vocalizations (whistles and a kind of "coughing"). He chases the female at a gallop. Sometimes he may temporarily gallop in front of her. The female also utters shrill whistles, and both partners splash urine in great quantities. In pauses during this driving, the animals stand in reverse-parallel position, sniffing each other's genitals and frequently pushing each other with their shoulders. The male tries to place his head under the female's belly or to bite her hind legs, and the female also tries to bite the male's legs. As both partners try to avoid being bitten by turning their hindquarters away, they begin to circle in reverse-parallel position. In fierce interactions, they may even sit down to protect their hind legs from being bitten. (All these behaviors strikingly resemble the fighting among zebra stallions.) Usually these interactions end with a renewed chase at a gallop. As the partners become more acquainted with each other (all observations on mating behavior of tapir were with captive animals), the driving actions become less violent. The male now tries to place his head on the female's croup (Fig. 121) as a preparation for mounting. When initiating the driving, the male Malayan tapir has sometimes been seen jumping to and fro in front of the female, throwing his head upward and waving it to the right and the left ("dance"—von Richter 1966).

According to Schenkel and Lang (1969), the mating behavior of the Indian rhinoceros (which also was observed exclusively in captivity) is in principle similar to that of the Malayan tapir. Here, too, the bull drives the cow at a gallop in the beginning, and the roles may occasionally change, with the bull temporarily running in front of the female. The cow breathes with whistling sounds, and both partners utter grunting vocalizations. The female splashes urine, and the bull urinates more frequently than usual. In driving, the bull tries to place his head under the female's belly and to lift her up, and he often bites her flank and hindquarters. In pauses during driving, the animals frequently stand facing each other and may fight with their horns or bite each other. Sometimes they also stand in reverse-parallel position and suddenly both swing their heads toward each other's flank. As with the tapir, both may simultaneously step aside with their hindquarters

Fig. 121. Male Malayan tapir (*Tapirus indicus*) places his head on the female's croup as a preparation for mounting. (von Richter 1966. Photo: W. von Richter. Nuremberg Zoo.)

and circle in reverse-parallel position. When standing together, the female may also assume a sagittal T-position and place her snout under the male's inguinal region, or she may position herself behind him and place her snout between his hind legs.

Schenkel and Lang (1969) interpret these last behaviors as infantilism, i.e., "symbolic suckling" by the female. Other authors have expressed similar views with respect to a few other ungulate species in which either the male or the female sometimes behaves this way. It is my opinion that most of these interpretations (a possible exception is discussed later) are vulnerable or at least premature. When the *female* places her nose under the *male's* abdomen—as is the case in Indian rhino—it is unlikely that her "symbolic suckling" should have any meaning for the male who never nurses the young. Furthermore, a female may show the same posture when sniffing or touching the male's genital region, i.e., an olfactory testing or a tactile sexual stimulation. Finally, in both male and female placing the head under the other's belly can be an intention movement for lifting up the other (as actually happens in aggressive interactions of tapirs, rhinos, swine, and some other ungulates). These possible alternatives are routinely ignored by those who interpret the behavior as "symbolic suckling."

In black rhinoceros (Schenkel and Lang 1969), the bull may follow the tracks of an estrous cow and finally approach her at a distance. When she rushes toward him, he usually retreats but remains in the vicinity. These behaviors are followed by a tending phase in which bull and cow stay close together. The male may perform the "complex bull's ritual" described in previous chapter, in which aggressive components (object aggression) are recognizable. Occasionally a bull may gently push the female with his horns, but no true fighting between the partners has been observed in the mating rituals of black rhino in the wild.

The same tending bond is also found in the square-lipped rhino (Owen-Smith 1974, 1975). Here, too, some mild aggressions may occur in the beginning of the interactions between male and female. The bull makes a frontal approach accompanied by hic-throbbing sounds, and stands staring at the female from a range of a few meters. The cow reacts to such an approach by snorts or the snarl-threat and will sometimes drive a bull back with a clash of horns. The bull readily responds to the female's threats and attacks by giving way. Later, when the male approaches the female from behind with his head held high, the cow may again initially ward him off with snorts, the snarl-threat, or a clash of horns. However, the bull now continues his advance until he finally rests his chin on her rump and starts mounting attempts. The cow responds by ejecting a squirt of urine, which is sniffed by the bull, and she will stand to receive his mount.

In summary, the mating rituals of tapirs and rhinos include vocalizations, typical of high-intensity excitement, by both sexes, and in at least some of the species the sounds are quite loud. Urination plays a much greater role than is the case with most of the other ungulates, and it occurs in both sexes. In tapirs and Indian rhino, urine is splashed during the entire ritual, indicating the importance of olfactory stimuli. As in all the ungulates, the female's urine probably contains components indicative of her estrous condition, i.e., an "information" which is simply given by the animal's physiological state. Tactile stimulation is also present. The male's placing his head on the female's croup, as an initiation of mounting and copulation, appears to be very typical in all the species under discussion. Furthermore, the involvement of aggressive actions is very clear. Most of them (chasing, biting, pushing with shoulders, horn-to-horn clashes) are only slightly ritualized fighting behaviors, i.e., their intensity may be somewhat diminished as compared to their use in encounters among opponents. Most striking is the fighting between male and female in (captive) Malayan tapir and Indian rhino, although it is not entirely absent in any of the described species. Threat displays, such as the snarl-threat in female white rhino, are identical with the threats in agonistic encounters. Special and elaborate visual displays of the males are infrequent and more or less dubious with respect to their character of courtship displays. In Malayan tapir, there is the possible exception of the male's "dance," but this could also be some kind of threat or dominance display, since it may possibly occur in encounters between opponents of the same sex (which were not observed in the captive animals). In black rhino, the "complex bull's ritual" also occurs in situations other than mating and is not directed only toward females (Schenkel and Lang 1969), so one can hardly speak of it as a special courtship display. Owen-Smith (1974) mentions a raised-head posture in the white rhino bull and interprets it as an intention movement for placing his head on the female's back and for mounting her. Schenkel and Lang (1969) describe the same or a very similar posture in black rhino that apparently also occurs in encounters with male rivals. Typically, the initiation of mounting by placing the head on the partner's back belongs to the category of "sexual" behaviors with at least an undertone of aggression. Mounting and all intention movements for it, in ungulates, have this aggressive undertone, since "mounting" as a fighting technique—throwing the weight of the body on the opponent in order to bring him down—occurs in quite a number of species.

In horses and their relatives, certain behaviors of the male, mainly the head-low posture of the stallion, have been categorized as "courtship displays," but they seem primarily to belong rather to herding than to sexual behavior, and they are not different from threats in agonistic encounters. Possibly one posture of the (domestic) horse stallion, with the head pulled acutely toward the neck and a kind of prancing trot (Zeeb 1963), may be somewhat closer to courtship, but this is not certain either. The mating ritual of horses and zebras generally consists of naso-nasal greeting and naso-genital testing. Grooming of the mare by the stallion and reciprocal grooming between both partners are frequent; however, as Klingel (1967) emphasizes, at least in plains zebra, such "grooming associations" between the stallion and a particular mare also occur when the female is not in estrus.

In Grevy's zebra (Klingel 1972), the stallion drives the mare for a while, "steering" her with his head or cutting her path when she approaches the boundary of his territory. He lowers his head, raises his tail and loudly roars during driving and mounting. Violent chasing by the stallion to the exhaustion of the mare has been mentioned in wild and domestic ass in earlier literature but has not been confirmed by recent studies (Klingel 1975, Lang 1980). The stallion mounts the mare several times without intromission before he copulates. A special facial expression of the copulating Grevy's male (Fig. 122—Zeeb and Kleinschmidt 1963) resembles a diminished version of the estrous face of the mare. In Grevy's zebra, the stallion frequently bites the mare's nape in copulation (Klingel 1972).

Fig. 122. "Copulation face" of the mounting stallion and estrous face (maximum intensity) of the mare in Grevy's zebra. (Zeeb and Kleinschmidt 1963. Photo: K. Zeeb. Stuttgart Zoo.)

In all Equidae species, when the mare is not fully receptive she may ward off the stallion by kicking with her hind legs. Except for domestic horses, the receptive Equidae mares show the estrous face. The estrous females stand with their hind legs apart and their tails raised at an angle of about 45°. This posture is most conspicuously displayed by young mares of plains zebra (Klingel 1967) and by horse mares (Tyler 1972), even when there is no stallion in attendance. The males are attracted from a distance by this female posture. In plains zebra, this results in the abduction of the young mares from the parental harem groups by young stallions who are in the process of establishing harems of their own. It has been proved that the posture, not the smell, is the decisive stimulus, since plains zebra under the influence of certain drugs (injected by "capture gun" to immobilize them for artificial marking) display the same posture, and are courted and even mounted by stallions (Klingel 1967).

In summary, in the mating rituals of the Equidae, olfactory testing of the other's condition, particularly the male's sniffing of the female's vulva and urine, followed by his *Flehmen*, are recognizable. Urination by the mare may be induced by the male's presence and/or his driving actions, but there is no continuous splashing of urine comparable to that in tapirs and Indian rhino. (These behaviors are the same in the ungulate species yet to be discussed; therefore, they will not be repeated.) Vocalizations—at times and in certain species, very loud vocalizations—particularly by males are present, but they are more or less the same as those in position advertising and/or calling for social contact. Similarly, tactile contacts, such as in greeting and grooming the partner, obviously play an important role in courtship but are not restricted to the mating rituals in Equidae: they generally occur among social partners who are "on good terms." One may see specific sexual tactile stimulations in the male's placing his chin on the female's croup and his repeated mounts before copulation, but these behaviors are so closely linked to the execution of the sexual act that they can hardly be considered expressive displays. In like fashion, the female's striking estrous stance is not primarily a communicative display that addresses a partner since, as mentioned above, it also occurs in the absence of any male. Of course, when a male is present, it releases strong reactions in him. This is the first case of a clearly visual sexual stimulus which we encounter in our discussion of mating rituals in odd-toed ungulates. Aggressive acts such as chases, the female's defense against the male's close approach, and the male's biting the female's nape during copulation occur in some of the species, but usually there is no fighting between the partners comparable to that described in tapirs and Indian rhino. If such fights occur at all (as has been suggested in the case of the ass by certain authors), they apparently represent exceptional disagreements between individual partners and not obligatory parts of the mating ritual. The mare's estrous face probably evolved from a threat behavior, but it is uncertain whether it functions as a definite signal to the male. No specific and elaborate courtship displays of the males are known in Equidae. Threat displays may occur in courting stallions, but are considerably more frequent and typical of herding behavior.

I must begin our consideration of even-toed ungulates with the statement that no detailed descriptions of mating behavior of hippopotamus are known to me. In some Nonruminantia, especially swine, tactile, vocal, and olfactory stimuli seem to be particularly important in the male's courtship to induce the female to stand still. This is most striking in the domestic pig (Signoret et al. 1960), where the male's nosing of the female's vulva, body, and sides, and his weight on her back in mounting, release an immobilization reflex in the estrous sow. In about 50 percent of the animals, this reflex can be released experimentally by exerting pressure on the estrous female's back, even when no male is present. The male's scent and his grunting, uttered while he is following her and throughout the whole mating ritual, can have the same effect. Of course, the immobilization reflex is most reliably released when the sow can simultaneously smell the male's scent, hear his "mating song," and feel his touch (rule of heterogeneous summation—Seitz 1940), as is normally the case.

In warthog (Frädrich 1974) as well as in wild boar (Beuerle 1975), the male also follows closely behind the female, trying to keep his snout disk in contact with her vulva. He utters rhythmical vocalizations which Frädrich (1974) adequately compares to the sound of a running motor, "massages" her body with his snout disk, and finally places his chin on her back before he mounts. Furthermore, the males of both species show a broadside display, with raised head and erected mane, in reverse parallel position (Simpson 1964) or in lateral T-position, in front of the female (Beuerle 1975). These displays are similar to dominance displays in agonistic encounters. At least in the wild boar, there occur other aggressive behaviors, particularly on the part of the male, which might elucidate the aforementioned "massaging" of the female's body.

According to Beuerle (1975), the male wild boar follows the female's tracks with deeply lowered head. When he has reached her, he lifts her tail with his snout disk and smells and licks her vulva. When this olfactory test indicates estrus and the sow does not run away, the male positions himself beside her or laterally in front of her. He places his snout under her belly and sometimes lifts her up. Moving his head upward from a head-low posture, he pushes the sow's belly, flank, and the underside of her neck with his snout. In this "massaging" as well as in lifting up the female's body, the male's head movements are basically the same as during a fight with a male rival but are considerably diminished in intensity. Occasionally, the male may gently bite the female's legs, or, standing more or less face to face with her, may breathe out at her. In the beginning of the mating ritual the sow usually runs away when approached by the male. The male then drives her with the aforementioned rhythmical grunting which, however, does not have an immediate immobilizing effect upon the wild boar female. Thus, the pair may trot over considerable distances.

In wild boar, the driven female reacts to the male's chin leaning upon her back by turning around and facing him; he responds by naso-nasal contact and breathing out at her. She may vehemently beat with her head against the male's head or bite him. Young males may be put to flight, but strong adult males simply accept the female's aggression without defending themselves. The same disregard by adult courting males for the females' aggression can also be observed in a number of ruminant species.

In peccary (Sowls 1974), naso-nasal contacts, sniffing of the partner's scent gland on the back, and reciprocal nuzzling and grooming initiate male-female encounters as well as most meetings between friendly partners. The actions entirely associated with reproduction are similar to those of swine and also show some aggressive features.

The male sniffs the female's vulva, the female sniffs the male's penis, and both male and female may nip the partner's neck and shoulders.

In summary, for the mating rituals of swine and peccary, scents, vocalizations, and, above all, tactile stimuli play important roles, and may even release an immobilization reflex in the female. It is of interest that this immobilization reflex is considerably less pronounced in the wild forms than in domestic swine. Tactile stimulations of the female, such as the "massaging" of her body by the male, the driving male's lengthy tactile contacts with her vulva, and the placing of the male's chin on her back, are more prominent than in any other group of ungulates. Beuerle's (1975) observations on wild boar suggest that this "massage" is a strongly ritualized (diminished) form of fighting behavior. Occasionally the female may defend herself by biting, and, at least in warthog, bush pig, and wild boar, the males may show broadside displays very similar to those used as dominance displays in agonistic encounters.

In contrast to all the other ungulates, tylopods copulate lying down. According to Pilters (1954, 1956), male camel and dromedary show the same threat and dominance displays toward the females that they use in aggressive interactions with other males. The female may approach the male and place herself in reverse position in front of him, spreading her legs, curling up her tail, and urinating. The male dromedary sniffs her urine and performs *Flehmen*. He may place his neck over her neck (neck-fighting), bite her legs, and/or jump at the female ("mounting") to force her down to the lying position. When she runs away, he drives her and tries to stop her by biting her hind legs. Sometimes, a female may defend by the same behaviors, and then the mating ritual, at best, differs from true fighting only in intensity. Female dromedaries roar loudly during copulation.

In the New World tylopods, the guanaco and its wild and domesticated relatives, the males may show threat displays toward the females similar to those in encounters with rivals. This is particularly frequent when a female tries to ward off the male or when, in captivity, the male is separated from the female so that he can see her but not come to her. The courting male approaches the female with ears laid back and clicking vocalizations. Before he drives her, he sniffs her genital region. A receptive female also utters clicking sounds and sniffs the male's genital and anal region. A nonreceptive female defends by kicking with a hind leg, spitting, or even attacking him. In driving, the male follows the female, walking, or chases her at a gallop, depending on her resistance. He erects his neck and utters very typical grunting vocalizations (Pilters 1956). Frequently, he circles her and snaps at her forelegs, or he mounts in order to wrestle her down to the lying position. If the female is not cooperative enough, the male can bite her quite severely, and he presses her neck down or bites her nape. If the female flees, he may try to bite her tail or hind legs. In domestic llama, all the male displays and acts of aggression can be lacking. The male simply mounts the female again and again until she lies down (Pilters 1954, 1956).

In summary of mating rituals of tylopods, olfactory testing and vocalizations certainly are not absent; however, the prominent feature is the aggression by the male toward the female. In the case of the female's defense, it can easily result in true fighting between the partners. The male's displays are the same as or very similar to the threats in hostile interactions among males. His acts of overt aggression consist of biting (her legs), neck-fighting, jumping at the female, and pressing her down with the weight of his body. When the male jumps at the female from behind, which is quite frequent since the driving male follows behind the female, his behavior corresponds phenotypically to the sexual mounting and the copulatory behavior of other ungulates. In tylopods, however, it is not copulation but an aggressive attempt to bring the female down to a lying position.

When we now proceed to the discussion of courtship behavior in the Ruminantia, it must be emphasized that their most primitive group, the Tragulidae, appear to be more primitive in many regards—one of which is their mating behavior—than all the recent odd-toed ungulates and the tylopods.

Three of the four Tragulidae species have been studied up to now and relatively great differences have been found within them. For example, Dubost (1975) describes a suckling-like licking of the female's udder region by the male as an obligatory part of the courtship of the African water chevrotain. Robin (1979) observed this behavior only occasionally in lesser Malayan mouse deer, and Ralls et al. (1975) do not mention it at all in the larger Malayan mouse deer. In water chevrotain, the female freezes in response to the male's squeaking vocalizations, and only this swinelike immobilization reflex of the female makes bodily contact possible among the partners (Dubost 1975). Apparently Robin (1979) did not find an immobilization reflex in lesser Malayan mouse deer, and Ralls et al. (1975) even emphasize that the female larger Malayan mouse deer does not freeze in a reflexlike response to each cry of the male, as described for water chevrotain. On the other hand, the same authors found a marking of the female by the male with his intermandibular (inter-ramal) glands in larger Malayan mouse deer, and Robin (1979) vividly describes how the male of lesser Malayan mouse deer marks the female, places his chin on her back, and presses her hindquarters down before mounting her, whereas the marking of the female is completely lacking in water chevrotain, according to Dubost (1975). Ralls et al. (1975) mention that females of larger Malayan mouse deer, when sexually pursued by a male, often flush their tails, squeal, and emit a squirt of urine to the rear, and Robin (1979) observed a pulling back of the corner of the mouth in the female of lesser Malayan mouse deer when she was trying to escape from the male's approach. Again, these behaviors were always described from only one of the Tragulidae species, but not from the others.

Since all these studies of mouse deer behavior were made in captivity and with relatively few specimens, it is, in my opinion, uncertain whether the described differences are truly species-specific or whether they are caused by different captive conditions (e.g., differences in the familiarity of the partners with each other). I am particularly cautious with respect to the male's suckling behavior. A partner placing his nose under the other's belly is a behavior that occurs in the mating rituals of several ungulate species, and it has been readily—often too readily—interpreted as an infantilism and a "symbolic suckling." In contrast to other cases (p. 263), the observations of suckling-like behavior by the males in water chevrotain and lesser Malayan mouse deer are clearly correct, since the female "supports" the male's "suckling behavior" by lifting a hind leg as she does when nursing a fawn. Thus, I do not challenge Dubost's and Robin's observations, and I certainly am not among those who think that the behavior of captive animals would always and necessarily be different from that of wild animals of the same species. However, I know from my own experience with various species that suckling is a behavior which can be continued in captivity for considerably longer periods than under natural conditions and that there sometimes are fully adult animals which suckle or at least try to do so when an opportunity is given and the female does not strongly reject it. This can occasionally happen with almost any species, and it obviously is a phenomenon linked to the captive conditions.

In summary, certain vocalizations and scents, which are more or less physiologically linked to the animal's mating condition, and certain tactile stimulations of supposedly erogenous zones of the partner's body, seem to be the prominent features of the mating ritual in Tragulidae. Apparently these stimuli release rather fixed sexual reactions in the partner, such as the female water chevrotain's immobilization reflex, strongly resembling that of the domestic sow. The male's pressing down the female by his chin could be interpreted as a somewhat aggressively toned behavior but it could also be said to be more closely related to the marking behavior of these animals. The female's occasional "grimacing" (pulling back the corner of the mouth) in lesser Malayan mouse deer might be related to the facial expression of a threat, like the estrous face in certain equids. Otherwise there is apparently no aggression between the sex partners, and no special male courtship postures or gestures have been described.

The courtship rituals of the other Ruminantia, the highly evolved Pecora, have one feature in common with those of the Tragulidae. Fights between male and female are not obligatory components of the mating ritual in any of the species. If they occur at all, they are brief and relatively mild fights which may occasionally develop from the female's defense against the male's approach. In many species, even such brief, occasional fights between the sex partners are entirely lacking. If a female becomes aggressive toward a courting male, he usually ignores it (Fig. 130b) continuing his courtship as if nothing had happened. One-sided, more or less ritualized, physical aggressions of the male toward the female occur in only a few species. For example, driving giraffe bulls may sometimes push the female's shoulder, flank, and hindquarters with their "horns" (Backhaus 1960a). Even chasing the female at a gallop is by no means frequent in the mating rituals of the Ruminantia (it can be different in herding).

Olfactory testing of the female's genitals and/or her urine is found in all ruminants, and is followed by the male's *Flehmen* in most of the species. Tactile stimulation of the female's genital region and hindquarters by licking and touching her with the tongue, nose, chin, or neck is also widespread. In at least some of the cervid species, the male regularly licks the female from her rump, along her back, and up to her neck before he mounts her. In bovids, tactile stimulation varies considerably, from species where courting males frequently and intensively touch the females (for example, nilgai bulls by intensive licking of the female's croup, or greater kudu bulls with their ritualized neck-fight), to species in which the males hardly touch the females during the entire mating ritual (for example, Grant's and Thomson's gazelle) including mounting and copulation, where touch is restricted to the partners' genital regions. Likewise, the male's placing his head or neck on the female's back before mounting is found in quite a number of the Pecora species but far from all of them, and appeasement by licking the face, neck, withers, and shoulders is even rarer. In short, the importance of tactile stimulation during courtship varies widely.

In addition to male marking of the female in certain species, which was discussed in a previous chapter, the males of some species presumably emit odors from glands opened widely during courtship. These are predominantly the preorbital glands (Fig. 4) in most of the species, the subauricular glands in pronghorn, and possibly the interdigital glands opened in connection with the foreleg kick in certain species. Whether tail movements or postures of the male are connected to the emission of scents (e.g., from circumanal glands) remains unknown. In contrast to the female ruminants which usually lift their tails, at least when they have reached the peak of the heat, males show a whole spectrum of tail postures during courtship. These range from species in which the posture of the tail does not differ at all from the usual (e.g., kudu) to species which stretch it more or less horizontally (e.g., blesbok), raise it vertically (e.g., nilgai), or even curl it forward over the back (e.g., Indian blackbuck). It is unlikely that these tail movements or postures play a role as visual signals to the females since the courting male usually is oriented with his head toward the female and thus she cannot see much of his tail. Vocalizations of the courting males are probably present in all the species, and they often are quite situation-specific; one may speak of "rutting calls," but they greatly vary in loudness. At one extreme are the loud roars from an open mouth, e.g., the roaring or "bellowing" in a number of cervid species (one may question whether these vocalizations belong to the mating ritual since they also occur in other situations during rutting season and may often come closer to position advertisements). At the other extreme is the soft grumbling with closed mouth and an even softer clicking with the tongue. Generally, tongue movements, particularly a flicking of the tongue in and out of the mouth, are frequent in courting Ruminantia males. Vibration sounds uttered through the nose may also range from relatively loud sounds to those so soft that one cannot hear them unless standing very close to the vocalizing male. Even then, one may still mistake male courtship calls for other sounds, such as the vocalizations of a bird, because their softness is so "out of proportion" to the size of these animals. For example, when watching the mating behavior of bushbuck in a zoological garden for the first time, it took me quite a while to realize that the twittering sounds I was hearing did not come from a little bird in the vicinity but were vocalizations of the courting bushbuck male.

The tactile stimulations, scents, and vocalizations seem to be of only secondary importance in Pecora males. Their most prominent and striking courtship behaviors are visual displays—movements and postures, particularly those of head and neck and sometimes also of the forelegs. Only a few of the behaviors are threats, but most of them are dominance displays or courtship displays in the strict sense outlined above.

Let us first discuss a few behaviors which are only slightly ritualized forms of aggression. Although chasing the female at a trot or gallop may occasionally occur in quite a number of the species under discussion, it is an obligatory component of the mating ritual in only a few of them. For example, it is mandatory for certain cervids, such as axis deer (Fuchs 1976) and roe deer, and it is also frequent in pronghorn. In these species, a female will sometimes make a "teasing run" to release the male's chase. More commonly, the male drives the female ahead at a walk, as he would an inferior male opponent after a hostile encounter. This mating march is a ritualized withdrawal of the female from the pursuing male which can turn into a true withdrawal or flight if the female has not yet reached the peak of the heat. The mating march is a basic component of the mating rituals in many of the species.

In oryx, addax, and sable and roan antelope, the mating march has been largely replaced by a more stationary performance, the mating whirl-around (*Paarungskreisen*—Walther 1958a). The male and the female step around each other in reverse-parallel orientation (a behavior that also occurs in agonistic encounters between male opponents in these species), the female showing a head-low posture like a subordinate male (Fig. 123).

In oxen, the mating ritual has become even more stationary. Here, male and female stand in parallel (Fig. 124) or reverse-parallel position most of the time (McHugh 1958, Schloeth 1961a, Schaller 1967). During this tending, the male seldom shows a special display, but he remains side by side with the female while executing the usual maintenance activities (standing, grazing, moving, resting, etc.). Tending is also common in a number of cervid species such as caribou (Bergerud 1974) and axis deer (Fuchs 1976).

As we know from previous discussions, broadside orientations commonly can be considered to be dominance displays in hoofed mammals, and such lateral positions also frequently occur in the mating rituals of Pecora species. They may occur in parallel or reverse-parallel orientation as in the tending of oxen and in the mating whirl-around of the oryx-related species, or with the male blocking the female's path in lateral T-position of bison and greater kudu, or in walking in lateral escort with the female as in the spiral-horned antelopes (genus *Tragelaphus*).

Most of the behaviors mentioned up to now show fairly obvious relationships and resemblances to behaviors used in agonistic

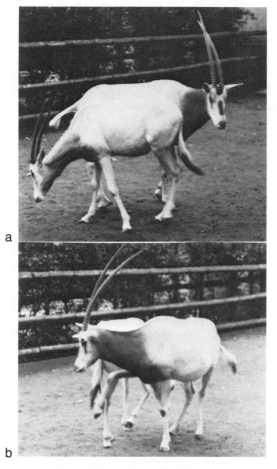

Fig. 123. Mating whirl-around in scimitar-horned oryx (*Oryx dammah*). a. The female (foreground) remains in head-low posture during circling in reverse-parallel position. b. "Knock-kneed" foreleg kick of the male (Walther 1966*a*. Hanover Zoo.)

encounters. However, even when we now come to other, more specialized courtship displays, there are hardly any gestures or postures that do not occur as threat and dominance displays in other ungulate species.

The neck-stretch (head-and-neck-stretched-forward posture = *Kopf-Hals-Vorstrecken* in Walther 1964*b*, 1968*a*, *Überstrecken* in Walther 1958, low-stretch in Geist 1971) is one of the commonest atti-

Fig. 124. Tending in parallel position in yak.
(Walther 1979. Zurich Zoo.)

tudes of courting Pecora males. It has been found in all the Cervidae
species investigated up to now, where the neck-stretch almost always
occurs when a courting male approaches a female (Fig. 125), particularly, although not exclusively, when he approaches the female from
behind to touch, sniff, or lick her genital region. Thus one may come
to the conclusion that here the neck-stretch is predominantly the expression of an intensified approach and, perhaps even more specifically, a (ritualized) intention movement for olfactory and/or gustatory testing. Even here, however, there are some indications for the
possible involvement of aggressive tendencies. For example, Pruitt
(1960) interprets the neck-stretch as a courtship display in male
caribou but as a threat in caribou females. When the neck-stretch is
used as an agonistic display by the females, a suspicion that it is not
completely free of aggressive components when used by courting
males of the same species may be justified. Moreover, in a number of
cervid species, such as caribou (Bergerud 1974) and axis deer (Fuchs
1976), the males also assume the neck-stretch attitude when standing
or moving parallel to the female, in a position from which they cannot sniff or lick the female's vulva and where something other than
mere approach tendencies appears to be involved. As a third variation, in certain cervid species (e.g., sika deer), the courting male may
raise his nose from a neck-stretch posture and gnash his teeth as in
certain aggressive displays.

In the horned ungulates the neck-stretch is also very common in
the courtship rituals, but with certain species-specific differences. In

Fig. 125. Moose bull (*Alces alces*) following the cow with head-and-neck-stretched-forward attitude.

all the Bovidae species, the male may occasionally stretch head and neck forward when touching, licking, or sniffing a female's vulva. In some species, such as oryx antelope, this movement apparently is used only for this purpose and in this situation. It is neither an obligatory component of the courtship ritual nor a special display. In some other species, such as sheep and goats, nilgai, hartebeest, blesbok (Lynch 1974), bontebok (David 1973), impala, and mountain goat (Geist 1965), the neck-stretch is a special display, frequently combined with tongue flicking or other species-specific additions. These include a vertical erection of the tail in nilgai, flapping the tail over the back in ibex, roaring or snorting vocalizations and/or rotating the head around its long axis (twist) and foreleg kicks (see below) in sheep and goats, raised hair crest (on the forehead—Fig. 126) and stiff-legged walking in dikdik (Tinley 1969).

In the spiral-horned antelopes (*Tragelaphus*), the neck-stretch (Fig. 127) is an intention movement for neck-fighting. It is combined with very soft vocalizations ("imm-imm-imm"), but in bongo sometimes with loud bleating (Hamann 1979), and occasionally with tongue flicking or, at least in lesser kudu (Leuthold 1979) and bushbuck, with symbolic snapping. In greater kudu, a driving bull accompanies the female in lateral escort (alternating with following behind her), and places his neck over hers from time to time (Fig. 128a). He may also frontally approach her and place his neck over hers from the neck-stretch posture (Walther 1958a, 1964b). Likewise, in nyala, the male maneuvers the female into a submissive (head-low) posture by pressing her neck down with his own (Anderson 1980).

Fig. 126. Neck-stretch in a courting Kirk's dikdik male (*Rhyncho-tragus kirki*). Note the raised crest and the anteriorly extended nose. (Redrawn from Tinley 1969.)

Fig. 127. Neck-stretch of a greater kudu bull in lateral escort of the female (Walther 1964*b*.)

This ritualized neck-fight during courtship is less frequent and pronounced in other *Tragelaphus* species (lesser kudu, bushbuck, sitatunga), although it may occasionally occur in all of them. These males frequently rub the sides of their stretched necks with winding movements on the female's hindquarters (Fig. 128b), and show a pronounced neck-stretch during lateral escort. Thus, their neck-stetches still appear to be related to neck-fighting, and a connection to mere naso-genital testing is unlikely. The relation between the neck-stretch display and neck-fighting, of course, is not impossible in other bovids, but it is often not as clear and obvious as in the spiral-horned antelopes.

In many sheep and goat species (Fig. 129), the neck-stretch (low

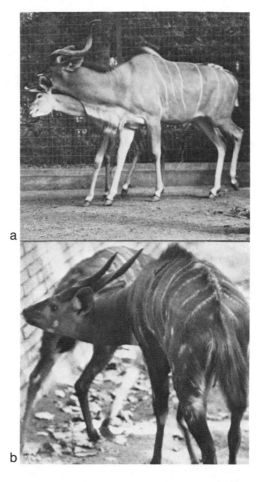

Fig. 128a. Greater kudu bull (with broken right horn) places his neck over the cow's nape (ritualized neck-fighting) while driving her in lateral escort. b. Driving bushbuck male (*Tragelaphus scriptus*) rubs his stretched neck and head at the female's hindquarters. (Walther 1964*a*. Frankfurt Zoo; Rome Zoo.)

stretch—Geist 1971) is often combined with a twist of the head, a turning of the head around its long axis so that one cheek points more or less to the ground. When the twist is performed during the male's lateral escort with the female, his chin is always turned toward her (Fig. 129b). It is certain that this twist has nothing to do with "symbolic suckling." The male's position relative to the female does not agree with this "suckling hypothesis," and only Equidae foals twist their heads in suckling. Young bovids do not. On the other hand, for example, red deer may stretch head and neck forward and twist their heads when aggressively snapping at an opponent. This behavior phenotypically corresponds very well to that of courting goat and sheep males. Thus, neck-stretch and twist in sheep and goats may possibly have evolved from ancestral biting behavior.

Fig. 129a. Neck-stretch with tongue flicking, tail flapped over the back, and ("knock-kneed") foreleg kick in ibex (*Capra ibex ibex*—the male can also stiffly stretch his foreleg during the kick in this species). The (resting) female responds with symbolic butting in this case. b. Neck-stretch with head-twist and foreleg kick in Afghan urial during lateral escort. (Walther 1977a.)

The neck-stetch is also a courtship display in a number of gazelle species but, in contrast to sheep and goats, the gazelle males do not twist their heads. Tongue flicking is also rare. In Thomson's gazelle (Fig. 4), the neck-stretch frequently transforms into or alternates with a head-and-neck-forward/upward posture or with a nose-up posture (Walther 1964a). This sequence, i.e., the nose-up following the neck-stretch, also does not support the hypothesis that the neck-stretch is derived from naso-genital testing. An apparently somewhat similar alternation between lowering the head and bobbing it up is described in mule deer (Geist 1966a).

Two other male courtship displays found in a number of Pecora species are the erect posture (Fig. 130, 131b) and the head-and-neck-forward/upward posture (Fig. 131a). Both can be temporarily exaggerated by a nose-up movement in which the nose points almost vertically upward (Fig. 4b). In principal, all three are displays in their own right, and in certain species, such as okapi (Walther 1960b), they are easily distinguishable (Fig. 131). On the other hand, for example, gazelles and their relatives frequently display during walking, and, since the male's neck leans somewhat forward when he walks it is hard to say whether this is now a head-and-neck-forward/upward

Fig. 130a. Erect display of a lesser kudu male in frontal right angle position to the female. (The male mounts with head and neck lowered to the female's back in this species.) b. If the female attacks the displaying male (by boxing his shoulder with her forehead), he keeps his erect broadside posture "unshakable." (Walther 1966a.)

Fig. 131a. Head-and-neck-stretched-forward/upward posture in a courting okapi bull (right). The female responds by a head-low posture. Compare these postures to those of the dominant and the subordinate opponent in neck-fighting (Fig. 95). b. Erect posture of the male behind the female. c. Lifted-nose posture combined with foreleg kick. (Walther 1960*b*.)

posture or a modification of the erect posture due to its performance during walking. Perhaps even more difficult is the distinction between the head-and-neck-forward/upward posture and the nose-up; often the latter appears to be nothing but an exaggerated form of the former.

The pure erect posture (i.e., neck vertically erected with head held horizontally) may occasionally be seen in mating rituals of many species since, as an intention movement for rising onto the hind legs, it can be related to mounting. However, as an elaborate display, which not only momentarily precedes mounting but is retained during large parts of the mating ritual, it is not quite as widespread. For example, it is very striking in the courting giraffe bull (Fig. 132).

Fig. 132. Erect posture of the driving giraffe bull. Compare this posture to that of the dominant in an agonistic encounter in Fig. 114. (Walther 1960*b*. Frankfurt Zoo.)

Erect postures, head-and-neck-forward/upward postures, and/or nose-up postures are typical of courting males in axis deer (Schaller 1967), brow-antlered deer (Blakeslee et al. 1979), pronghorn (Bromley 1974), many gazelle-related species (Antilopinae—Walther 1968*a*), Uganda kob (Buechner and Schloeth 1965), and many others. In kongoni (Gosling 1974), tsessebe (Joubert 1975), and topi, it is combined with an "ear-drop" typical of courting males in the Alcelaphinae subfamily. Assuming an erect posture, courting male chamois either stand silently or utter strange grunting sounds ("*Blädern*" in the terminology of German hunters).

The nose-up gesture is frequently combined with foreleg kicks (see below) in okapi (Fig. 131c) and in gazelles and their relatives (Antilopinae). In some other bovid species, the erect attitude is combined with exaggerated, stiff-legged walking. The most pronounced case of this kind is perhaps the high and slow lifting of the angled forelegs in the courting topi bull (Fig. 133—Walther 1968*b*, 1979).

In many Pecora species, a driving male may occasionally show a turning of the head sideward at angles of 45° or 90°, frequently in combination with the erect posture, when he is standing behind the female. In some species, such as eland antelope, these head-turns are frequently and regularly seen during the mating ritual; however, I am aware of the sideward turn of the head (alternately to the right and the left) as a truly striking and elaborate display only in pronghorn (Gregg 1955), where bucks show this "head-waving" when approaching a female and when following her (Fig. 134) during rutting season. Possibly this behavior is linked to the black patch on the male's cheek and/or the presence of a subauricular gland.

Another typical male courtship display is kicking with the foreleg (*Laufschlag* or *Laufeinschlag*—Walther 1958*a*) which occurs in okapi and a large number of Bovidae species (Walther 1960*b*, 1979). With respect to the possible development of courtship displays from ancestral fighting techniques, it is of interest that the foreleg kick as a courtship display is not found in the Tylopoda and, above all, the Cervidae, those groups of recent artiodactyls that fight with their forelegs. In pronghorn as well as in some cervids, such as fallow deer, white-tailed deer, and axis deer, kicking with the forelegs occurs (apparently without function) in the young during suckling. This is not for soliciting milk when the young is following behind its mother as

Fig. 133. Head-up posture with ear-drop and high lifting of the angled forelegs in the courting topi bull.

Fig. 134a.–c. Head-waving of the courting pronghorn buck.
(Walther 1979. National Bison Range, Montana.)

happens in certain bovids, but while the fawn is actually nursing. It is presently unknown whether this behavior of young cervids and pronghorn might be related to the foreleg kick in the courtship of certain bovids, and, if so, how to interpret this relationship.

Bovidae groups which do not kick with the forelegs include all the oxen, nilgai, spiral-horned antelopes, wildebeest, impala, and aoudad. It is also lacking (or infrequent and weak) in hartebeest, chamois, and some of the *Damaliscus* species, such as bontebok and blesbok. The foreleg kick does occur in the majority of goats and sheep (Fig. 129), gazelles and their relatives (Fig. 135b), some dwarf antelopes (Neotraginae), duikers, roan, sable, addax, and oryx antelopes (Fig. 135a), waterbucks, mountain goat, and topi. It is most frequently seen when the male is standing or walking behind the female, but it also occurs occasionally when he is face to face with her or is oriented frontally toward her flank (sagittal T-position). In oryx, addax, roan and sable antelope, the males often perform the kick with the foreleg during the mating whirl-around in reverse-parallel position (Fig. 123b). Sometimes the male touches the female's hind legs and, occasionally, even her belly with his foreleg. More often the female is not touched. The male moves his foreleg between her hind legs (*Laufeinschlag* = kick-in-between) in certain species, or he does not raise his foreleg high enough (Fig. 131c), or he performs the foreleg kick at a distance from which he cannot possibly touch her (Fig. 135c).

The most pronounced performances (raising one foreleg to approximately 90°) are seen when the male is standing. However, he also can deliver the foreleg kick while walking, but then the leg is usually raised up to only about 45°. In some species, such as Grant's gazelle and blackbuck, the foreleg kick is reduced to a big, stiff-legged step. (The full foreleg kick was observed in juvenile males of blackbuck— Benz 1973). Sloppy, "knock-kneed" performances of the foreleg kick occasionally happen in any species (Fig. 129a). In addax antelope (Huth 1980, Manski 1979) and scimitar-horned oryx (*Oryx dammah*—Huth 1980), they are even the rule (Fig. 123b); otherwise, the foreleg is rather stiffly stretched in a "good" kick (Figs. 129b, 135b,c).

In all bovid species under discussion, the foreleg kick can be delivered when the male is standing or walking in a "normal" or an erect attitude. In the oryx-related, the roan and sable antelopes, and the waterbuck species, this is the rule. In a very few species, such as dama gazelle (*Gazella dama*—Mungall 1980), the male may sometimes kick with his foreleg while his nose is touching the female's croup. In some species, such as topi and oryx antelope, the foreleg kick can be combined with mounting intentions (bending the hind

Fig. 135a. Foreleg kick (*Laufschlag*) in the courtship of
South African oryx. b. *Laufschlag* in the courtship of springbuck.
c. A male springbuck approaches a resting female and tries to
bring her up with (symbolic) foreleg kicks. (Walther 1981. Etosha
National Park.)

legs). In sheep and goats, it is frequently combined with neck-stretch and twist (Fig. 129b), while in okapi and many gazelle species, there is a tendency to combine it with a nose-up movement (Fig. 131c).

Generally the mating kick can be interpreted as a kind of "final test": when the female does not react to it, she is ready to accept and tolerate the male's mounting. For those species which mount and copulate during a brisk walk (predominantly some of the gazelle and their relatives), the foreleg kick can also be used to make the female continue moving after she has stopped walking during the mating march or the mating whirl-around.

As mentioned above, the kick with the foreleg is often combined with the neck-stretch in sheep (Fig. 129b). The two behavior patterns may also be used in combination or independently in encounters between males in sheep (Geist 1971). This is the only presently known case in which behaviors primarily or exclusively serving as courtship displays in most bovid species play an important role in agonistic encounters. Here they obviously serve the same function as dominance displays, since they typically are shown by dominant rams in encounters with inferior ones. (Usually the opposite is true, i.e., dominance displays in agonistic encounters among males may also occur in encounters of courting males with females.)

In view of the apparent relevance of visual courtship displays in Pecora, it is surprising that the list of the most important postures and gestures is so short: neck-stretch, head-and-neck-forward/upward posture, erect posture, nose-up movement, head-sideward turn, and foreleg kick. Obviously the species-specific character of courtship rituals in these animals is not demonstrated by a multitude of different displays but by differences in frequency of single displays (i.e., some species show three to five of these displays, but other species may show only one of them), by differences in the elaboration, and by combinations within these relatively few displays. The degree of specialization achieved in this simple way is astonishing. Of course, the species-specific differences become more pronounced when one takes into account additional features, such as ear and tail movements. However, it is possible to characterize the courtship behavior of many species by simply using the postures and movements listed above, and, particularly in closely related species, there are hardly two in which the courtship ritual looks completely alike.

In summary, in the mating rituals of Pecora (i.e., pronghorn, the giraffe-related species, and above all the deer and the many horned ungulates) visual displays on the part of the males are so prominent that the olfactory, tactile, and acoustical behaviors become secondary. Although fighting between male and female does not form an obligatory component in the mating rituals of these animals, most of said displays appear to be related to aggressive behaviors. True threats of the males toward the females do occur in certain species, but on the whole they are infrequent during courtship. The males more commonly use the same dominance displays as in agonistic encounters between rivals of the same species. Finally, there are "courtship displays" in the strict sense, which are predominantly or exclusively used by adult males in encounters with females, but do not commonly occur in agonistic encounters among male opponents of the same species. However, there is hardly one of them which would not occur as a threat or dominance display in another ungulate species. This points to the possibility that these courtship displays in the strict sense also originated from ancestral aggressive behaviors. Generally, the relatively small proportion of obviously genuine sexual displays in the mating rituals of the animals under discussion is surprising. One may say the relationship of the sexual drive and the courtship displays is here analogous to that of the French nation and the Foreign Legion. The legionnaires served and fought for France, but most of them were not French. Correspondingly, although the courtship displays occur in the service of the sexual drive, many of them are not sexual behaviors.

15. SUBMISSIVE DISPLAYS

When speaking here of submissive displays, I do not mean all kinds of inferiority or appeasement behavior. For example, flight and withdrawal are behaviors of inferiority, and licking the partner may function as an appeasement in certain cases. These behaviors have been mentioned and at least partially discussed in previous chapters. In this chapter, we will focus on special gestures and postures of submission.

Most submissive displays in hoofed mammals are in every way the antithesis of dominance displays and offensive threat displays. They indicate the acceptance of the inferior role. In a sense, they anticipate defeat and lack features that could possibly challenge an opponent and release his aggression. The effects on a superior opponent range from a diminution to a complete cessation of his aggression. On the other hand, there are sometimes cases in which a submissive display of a subordinate does not work, does not stop the dominant's aggressiveness. This is more or less to be expected, since expressive behavior generally does not work with absolute reliability; threat and dominance displays, too, can sometimes be ignored by the recipient. Moreover, outrageous aggressiveness may be particularly resistant to moderating influences—as we know well enough from our own experiences in human life. Thus, one should not be too surprised when occasionally a superior aggressor continues attacking an inferior opponent in spite of the latter's submission, but one has every reason to be surprised how frequently submissive displays do stop or at least markedly diminish the aggressiveness in the animals under discussion.

In contrast to flight and withdrawal, submissive displays enable an inferior animal to remain with a group and/or in the same area as before despite the presence of very dominant and aggressive conspecifics. This is important for females in the courtship ritual; and for juvenile and subadult animals, it may often be essential for their survival chances.

I once had a particularly impressive demonstration of these functions of submissive behavior in the little Kirk's dikdik. A pair had their territory around my bungalow in Serengeti National Park, and a young male was born there. Growing fast, at about five months of age, he had almost reached the size of an adult, and his presence began to "annoy" the father. As the pair roamed through the large territory, it quite frequently happened that the young male tried to join them and to approach the female—presumably still with more or less infantile intentions. However, the adult male "took offense," erected the crest of long hair on his forehead, stretched head and neck horizontally forward, and rushed toward his son. The young male promptly assumed a head-low attitude or even lay down, with head and neck stretched forward, flat on the ground. The adult buck stopped his rush, watched the submissive son at close range, his ruffled crest went down, and he turned and joined his female. After a while the young male stood up and approached the pair again. Again the father turned toward him, raised his crest and rushed toward him; and again the young went down in submission and the father stopped. I once counted forty such encounters during one bright moonlit night. In this way, the young male managed to stay two or three more weeks in the familiar, parental territory before he eventually left it and established a territory of his own in the vicinity. In these fast-growing little creatures, a few weeks may make a significant difference with respect to the survival chances of the young.

No submissive postures or gestures are known from tapirs (von Richter 1966). As for rhinoceroses, only squeals of fleeing animals have been mentioned in the literature (Player and Feely 1960, Ullrich 1964, Schenkel and Lang 1969). In horse-related animals, we find a facial expression of submission (mainly, although not exclusively, in subadult animals—Zeeb 1959, Klingel 1972, 1977) which has been described and discussed in another context. According to Frädrich (1967), submissive gestures and postures are unknown or doubtful in swine and hippos. Sometimes the distress cries of swine may have an inhibitory effect upon aggressors. Bourlière and Verschuren (1960) describe a case in which a young but fully adult and sexually active hippo bull lay down and remained motionless when a gigantic rival approached. In peccary, Schweinsburg and Sowls (1972) mention that a subordinate may hold his snout and forequarters low, sometimes kneeling with the forelegs, in an encounter with a dominant opponent, and that a subordinate may even lie down completely (in captivity).

On the whole, submissive displays do not appear to be very frequent and striking in odd-toed ungulates and in the Nonruminantia. In the ruminants, they are present in the most primitive species, the mouse deer. According to Robin (1979), a submissive lesser Malayan mouse deer lowers head, neck, and anterior part of his body, turns the ears back, and flips the tail over the back. This posture is not only used to prevent the attack of a superior combatant, but is also assumed by animals, particularly females, when they are bitten. As Robin (1979) emphasizes, these animals remain completely motionless while being bitten.

In cervids and bovids, submissive displays are quite common, especially in females and subadult males. To name a few examples, they are reported from muntjac (Dubost 1971, Barette 1977), fallow deer (Freye and Geissler 1966), brow-antlered deer (Blakeslee et al. 1979), red deer (Burckhardt 1958a), elk (Geist 1966a), bighorn sheep (Geist 1971), sable antelope (Huth 1970), roan antelope (Joubert 1974), domestic sheep (Grubb 1974), domestic cattle (Schloeth 1961a), bongo (Hamann 1979), gerenuk (Walther 1961c, Leuthold 1971), dik-dik, dorcas gazelle, Grant's gazelle, eland antelope, oryx antelope, black wildebeest, sitatunga, kudu (Walther 1958ab, 1964b, 1965b, 1966ab, 1968a, 1978d), and many other species.

The intensity, frequency, and importance of such submissive displays vary according to situations and/or with species. The commonest forms of submission in bovids and cervids, which may occur singly or in combination, are lowering the head, turning the hindquarters toward the opponent, and lying down with the head and neck stretched forward. Used in succession, they can express increasing degrees of submission.

In agonistic encounters, turning the hindquarters toward the opponent is frequently an intention movement for withdrawal or flight. One can consider it a special display only when it is combined with other features of submission (see below), and/or when the animal does not withdraw or flee but remains in the dominant's vicinity. Since females are oriented with their hindquarters toward the males in sexual encounters, certain authors maintain that a subordinate male may mimic a female and thus take advantage of the dominant male's inhibition about attacking an (estrous) female. However, the same submissive behavior can also be seen in encounters among females. It is unlikely that a subordinate female would "mimic" a female—which she is, after all—in an encounter with another female. At least in hoofed mammals, the reverse is more probable with respect to the hindquarters orientation and other submissive behaviors. That is, they are behavior patterns of inferiority by origin and nature, and thus they may also occur on the part of the female in sexual encounters because she is inferior in strength to an adult male in most of the species under discussion.

The single serious counterargument to this view that I can think of, is the dominant's occasional mounting of a submissive male. First, it must be stated that this is absolutely exceptional in most undomesticated ungulates. It seems to be comparatively frequent in sheep

(Geist 1971) and in at least some of the wild oxen. However, one may argue that mounting is not a sexual behavior beyond any possible doubt in hoofed mammals, and that mounting a subordinate animal of the same sex may be more related to an act of aggression (jumping at the other and throwing the weight of the body on him) and come close to a demonstration of dominance in agonistic interactions.

According to Lott (1969), a submissive bison frequently does not fully turn away from the dominant opponent but remains in a broadside position. This means he takes the same position as in a lateral dominance display. However, the latter can be clearly distinguished from the position of submission in this species because, in the dominance display, head and body form a straight line and the head is carried at about the elevation normally associated with walking or somewhat higher. By contrast, in submission, the head is dropped close to the ground, as in grazing.

Lying down with the head and neck stretched forward on the ground, often but not necessarily with the hindquarters toward the opponent (Figs. 136, 138a), apparently occurs considerably less frequently in the wild than in captivity, where the spatial limitations often exclude effective withdrawal. Sometimes the animal only drops to its "knees" as an intention movement for lying down (Walther 1961c, 1966b). In free-ranging animals, one can see the full submissive lying relatively frequently when females, presumably not yet in heat, are sexually approached by males.

The most extreme case of lying in submission was observed in captive black wildebeest (Walther 1966b). An old cow whose condition had deteriorated due to a miscarriage was frequently and severely harassed by a younger female who previously had been subordinate

Fig. 136. Lying down in full submission with head and neck on the ground and with hindquarters oriented toward the dominant in black wildebeest. (Walther 1966b.)

to her. When cornered and continuously attacked by the young female, in spite of her lying flat on the ground in submission, the old female rolled on the side, turning her belly toward the attacker. In this and similar cases, one is reminded of Lorenz's (1949) hypothesis (mainly based on the behavior of wolves, dogs, and certain birds) that the submissive animal presents the most vulnerable part of its body to the dominant. However, according to my experience with hoofed mammals, the primary tendency of submissive animals seems to be to turn the weapons (e.g., the horns in the case of a horned ungulate) away from the opponent which in some cases—such as that of the old wildebeest cow—may lead to exposing a vulnerable body region simply because the weapons are on an opposite side of the body.

Since lying down, including lying with head and neck stretched forward on the ground, is a quite normal resting behavior in these animals, the question arises whether the usual lying down for rest can sometimes be "mistaken" for submission by conspecifics. Indeed, there are some observations which indicate that normal lying down can occasionally result in a temporary "loss of rank." It sometimes happens that a high-ranking group member, while resting, is pestered by an otherwise absolutely subordinate animal. Of course, the subordinate immediately stops his (usually not very severe) aggressions as soon as the dominant arises. Thus, there appear to be connections between resting behavior and lying in submission (Walther 1966b).

In some species, such as black wildebeest, submissive lying down is sometimes accompanied by vocalizations frequently heard from calves (Walther 1966b). This and the resemblance to the infantile lying-out (lying-in-seclusion) behavior of certain Artiodactyla species makes it tempting to assume that an animal lying down in submission may be mimicking an infant (Burckhardt 1958b). However, there are several objections to this hypothesis. It is rather obvious that the animals under discussion can distinguish an adult conspecific from an infant (by visual appearance and scent) regardless of his posture and position. Thus, it is unlikely an adult animal can assume a baby's identity simply by lying down. It is also doubtful that certain vocalizations in Artiodactyla are so typical of juveniles that they definitely identify an animal as an infant (except, of course, by pitch—but the pitch of the voice is different in an adult ungulate anyway). The vocalizations uttered in connection with submissive behavior are usually distress cries. These are heard particularly frequently from juveniles, but they are by no means restricted to them. Moreover, neither submissive lying down nor other forms of submission are necessarily combined with vocalizations; on the contrary, silence is quite common. Furthermore, submissive lying down is a behavioral response to threats from very dominant conspecifics, frequently adult males. In most of these species, however, adult males have hardly any contact with infants and pay little attention to them; why such a male should react to infantile behavior remains obscure. Finally, submissive lying down is also shown by species, such as black wildebeest, whose young do not lie out. In short, it is more probable that lying down with head and neck stretched forward functions as a submissive behavior simply because it is the perfect antithesis of the self-exposure and emphasizing of an animal's presence in dominance and offensive threat displays, and because the inferior animal blends into the ground and, in a sense, leaves little for its opponent to attack.

Lowering the head ranges from performances identical to the head-low posture (Fig. 1) described as a defensive threat to postures in which the animal stretches its head and neck more forward-downward (Fig. 109), or turns its head somewhat away from the challenger (Fig. 137c), or holds its neck in a rather strikingly curved fashion (e.g., guanaco—Pilters 1956). The head-low posture is the most common form, found in many bovids and cervids. In a few species and/or cases, the back may appear slightly humped in this posture. As mentioned in another context, in certain species, such as fallow deer and eland antelope, submissive females may perform snapping movements with the mouth when lowering the head or lying down in submission. As in the aggressive (defensive) head-low posture, submissive lowering of the head may sometimes change into grazing. It is often shown during withdrawal (Fig. 54a) and sometimes during flight (Fig. 66). The most pronounced and even exaggerated performances, however, can be seen when an animal does not withdraw but remains close to the dominant partner. In this case, the lowering of the head can be combined with assuming a reverse position, but it may also be displayed in any other orientation relative to the dominant, including a frontal orientation.

The frontal orientation is by no means rare in submission, and it can even happen in certain situations and in certain species that the submissive animal approaches the dominant. This is particularly common in species in which the submissive animals tend to stretch head and neck more forward and downward. For example, a submissive chamois lowers the body somewhat, stretches the lowered head and neck more forward than downward toward the dominant (Burckhardt 1958b). Occasionally, this approach may lead to naso-nasal contact (Krämer 1969). However, more commonly, after an initial approach the subordinate turns and runs away, or he continues past the dominant. Likewise, in roan antelope (Joubert 1974), sable antelope (Huth 1980), or oryx antelope (Walther 1978d, 1980), a submissive animal may sometimes stretch head and neck more forward than downward, and then approach the broadside-displaying dominant and try to pass past the dominant's rear.

Also, in the African buffalo, a submissive animal stretches the lowered head and neck horizontally forward and approaches the dominant, but then the subordinate places his muzzle under either the neck or belly or between the hind legs of the dominant (from behind). Immediately afterwards the subordinate abruptly turns and jumps away, uttering a loud bellow. Sinclair (1974) is inclined to interpret this behavior as a (symbolic) suckling. However, when observing such events, this possibility never occurred to me. Although I cannot give a final explanation of this behavior, I think such an interpretation is at least premature.

The possibility or even likelihood of a developmental connection between submissive displays and threat behavior, as well as the occasional switch from a submissive behavior to a threat display and vice versa, has been considered several times in ethological literature (Lorenz 1935, Tinbergen 1959). The comparative study of artiodactyl behavior may possibly provide further insight into this "mechanism."

As mentioned above, the head-low posture occurs as a defensive threat in certain bovids. When an animal challenged by another's offensive threat or dominance display (high presentation of horns, erect posture, broadside display, etc.) shows a defensive head-low threat, this means that it does not "dare" respond to the challenge in an equivalent way, but is only ready to defend itself if attacked. Hence, a defensive threat, when used in response to a challenger's offensive threat or dominance display, comes very close to a behavior denoting inferiority. Furthermore, in the particular case of the head-low posture, the animal has only to stretch its lowered head and neck somewhat more forward and/or turn its horns somewhat away from the opponent to assume a more pronounced submissive attitude. Thus, the difference between these is only marginal.

In oryx antelope, the transition of the head-low posture from a defensive to a submissive display can sometimes be observed sequentially in the same animal (Walther 1978d). When approached by a dominant challenger, the subordinate may first lower the head with the horns pointing straight up (Fig. 137a). If he is attacked, this head-low posture allows him to counteract with a butt which, although it is not equal to the offensive downward-blow from medial or high horn presentation (commonly used by the attacker in this species), is a technique which can be used in offensive and in defensive fighting. If the dominant does not immediately attack but comes closer and reinforces his display, the subordinate may lean his horns

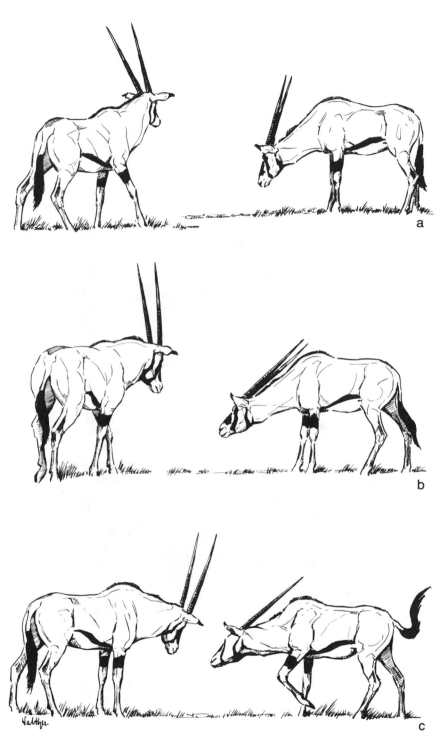

Fig. 137. Transition from a defensive threat to submission in response to the dominant's intensified threat in East African oryx. a.
Head-low posture of the subordinate (right) with horns pointing straight
up. b. Head-low with horns leaning back toward the nape. c. Head-low
with turning the horns sideways away from the opponent.

back toward his nape so that his head and neck are stretched forward and downward (Fig. 137b). From this posture, he cannot fight back as easily, but he can still effectively parry the other's blow with his horns. Thus, this head-forward/downward posture indicates the readiness for pure and more passive defense. If the dominant still does not attack but continues and further reinforces his threat, the subordinate may turn his horns sideways (Fig. 137c) so that they cannot

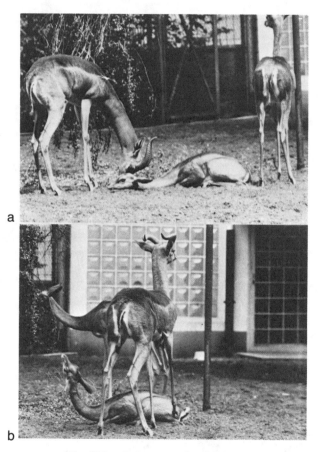

Fig. 138a. Submissive lying of a gerenuk female (*Litocranius walleri*) threatened by the male's low presentation of horns. b. Neck-winding of a gerenuk female during submissive lying when the buck tries to bring her up by foreleg kicks. Note the spreading of hooves of the male's kicking leg. (Frankfurt Zoo.)

catch the blow in the case of the other's attack. This indicates the abandonment of any kind of defense and is totally submissive.

It may be mentioned here that in the behavioral inventory of a species there are also other relationships between threat and submissive displays which apparently depend on species-specific peculiarities. This is easy to understand in species where the head-low posture can be a very severe and offensive threat, such as chamois and pronghorn. In such cases, the submissive posture must be different according to the principle of antithesis. As mentioned above, a submissive chamois stretches head and neck straight forward, and in pronghorn (Kitchen 1974), a submissive animal erects the neck and (slightly) hunches its back. On the other hand, there are submissive postures, deviating from the usual, for which we have no good interpretation up to now. In this context, I am thinking primarily of the hartebeest species (or subspecies) and the topi and its relatives, where, instead of a head-low posture, an attitude very similar to the medial presentation of horns serves as an expression of submission. Another somewhat difficult case is the neck-winding and twisting movements of submissive females in certain species. In some of these species, such as sitatunga, one could think of (symbolic) neck-fighting. However, similar movements of the neck also occur in females of species such as gerenuk (Fig. 138b), in which neck-fighting is unknown.

Finally, there are cases of mosaiclike combinations of threat and submissive displays—as in humans, when an inferior individual may withdraw and/or bow when charged by a feared superior, but may curse and clench the fists at the same time. For example, in okapi (Walther 1962), submissive lying down may be combined with vertical erecting of head and neck, which is a (defensive) threat behavior (related to neck-fighting) in this species. Also, a subordinate oryx bull, withdrawing with submissively lowered head from a dominant challenger, may throw his head up and down as a threat behavior ("grumbling to oneself"). Corresponding events can occasionally be observed in many species.

16. "HERDING" AND RELATED BEHAVIORS

The discussion of activities which have loosely been termed "herding" is a direct continuation of chapter 11, on orientations relative to the partner and direction signaling. Since threats, dominance and courtship displays, and submissive behaviors, often play an important role in the herding activities, it was necessary first to familiarize the reader with them before delving into a discussion of herding.

Problems arise in this discussion for at least three reasons—one is more or less "historical," another is due to our old "Tower of Babel" confusion of terms, the third is given by the subject. For a long while ethologists did not distinguish between herding and courtship (I admit that I have been among the "sinners" in a few earlier publications). However, this distinction appears to be necessary for several good reasons. Male courtship behavior is always directed toward a female in estrus or at least serves to find out whether a female is in estrus. However, herding is not necessarily restricted to sexual motivations. In some species, the males herd females regardless of whether they are in estrus. In certain species and/or situations, a male may herd not only females but also other males. Furthermore, the males show dominance displays, threats, and even physical aggressions in herding, in addition to courtship displays.

In part, this depends on whether the males of a given species have the same or a different behavioral inventory in encounters with females and among themselves. The males of a given species, e.g., Thomson's gazelle, may use certain displays in encounters with females that largely differ from those used in encounters with other males. When this occurs, the courtship and the herding of females may look very much alike; but interactions with other males in all-male groups and mixed herds, more or less comparable in their functions to herding (Walther 1978a), may look entirely different. In other species, e.g., oryx antelope, males perform a variety of displays in encounters with partners of either sex but have only a few displays (in oryx, mainly the foreleg kick) that are restricted to sexually motivated encounters with estrous females. In such species the courtship may differ from the herding of females, but the herding of females and of other males may look very much alike. Finally, considering only the interactions of males with females, there are species in which the males use different displays in herding and in courtship but their herding is more striking than their courtship behavior. In such cases, herding has often been mistaken for courtship. For example, for centuries the red deer stag's herding behavior ("*Sprengen*" in German literature) was mistaken for mating behavior (Bützler 1974).

Confusion may also arise because the term "herding" is frequently applied to different situations. It sometimes means that the sender tries to make the herded animal or animals remain at the spot or at least to prevent them from moving ahead in a given direction. However, one also speaks of herding when the sender tries to make the others move, move faster, or move in a definite direction. Finally, the term is also used when an animal rounds up the others—be it at the spot or while moving. Although it may be wise to distinguish these different cases by different terms, I will not do so here but will retain the term "herding" for all three situations as has been done up to now in the literature.

Finally, there are several forms of herding in hoofed mammals. One form is closely related to sexual behavior, particularly to the often temporary "tending bond" between a male and a female. This is known as a typical rutting behavior in a number of cervid species, e.g., axis deer (Fuchs 1976), and also in certain bovids, particularly wild oxen such as bison (McHugh 1958, Lott 1974). When being tended, the estrous female is usually prevented by the tending male from following the others. He not only keeps other males away from her but stands and walks beside her constantly and stops her, if necessary, by moving into a lateral T-position in front of her.

In other species, predominantly certain cervids, where a male, without being territorial, temporarily associates himself with a group of females during rutting reason, the male's herding activity may primarily serve to keep such a harem together and to prevent single females from splitting off from it. Bützler (1974) describes the situation in red deer. When a female red deer strolls away from the others during rutting season, the stag leaves the temporary harem, runs toward the isolated female, passes her and circles her, walking in a prancing gait with erected neck and lifted nose ("canine threat"!). The cow turns away from the stag, and thus back toward the group. Then, the stag approaches her and chases her in straight line back to the group. Occasionally he may threaten her by presenting his antlers and symbolic butting, and he usually utters staccato-like vocalizations during the chase. When the female has joined the harem, the stag stops running, stands, and roars.

In principle, the same situation occurs in elk. However, according to Geist (1966a), the male's herding posture is different. When retrieving cows straying from the harem, the elk stag assumes a stretched posture. His nose points forward and up, and his antlers are consequently laid on his back. The stag approaches the cow tangentially, not frontally. He may turn his head away from the female, if his body axis is oriented toward her. The latter seems to be some kind of swing-out movement. Geist (1966a) reports that the stag may suddenly turn his head toward the cow from this position, lower his antlers, and charge her. The behavior of caribou is similar (Pruitt 1960, Bergerud 1974). In short, these herding activities serve to round up the females in a bunch during rutting season.

A different type of herding is found in territorial species, although not without transitions. For example, a territorial impala buck may round up the females in a rather tight bunch within his territory. However, more frequently in hoofed mammals, the females can disperse as much as they like within a territory, and the territorial male does not drive them together in a bunch. He herds them from the boundary area toward the center of his territory, and, above all, he herds them back when they try to leave his territory. Thus, this territorial herding serves not to keep the group together but to keep the females inside the territory.

Territorial herding occurs in all ungulate species where the males are territorial but the females are not and roam through their (usually large) home ranges visiting the stationary owners of territories only for a few hours per day (wildebeest, hartebeest, topi, gazelles, etc.). Here, a territorial male approaches the females coming into his territory, and—using the same displays as in courtship in most of the species—he herds them toward the center of his territory. Later, when the females move ahead to continue their daily circuit, the male tries to prevent them from leaving by herding them back from the boundary. Vehement chases may occur in this situation during which the male always tries to pass the female and to position himself between her and the boundary. Typically, he always directs his herding activities toward one female at a time, even when there are many of them, usually toward that one which has come closest to the boundary. It must be emphasized that this territorial herding is not restricted to females in estrus; all females entering a territory are treated this way regardless of their physiological condition.

A very comparable type of territorial herding is also found in white rhino (Owen-Smith 1974) and Grevy's zebra. Klingel (1974) observed an interesting herding technique in the latter species in addition to the usual blocking of the mare's path and driving her ahead by threat displays. The Grevy's stallion may make the mare move ahead by placing his head on her croup, and he may turn her to the right by pressing his head against her left flank, or to the left by pressing his head against her right flank, respectively, while pushing her hindquarters with his chest. This "steering" of the mare is also possible during a gallop.

As was emphasized from the beginning and is obvious from the descriptions above, the sender's orientation relative to the recipient plays an important role in all types of herding. Frequently the sender's orientations are combined with expressive displays—threat displays, dominance displays, or courtship displays, depending on species and/or situation. Besides combinations of distinct displays with certain orientations, herding can also be executed by mere orientations, i.e., the male signals to the females "where to go or not to go" merely by his orientation relative to them. This "silent herding" is very inconspicuous to the human observer and, probably for this reason, has seldom been studied and described. One may presume that it is present and plays an important role in many ungulate species. I know it particularly from Grant's gazelle. Under certain local conditions (Walther 1972a,b), a relatively stable harem (usually ten to twenty females with or without offspring) can be with a male during his entire territorial period (about five months per year) in this species. However, only the Grant's male is territorial and only he is aware of the territorial boundaries. Thus, the females will transgress the boundaries without hesitation if the buck does not prevent them from doing so. When females are at the point of leaving the territory, the male blocks their path and herds them back, using dominance displays, threats, and chases. Thus these herding efforts are very striking. However, it took me a shamefully long time to realize that these were only extreme cases, and that the buck commonly tries to direct the females' course long before they near the boundary of his large territory. He does this simply by placing himself between the females and the boundary, and by assuming definite orientations (Figs. 50, 53, 56, 58a) toward the females while he is standing, resting, moving, or grazing. The females clearly react to the male's "silent herding" (unless they are trying to leave him and the area deliberately), and this permanent direction signaling works very effectively.

Herding the females also occurs in species which are not territorial but form very stable harem groups which remain in existence over long periods, frequently for years. This situation is found in several equid species such as plains zebra, mountain zebra, and horse (Klingel 1972). The herding activities of the stallion serve to keep the group together and to direct its course during moves (Fig. 139). As

Fig. 139. Stallion (right) of East African plains zebra herding the mares of his harem. (Klingel 1972. Photo: H. Klingel. Ngorongoro Crater, Tanzania.)

with most wild ungulates, these harem groups wander in file formation, one animal behind the other. According to Klingel (1972), in plains zebra, the highest-ranking mare leads the file, and the other mares follow her in the order of their dominance. Any mare who walks in front of a higher ranking one will be attacked and threatened by that animal until she takes her proper place. Each foal follows behind its mother. The stallion is not bound to a definite place. Usually he walks at the rear or beside the marching file. On relatively rare occasions he may also take the lead. The leading mare usually determines the direction and the speed of the move but sometimes the stallion intervenes and speeds up the mares or directs them to take another course, althouth he marches at the rear. He then walks faster than the others—if necessary he trots or gallops—moving in threat posture sideways along the file toward its head. Each individual animal responds to the stallion's threat by turning away from him. The leader mare finally moves into a new direction "demanded" by the stallion, and the other animals again form a file behind her and follow her (Fig. 140).

In spite of all their differences, the types of herding discussed so far have one point in common. They all concern the herding of females by males. However, there are also situations and species where males herd females *and* other males. Particularly in all-male groups and mixed herds of gregarious horned ungulates, it happens quite frequently that animals, usually adult males, involved in a given activity

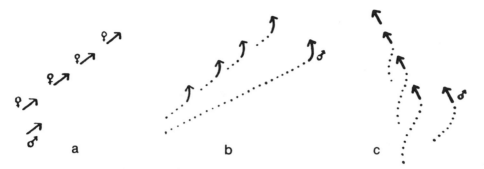

Fig. 140. Direction change of a marching zebra harem due to the herding activity of the stallion. a. The group is marching in file with the stallion at the rear. b. The stallion moves in threat posture along the file. Each mare responds to the stallion's threat by turning away. c. They again form a file with the stallion at the rear, now moving in the new direction. (Klingel 1972.)

may "take offense" at deviating activities of group members. For example, at the end of a resting period, some animals which are already on their feet may begin to threaten others which are still resting (Fig. 141). Likewise, at the beginning of a move, animals moving in a given direction may display toward group members moving in another, particularly the opposite, direction ("voting" on marching direction); or, during a move, a male may "push" the animal in front when it slows down (Walther 1978a, c). Of course, this "taking offense" at deviating activities of group members is quite impartial in character, and may be considered as a somewhat primitive and imperfect type of herding insofar as it is restricted to group members right in front of the performer's nose. However, it can considerably contribute to the coordination of group activities, and it is extended to both males and females.

The most elaborate and individualized cases of herding that I have observed in ungulates occurred in migratory herds of fringe-eared oryx antelope (*Oryx beisa callotis*) in East Africa. There often seems to be a well-established and individualized social hierarchy within the oryx herds with (in the cases of all-male groups or mixed herds) a strong adult male at the top of the hierarchy (alpha animal). Apparently even then it requires a somewhat special situation for an alpha bull, with his herding activities, to become the very life and soul of a herd. Such special occasions occurred when migratory oryx herds invaded Serengeti National Park (Walther 1978d). These herds came from afar and passed through a terrain that was not particularly familiar to them. In these cases, the alpha bull, usually walking at the rear

a

b

Fig. 141a. At the end of a resting period, some members of an all-male group of Thomson's gazelle are still lying while others are already on their feet. A buck interrupts grazing and threatens one of the still-resting males ("taking offense"). b. The resting buck "obeys" the threat and rises. (Walther 1978c. Serengeti National Park.)

of the marching file, not only induced activity changes, kept the group together, and sped up the others when they slowed down, but also hurried to the top of the marching file and, assuming a broadside position in front of the foremost animal, blocked the path when the herd was deviating from its course, or he placed himself temporarily at the top of the file leading the herd into a desirable direction, or he left the herd and walked back over quite remarkable distances to pick up stragglers (Fig. 142; see also Figs. 1, 54a).

Fig. 142. The alpha bull of a migratory mixed herd of East African oryx picks up a straggler. a. A subordinate bull (left) has remained behind while the herd was moving on. The alpha bull (center) walks back and approaches him in erect posture with his head slightly turned away and a "pointing" ear. The addressee responds with a head-low posture. b. The alpha bull (left) has stopped in front of the subordinate and has turned his head toward him. The subordinate bull (center) follows the herd, keeping his head low. (Walther 1978d. Serengeti National Park.)

In this way all members of the group were herded by one animal, and one could compare the situation to the herding of a plains zebra harem by its stallion. However, the important difference was that these oryx herds were not harems but mixed groups that included several adult males. Perhaps the best way to give the reader an adequate view may be to briefly describe the activities of one of these oryx herds during one day of the "invasion" of Serengeti National Park. This particular herd consisted of six adult bulls and nine adult cows, and it was observed on 4 September 1974 (Walther 1978d).

At 0700 hours, this herd was grazing and moving about 4 kilometers south of the Gol Kopjes. Later some of the animals bedded down. At 0935 hours, they started moving in a southeasterly direction (toward Olduvai Gorge), and kept this general direction in all their moves throughout the day. When they changed from resting or grazing to moving, the alpha bull threatened (angle horns) a subordinate bull, and then placed himself at the rear of the file. After a while, two bulls which had been somewhat apart from the others started an intensive sparring match and remained behind.

At 0956 hours, the cow in front of the marching file deviated from the previous course at an angle of about 45° to the east and the others followed. The alpha bull hurried to the front, stopped the march by assuming a lateral T-position in front of the foremost animal, and chased the first animals back by threats and short rushes toward them. It was apparently at this time, that he became aware of the two fighters, now more than 200 meters behind. He left the herd and headed toward them. Upon his arrival, the two bulls stopped fighting. The alpha bull circled them, took an erect stance in broadside position in front of one of them, turned his head toward him and slowly lowered his horns against him. The threatened bull immediately responded by a head-low posture. Then both subordinates galloped toward the group, with the alpha bull following at a walk. Upon his arrival, the march was continued.

At 1011 hours, the march had come to a standstill, and a solitary bull approached the group from the east. The alpha bull charged him at a gallop. After an initial flight, the solitary bull stopped, turned, and after some reciprocal displays (erect posture, high presentation of horns), the two strenuously fought each other. At 1033 hours, after both were apparently exhausted, the alpha bull left his opponent standing and herded his group in the opposite direction (west). Several times he prevented herd members from walking back by threatening and chasing them. At 1041, the mixed herd resumed its march to the southeast with the alpha bull as the last animal of the file.

At 1125 hours, the herd had changed to grazing, standing, and lying. Two bulls were engaged in an intensive, long-lasting sparring match, ending with a chase at a gallop. The alpha bull intervened and stopped the pursuer in broadside position. The latter responded by submission and fled at a gallop. At 1241, the last animals stopped grazing, and a resting period began. During this pause, the alpha bull remained standing, circling with one of the cows in reverse-parallel position ("mating whirl-around") most of the time.

At 1520 hours, some of the animals stood up. The alpha bull left the cow and walked into the midst of the group. He displayed (head-low posture, head-throwing, and erect posture in lateral position) toward three lying bulls, all three of which arose immediately. At 1524, the herd formed a single file and marched to the southeast. One of the subordinate bulls remained behind, and the alpha bull had a full dominance encounter with him (erect stance, broadside position, averted head, etc., on the part of the alpha bull, head-low posture on the part of the subordinate). Finally, the subordinate walked after the moving herd, and the alpha bull followed. On the way, the subordinate slowed down, at which time the alpha bull caught up to him and displayed again. The subordinate fled at a gallop, pursued by the alpha bull, and both rejoined the herd. At 1528h, the animals grazed; at 1535, they marched again. Two bulls remained grazing. The alpha bull had a dominance encounter with one of them and followed him when he walked toward the herd. He ignored the second bull, who remained behind, still grazing. After a march of about 100 meters, the alpha bull stopped, turned, and walked back. He displayed to the grazing bull and made him follow the herd. He hurried him several times, and upon reaching the group he had a dominance encounter with another bull who had stopped.

At 1553 hours, the animals began to graze, and the alpha bull had another dominance encounter with one of the subordinate males. At 1624, three animals bedded down. The alpha bull approached one of them (in erect posture, with head averted and "pointing" ear), and it stood up. During the next five minutes, the group grazed and moved, and the alpha bull had three encounters with animals lagging behind. All ended by the recipients' following and catching up with the herd.

At 1725 hours, the herd was in a determined march, with the alpha bull walking 50 meters behind the others. At 1745, one of the sub-adult bulls straggled about 100 meters behind the alpha bull. The alpha bull stopped, returned to him, displayed, and brought him back to the herd, speeding him up to a gallop on the way. At 1758 hours, the beta bull, who had been the third animal in the file, suddenly galloped to the front, blocked the first cow's path in lateral T-position, threatened several arriving animals, and brought confusion to the group. Upon the alpha bull's arrival, a long dominance encounter with the beta bull ensued, ending with the latter's full submission and following the herd which, meanwhile, had continued moving.

Shortly before 1900 hours, I observed the last display of the alpha bull toward a member of the group who had slowed down. After this point, I could no longer recognize displays because of the darkness.

After these descriptions of herding behavior, the reader may now better understand why I have stressed several times in this book my disagreement with the opinion that the displays of animals such as hoofed mammals are only able to signal their internal state, not what they expect the recipient to do. They convey to him very well what they expect him to do, and they not only make him move but they also make him move in the direction they want him to go. Herding behavior offers particularly impressive examples of this direction signaling by the sender's aggressive displays and by his position relative to the recipient.

When a mammal is used to reacting to such (in the opinion of many people) relatively inconspicuous signals of its conspecifics, it often also is able to transfer its reactions to somewhat similar signals given by animals of another species, including humans. This is the story behind the famous "Clever Hans" experiment: the horse was erroneously presumed to have learned to count and to calculate, but in truth had learned to react to slight and completely unintended movements of the human trainer (Pfungst 1907, Hediger 1980). It also generally plays a basic role in man-animal communication and, above all, in the domestication of animals, as we will discuss in more detail in a following chapter.

17. COMPARATIVE DISTRIBUTION OF CERTAIN COMMUNICATIVE BEHAVIORS AND DISPLAYS

In our previous discussions, we have occasionally mentioned certain aspects of the distribution of communicative and expressive behaviors over the species. A thorough review of this subject would take a book of its own. Thus, I will only summarize here a few points and illustrate some special problems by a few selected examples. Such problems are quite numerous and many of them are true problems, i.e., a final answer is not known.

As a rule of thumb, one may say that in comparatively primitive species, olfactory and acoustical signals and (at close range) tactile stimulations play the major roles, whereas visual signals are few and often appear to be of minor importance. The opposite is the case in more advanced species: although tactile, olfactory, and acoustical signals are still in effect, visual signals—postures and gestures—become more and more numerous and important and vocalizations and the emission of odors appear to be mere accompaniments of the visual displays. In some cases, one may even get the impression that visual signals have replaced certain olfactory, tactile, or acoustical signals.

Some authors maintain that visual signals are mainly found in open plains animals, whereas communication by acoustical and/or olfactory means is typical of forest animals. There is some truth to this. However, on the whole, I think it misses the point. The primary factor for the prevalence of either acoustical and olfactory signals or visual displays seems to be the degree of advancement of the species in question. Acoustical and olfactory signals prevail in primitive ungulate species, and many of them are forest dwellers. However, a comparatively advanced species that happens to live in the forest will usually show about as many visual displays as any open plains species. For example, in the mating ritual of the okapi (an inhabitant of one of the densest tropical rain forest habitats to be found on earth), the male has a considerable repertoire of visual displays, such as erect posture, head-and-neck-stretched-upward/forward posture, head-throwing, foreleg kick, combinations of the latter with erect posture, etc. (Walther 1960*b*)—more than are shown by certain open plains species, such as bison (Lott 1974). In short, evolutionary and taxonomic aspects appear to be more persuasive than ecological aspects in explaining the distribution of communicative and expressive behaviors in ungulates.

On the other hand, the taxonomically oriented researcher will also find more than one "tough nut" in the distribution of communicative displays of hoofed mammals. Some of them, of course, are quite group specific. For example, the combination of the neck-stretch with the twist and/or the foreleg kick in courting males seems to be typical of goats and sheep. The neck-stretch occasionally occurs in combination with a foreleg kick in the courtship of only a few other horned ungulates, and in such cases it is usually not combined with a twist. Thus, this combination, and particularly this triple combination, distinguishes sheep and goats from other ungulates. However, in Thomson's gazelle, the courting buck displays the neck-stretch, the nose-up, the foreleg kick, and a combination of the foreleg kick with a lifted nose posture. Almost all these behaviors are also found in the aforementioned okapi bull, but none of them in, e.g., the bison bull—although the gazelle and the bison are in the same taxonomic family, the Bovidae, whereas the okapi belongs to a different family, the Giraffidae. (It is obvious that the "environment hypothesis" is no help here either, since Thomson's gazelle, like bison, is a typical open plains species.) In short, aspects of classification and phylogenetic relationships bring us a step forward in understanding the distribution of communicative and expressive behaviors in hoofed mammals, but they do not provide us with a final and truly reliable key. Many problems of this distribution must remain unsolved at present.

Presented below in the form of four tables (Tables 3-6) are a few selected examples of the distribution of certain communicative behaviors and expressive displays, as mentioned and described in previous chapters. These examples are mainly taken from behaviors that are neither so common as to be found in almost all of the species nor so rare as to be confined to only one or two of them. Taxonomic units (subfamilies, genera) for which our present knowledge does not allow definite statements on the majority of the behaviors under discussion have not been included. The tables mainly present the distribution of the behaviors at the level of genera. Subgenera or species are only mentioned when a genus includes a number of species and sufficient behavioral data are only available in one or a few of them.

Behaviors that leave marks in the environment. Table 3 presents certain behaviors that leave marks in the environment and thus may function as advertisements of the animal's presence, position, sex, or social status and may sometimes also serve as space claim displays. These include wallowing, the establishment of dung piles, marking of inanimate objects by secretion of glands on the head, and combinations of the aforementioned behaviors with scraping the ground. Urination is only mentioned when the performance is strikingly specialized, as in splashing the urine backwards, rub-urinating, urinating in (frequent) combination with pawing the ground, and urinating and defecating combined in a strict sequence and/or performed in extremely exaggerated postures. Object aggression (which also may leave visible spoor in the environment) is not included in this table because it occurs in so many species (in almost all the ruminants for example). Some types of object aggression (e.g., pawing the ground as a threat display) are presented in other tables. Special attention is paid in Table 3 to scraping the ground with forelegs or hind legs, but only insofar as it is combined with wallowing, urination, defecation, or gland marking. It does not include scraping the ground in search of food, prior to lying down, in combination with object aggression, or as a threat display of its own.

Within the odd-toed ungulates (Perissodactyla), all the more primitive forms, the tapirs and rhinoceroses (Ceratomorpha), wallow in sand and dust (black and square-lipped rhino) or in mud. (In Indian rhino and tapirs, wallowing may sometimes be difficult to distinguish from mere resting in muddy water). All of these species establish dung piles (the tapirs to a lesser extent than the rhinos because they frequently defecate while in the water), and they spray the urine backward. Defecation, but also sometimes spray urination, may be combined with backward scraping (wiping) movements of the hind legs in males, sometimes before but more often after the defecation or urination process (in Indian rhino, this is apparently less frequent and pronounced than in the others).

In the more advanced group (Hippomorpha) of the odd-toed ungulates, the horses and their relatives (Equidae), wallowing (mainly in sand and dust) is found in all the species. Marking with skin glands is lacking. In Grevy's zebra and in African and Asiatic wild ass, the territorial stallions establish large dung piles (Klingel 1969, 1974, 1977). In the nonterritorial equids (horse, plains and mountain zebra), dung piles are much smaller. In all the points mentioned so far, the behavior of Hippomorpha does not differ markedly from that of Ceratomorpha. However, scraping with the hind legs is lacking in the horse-related species (although they use their hind legs quite exten-

Table 3: Distribution of Certain Behaviors Suitable to Leave Marks in the Environment

Order Family Subfamily Genus (or Subgenus and/ or Species)	a	b	c	d	e	f	g	h	i	j
Perissodactyla										
Tapiridae										
Tapirus tapirs	++	-	++♂	+	+	-	-	-	-	-
Rhinocerotidae										
Rhinoceros unicornis Indian rhinoceros	++	-	?♂	inf.♂	++	-	-	-	-	-
Diceros black rhinoceros	++	-	+♂	++♂	++	-	-	-	-	-
Ceratotherium square-lipped rhinoceros	++	-	+♂	++♂	++♂	-	-	-	-	-
Equidae										
Equus horse, asses, zebras	++	+	-	-	++♂/+	+♂	-	-	-	-
Artiodactyla										
Suidae										
Sus scrofa wild boar	++	-	-	-	?	-	-	(+)♂	(+)♂	(+)♂

	1	2	3	4	5	6	7	8	9	10
Phacochoerus warthog	–	–	–	–	–	?	–	–	–	++
Tayassuidae										
Tayassu tajacu collared peccary	(++)	(+)	–	–	–	+	–	–	–	++
Hippopotamidae										
Hippopotamus hippopotamus	–	–	–	–	–	(++)♂	–	–	–	??
Camelidae										
Camelus camel, dromedary	+♂	–	–	–	–	–	–	–	–	?
Lama guanaco, vicuna	–	–	–	–	(++)	++	–	–	–	+
Tragulidae										
Hyemoschus water chevrotain	–	–	–	–	–	?	–	–	–	–
Tragulus mouse deer	++♂	–	–	–	–	?	??	–	–	–
Cervidae										
Moschinae										
Moschus musk deer	(+)♂	–	–	–	–	+	–	–	–	–
Odocoileinae										
Odocoileus (*Odocoileus*) white-tailed deer, mule deer	+♂	+♂	inf.	–	–	–	–	(++)♂	–	–
Capreolus roe deer	++♂	++♂	–	–	–	–	–	–	–	–

Table 3. (cont.) Distribution of Certain Behaviors Suitable to Leave Marks in the Environment

Order / Family / Subfamily / Genus (or Subgenus and/ or Species)	a	b	c	d	e	f	g	h	i	j
Alcinae										
Alces moose	–	(+)♂	–	–	–	–	–	(+)♂	–	–
Rangiferinae										
Rangifer reindeer, caribou	–	–	(++)♂	–	–	–	–	–	–	–
Muntiacinae										
Muntiacus muntjacs	–	–	–	–	–	–	–	–	–	++♂
Cervinae										
Dama fallow deer	–	–	–	–	–	–	–	–	–	–
Axis axis deer	–	–	–	–	–	–	–	inf.♂	++♂	+♂
Cervus red deer, elk, sambar, barasingha, etc.	+	++♂	–	–	–	–	–	inf.♂	++/+♂	+♂
Giraffidae										
Okapia okapi	–	–	–	–	–	–	–	–	–	–

	1	2	3	4	5	6	7	8	9	10
Giraffa giraffe	–	–	–	–	–	–	–	–	–	–
Antilocapridae										
Antilocapra pronghorn	++♂	–	–	++♂	–	–	–	–	–	–
Bovidae										
Cephalophinae										
Cephalophus maxwelli Maxwell's duiker	++		–	–	–	?	–	–	–	–
Neotraginae										
Madoqua (Rhynchotragus) kirki Kirk's dikdik	++	?	–	++♂	–	++	–	–	–	–
Oreotragus klipspringer	++	–	–	(+)	–	+	–	–	–	–
Raphicerus (Raphicerus) steenbok	?	–	–	++	–	+	inf.	–	–	–
Ourebia oribi	++♂	–	–	+♂	–	+	–	–	–	–
Tragelaphinae										
Tragelaphus (Tragelaphus) kudu, bushbuck, nyala, sitatunga, etc.	–	–	–	–	–	–	–	–	–	–
Tragelaphus (Taurotragus) oryx eland antelope	–	–	–	–	–	–	–	–	–	–
Boselaphus nilgai antelope	–	–	–	–	–	+	–	–	–	–

Table 3. (cont.) Distribution of Certain Behaviors Suitable to Leave Marks in the Environment

Order Family Subfamily Genus (or Subgenus and/ or Species)	a	b	c	d	e	f	g	h	i	j
Bovinae										
Bubalus (Bubalus) water buffalo	++	+	–	–	–	+	–		–	–
Syncerus African buffalo	++	inf.	–	–	–		–		–	–
Bos (Bibos) gaurus gaur	inf.	inf.	–	–	–		–	–	–	–
Bos (Bos) primigenius (Camargue) cattle	–	(++)	–	–	–	(+)	–	??	–	–
Bison bisons	++	++♂	–	–	–		–		–	–
Alcelaphinae										
Connochaetes wildebeests	+	++	–	–	+·♂	++♂	–	–	?	(+)
Alcelaphus hartebeests	–	(++)	–	–	++♂	++♂	–	–	–	+
Damaliscus topi, tsessebe, blesbok, etc.	–	(??)	–	–	++♂	++♂/–	–	–	inf.	++

Taxon										
Reduncinae										
Kobus — waterbucks, kobs, lechwes, etc.	–	–	–	–	–	–	–	–	–	–
Redunca — reedbucks	–	–	–	–	–	–	–	–	–	–
Hippotraginae										
Hippotragus — roan and sable antelope	–	–	–	–	+♂	–	–	–	–	–
Oryx — oryx antelopes	–	–	–	→(++)♂	–	+♂	–	–	–	–
Addax — addax antelope	–	–	–	→(++)♂	–	+♂	–	–	–	–
Antilopinae										
Gazella — gazelles	++♂/–	–	–	++♂	–	++♂	–	–	–	–
Antilope — Indian blackbuck	+♂	–	–	++♂	–	++♂	–	–	–	–
Litocranius — gerenuk	+♂	–	–	+♂	–	+♂	–	–	–	–
Ammodorcas — dibatag	?♂	–	–	+♂	–	+	–	–	–	–
Antidorcas — springbuck	–	–	–	++♂	–	++♂	–	–	–	–
Aepycerotinae										
Aepyceros — impala	(+)♂	–	–		–	+	–	–	–	–

Table 3. (cont.) Distribution of Certain Behaviors Suitable to Leave Marks in the Environment

Order Family Subfamily Genus (or Subgenus and/ or Species)	a	b	c	d	e	f	g	h	i	j
Caprinae										
Capra wild goat, ibex, markhor	–	–	–	–	–	–	–	–	–	–
Hemitragus tahrs	–	–	–	–	–	–	–	–	–	–
Ammotragus Barbary sheep	(+)	(+)	–	–	–	–	–	–	–	–
Ovis argali, urial, bighorn sheep, etc.	–		–	–	–	–	–	–	–	–
Rupicaprinae										
Rupicapra chamois	–	–	–	–	–	–	–	–	–	++♂
Oreamnos mountain goat	–	(++)♂	–	–	–	–	–	–	–	+
Ovibovinae										
Ovibos musk ox	–	–	–	–	–	–	–	–	–	(+)

a = wallowing in mud, sand, or dust
b = scraping the ground with foreleg before wallowing
c = scraping the ground with hind legs before and/or, more commonly, after urination
d = scraping the ground with hind legs before and/or, more commonly, after defecation
e = establishment of dung piles
f = scraping the ground with foreleg before defecation
g = scraping the ground with foreleg before urinating and defecating in a sequence and in striking postures
h = scraping the ground with foreleg before urination
i = scraping the ground with foreleg in combination with secretion marking by glands of the head region
j = marking of inanimate objects by special gland organs of the head region

SIGNS: + = clearly present
       ++ = very pronounced and/or frequent
       (+) = aberrant or strongly reduced performance
       +♂ = predominantly or exclusively in (adult) males
       inf. = present but infrequently used
       ?? = similar behavior present but dubious whether identical with behavior under discussion
        ? = not observed beyond reasonable doubts but possibly present
    blank = not observed or described; negative statement appears premature due to insufficient data
        – = never observed or described, lacking with great probability

For more explanation see text.

In this and the other tables on distribution of certain behavior patterns, the data on tapirs were mainly taken from Richter (1966), those on Indian and black rhinoceroses from Schenkel and Lang (1969), those on equids from Klingel (1972), those on wild boar from Beuerle (1975), those on warthog and hippopotamus from Frädrich (1967), those on peccary from Schweinsburg and Sowls (1972), those on camels and llamas from Pilters (1956), those on water chevrotain from Dubost (1965), those on mouse deer from Robin (1979), those on musk deer from Schäfer (1960), those on white-tailed deer from Hirth (1977), those on mule deer, moose, elk, bighorn sheep, and mountain goat from Geist (1965, 1966a, 1971), those on reindeer from Espmark (1964), Pruitt (1960), and Bergerud (1974), those on muntjacs from Dubost (1971) and Barette (1977), those on axis deer, sambar, barasingha, gaur, wild goat, tahrs, and blue sheep (bharal) from Schaller (1967, 1977), those on Maxwell's duiker from Aeschlimann (1963) and Ralls (1974), those on nyala from Anderson (1980), those on bongo from Hamann (1979), those on water buffalo from Wünschmann (1968), those on African buffalo from Sinclair (1974), those on (Camargue) cattle from Schloeth (1961a), those on American bison from Lott (1974), those on tsessebe from Joubert (1972), those on Uganda kob from Buechner and Schloeth (1965), those on lechwe from Lent (1969), those on reedbuck from Jungius (1970), those on roan and sable antelope from Huth (1980), those on addax from Manski (1979), those on impala from Schenkel (1966b) and Jarman & Jarman (1974), and those on musk ox from Gray (1973).

Table 4: Distribution of Certain Threat Displays (Mainly in Males)

Order **Family** **Subfamily** **Genus** **(or Subgenus and/ or Species)**	a	b	c	d	e	f	g	h	i	j
Perissodactyla										
Tapiridae										
Tapirus tapirs	+	–	–	–	–	–	–	–	–	–
Rhinocerotidae										
Rhinoceros unicornis Indian rhinoceros	?		–	–	–	(+)D??	–	(+)	← ++	–
Diceros black rhinoceros	–	+	–	–	–		–	(+)	← ++	–
Ceratotherium square-lipped rhinoceros	–	+	–	–	–	(+)D	–	(+)	← ++	–
Equidae										
Equus horse, asses, zebras	++	→ ++	+	++	++	++(D)	(+)(D)/–	(+)	← ++	–
Artiodactyla										
Suidae										
Sus scrofa wild boar	(++)	++		inf.	–	–	–	(+)	← ++	–

Taxon										
Phacochoerus warthog	−	−	−	−	−	−	−	?	?	−
Tayassuidae										
Tayassu tajacu collared peccary	(++)	−	−	−	−	(+)	−	−	+	−
Hippopotamidae										
Hippopotamus hippopotamus	(++)	−	−	??(D?)	−	−	−	−	−	−
Camelidae										
Camelus camel, dromedary	+	→ +	+	inf.	inf.	++D	−	−	−	−
Lama guanaco, vicuna	+	−	−	++	+	++(D)	+	−	+	−
Tragulidae										
Tragulus mouse deer	+	→ (+)	(+)	−	−	(+)(D?)	−	−	??	−
Cervidae										
Odocoileinae										
Odocoileus (Odocoileus) white-tailed deer, mule deer	−	??	(+)	+	+	++(D)	−	+	++	−
Capreolus roe deer	−	−	++		??	+(D)	−	+	++	−
Alcinae										
Alces moose	−	−	−	+	+	++	inf.	+	++	−
Rangiferinae										
Rangifer reindeer, caribou	−	+?(D?)	−	+?	?	−	++	?	++	−

Table 4. (cont.) Distribution of Certain Threat Displays (Mainly in Males)

Order
Family
  Subfamily
    Genus
    (or Subgenus and/
    or Species)
	a	b	c	d	e	f	g	h	i	j

Muntiacinae										
Muntiacus muntjacs	(++)/+♀→	+♀	–	–	–	–	–	++	–	–
Cervinae										
Dama fallow deer	+/(++)♀	??	–	+	–	+D	–	++	–	–
Axis axis deer	+/(++)D	+	(+)	+	+	++(D)	–	++	–	–

Cervus
  red deer, elk,
  sambar, sika, etc.
	+(?)/(++)D	+(♀)	inf.	+	+	++(D)	–	++	–	–

Giraffidae										
Okapia okapi	–	+	inf.	–	?	++(D)	–	(+)	←	++
Giraffa giraffe	–	++	–	–	inf.	++(D)	–	(++)	←	(+)
Antilocapridae										
Antilocapra pronghorn	–	?	–	–	–	–	–	(+)	←	++

Taxon									
Bovidae									
Cephalophinae									
Cephalophus nigrifrons	+	−	−	−	−	−	−	+	−
blackfronted duiker									
Neotraginae									
Madoqua (Rhynchotragus) kirki	−	??D	−	−	−	−	−	+	+
Kirk's dikdik									
Oreotragus	+♀	−	−	−	−	−	−	+	+
klipspringer									
Raphicerus (Raphicerus)	−	(+)	−	−	−	−	−	?	?
steenbok									
Tragelaphinae									
Tragelaphus (Tragelaphus)	+♀	(+)♀	−	−	−	??♀	−	++	++
kudu, bushbuck, nyala, etc.									
Tragelaphus (Taurotragus)	(++)♀	−	−	−	−	??♀	−	++	++
eland antelope, bongo									
Boselaphus	+♀	++(D)	−	inf.♀	−	inf.♀	−	inf.	(+)
nilgai antelope									
Bovinae									
Syncerus	−	−	−	−	−	−	−	++	+
African buffalo									
Bos (Bibos) gaurus	−	inf.	−	−	−	−	−	+	+
gaur									
Bos (Bos) primigenius	−	++	−	−	−	−	−	++	(+)
(Camargue) cattle									
Bison bison	−	++	−	−	−	??	−	??	−
American bison									

Table 4. (cont.) Distribution of Certain Threat Displays (Mainly in Males)

Order Family Subfamily Genus (or Subgenus and/ or Species)	a	b	c	d	e	f	g	h	i	j
Alcelaphinae										
Connochaetes wildebeests	–	–	++	–	–	–	–	+	??	++
Alcelaphus hartebeests	(+)	–	++	–	–	–	–	++	+	++
Damaliscus topi, tsessebe, blesbok, etc.	–	–	+	–	–	–	inf.	++	+	++
Reduncinae										
Kobus waterbuck, kobs, lechwes, etc.	(+)♀/–	??/–	–		–	??♀	+/–	++	++	–
Hippotraginae										
Hippotragus roan and sable antelope	–	–/??	?/+	–	–	–	+	++	++	+
Oryx oryx antelopes	–	–	+	–	–	++D/–	+	++	++	+
Addax addax antelope	–	–		–	–	–	?	++	++	+

Taxon										
Antilopinae										
Gazella gazelles	–	–	+/inf.	–	–	–	++/+	++	+/inf.	–
Antilope Indian blackbuck	–	–	–	–	–	–	–	++	+	–
Litocranius gerenuk	–	–	?	–	–	??:	–	++	++	–
Antidorcas springbuck	(+)	–	–	–	–	–	–	+	++	–
Aepycerotinae										
Aepyceros impala	–	–	–	–	–	–	?	++	++	–
Caprinae										
Capra wild goat, ibex, markhor	–	–	(inf.)	++	–	inf.(D)	(++)	++	+/–	–
Hemitragus tahrs	–	–	(+)	inf.	–	–	–	+	↓ ++	–
Ammotragus Barbary sheep	–	–	–	inf.	–	–	–	++	?	–
Pseudois blue sheep	–	–	(inf.)	+	–	+(D)	–	++	++	–
Ovis argali, urial, bighorn sheep, etc.	–	–	+/(inf.)	++/inf.	–	++(D)	inf./?	++	inf.	–
Rupicaprinae										
Rupicapra chamois	–	?	–	??:	–	–	–	++	++	–

Table 4. (cont.) Distribution of Certain Threat Displays (Mainly in Males)

Order Family Subfamily Genus (or Subgenus and/ or Species)	a	b	c	d	e	f	g	h	i	j
Oreamnos mountain goat	–	–	(++)		–	–	–	+♀(++)→ (+)	(+)	–
Ovibovinae										
Ovibos musk ox	–	–	+		–	–	?	++	??	–

a = bite-threat and related behaviors
b = neck-stretch
c = scraping the ground with foreleg (excluding cases prior to defecation, urination, wallowing, etc.)
d = (symbolic) rising on hind legs
e = (symbolic) foreleg kick
f = erect posture (including lifted-nose posture, nose-up, head-and-neck-stretched-forward/upward posture, etc.)
g = high presentation of horns or antlers
h = medial (and low) presentation of horns or antlers
i = head-low posture
j = (symbolic) kneeling posture

SIGNS: +♀ = predominantly or exclusively in females
        +(♀) = in females more frequent than in males
        +(D) = threat display with a minor dominance display component in it
        +D = strong dominance display component
        ← = strong connection or transition

Other signs and comments see Table 3.

Table 5: Distribution of Certain (Predominantly Male) Dominance Displays Commonly Presented in Lateral Orientation

Order 　Family 　　Subfamily 　　　Genus 　　　(or Subgenus and/ 　　　or Species)	a	b	c	d	e	f	g	h	i	j
Perissodactyla										
Tapiridae										
Tapirus 　　tapirs	–	–	–	–	–	–	–	–	–	–
Rhinocerotidae										
Diceros 　　black rhinoceros	–	–	–	–	–	–	–	–	??f	–
Ceratotherium 　　square-lipped 　　rhinoceros	–	–	–	–	–	–	–	–	+F	–
Equidae										
Equus 　　horse, asses, zebras	(+)TF/?	–	–	–	–	–	++TF ←	+TF		–
Artiodactyla										
Suidae										
Sus scrofa 　　wild boar	–	(+)Tf	–	+Tf	–	–	(++)(T) ← (++)(T) ← (++)(T) ← (++)(T)	–	–	–
Phacochoerus 　　warthog	–	–	–	–	–	–	–	–	(+)(T)f	–

Table 5. (cont.) Distribution of Certain (Predominantly Male) Dominance Displays Commonly Presented in Lateral Orientation

Order
Family
  Subfamily
    Genus
    (or **Subgenus** and/ or **Species**)

	a	b	c	d	e	f	g	h	i	j
Tayassuidae										
Tayassu tajacu collared peccary	–	–	–	–	–	–	+TF	–	–	–
Camelidae										
Camelus camel, dromedary	–	–	–	–	–	–	++(T)F	–	–	–
Lama guanaco, vicuna	–	–	–	–	–	+TF	++TF	–	–	??
Tragulidae										
Tragulus mouse deer	–	–	–	–	–	–	–	??T	–	–
Cervidae										
Odocoileinae										
Odocoileus (*Odocoileus*) white-tailed deer, mule deer	+T	–	–/+	–	–	–	–	++T/?	–	–
Capreolus roe deer	–	–	–	–	–	–	–	+	↓ +	–

Taxon	C1	C2	C3	C4	C5	C6	C7	C8	C9
Alcinae									
Alces — moose	?T	–	–	–	–	–	++TF		–
Rangiferinae									
Rangifer — reindeer, caribou	–	–	–	??(T)F♀	–	–	–		–
Muntiacinae									
Muntiacus — muntjacs	–	–	–	–	–	–	–		–
Cervinae									
Dama — fallow deer	(+)T	–	–	–	–	–	(+)Tf	(++)	–
Axis — axis deer	??T	–	–	+Tf	–	++Tf	++Tf		–
Cervus — red deer, elk, barasingha, etc.	(+)T	–	–	+Tf → +Tf	–	++TF	++TF	+	–
Giraffidae									
Okapia — okapi	–	–	–	+TF → ++Tf	+(T)F	+(T)F	–		–
Giraffa — giraffe	–	–	–	+Tf ↓ +(T)f	+(T)f	++	++		–
Antilocapridae									
Antilocapra — pronghorn	–	–	+	+	↓	+	+		+C
Bovidae									
Cephalophinae									
Cephalophus nigrifrons — black-fronted duiker	–	–	–	–	–	–	?		–

Table 5. (cont.) Distribution of Certain (Predominantly Male) Dominance Displays Commonly Presented in Lateral Orientation

Order / Family / Subfamily / Genus (or Subgenus and/or Species)	a	b	c	d	e	f	g	h	i	j
Neotraginae										
Madoqua (Rhynchotragus) kirki — Kirk's dikdik	–	–	–	–	–	–	–	–	–	–
Raphicerus (Raphicerus) — steenbok	–	–	–	–	–	–	–	?	–	–
Tragelaphinae										
Tragelaphus (Tragelaphus) — greater & lesser kudu, nyala, etc.	–	–/? ←	++/– →	?/–	inf.	??$_+$	++f ←	++f	–	inf.F
Tragelaphus (Taurotragus) — eland, bongo	–	–	–	–	inf./++f →	??$_+$	–/+f ←	++F	–	inf.F
Boselaphus — nilgai antelope	–	–	inf.T ←	+T ←	++T →	+T	–	??	–	–
Bovinae										
Syncerus — African buffalo	(+)T →	(+)T	–	–	–	–	–	–	+	–
Bos (Bibos) gaurus — gaur	+T ←	(+)T ←	++ →	+	–	–	–	–	–	–

Species							
Bos (Bos) primigenius (Camargue) cattle	(+)T ←	–	–	–	–	+	(+)f
Bison bison	??T	–	–	–	–	??	(+)f
American bison	(++)	–	–	–	–	+	(+)f
Alcelaphinae							
Connochaetes wildebeests	–	–	–	–	–	+++F →	++F
Alcelaphus hartebeests	–	–	–	–	–	++F →	+F
Damaliscus topi, tsessebe, blesbok, etc.	–	–	+/– ←	+f ←	++f	+F →	++F
Reduncinae							
Kobus waterbuck, Gray's waterbuck, kob, etc.	–	??:/–	??/–	+/inf.F	++/inf.F	+F	++/?
Hippotraginae							
Hippotragus roan and sable antelope	++T	–	–	–	–	+	–
Oryx oryx antelopes	–	–	–	+(T)/– ←	++/+(T)	++(T)	+f
Addax addax antelope	–	–	–	–	–	+	+f
Antilopinae							
Gazella gazelles	–	–	–	++/–	++f/–	+TF/–	++f/–
Antilope Indian blackbuck	–	–	–	–	++f →	+f	–

Table 5. (cont.) Distribution of Certain (Predominantly Male) Dominance Displays Commonly Presented in Lateral Orientation

Order
Family
Subfamily
Genus (or Subgenus and/or Species)

	a	b	c	d	e	f	g	h	i	j
Litocranius gerenuk	–	–	–	–	–	–	++F ←++F	–	–	+F
Antidorcas springbuck	–	–	–	–	–	–	–	–	–	–
Aepycerotinae										
Aepyceros impala	–	–	–	–	–	–	–	+F → +F	–	++F
Caprinae										
Capra wild goat, ibex, markhor	++T/-→ +T/- → inf./-	–	–	–	–	–	–	–	–	–
Hemitragus tahrs		+T ← ++f		?	(+)/–				?	
Ammotragus Barbary sheep	–	–	–	–	–	–	–	–	–	–
Pseudois blue sheep	–	+T ← +f			++fC		–	+T		–
Ovis argali, urial, bighorn sheep, etc.	–	–	–/inf.	–	++CF	–	+TF/–	++TF	–	+F

Rupicaprinae
  Rupicapra
    chamois
  Oreamnos
    mountain goat

	a	b	c	d	e	f	g	h	i	j
Rupicapra chamois	—	—	(+)'T ←	(+)'T ←	(++)'T	—	??	??'T	?	??(+)
Oreamnos mountain goat	—	—	—	—	—	—	—	—	—	—

a = medial presentation of horns or antlers in broadside position
b = low presentation of horns or antlers in broadside position
c = humped-back posture (hunch)
d = head-low posture
e = neck-stretch
f = head-and-neck-stretched-forward/upward posture and/or nose-up posture
g = lifted-nose posture
h = erect posture with nose pointing horizontally forward
i = erect stance with moderately erected neck and nose pointing forward-downward
j = sideward-turn of the head

SIGNS: +(T) = dominance display with a minor threat display component in it
    +T = strong threat display component
    +C = primarily used as a courtship display
    +f = sometimes also displayed in frontal orientation
    +F = predominantly displayed in frontal orientation

Other signs and comments see Tables 3 and 4.

Table 6. Distribution of Certain Male Courtship Displays

Order / Family / Subfamily / Genus (or Subgenus and/or Species)	a	b	c	d	e	f	g	h	i	j
Perissodactyla										
Tapiridae										
Tapirus tapirs	+		+	−	−	−	−	??	−	−
Rhinocerotidae										
Rhinoceros unicornis Indian rhinoceros	+	−	+	−	−	−	−	??	−	−
Diceros black rhinoceros	−	−	+	−	−	−	−		?	−
Ceratotherium square-lipped rhinoceros	−	−	+	−	−	−	−	??	(+)	−
Equidae										
Equus horse, asses, zebras	−/(??)		??		−	−	−		?	−
Artiodactyla										
Suidae										
Sus scrofa wild boar	(+)		+	−	−	−	−		(+)	−

Taxon										
Phacochoerus warthog	−	??:	−	−	−	−	−	+	−	−
Tayassuidae										
Tayassu tajacu collared peccary	−		−	−	−	−	−	+	−	(+)
Camelidae										
Camelus camel, dromedary	−	+ ↑	+	−	−	−	−	??	? ↑	+
Lama guanaco, vicuna	−	+ ↑	++	−	−	−	−	??	? ↑	+
Tragulidae										
Tragulus mouse deer	−	−	−	−	−	−	−	(++)	−	(+)
Cervidae										
Odocoileinae										
Odocoileus (*Odocoileus*) white-tailed deer, mule deer	−	−	−/(+)	−	−	−	−	++	−	−
Capreolus roe deer	−	−	−	−	−	−	−	++	−	−
Alcinae										
Alces moose	−	−	−	−	−	−	−	++	−	−
Rangiferinae										
Rangifer reindeer, caribou	−	−	−	−	−	−	−	++p	(+) ←	(+)

Table 6. (cont.) Distribution of Certain Male Courtship Displays

Order Family Subfamily Genus (or Subgenus and/ or Species)	a	b	c	d	e	f	g	h	i	j
Muntiacinae										
Muntiacus muntjacs	–	–	++	–	–	–	–	–	–	–
Cervinae										
Dama fallow deer	–	–	++	–	–	–	–	–	–	–
Axis axis deer	–	–	++	–	–	–	–	+p	+p	–
Cervus red deer, elk, sika, etc.	–	–	++/–	–	–	–	–	–	–/+	–
Giraffidae										
Okapia okapi	–	–	(+)	–	+	++	?	++	+	–
Giraffa giraffe	–	–	–	–	–	–	–	+	++	–
Antilocapridae										
Antilocapra pronghorn	–	–	–	–	–	–	–	+	++	++

Taxon								
Bovidae								
Cephalophinae								
Cephalophus nigrifrons black-fronted duiker	+	++	−	−	−	−	?	−
Neotraginae								
Madoqua (Rhynchotragus) kirki Kirk's dikdik	++	−	−	−	−	−	−	−
Raphicerus (Raphicerus) steenbok	+	++	−	−	−	−	+	−
Tragelaphinae								
Tragelaphus (Tragelaphus) kudu, sitatunga, nyala, etc.	−/(+)p ← (+)p ← ++p	−	−	−	−	++/−	++/−	inf.
Tragelaphus (Taurotragus) eland antelope, bongo	(+)p ← +/++p	−	−	−	−	−/?	+	+/?
Boselaphus nilgai antelope	(+)	−	−	−	−	−	−	−
Bovinae								
Bos (Bibos) gaurus gaur	−	−	−	−	−	−	−	−
Bos (Bos) primigenius (Camargue) cattle	??	−	−	−	−	−	??	−
Bison bison American bison	??	−	−	−	−	−	??	−
Alcelaphinae								
Connochaetes wildebeests	+	−	−	−	−	−	−	−

Table 6. (cont.) Distribution of Certain Male Courtship Displays

Order
Family
Subfamily
  Genus
  (or **Subgenus** and/
  or **Species**)

	a	b	c	d	e	f	g	h	i	j
Alcelaphus hartebeests	–	–	++	–	–	–	–	(+)	–	–
Damaliscus topi, tsessebe, blesbok, etc.	–	–	??/++	–	+/–	–	–	++/– →	+/–	inf.
Reduncinae										
Kobus waterbuck, kobs, lechwes, etc.	–	–	(+)/–	–/+	++/(+)	–/+	–	++/–	+?	inf./–
Redunca arundium southern reedbuck	–	–	+	–	–	–	–	–	?	–
Hippotraginae										
Hippotragus roan and sable antelope	–	–	–	–	++rp	–	–	–	++rp	–
Oryx oryx antelopes	–	–	–	–	++/(++)rp	–	–	–	+/(+)rp	–
Addax addax antelope	–	–	–	–	(++)rp	–	–	–	(+)rp	–

Antilopinae	-									
Gazella gazelles	-	-	++/??	-/(+)	++/-	++/-	+/-	++/-	++/inf.	inf.
Antilope Indian blackbuck	-	-	-	-	-	(+)	++ ↓	++ ↓	(+) ↑	-
Litocranius gerenuk	-	-	-	+	++	++	inf.	++ ↓	++	+
Antidorcas springbuck	-	-	+	-	++	-	-	+	+	+
Aepycerotinae	-									
Aepyceros impala	-	-	++	++	-	-	-	-	?	
Caprinae	-									
Capra wild goat, ibex, markhor	-	++/inf.p	←++p	→++p	++	-	-	-	-/?	-
Hemitragus tahrs	-	+	+	-	+	-	-	(?)-	-	-
Ammotragus Barbary sheep	-	+	+	+	-	-	-	-	-	-
Pseudois blue sheep	-	inf.	++	+	+	-	-	-	-	-
Ovis argali, urial, bighorn sheep, etc.	-	++p	←++p	→++p	++	-	-	-	+	inf.
Rupicaprinae	-									
Rupicapra chamois	-	??	??	-	-	-	-	+	←++	-

Table 6. (cont.) Distribution of Certain Male Courtship Displays

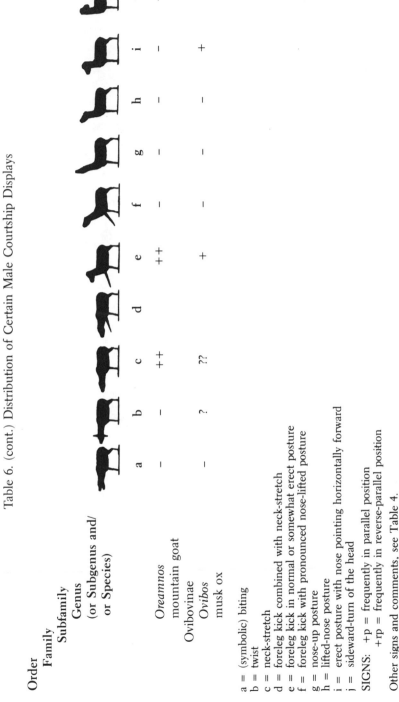

Order Family Subfamily Genus (or Subgenus and/ or Species)	a	b	c	d	e	f	g	h	i	j
Oreamnos mountain goat	–	–	++		++	–	–	–	–	–
Ovibovinae *Ovibos* musk ox	–	?	??		+	–	–	–	+	

a = (symbolic) biting
b = twist
c = neck-stretch
d = foreleg kick combined with neck-stretch
e = foreleg kick in normal or somewhat erect posture
f = foreleg kick with pronounced nose-lifted posture
g = nose-up posture
h = lifted-nose posture
i = erect posture with nose pointing horizontally forward
j = sideward-turn of the head

SIGNS: +p = frequently in parallel position
+rp = frequently in reverse-parallel position

Other signs and comments, see Table 4.

sively in hostile interactions). Instead, pawing the ground with a foreleg may precede wallowing and, in stallions, sometimes defecation as well. In this regard, the horses have much less in common with the other odd-toed ungulates than with certain species of even-toed ungulates. This is probably due to similarities in morphological and anatomical structure.

In even-toed ungulates (Artiodactyla), all the Nonruminantia (swine, peccaries, and hippos) wallow in mud. This may be somewhat questionable in hippos but they are at least sometimes found in very muddy water. Male hippos distribute their dung by propelling movements of the tail at definite places, which may be said to be a special form of dung piling. In swine, dung piles apparently are not regular institutions but sometimes concentrations of dung may be found (Frädrich 1967). The presence of dung piles is mentioned in peccary (Sowls 1974). Scraping the ground with the forelegs does not appear to be combined with defecation in the Nonruminantia, and it also is not very prominent in combination with urination and gland marking. We encounter object marking with gland secretion for the first time in a Nonruminantia species, the peccary. However, it is still different from the marking with head glands that is so striking and frequent in certain ruminants. Perhaps one could also mention the foam (saliva) marking of wild boar in this context. (Wild boar possess preorbital glands but nothing is known of their use in object marking.)

In the Tylopoda, the camels and llamas (Camelidae), wallowing is present in the *Lama* species. (I did not find any mention of its presence or absence in camels in the literature available to me, and do not know enough about their behavior to make an authoritative statement.) Dung piles are not found in camels but are prominent in vicuna and guananco. Defecation and urination are usually combined in the wild llamas; however, they first defecate and then urinate. Consequently, the initial scraping precedes the defecation rather than the urination in this case. Moreover, the movements of their forelegs before elimination are better described as stamping than scraping. In these details, the behavior of llamas at their dung piles differs from that of certain ruminants, which show a urination-defecation sequence (i.e., they urinate before they defecate, and they do not stamp but scrape the ground). Thus, this behavior of llamas is not homologous to that of the said ruminants. In camels, we encounter a clear case of object marking with a head gland. However, in contrast to all other ungulates, in camel this is done with an occipital gland.

The Tragulidae, the most primitive of recent Ruminantia, do not wallow. The occurrence of dung piles appears to be questionable in their case. Dubost (1975) did not find that free-ranging African water chevrotain established dung piles, but captive animals localized their feces. Thus, the concentration of dung may be linked to the captive condition in these animals. Scraping the ground with the forelegs is not reported from tragulids. However, at least lesser Malayan mouse deer may lift the hind legs alternately before defecating so that one could possibly think of a remote "resemblance" to the scraping the ground with the hind legs in Ceratomorpha. (One also should not forget that mouse deer stamp the ground with all four legs, and even particularly with the hind legs, in "drumming"—not mentioned in Table 3.) Interestingly, even in at least some of these very primitive ruminant species, we find a behavior which we have encountered only once in all the animals mentioned previously: object marking with special head glands, in this case the interramal (or intermandibular) glands. The lesser Malayan mouse deer also marks with proctodeal glands (not mentioned in Table 3), which is absolutely unique in hoofed mammals.

In deer (Cervidae), wallowing occurs in the genus *Cervus* (with all of its subgenera: *Cervus, Rusa, Rucervus, Sika*), i.e., red deer, elk, sambar, barasingha, and sika deer. They frequently paw the ground with their forelegs in this connection. In moose, the establishment of rutting pits may be somewhat related to wallowing. All the many other cervids, such as musk deer, muntjac, roe deer, mule deer, fallow deer, axis deer, etc., do not wallow. The primitive musk deer establish dung piles. In the more highly evolved Cervidae species, dung piles are unknown. Urine seems to play a somewhat more important role than dung in their social life. Besides self-impregnation by urine in stags during rutting season (not shown in Table 3), stags of the *Cervus* species may urinate in the wallowing places. Furthermore, rub-urination is found in the genus *Odocoileus* (e.g., mule deer and white-tailed deer) and in reindeer. Although rub-urination appears to be primarily a kind of self-impregnation, it is likely that some fluid also runs onto the ground, and the whole performance may very remotely resemble the hind leg scraping in combination with urination in Ceratomorpha; at least movements of the hind legs are involved. However, this does not bespeak a phylogenetic relationship. (In Table 3, it is placed in the same column mainly to save space.) Finally, urination may also, although infrequently, be combined with foreleg scraping in a few cervid species such as axis or white-tailed deer. The connection of pawing with a foreleg to gland marking is more pronounced in species such as roe deer (Müller-Using and Schloeth 1967), and in "preaching" species such as axis deer or sambar (Schaller 1967). In cervids, the strongest connection of pawing the ground seems to be with object aggression (thrashing vegetation) with the antlers (not presented in Table 3). The gland marking of musk deer, the most primitive species within the Cervidae family, deviates from the usual in that male musk deer mark branches with the secretion of the circumcaudal glands at their very short tails (Schäfer 1960). Roe bucks mark with their frontal gland. All the other cervid species, to the extent that they show marking with head glands, use their preorbital glands: male muntjac, white-tailed deer, red deer, sambar, barasingha, axis deer, etc. On the other hand, there are also Cervidae species, such as moose and reindeer, in which any comparable gland marking is lacking.

In the Giraffidae, okapi and giraffe, all the behaviors under discussion are absent. Some kind of urine marking in okapi bulls has been described by Lang (1956) but it apparently is not combined with any form of scraping with legs.

In the Antilocapridae, the pronghorn, wallowing is lacking. Adult males urinate and defecate in sequence and in striking postures, and this sequence is more or less regularly initiated by pawing the ground with a foreleg. However, even in territorial bucks, it apparently does not result in the establishment of sizable dung piles. Otherwise the details of this urination-defecation sequence in pronghorn agree so strikingly with the corresponding behavior of gazelles and certain dwarf antelopes (see below) that I find it hard to believe in a mere analogy, although, of course, there is a relative taxonomic distance of pronghorn to these other species. In contrast to all other ungulates, pronghorn bucks mark by means of their subauricular glands.

Things become most interesting but also most complicated when we come to the horned ungulates (Bovidae), as is to be expected considering the great number of species and the great differences in size, body structure, habitats, etc., within this group. Wallowing is mainly found in two subfamilies: the oxen (Bovinae) and the wildebeest and their relatives (Alcelaphinae). In all these species, it is quite frequently combined with scraping the ground with the forelegs. The Bovinae run the gamut from species such as bison in which wallowing is very pronounced and frequent, to species such as gaur where it apparently is present but rather infrequent, to species such as domestic cattle (as descendants of the extinct wild form, the aurochs— Table 3 presents the situation for Camargue cattle, a domestic breed which appears to be relatively close to the extinct wild form), which, although they do not wallow in the true sense, show some behaviors that can be considered phylogenetic relics of wallowing. Thus, in the oxen as a group, wallowing is present, but with indications of some diminution. This diminution is even more obvious in the Al-celaphinae. Of the three genera of this group, only the wildebeests (*Connochaetes*) truly wallow. The other two genera, the hartebeests (*Alcelaphus*) and the topi-related species (*Damaliscus*), only show a behavioral sequence, described in previous chapters, in which pawing the ground plays an important role, that more or less corresponds to wallowing in wildebeest. However, these animals do not roll on the ground. Otherwise, wallowing-like behavior shows up sporadically in only two other Bovidae species. (I have disregarded the occasional rubbing of head and neck on the ground while an animal is resting with head and neck stretched forward. This can occasionally happen in almost all the ungulates and is not presented in Table 3). Barbary sheep (as the single species of the Caprinae subfamily) wallow in mud but they do so in a very special form by kneeling or lying down and throwing mud on their backs with their horns. Mountain goats do not wallow but the males may sit down like dogs and dig pits during rut-ting season. The mountain goat's closest relative, the chamois (living in a similar habitat), does not show any comparable behavior. None of the many other Bovidae species wallow, and in these, consequent-ly, there is no connection with pawing the ground. Thus, on the whole, wallowing is the exception rather than the rule in horned un-gulates.

Dung piles are found in a number of Bovidae species, predomi-nantly in those belonging to the subfamilies of dwarf antelopes (Neo-traginae), the gazelles and their relatives (Antilopinae), and the hartebeest-related (Alcelaphinae). In a number of dwarf antelopes, such as dikdik and klipspringer, which have pair territories, male and female eliminate on the same dung pile. However, e.g., in steenbok, where male and female often live separated from each other, each animal establishes dung piles of its own. In Antilopinae and Al-celaphinae, the establishment of dung piles is restricted to males (with the possible exception of the dibatag), and in the overwhelming majority of the cases to territorial males. The situation seems to be similar in addax and oryx antelopes (except that territoriality is not as well proven in these animals as in Antilopinae and Alcelaphinae). On the other hand, the fact that territorial behavior does not necessarily lead to the establishment of dung piles in hoofed mammals is dem-onstrated by the waterbuck and its relatives (Reduncinae), where males are territorial but do not establish dung piles. In the duikers (Cephalophinae), where only one (Maxwell's duiker) of the many species has been sufficiently investigated to allow statements on such details of behavior as are of interest here, concentrations of dung have been reported from animals in captivity (Aeschlimann 1963).

Somewhat suprisingly, dung piles also occur in nilgai antelope, which is not closely related to any of the aforementioned Bovidae groups. Whether this is linked to territorial behavior is doubtful in this case (p. 94). Besides the aforementioned reed- and waterbucks (Reduncinae), dung piles are lacking in many other bovid species such as spiral-horned antelopes (genus *Tragelaphus*, including the subgenus *Taurotragus*, within the subfamily Tragelaphinae); oxen (Bovinae—although the cow dung may sometimes resemble a "dung pile," this is not through the accumulation of successive eliminations); goats, sheep, and their relatives (Caprinae); chamois-related species (Rupicaprinae); and musk ox (Ovibovinae). Also, no striking dung piles have been found in roan and sable antelope (genus *Hippotragus* of the Hippotraginae subfamily).

Urination and defecation in sequence and in exaggerated postures, frequently initiated by pawing the ground with forelegs, is typical of adult males in gazelles and related species (Antilopinae), and in dwarf antelopes (Neotraginae). In the latter, the urination-defecation sequence is also found in the females of some species, e.g., dikdik and steenbok. Steenbok males and females have the peculiar habit of scraping the ground not only before but also after the performance of said sequence, and also with their hind feet. Pawing with forefeet before defecation mainly occurs in males of those species—besides Antilopinae and Neotraginae—which establish dung piles in their territories, i.e., primarily the Alcelaphinae. However, this is not the case in all of them, e.g., bontebok (David 1973). Dominant bulls of addax antelope and all the oryx species (or subspecies, depending on the classification system used) show a combination of pawing the ground with a striking defecation posture. The defecation postures of wildebeest, hartebeest, and topi bulls are not strikingly exaggerated. Pawing the ground before defecation also occurs in male roan and sable antelope, which are not known to establish dung piles. Likewise, cattle may defecate in small portions while scraping the ground (in agonistic encounters) without establishing dung piles.

With the exception of scraping the ground before the urination-defecation sequence of gazelles and dwarf antelopes, pawing with the forelegs before urination is exceptional in Bovidae. It is known mainly from cattle, and then only in extremely stressful situations, e.g., in a bullfight arena (Schloeth 1959). Scraping the ground in combination with gland marking occurs in only a very few Bovidae species, and even then infrequently.

About 50 percent of the Bovidae species mark with special glands of the head region. This is lacking in oxen (Bovinae), spiral-horned antelopes (Tragelaphinae), reed- and waterbucks (Reduncinae) and sheep and goats (Caprinae). Some of these animals simply do not have functional specialized gland organs of the head region. Impala also does not have specialized gland organs on the head (Haltenorth 1963), but Jarman and Jarman (1974) speak of a "glandular area" on the forehead of the males, and they found oily secretion from it deposited on vegetation. In duikers (Cephalophinae), dwarf antelopes (Neotraginae), hartebeest-related species (Alcelaphinae), gazelles and their relatives (Antilopinae), chamois-related species (Rupicaprinae), and also some smaller groups such as musk ox (Ovibovinae), marking with glands on the head is common.

Threat displays. Table 4 presents certain examples of gestures and postures functioning as threat displays in hoofed mammals, particularly in males. Dominance displays are generally excluded, but a few transitional cases, i.e., threat displays with a dominance display component, are included. Furthermore, pure pawing the ground (i.e., pawing which neither precedes wallowing, nor urination and/or defecation) in agonistic encounters is included in this table since it may at least come close to a threat display (strictly speaking, it is more of a space-claim display). Table 4 also presents (symbolic) biting and related behaviors, neck-stretch, (symbolic) rising on the hind legs, (symbolic) foreleg kick, erect posture, high presentation of horns or antlers, medial presentation of horns or forehead, head-low posture, and (symbolic) kneeling. Most of these displays are self-explanatory and have been extensively described in previous chapters. The threat jump, which at least occasionally occurs in almost all the species, is not included in "rising on the hind legs." The latter means that the animal truly stands on its hind feet for several seconds and the body is almost vertically erected. It includes the intention to throw the body on the opponent as well as to flail with the forelegs and to "dive" down into a horn clash. "Foreleg kick" and "scraping the ground with a foreleg" are presented regardless of combinations with special postures of head and neck. "Erect posture" includes all kinds of erect stances. It includes cases in which the head is not raised above the horizontal level as well as the lifted-nose posture, the full nose-up, and the head-and-neck-stretched-forward/upward posture. The relatively infrequent cases of low presentation of horns are included in "medial presentation" in Table 4.

As far as our still rather fragmentary knowledge of agonistic behavior in tapirs goes, the only threat displays in these animals seem to be related to biting. The most detailed study of tapir behavior is that of von Richter (1966). He does not specifically mention symbolic biting, but it may be presumed that it exists in tapirs since biting is their major fighting technique. In any case, von Richter describes and documents a facial expression in the lowland tapir that is obviously a ritualized form of biting behavior.

Similarly, symbolic biting has not been literally described in the Indian rhinoceros. However, they also bite frequently in their fights, and judging from a photo in Schenkel and Lang (1969), it is likely that symbolic biting or a presentation of the open mouth may occur as a threat display in this species. By contrast, biting is lacking as a fighting technique in the two African rhinos, and there are no indications of a threat display related to biting in them. All rhinos assume a head-low threat as an intention movement for throwing the head upward in fighting with their horns. This threat posture may sometimes approximate that of medial or low presentation of horns or antlers in Bovidae and Cervidae. Furthermore, rhinos can throw their heads upward in a symbolic form, and this behavior may somewhat resemble the erect posture of other species. Of course, there are other behaviors, such as the rush, the symbolic chase, and certain movements of the ears, which are not listed in Table 4. However, their inclusion would not "proportionally" change very much as compared to other ungulate species since these behaviors are widespread. On the whole, visual threats are comparatively infrequent and poorly developed in Ceratomorpha.

This picture changes drastically when we come to the more advanced Hippomorpha. Facial expressions derived from biting are numerous in horses, asses and zebras. A neck-stretch posture, frequently with the mouth still closed, is an intention movement to bite, and the head-low posture so typical of Equidae stallions in herding and hostile encounters can probably also be related to biting. As in the Ceratomorpha, this head-low may occasionally resemble the posture of medial or low presentation in horned or antlered ungulates. In all the Equidae, fighting stallions often rise on their hind legs. Since they can bite, kick with their forelegs, throw their body onto the opponent, and/or initiate a neck-fight from this posture, the corresponding symbolic performance can be related to all these fighting techniques. The erect stance, usually with the nose somewhat lifted above horizontal level, but sometimes approximating the posture of high presentation of horns in bovids is an intention movement for rising on the hind legs and/or for kicking with the forelegs in horses and zebras. One could possibly relate a certain dominance display component to it. Basically, however, it is the intention movement for actual fighting, and thus a threat display in these animals. The kick with a stiffly stretched foreleg while standing on three legs, is another fighting movement of horse-related animals which also occurs in symbolic form. Finally, horses may scrape the ground with a foreleg (redirected aggression) in agonistic encounters. In short, in contrast to tapirs and rhinos, the horses and their relatives have kept the "old" biting displays and have elaborated on them. They have also incorporated "new" displays related to the aggressive use of the forelegs and to rising on the hind legs.

In the Nonruminantia, the more primitive group of the even-toed ungulates, the situation is on the whole similar to that of Ceratomorpha. In swine and peccaries, head-low and related postures play an important role as intention movements for throwing the head upward to lift up the opponent's body or to use the elongated and upward-curved canines. Only infrequently will a wild boar, for example, symbolically rise on its hind feet as an intention movement for throwing its body onto the opponent. (This behavior may be somewhat more common as a direct fighting technique.) Also, the hippo's raising its body high up and plunging it back into the water only remotely resembles the rising on the hind legs and is probably more of a space-claim display than a threat. On the other hand, displays derived from biting are very prominent, although, through ritualization, they often deviate considerably from the original symbolic snapping. The reader may be reminded of the more or less rhythmical clapping with the jaws which may result in saliva foaming, and the grinding of teeth in several swine species and peccary, as well as yawning-like performances in peccary and above all hippo. A head-up posture in peccary was also interpreted as an intention movement for biting (with the side of the mouth) by Sowls (1974), and the neck-stretch of wild boar is an intention movement for pushing with mouth shut which, although not direct biting, is not too far from it.

The situation in Tylopoda, the camels and llamas, resembles on the whole that of horses and their relatives. The biting is less ritualized and occurs only in the form of actual and symbolic snapping. In camels, a neck-stretch posture is frequently combined with biting, and a dromedary may approach an adversary in this attitude from quite a distance. At least in guanaco and vicuna there is a head-low posture as a rather severe threat display of males which appears to be related to biting (the opponent's legs). As is the case with horses, furthermore, llamas may rise on their hind legs in actual fighting as well as in symbolic threat performances. This behavior can also be related to biting, but more often it is an intention for throwing the body onto the other and/or for neck-fighting in tylopods. In contrast to horses, they do not kick with their forelegs from the bipedal stance. They may kick with a foreleg while standing on three legs, but this is not as frequent as in the equids. Thus, the use of forelegs is present in tylopods, but to a considerably lesser extent than in horses. Consequently, the frequent erect stance with lifted nose of tylopods, which also includes here the nose-up and the head-and-neck-stretched-forward/upward posture, has little if anything to do with kicking with the forelegs, but it is primarily related to rising on the hind legs. Moreover, in llamas, it is often also an intention movement to spit, and in camels, it sometimes can be combined with the display of the gular bag.

In the Ruminantia, the situation of the very primitive mouse deer (Tragulidae) approximates that of tapirs and swine. There is no use of the forelegs and no rising on the hind legs. Approaching the opponent with wide-opened mouth and symbolic snapping are the major threats. In at least one species, the lesser Malayan mouse deer, there is a facial expression that appears to be a ritualization of biting. The "shooting" forward of head and neck in the direction of the opponent when applying a bite somewhat resembles the neck-stretch of other species. It is initiated by an erect stance as a swing-out movement. A head-low posture seems to be present but, in contrast to the head-low postures in rhinos, swine, horses and llamas, it is a defensive threat or perhaps even a submissive posture in mouse deer.

In the numerous Cervidae species, the role of displays related to biting varies in different species. In most of the Telemetacarpalia, there is only some grinding of the teeth (Müller-Using and Schloeth [1967] also mention chewing movements in moose), but clear and more specialized displays related to biting are lacking, as is biting as a fighting technique. In the other large group of Cervidae, the Plesiometacarpalia, biting (frequently applied by stretching head and neck forward combined with some twisting of the head) is quite common in agonistic encounters, as is symbolic snapping. However, it is more frequent in females than in males, and, e.g., in female fallow deer, it has been ritualized into a "rhythmical" sequence of fast snapping movements which seems to be a submissive behavior. In most of the Plesiometacarpalia males, grinding of teeth is very pronounced and results in facial expressions which more or less directly transgress into a "canine display," combined with raising the muzzle (more pronounced in some species than in others). Since the stags do not bite from this posture, and since even in actual biting the canines do not play any particular role in these animals, the "canine display" apparently is a phylogenetic, behavioral relic in them, and for these reasons may be considered as a dominance display. On the whole, threats related to biting are present in many Cervidae species but, as compared to odd-toed ungulates, Nonruminantia, Tylopoda, and Tragulidae, they are diminished.

With the apparent exception of a few relatively primitive species, such as muntjac, rising on the hind legs is very common in cervids and is always combined with actual or symbolic flailing with the forelegs. Also, striking out with a stiffly stretched foreleg (sometimes combined with neck-stretch and head-twist as biting intentions) while standing on three legs is found in the majority of the species. (In roe deer, I know it only from defense against small predators such as foxes.) In all these features, the Cervidae have much in common with the horses and the llamas. The situation with regard to scraping the ground with a foreleg is somewhat different. The full perform-ance occurs in agonistic encounters (in addition to other situations) in only a few species, such as roe deer. In most species it is reduced to a stamping, and there are considerable species-specific differences in frequency. Perhaps one could argue that here pawing the ground primarily is a form of redirected aggression and, in their antlers, the cervids possess "better" means for object aggression. This may explain the comparatively minor role of scraping the ground as an agonistic display in the deer species. Corresponding to the great role of rising on the hind legs and kicking with the forelegs, erect stances (includ-ing lifted-nose postures and a full nose-up in some cases) are found in many cervids. A dominance display component may be involved, and, as mentioned above, there are also relations to the "canine threat." Primarily, however, the erect postures appear to be intention movements for rising on the hind feet in Cervidae, and since the latter is a recent fighting behavior in these animals, the corresponding intention movements and the postures derived from them are basic-ally threat displays.

As compared to camels and llamas, typical "new inventions" of the deer species are the threat displays by presenting the antlers, usually in the form of medial and sometimes also low presentation, in frontal orientation. The high presentation of antlers, has been described, e.g., in moose, but it does not seem to be frequent in Cervidae. A pronounced head-low posture has only been reported from moose to date, but it may be that the absence of concrete data from other Cervidae species is simply due to superficial observation and incom-plete reporting. In contrast to the odd-toed ungulates, Nonruminan-tia, and Tylopoda, in moose the head-low posture is a defensive threat, and, if it should be present in other cervids, the same can be presumed for them.

In short, the threat displays in Cervidae resemble the situation in horses and llamas, with a diminution of displays related to biting and an increase of displays related to rising on hind legs and kicking with forelegs. In addition, there is the (medial) antler presentation as an intention movement for butting as a "new invention."

In giraffe and okapi, rising on the hind legs is lacking. In okapi, Grzimek (1958) mentioned occasional slapping the ground with the forelegs in agonistic situations, and aggressive foreleg kicks can exceptionally be seen in giraffe. However, on the whole, these actions are so rare in the Giraffidae that their erect postures cannot be understood as intention movements for rising or kicking. The most important threat display of giraffe is a neck-stretch-like posture that is an intention movement for a heavy sideward and upward blow with the long neck. Sometimes a giraffe may even lower the head further, approximating the head-low or the posture of low presentation in horned ungulates. An erect posture with strongly raised head (nose-up) could possibly also be related to a (defensive?) use of the neck in fighting giraffe. Likewise, in okapi, the head-low posture, sometimes transgressing into a low presentation of horns, is a swing-out movement for throwing head and neck upward. A very pronounced head-and-neck-stretched-foward/upward posture and—apparently as a diminution of it—a neck-stretch posture may include dominance display components but are basically intention movements for placing the neck over that of the opponent and pressing him down. Since this sort of neck-fighting definitely exists in okapi, these postures must be considered primarily threat displays in this species. Thus, when compared to the Cervidae, the Giraffidae show an absolute lack of threat displays related to biting, and also a very strong diminution of those related to the use of forelegs. Horn presentation likewise plays a minor role at best. Most of the threat displays in giraffe and okapi can be understood as intention movements for the aggressive use of the neck. In this regard, there are similarities only to the behavior of llamas and some remote resemblances to certain displays in odd-toed ungulates.

In Antilocapridae we find the same absence of threat displays related to biting, rising on the hind legs, and the use of the forelegs as in Giraffidae. The head-low posture is a well-pronounced display in pronghorn which may sometimes approximate a medial or low horn presentation and, apparently in a low-intensity form, may vaguely resemble a very slack neck-stretch (i.e., head and neck are almost in normal posture). In contrast to giraffe, these postures have nothing to do with the aggressive use of the neck but are intention movements for butting in pronghorn.

In the very numerous Bovidae species, actual as well as symbolic snapping occurs predominantly in certain relatively primitive forms and in the hornless females of certain more highly evolved species. A sequence of snapping movements, comparable to that of submissive female fallow deer, is found in female eland antelope and waterbuck, and, strangely enough, as a very inconspicuous—at least to the human observer—threat in male (!) springbuck. However, in the majority of the Bovidae species, threat displays related to biting behavior are missing completely.

The same is largely true for the neck-stretch as a threat display, except for its occurrence in *Tragelaphus* females and, above all, in nilgai bulls, where it apparently is an intention movement for neck-fighting and probably includes a dominance display component. The neck-stretch in encounters of sheep is apparently more of a dominance than a threat display and therefore is not included in Table 4.

Scraping the ground in agonistic situations plays a role in some but not all of the oxen (Bovinae), the Alcelaphinae (wildebeest, hartebeest, etc.), the Hippotraginae (roan and sable antelope, addax, and the oryx species), to a minor extent in some of the gazelle species, in mountain goat, and some goats and sheep. In the latter, however, stamping is more common, and it is debatable whether this behavior is some kind of threat display or more of an excitement activity. On the whole, mere pawing the ground (i.e., not followed by urination and/or defecation or wallowing) and related behaviors in agonistic situations are present in barely 50 percent of the species under discussion.

Rising on the hind legs as a fighting behavior as well as a threat display has been occasionally observed in encounters among female nilgai antelopes. Otherwise, it is restricted to one subfamily of horned ungulates: the Caprinae. Even here there are species, such as Barbary sheep and the tahrs, in which it is very exceptional. It also is infrequent in the smaller sheep, such as mouflon and the urials. It is very common in all the goat species (genus *Capra*), in the American sheep, such as bighorn, and in the larger Asiatic sheep, such as Marco Polo sheep and argali. In contrast to all other ungulates which show rising on the hind legs as a fighting behavior, it is an initiation of horn fighting in goats and sheep.

Kicking or striking with the forelegs as a fighting technique and/or a threat is absent in all horned ungulates. Foreleg kicks occur in the agonistic encounters of sheep but they are more dominance displays than threat displays.

Because of this absence of rising on the hind legs and kicking with the forelegs, erect postures with or without lifting the nose are not related to recent and actual fighting techniques and thus are not threat displays in the overwhelming majority of the horned ungulates. One could think of the erect stance as being a threat display in sheep because here it can be considered as an intention movement for rising on the hind feet as a fighting behavior. However, a dominance display component may be involved in it. Similarly, the erect attitude in some of the oryx species could be considered as a swing-out movement for a strong downward-blow with the horns—a common fighting technique in these animals—and thus as a threat display. However, the dominance display component certainly is very strong here. The few cases of erect postures as threat displays in other species are even more doubtful. For example, the (hornless) *Tragelaphus* females as well as females of nilgai, waterbuck, Gray's waterbuck, and gerenuk may raise the muzzle to an almost vertical position, and one may sometimes get the impression that in their case it is some kind of defensive threat, possibly related to neck-fighting. Also, the upward swinging of the head in agonistic encounters of bison may remotely resemble a very brief erect stance. On the whole, however, erect postures do not play a great role as threat displays in horned ungulates. The interesting fact is that erect postures, with or without raising the muzzle, neck-stretch postures, and foreleg kicks, do definitely belong to the behavioral inventories of many Bovidae species. However, they are not threat displays.

The most prominent threat displays of horned ungulates are the presentations of horns. The medial horn presentation is hardly lacking in any species. In a few species, such as nilgai or mountain goat, it is comparatively infrequent, and in a few species, such as bison, it is somewhat difficult to recognize because the normal posture of the animal comes very close to it. However, in the majority of the species, it is the most elaborate and most frequent form of threat. The high presentation of horns is not as common. However, in some of the gazelle species, such as Thomson's gazelle and dorcas gazelle, it is *the* typical threat display of adult bucks. The head-low posture is very common in horned ungulates. In contrast to some other hoofed mammals (see above), it is related to horn fighting in the Bovidae, and it usually is a more or less defensive threat (with only a few exceptions, e.g., chamois) approximating a submissive behavior in quite a number of the cases and species. Dropping down to the "knees" as a threat display is also related to horn fighting in bovids. In nilgai, the symbolic performance is much rarer than is the use of the "kneeling" posture in actual fighting. In oryx, addax, roan and sable antelope, the "kneeling" posture (in addition to overt fighting) is frequently combined with object aggression. "Kneeling" is most pronounced as a threat display in the agonistic encounters of Alcelaphinae.

In short, the threat displays of horned ungulates differ quite considerably from those of all other hooofed mammals—except pronghorn—in that all those postures and gestures which are related to biting, neck-fighting, rising on hind legs, and kicking with the forelegs are infrequent or lacking completely. Instead, the bulk of their threat displays are intention movements for horn-fighting, in which the different forms of horn presentation play a particularly prominent role. Even when certain display forms (such as head-low posture, kneeling down, and rising on the hind legs) which also occur in other ungulates are present in the Bovidae, they are connected to the use of horns.

Dominance displays. Table 5 presents examples of postures and gestures which may be considered dominance displays in agonistic encounters among males. The displays shown in this table primarily concern postures and movements of head and neck as they occur when the animal is laterally oriented toward the opponent (broadside displays). Table 5 largely presents the same gestures and postures presented in Table 4 (threat displays), with the exception of those exclusively used as threats (biting intention, rising on the hind legs, kicking with forelegs, kneeling, etc.).

Postures corresponding to the medial and low presentations of horns or antlers in Bovidae and Cervidae are treated only insofar as they occur in combination with well-pronounced broadside displays (lateral T-position, reverse-parallel orientation, and lengthy parallel march). High presentation and sideward-angling of horns are not included in Table 5. The high presentation of horns occurs in relatively few species (Table 4), and there always seems to be a small or not so small dominance display component in it. The sideward-angling of horns is so common that it occurs, at least occasionally, in all species which present their horns, and, of course, even more so in those in which any form of horn or antler presentation is combined with a pronounced broadside orientation. Furthermore, Table 5 presents the humped-back posture (hunch) which was not mentioned in Table 4 because it apparently is a dominance display in most of the species. Head-low posture and neck-stretch are the same as in Table 4. Within the general category of erect displays, several postures are shown separately that were combined into one category in Table 4: the head-and-neck-stretched-forward/upward posture (which also includes here the vertical nose-up), the erect stance with lifted nose, the erect stance with (strongly) vertically raised neck but nose pointing horizontally forward, and an erect stance with moderately erect neck (mainly in those species in which a vertical erection of the neck is impossible due to their anatomical structure). Finally, Table 5 shows the sideward turn of the head, but only for those species in which it truly is a striking and/or frequent display. Occasional and slight sideward turns of the head, as they may occur in almost all the species, are not included.

No dominance displays have been found in tapirs (von Richter 1966). Schenkel and Lang (1969) consider an erect stance of black rhino to be a dominance display (*Imponierhaltung*); however, its character as a dominance display appears somewhat questionable (see p. 256). Owen-Smith (1975) describes a "reciprocal horn to horn stare" of square-lipped rhino bulls which possibly may be some kind of dominance display. In horses and their relatives, erect postures with more or less lifted nose as well as (apparently only in horses) the tucking of the chin toward the throat may include a dominance display component but basically they are threat displays as are (symbolic) rising on the hind legs and (symbolic) foreleg kicks in these animals. The single point that may speak in favor of a dominance component in such displays is that they sometimes occur in lateral (parallel) orientation, as, e.g., in the "departure jump" of plains zebra.

Thus, in the few cases in which one could think of dominance displays in odd-toed ungulates, either the display character is somewhat doubtful, or they are primarily threats, with only a component of dominance display. Dominance displays without any possible restriction are rarely found in Perissodactyla.

In the Nonruminantia, the data on hippopotamus appear too meager to allow any conclusions on dominance displays. In peccary, a frontal stance with lifted muzzle is basically a threat display, but shows a dominance display feature in that, in an encounter between unequal opponents, the stronger one raises his head higher than the subordinate (Sowls 1974). Somewhat different is the situation in swine, where broadside displays occur in several species (including the bush pig, which is not presented in Table 5). In wild boar (Beuerle 1975), the head-low posture is basically a threat display but may also occur in lateral T-position from which lateral fighting (which otherwise is found in wild boar) is unlikely. The dominance display character of an erect attitude in lateral orientation is even clearer. Thus, one may say that some dominance displays are present in Suidae.

In camels and llamas, the situation is similar to that in horses and their relatives; a dominance display component can be attributed to erect displays with lifted nose as well as to the nose-up and the head-and-neck-stretched-forward/upward posture, but these are basically threat displays.

In the Tragulidae, the most primitive group of Ruminantia, an erect stance has been described in the lesser Malayan mouse deer. Robin (1979) is inclined to consider it a dominance display since the white color patterns at the neck are strikingly presented in this posture. On the other hand, this erect stance frequently initiates the forward "shooting" of the head and neck for biting, i.e., true fighting, in mouse deer, and thus it seems to be more of a threat display in these animals.

In the Cervidae there are species such as muntjac and reindeer in which either no dominance displays have been found to date, or the displays appear to be primarily threat displays with at best, a slight dominance display component. Also, in the other deer species, there are numerous cases of basic threat displays with a more or less pronounced dominance component. They center around two "trends." One consists of (medial) antler presentation—unmistakably a threat display, but delivered during a parallel stance or, more frequently, a parallel march, i.e., in a broadside orientation which does not imply immediate use of the antlers. In species such as mule deer (Geist 1966a), the antler presentation in broadside position is combined with a humped-back posture (hunch) which reinforces the dominance display character. The slow and somewhat stiff-legged (prancing) parallel march may come closest to a pure dominance display in those cases in which the medial antler presentation is reduced to a head-nodding in otherwise "normal" or somewhat erect posture, as is the case in red deer and even more so in fallow deer.

The other "trend" in the dominance displays of cervids is the combination of the "canine threat" with raising the muzzle and species-specific neck postures, ranging from an almost horizontal neck-stretch to a pronounced erect posture and even a full nose-up. All these postures are primarily threat displays in cervids. They come closest to dominance displays when shown in reverse-parallel position such as in the "sidle" of white-tailed deer (Thomas, et al. 1965). Also, the dominance display character of the canine threat is not unambiguous, since it refers to the aggressive use of the teeth, and biting is a fighting technique in many deer species. On the other hand, the stags normally do not bite from this display. Thus there is at least no direct and immediate connection from the canine display to (recent) fighting. On the whole, one may say that there are dominance displays in the Cervidae, but they are still closely related to threat displays and of a somewhat "transitional" character.

In principle, the situation in giraffe and okapi is not too different from that in cervids, i.e., there are primarily threat displays with more or less pronounced dominance display components involved. The posture with vertically erected neck but without raising the muzzle above horizontal level may perhaps be an almost pure dominance display in the Giraffidae.

In pronghorn an erect stance with somewhat lifted nose apparently is a dominance display. Pronounced turns of the head alternately to the right or the left can sometimes be combined with it, but this is more frequent and typical in the courtship ritual of this species.

In the horned ungulates (Bovidae), there are again some species in which dominance displays are lacking or are of rather doubtful character. This is mainly the case in primitive species such as duikers and dwarf antelopes (Neotraginae). It is also true in some species, such as springbuck and Barbary sheep, where the lack of dominance displays cannot be attributed to a comparatively primitive general state. If we furthermore consider the incomplete separation of dominance displays from threat displays to be an indication of primitiveness in the development of dominance displays, we must mention in particular the situation in oxen (Bovinae), goats and sheep (Caprinae) and some groups which taxonomically are not too distant from the latter, such as mountain goat and chamois (Rupicaprinae). Erect postures are not particularly common in most of these animals. In species in which they occur, such as sheep, one can relate them to rising on the hind legs as a fighting technique. Their combination with sideward turns of the head (in frontal orientation) as well as their frequent performance *after* a horn clash may somewhat "cut" the direct connection to fighting and indicate the existence of a dominance display component. The neck-stretch, often combined with head-twisting, and the foreleg kick (not presented in Table 5) in agonistic encounters are confined to the sheep. One may consider them as dominance displays; however, they are somewhat aberrant in that they apparently have (recurrently?) developed from courtship behaviors.

Other possible dominance displays in Rupicaprinae, Caprinae, and Bovinae are medial and low horn presentations or head-low postures, i.e., threat displays, in combination with broadside positions. Thus, it is about the same situation as in some of the deer species. Also, the hunch occurs again but in more species and often in a more pronounced performance than in the cervids.

Interestingly enough, a corresponding posture, with hind legs placed forward under the belly and a more or less humped back, also occurs in at least some of the oxen, such as gaur and domestic cattle (the latter cannot hump the back very much due to their anatomical structure, but they place the hind legs correspondingly under the belly). From this, there is apparently a "trend" to nilgai and the *Tragelaphus* species; however, with a rather typical change. In cattle, the lateral humped-back posture may still be combined with a medial horn presentation (directed forward into the air), but in nilgai and the spiral-horned antelopes, this connection to the medial horn presentation is absent. In nilgai, the placing of the hind legs forward is only occasionally seen, but the humping of the back is frequent and typical. The neck postures seem to be related to neck-fighting and since the latter definitely is a fighting technique in nilgai, the broadside display includes a strong threat component in this species. In the genus *Tragelaphus*, there is no connection between the humped-back display and neck-fighting. Here, therefore, it appears to be a pure dominance display. Greater kudu shows a pronounced humped-back posture, always in lateral position, with hind legs placed forward under the belly, and head and neck somewhat lowered, although often not as much and as stiffly as in typical head-low. In other *Tragelaphus* species, such as nyala and bushbuck, the hind legs are not placed forward as far, but the humping of the back (with erection of the mane along the back) is well pronounced. Bushbuck sometimes carry head and neck in normal or even slightly erect posture in this display.

The erect posture, with or without raising the muzzle above horizontal level (depending on species), but without any humping of the back, occurs (as another dominance display) in some of the *Tragelaphus* species, such as greater and lesser kudu. Erect postures—commonly combined with broadside orientation, but sometimes also independent, i.e., in frontal position—make up the bulk of the dominance displays in other groups of horned ungulates, such as Alcelaphinae (wildebeest, hartebeest, topi, blesbok, etc.), Hippotraginae (oryx antelopes, roan and sable antelopes, etc.), and Antilopinae (gazelles, blackbuck, gerenuk, etc.). Particularly in the oryx species, the erect posture may still include a threat component. Also, in oryx and other bovid species, the erect postures can be combined with sideward angling of the horns when displayed in lateral position. However, this is merely an additive combination of a threat display (angle horn) with a dominance display (erect posture). Otherwise the erect postures and their derivates have no connection to any recent fighting technique in these horned ungulates; they are pure dominance displays.

Head-turns (away from the recipient) occur, often in combination with erect postures, in many bovid species. In part, they are "abbreviations" of broadside displays; in part, they are swing-out movements for turning toward the recipient. The head-flagging of Grant's gazelle as a particular elaboration of an erect dominance display has been extensively described in a previous chapter.

Finally, it may be advisable once more to draw the reader's attention to the sporadic distribution of certain displays. For example, as pointed out above, the combination of a broadside position with a medial horn presentation is present in certain oxen, and it also occurs in some goat species. Otherwise, this combination is lacking in most of the horned ungulates. However, it sporadically occurs as a pronounced display in parallel marches of sable antelope, which are not particularly closely related to either the goats or the oxen.

On the whole, of all the hoofed mammals, it is the horned ungulates that provide us with the clearest examples of dominance displays, and in which the separation of dominance displays from threat displays is greatest. This is to be expected under the presumption that dominance displays evolved from ancestral fighting behaviors which were lost after the "invention" of "new" weapons (the horns) and corresponding "new" fighting techniques. Since animals such as tapirs, horses, and llamas, have not developed "new" and special weapons (such as horns) and, with them, "new" fighting techniques, they cannot replace anything. Thus, their aggressive displays remain in more or less direct connection with their recent fighting techniques, i.e., they are basically threats. In principle, the situation is not very different in cervids, whose "new" weapons, the antlers, cannot be used for a considerable part of the year, and who consequently have kept many of their "old" fighting techniques. Thus, the only criteria for the involvement of a dominance component in the aggressive displays of equids, tylopods, swine, cervids, etc., are their occurrence in orientations from which fighting is somewhat unlikely (e.g., an erect stance—as an intention for rising and/or kicking—but in lateral position), and/or their combination with another posture which makes them ineffective as fighting behaviors (e.g., grinding of teeth—as an intention for biting—but combined with a nose-up posture). These criteria certainly speak for the development of a dominance display from the original threat display, but they are not so convincing as the complete separation of the two.

Courtship displays. Table 6 presents some examples of postures and gestures used as male courtship displays in hoofed mammals. Sexual mounting and its immediate intention movements, behaviors by which the males test the estrous state of the females, and herding behaviors (insofar as they are not identical with the courtship displays) are not included. Again, essentially the same postures and gestures are presented here as in the tables of threat and dominance displays, but with a few modifications. The head-low posture and all the forms of horn presentation are omitted since they occur on the part of the courting males in only a very few of the species under discussion. The table presents (symbolic) biting; the twist; the neck-stretch; three combinations of the foreleg kick (with neck-stretch, with normal or somewhat erect posture, and with strongly lifted muzzle); three forms of the erect posture (nose-up, lifted nose, and erect neck but nose not raised above horizontal level); and the sideward-turn of the head. The presentation of the latter is restricted to cases in which it truly is a striking display.

In tapirs and Indian rhinoceros, biting plays a certain role in the mating ritual. Particularly when following the females, all the male tapirs and rhinos assume an attitude which may be said to be a neck-stretch posture, although one may have doubts whether it truly is a special display. The display character of the erect stance and the lifted nose posture is even more doubtful in these animals. Somewhat erect stances are usually assumed by these males when they place their chins on the females' backs prior to mounting. It is hard to say whether these erect postures are visual displays, but probably they are not. Thus, in tapirs and rhinos, the visual male courtship displays are, on the whole, as poorly developed as the dominance displays.

Interestingly enough, the same is also true for horses and their relatives: the stallions show many pronounced threat or threat-dominance displays (mainly during herding, but sometimes also in the beginning of the mating ritual) but almost no postures or gestures that could be considered special courtship displays.

In swine and peccary, the situation is not too different from that in odd-toed ungulates. More or less ritualized (diminished) biting plays a role in some of the species; erect postures occur but often are somewhat questionable in their display character; neck-stretch postures are quite pronounced but are restricted to the male's persistent following of the female in naso-genital contact.

Male camels and llamas bite the females during courtship and wrestle them down with their necks. Neck-stretches may occur, particularly in connection with snapping, but they are more than questionable as courtship displays. Erect postures with more or less lifted noses are very typical of courting male Tylopoda. They are the same or at least very similar to those used as threat or dominance displays in encounters with male opponents.

Also, in mouse deer, the male may still bite (in a somewhat diminished form) the female during the mating ritual, particularly when she is not being very cooperative. When marking her with his interramal gland and/or pressing her down prior to mounting, the male assumes a posture which may be likened to a neck-stretch. Otherwise, special courtship postures and gestures of the males are unknown in the Tragulidae.

No snapping or biting has been described from courting Cervidae males. Erect stances show up in some of the species, such as axis deer. Neck-stretches are typical male courtship displays in most of the Cervidae species. An exception is elk, where a neck-stretch posture is used by the stags when herding the females, whereas the courting elk stag shows an erect attitude (Geist 1966a). It is the opposite in red deer, which are so closely related to elk that many taxonomists consider the two to be subspecies of the same species. It certainly is not unreasonable to consider the pronounced neck-stretches of courting

Cervidae males as ritualized intention movements for sniffing the female's vulva. However, these postures are not as strongly related to naso-genital contacts as in swine, and possess certain features which indicate that something more may be involved. One might possibly think of the phylogenetic ritualization of biting intentions. In any case, the neck-stretches are the most prominent courtship displays of deer, whereas foreleg kicks have not been observed in the mating ritual of any of them. This fact certainly is noteworthy, since beating and kicking movements with the forelegs are by no means lacking in the cervids and play a great role as threat displays in their agonistic encounters (Table 4).

In contrast to the Cervidae, the neck-stretch is not a courtship display in giraffe. In okapi, it shows only up when the male is standing directly behind the female with his chest almost or literally touching her rump—possibly a ritualized intention movement for neck-fighting. (Okapi bulls mount with neck erected.) Striking erect postures with more or less lifted nose are typical for both giraffe and okapi bulls, and they are not significantly different from threat and dominance displays in agonistic encounters. However, the courting okapi bull frequently displays the foreleg kick in combination with an erect attitude or a head-and-neck-stretched-forward/upward posture. Giraffe bulls do not show the foreleg kick.

The erect stance, often with slightly lifted nose, is typical of the courting pronghorn buck, and he strikingly turns his head alternately to the right and the left. Although head-turns of 45° or 90° may occasionally occur in the courting males of other ungulates, no other species shows such a striking and pronounced head-waving in courtship.

Symbolic snapping on the part of the courting male is infrequently found in the numerous Bovidae species. Only in some of the *Tragelaphus* species, such as bushbuck and lesser kudu, do the males show some kind of symbolic snapping into the air during the neck-stretch when running beside the female in lateral escort. On the whole, the elaborateness of male courtship postures and gestures varies greatly among the horned ungulates and does not seem to be directly related to the degree of evolutionary advancement; the highly advanced oxen (Bovinae) are absolutely poor in this regard. Sometimes the attitude of a bull may approximate a neck-stretch, or the upward swing of his head may somewhat resemble an erect stance. However, there is hardly any striking and well pronounced courtship posture in these animals. Also, in wildebeest, there is only the neck-stretch (combined with the ear-drop in this and other Alcelaphinae species—not shown in Table 6) and possibly a somewhat erect attitude. The situation is similar in some other species, e.g., southern reedbuck (*Redunca arundium*—Jungius 1970). On the other hand, there are Bovidae species with three, four, or even more elaborate courtship postures or gestures of the males.

The neck-stretch is found in many, though not all, of the Bovidae. It is not a courtship display in the Hippotraginae (roan, sable, oryx, addax antelopes), and is also missing or somewhat doubtful in its display character in some of the gazelle species and their relatives (blackbuck, gerenuk). It is particularly well pronounced in Tragelaphinae, Caprinae, mountain goat, impala, and most of the Alcelaphinae. In the latter, it is the single very striking male courtship display in blesbok and bontebok. The situation in the genus *Tragelaphus* and in the Caprinae is especially interesting. In greater and lesser kudu, nyala, sitatunga, bushbuck, and bongo, the neck-stretch is the most prominent male courtship display. It sometimes merges into a moderate twist. Details in situation and performance strongly suggest that it originated from neck-fighting in these animals. In the Caprinae, the neck-stretch shows a strong connection with the well-pronounced twist, and it often occurs in combination with the foreleg kick. This combination of neck-stretch and foreleg kick is very rare in the other bovids and entirely lacking in the genus *Tragelaphus*.

As courtship displays, erect postures with more or less lifted noses are not quite as common in horned ungulates as are neck-stretches. They occur mainly in the *Tragelaphus* species, most of the gazelles and their relatives, some species of the waterbuck group (e.g., Uganda kob), some of the Alcelaphinae (hartebeest, topi), and some of the Hippotraginae. In the latter, however, there are great differences as to elaboration. For example, an erect stance of the bull is quite pronounced in sable antelope, but poorly pronounced in addax. Only in some gazelle species and in Indian blackbuck does the erect lifted-nose posture frequently merge into a full nose-up. Head-turns may sometimes occur in combination with erect attitudes; however, in most of the species, they are infrequent displays.

Foreleg kicks as male courtship displays occur in at least some of the duikers (besides the black-fronted duiker, presented in Table 6, I also have seen them in grey duiker [*Sylvicapra grimmia*] and blue duiker) and in some of the dwarf antelopes (Neotraginae). For example, they are present in steenbok but lacking in Kirk's dikdik. Furthermore, foreleg kicks are present and very typical of Antilopinae (gazelles and their relatives), Hippotraginae, many of the Reduncinae (waterbuck, Uganda kob, Gray's waterbuck, etc.), a very few of the Alcelaphinae (e.g., topi), most of the Caprinae (sheep and goats), mountain goat, musk ox, and also some species not listed in Table 6, such as serow (*Capricornis sumtraënsis—Schaller* 1977). Almost all the species display the foreleg kick in normal or somewhat erect posture. In addition, combinations with other postures may occur in some species. These are mainly the sheep and goats, where the foreleg kick may be combined with the neck-stretch and the twist, as mentioned above, and some of the gazelles and their relatives, where the foreleg kick frequently is combined with a lifted-nose posture or even a nose-up.

These foreleg kicks in the mating ritual offer a particularly impressive example of how such a behavioral "element" may occur in species of very different size (blue duiker and roan antelope), living in very different biotypes (oryx antelope and bighorn sheep), and in very different types of social organization (steenbok and topi). Sometimes, the foreleg kick shows up and is even combined with the same neck and head postures (e.g., erect posture with lifted nose), in species which are taxonomically as distant from each other as Grant's gazelle and okapi. On the other hand, there are whole subfamilies in which the presence or absence of the foreleg kick appears to be quite group specific, as can be taken from Table 6. However, in a group where the foreleg kick is generally present and quite uniform, even with respect to its combinations with other movements or postures, e.g., in the sheep and goats and their relatives, there suddenly may be a species among the others where it is missing, such as the Barbary sheep within the Caprinae. Likewise, in Rupicaprinae, only one of the two species belonging to this group, the mountain goat, displays the foreleg kick as a male courtship behavior; the other species, chamois, does not.

When several species belong to the same relatively small taxonomic category (e.g., a genus) and each species possesses several well-elaborated male courtship displays, a display which is particularly pronounced in one species is often poorly pronounced or even lacking in another. This is the reason why in Table 6 a behavior has occasionally been signified to be present *and* absent within the same genus.

18. ON INTERSPECIFIC COMMUNICATION

Communication works only when sender and recipient share a mutual, "agreed-upon" communication code. This is usually not a problem among adult animals of the same species; either their sending and receiving devices are genetically adapted to each other by phylogenetic evolution, or all the conspecifics have learned the same things during the course of their lives when growing up under approximately natural conditions. The situation is different when animals of different species have to communicate with each other. The natural innate or learned communication code basically "is made for" communication with conspecifics. It is species-specific. Consequently, when an animal of a given species has dealings with an animal of another species, there can be a communication barrier.

Apparently it is not easy for humans to rightly assess this communication barrier. It is frequently either underestimated or overestimated. As a general rule, this communication barrier is always present, and thus must always be taken into account. On the other hand, the "isolation" between the species often is not so hopeless that it is impossible to overcome the communication barrier to some extent.

Some etho-ecologists (e.g., Jarman 1974, Leuthold 1977) have proposed the hypothesis that ungulate societies were primarily shaped by feeding style and/or antipredator adaptations. I disagree with this opinion, particularly with respect to the presumably great role of predators in the life of these animals. When one studies an ungulate species such as Thomson's gazelle, which is preyed upon by a variety of predators (cheetah, wild dog, spotted hyena, leopard, lion, etc.), some of which are very numerous and all of which can be visible over large distances in an open plains situation (e.g., Serengeti Plains), it is often surprising how little attention they pay to the numerous predators around them. Even when a predator has attacked and made a kill, peace usually returns within a quarter of an hour. A tommy buck may begin to court a female or fight a territorial neighbor in full sight of the predator eating its kill not more than half a kilometer away. In general one may say that these animals care as little about their natural enemies as a hardened pedestrian in a big city cares about the car traffic. *Cum grano salis*, each species lives as if it were alone in the world.

The same is true for relations between different ungulate species. Again, I must destroy a widespread view which is largely derived from photos of African plains wildlife showing animals from different species together. Of course, such interspecific "aggregations" do occasionally occur. Except for a few special situations (see below), however, the animals do not seek out the company of the other species, but are brought together by reacting to the same environmental factors—a specific location with a preferred food, a water-hole, the shade of a single tree in otherwise open country, etc. In short, there usually is no social attraction and no social interaction among these ungulates of different species, and they come together more or less accidentally and temporarily. They simply do not fear the others; they tolerate their presence and move around them as if they were inanimate obstacles.

Thus, when approaching the problems of interspecific communication in hoofed mammals, we must at least start from the heuristic basis that in these animals only conspecifics are partners and companions by nature. If such an animal interacts socially with an animal of another species, this can only happen when it acts and reacts toward the other as if it were a conspecific.

Anybody who has read a few books or papers on animal psychology or ethology will have encountered the term "anthropomorphism." It refers to man's looking at animals, treating them, or interpreting their behavior as if they were humans—which is usually considered to be a serious mistake in the behavioral sciences. (It certainly is interesting that we also find the problem of anthropomorphism in a quite different branch of science: theology, where some people think of God as a human being—the "old man with the white beard.") One of Hediger's great scientific contributions was to point out that anthropomorphism is only a special case of the much more widespread "assimilation tendency" or "zoomorphism": that not only humans but many other higher animals under certain conditions tend to "consider," to treat, and to react to animals of another species (including humans) as if they were conspecifics.

This zoomorphism can develop in several ways. One of them is imprinting. For example, when a young animal has been raised and bottle-fed by humans, it may happen that it later prefers human partners over conspecifics, and it may be fixated in certain reactions (and not only infantile behaviors but also aggression, sexual behavior, etc.) to humans. Of course, a similar situation can also occur when the young animal is raised by animals of another species. Thus, this imprinting to another species involves a rather artificial situation, which usually occurs only under captive conditions.

Another factor favoring the assimilation tendency is the damming up of action-specific energy. This may occur when an animal of a given species has not been able to perform a special behavior (e.g., fighting, courting, etc.) with an adequate conspecific partner for a long period of time. Then it may become so "eager" to perform this behavior that it eventually directs it toward an animal of another species (including humans). This is particularly frequent under captive conditions, but it can also happen in the wild. Such damming-up processes, of course, are not restricted to infancy; they also are possible in fully adult animals.

Habituation is a third way in which animals of different species may become familiar with each other to such an extent that they finally "consider" each other almost to be conspecifics. This means that an animal is frequently exposed to animals of another species who do it no harm. Habituation appears to be a significant factor in familiarization, but it alone is usually not enough for the development of an assimilation process in the outlined sense. However, it provides the basis for another phenomenon which has been termed the "mutual fate" (*gemeinsames Schicksal*) factor by Gestalt psychologists (Metzger 1954), and which obviously can become very important in social assimilation. It means that those individuals may associate or even form special individual bonds who have something in common with respect to their social situation which, at the same time, distinguishes them from other individuals. This "mutual fate" factor plays an important role in the formation of all-male groups, age groups, mothers groups, etc., and it can become so strong under certain conditions that it even overpowers the species barriers. Then an animal of a given species may interact with an individual of another species as it would otherwise only interact with a conspecific.

For example, in a zoological garden where I once worked, we kept Marco Polo sheep, urial sheep, markhor goats, and several subspecies of ibex together in a large enclosure. The males of all these species are known to separate from their females outside the rutting season and to form all-male bands in the wild—of course, under natural conditions, only with conspecific males. In the captive situation there was only one adult male of each species or subspecies respectively, but each of them was in the same social situation, i.e., he tended to separate from the females and join other males. Consequently, all these males from the different species formed one all-male band.

In Serengeti National Park, I once observed a male Thomson's gazelle who kept his territory at a time when all the other Thomson's gazelle and almost all other game animals, except Grant's gazelle, had left the vicinity. When one day an all-male group of Grant's gazelle passed through his territory, the tommy buck tried to herd them. Normally a tommy buck herds only females of his own species, and is indifferent to nonconspecific animals passing through his territory. Thus, this tommy buck treated the male (!) Grant's gazelle as if they were conspecific females, obviously due to a "sinking of the thresholds" for herding behavior during his long period of isolation from conspecifics. Needless to say, the Grant's bucks did not show much "understanding" of his actions.

Since, under natural conditions, hoofed ungulates only defend their territories against conspecific rivals, it is not uncommon for the territories of males of different species to overlap each other completely or in part. For example, a kongoni bull and a topi bull may have overlapping territories. Under certain conditions (as when neither of them is visited by conspecifics for a while), they may stand, graze, move, or rest side by side (Fig. 143). Basically these species are gregarious. Thus, when males become territorial and leave the herds, they sometimes may be in an inner conflict between the tendency for territorial isolation and the tendency to rejoin the herds. When territorial males of different species—in our example, kongoni and topi—are in the same situation ("mutual fate"!) and together in the same area, they may satisfy their social needs by forming a group. Interestingly enough, the assimilation tendency works only insofar as the males of the different species unite but do not "consider" the other to be a territorial rival. The latter frequently happens in captivity, and, since on the whole, the assimilation tendency is considerably more frequent and stronger in captive animals (e.g., when the same individuals are together in a very limited space day after day and year after year), Hediger (1950) was originally inclined to consider the occurrence of zoomorphism to be restricted to captive conditions. However, comparable events occasionally happen in the wild, as shown by the last two examples. Furthermore, the example of territorial males from different species may point to the important conclusions that (a) the assimilation tendency may reach different degrees of perfection depending on situation, and (b) a partial assimilation process may sometimes allow friendlier relationships among the animals of different species than those which normally occur among conspecifics. A territorial bull or buck may fight any other territorial male of his own species, but he may be "on good terms" with a territorial male of another species (in the wild).

In regards to interspecific communication, I would like to distinguish between primary and secondary communication. In primary

Fig. 143. A territorial topi bull and a territorial kongoni bull (*Alcelaphus buselaphus cokei*), whose territories largely overlap, are standing together during a resting period at high noon; the topi bull stands exposed on a termite mound. (Walther 1979. Serengeti National Park.)

communication, the sender does not "know" (in the very broadest sense of the word) anything about the recipient's communication code; he just uses the same signs and signals that he uses in communication with conspecifics, due to the assimilation tendency. In secondary communication, either the sender adapts to the communication code of the recipient or, more commonly, the receiver adapts to that of the sender. (A third possibility would be that sender and recipient both use a communication code which is neither the original code of the sender nor that of the recipient. However, this possibility apparently is restricted to man-animal relations and even here usually to special situations in certain scientific experiments.) As far as I can see, secondary communication is always based on learning processes in hoofed mammals. For example, a horse may learn to turn to the right or to the left, or to stop, or to move ahead, on special verbal commands of the rider or the driver. However, this learning appears to be based on innate, species-specific learning dispositions. Frequently these species-specific dispositions limit the learning capacity. Sometimes, however, they may enable an animal to learn a considerable and—to humans—surprisingly great amount in a special area. In animals such as hoofed mammals, such a special field would be that of communicative expressions. The reader may be reminded of the famous "Clever Hans" experiment in which a horse learned to react to minimal and unintended movements of the human trainer. In the same way, an animal may also learn to react to certain gestures, postures, vocalizations, etc., of an animal of another species when it has had sufficient occasion to experience what the other is going to do after these expressions. This secondary interspecific communication certainly has very important practical aspects—not least in the training of animals by humans. Otherwise, it follows the usual pattern of learning, and, except for the problems of species-specific differences in learning dispositions, there is nothing too exciting about it.

Very interesting, however, are the problems of primary interspecific communication. As stated above, the sender of the one species addresses the recipient of the other species by the same—innate or learned—signs and signals which he uses in communication with conspecifics, and the recipient reacts by the same—innate or learned—responses which he uses in communication with partners of his own species, i.e., sender and recipient conform to the principles of the assimilation tendency. When one takes the species barriers into account, and considers that these gestures, postures, vocalizations, etc., are "made for" communication with conspecifics, not with strangers, it is not too surprising that this often does not work, and that mistakes and errors may happen. What is surprising is that it works at all, and relatively often at that.

Three factors are important for the success or failure of primary interspecific communication. One of them is a characteristic which instinctive and learned expressions have in common. It is usually not the whole (sending) animal which becomes effective in communication and releases a response but only a few very definite characteristics of it. These characteristics are more important in creating the impression on the recipient's part and/or for his reaction than anything else. A very simple but instructive example from the human field is the expression of laughing or crying in a primitive line drawing of a human face. The structure of one single line, representing the mouth, can be deciding for the impression of a smiling or a crying face (Fig. 144). The other facial structures are unimportant or at best of minor importance in this regard. With respect to primary interspecific communication, this means that the understanding of the expressive behavior of an animal of another species depends very much on the presence of such special features. It does not matter, or at least not too much, on how they are brought about or which organs are used to bring them about. These can be different in different species. However, when they result in phenotypically similar structures, at least the possibility is there that their message and meaning

Fig. 144a. "Laughing
face." b. "Crying face."

will be understood by animals of a different species. For example, we
may think of vocalizations linked to high levels of excitement. Quite a
number of these so-called alarm calls and all the distress cries are
relatively loud, short, abruptly beginning and abruptly ending. Provided a species possesses an—innate or learned—receiving "mechanism" which responds to these structural features of the vocalization,
it does not matter, or at least not very much, whether the vocalization is a bark, a roar, a whistle, or a squawk, whether it is uttered
through the mouth or the nose, often even not whether it is high or
low in pitch. The phenotypic structural features—relatively loud,
short, abruptly beginning and ending—release attention, alarm reactions, and sometimes even flight in animals equipped with a corresponding receiving mechanism. It need not even be a vocalization.
Sometimes, a mechanically produced sound—such as stamping the
ground with the feet and similar noises—may have the same structural features and thus the same effects. This dependence of definite
impressions and/or reactions on relatively few, very special, phenotypic features of an expressive behavior, and, on the other hand, the
remarkable independence from all the other qualities of the (sending)
object, considerably favor the spontaneous, primary understanding
between animals of different species.

The similarities of expressive postures, gestures, and vocalizations
in different species can be due to homologous (of mutual origin in
phylogenetic evolution) or analogous (adaptations to the same functions) developments. Both homologies, which are frequent in closely
related species, and analogies, which can show up in taxonomically
very distant species, favor the primary interspecific communication.
However, both homologies and analogies can also cause errors and
misunderstandings.

For example, (sudden) phenotypic increases in size and/or breadth
are widespread structural features of dominance displays, as discussed
in previous chapters. If an animal is able to recognize these features
in the displays of conspecifics, it often may recognize and correctly

respond to the corresponding displays of animals from other species, regardless of whether the similarity to the displays of its own species is due to homology or analogy. On the other hand, when certain gestures, postures, or vocalizations are phenotypically similar in two species but serve different functions, and thus have different meanings, it may become a source of misunderstanding, since the recipient reacts according to that meaning which the behavior would have when displayed by a conspecific. Again, this happens with homologous as well as with analogous displays.

Hediger (1950) reports a typical example of such an interspecific misunderstanding. He once put a kangaroo and a sika deer together in one enclosure (probably due to temporary spatial problems in his zoo). These two very different animals were not very interested in each other, and thus the situation was quite peaceful—as long as the kangaroo remained in a crouched posture. As soon as it assumed an erect posture by sitting on its hind legs, as kangaroo do as a usual maintenance activity, it was attacked by the deer. Deer do not sit on their hind legs, but taking an erect attitude and rising on the hind legs is an aggressive behavior in deer. Correspondingly, the stag mistook the kangaroo's sitting posture for a threat display and reacted aggressively to it.

Certainly similarities of expressive behaviors due to homology are very important in primary interspecific communication. As a rule of thumb, one may say that the more closely related two species are, the more homologous displays they have in common, and the better communication between them will work. Let me emphasize that good communication due to homologous behaviors does not necessarily imply that the animals would get along particularly well with each other. For example, certain threat displays may be homologous in two species. Then the animal of the one species can recognize the other's threat very well, take the challenge, and correctly react by aggressive behaviors, regardless of possible enormous differences in size, weight, and/or weapons, and/or fighting techniques (Fig. 145). This usually is a major problem in keeping different ungulate species together in a zoo. The presentation of horns, for instance, is a threat which almost all species of horned ungulates have in common, and it is probably a homologous behavior in all of them. Thus, it is understood whenever an animal of another species displays it. For example, when one male and several females of Thomson's gazelle are kept together with one male and several females of eland antelope in the same enclosure, so that they become sufficiently familiar with each other, the very aggressive little gazelle buck will predictably start displaying with presented horns toward the big eland bull. Since horn

a

b

c

Fig. 145. Interspecific agonistic encounter between an oryx and a wildebeest in captivity. a. The oryx gores the ground in "kneeling" posture. The wildebeest approaches and, since it "understands" this behavior, which is also present in the species-specific behavioral inventory of wildebeest, . . . b. . . . it responds with a corresponding object aggression. The oryx meanwhile scrapes the ground—also a display that is present in wildebeest. c. The opponents have "understood" the reciprocal challenge, and they start fighting in spite of the considerable difference in size and shape of their horns. (Walther 1965*a*. Munich Zoo.)

presentation is also a threat display in eland, the eland bull understands this challenge, may return the threat, and they may start fighting. A tommy buck has a weight of about 25 kg and an eland bull can weigh as much as 500 kg, so it does not require too much imagination to realize that such an encounter can be rather disastrous to the gazelle. Consequently, with respect to keeping animals in zoological gardens, it is often better not to keep closely related species together, and one may have fewer problems with rather distant species, e.g., an antelope species with certain birds such as crested cranes or flamingos. These birds have few behaviors in common with the antelope, so communication is poor, but hostile interactions are also infrequent.

I might add here that, in the wild, antelopes of different species only rarely interact with each other. This is not because they are unable to communicate with each other, but simply because each of them usually sticks to its own species; they satisfy their need for aggression, sexual behavior, etc., with conspecific partners, showing no great tendency to interact with animals of a different species (they live as if they were alone in the world, as I said above). Moreover, there are not too many situations that would require or favor such interactions.

As important as homologies in expressive behaviors may be in the communication of animals from different species, however, they do not absolutely guarantee the success of the communication. Homology means only that the behaviors of different species phylogenetically originated from a mutual root. It does not imply that nothing has changed during further evolution. For example, changes can occur in the functions of behaviors. Neck-fighting along with its intention movements is an aggressive behavior, but it has become a male courtship behavior in greater kudu. Furthermore, a divergent species-specific ritualization can take place in originally homologous behaviors so that eventually the originally homologous expressions may look rather different in different species. They may even become more similar to certain other gestures, with different meanings and origins, in the other species. In this regard—and perhaps generally in the investigation of interspecific communication—the study of misunderstandings and errors is often particularly instructive.

As an example, I may mention an event which I remember very well. It happened in the beginning of my career as an ethologist and it remained rather obscure to me at that time. I observed nilgai antelope (one male and several females) in a zoological garden where they were kept together with Scotch cattle in a large enclosure. (This somewhat strange combination was due to temporary spatial problems in this zoo.) The nilgai bull displayed to the cattle, and particularly to the Scotch bull, by assuming a broadside position in front of them (lateral T-position) with somewhat crouched back and head and neck stiffly stretched forward—in short, the usual threat-dominance display of this species (Fig. 94a). The cattle watched the nilgai bull but otherwise did not react to his display. Cattle have a broadside display (with hind legs somewhat under the belly) that is probably homologous to that of nilgai, but during the display their noses more or less point toward the ground. Apparently these differences in the head and neck postures in the broadside displays of cattle and nilgai are due to divergent species-specific trends in an originally homologous behavior. These behaviors have become so different in these different species that the cattle "did not know" what to make of the nilgai bull's display in the described situation. Since they did not react, the nilgai bull intensified his display to the highest (species-specific) extent by slightly raising his stiffly stretched neck and head so that they now not only pointed forward but also somewhat upward. At this point, the cattle regularly stampeded. In the beginning, I presumed that they were finally "getting the message." However, it soon struck me that their reaction was rather strange. Their flight always lasted several minutes; they galloped to and fro throughout the whole enclosure; and they even ran back toward the nilgai bull (who did not participate in the stampede). Later, when reading Schloeth's excellent studies on Camargue cattle, I learned that cattle may assume a stance with neck and head held forward and somewhat upward that closely resembles the attitude of the nilgai bull in the high-intensity display, and that Schloeth (1956b) interpreted as an "alarm posture; signal for group members to prepare for flight." It appears likely that, in the described situation, the Scotch cattle had mistaken the nilgai bull's threat-dominance display as a flight signal, according to the meaning of this posture in their species-specific repertoire.

Another interesting case of a misunderstanding caused by species-specific deviations following the same (I do not dare decide whether homologous or analogous) behavioral principle became evident when I once had occasion to interview a zookeeper who had been attacked by an oryx bull. Typically, the man was not the keeper who usually took care of these animals, but a substitute. He had been cleaning the large outdoor enclosure with a brush and a wheelbarrow in the presence of the antelopes, and said the reason the attack had been so dangerous was that it had come as a complete surprise. When I questioned him further it turned out that the keeper had felt some alarm when the oryx bull walked straight toward him, but then relaxed because instead of facing him it assumed a broadside position in front of him and stood there motionless for several minutes before the "surprise" attack. The man was astonished when I told him that this lateral position is an aggressive display in oryx. He assured me over and over that the bull was not facing in his direction. I, in turn, assured him as frequently that I did not doubt that. The principle of impressing an opponent by emphatically displaying the breadth of one's own body is also present in man. (As I said above, I do not dare decide whether it is homologous or analogous to the corresponding behavior of other mammals.) However, a man can best display the breadth of his chest and shoulders by assuming a frontal orientation toward the opponent. In oryx, as is generally the case in hoofed mammals, the silhouette of the body is small in frontal view; consequently they use a lateral orientation toward the recipient when displaying their breadth. In this case, the interesting point was that the obviously inexperienced and apparently not especially bright man was unable to recognize the principal feature (impressing the other by the breadth of the body) in the bull's display. He was absolutely fixated to the species-specific, human version of the performance, the frontal orientation in this case. Even when I had explained the matter to him in very simple terms and had demonstrated the corresponding human behavior, which he knew very well, he continued to insist that the bull had not been facing him.

A final aspect of primary interspecific communication concerns the distribution and reliability of certain expressions. Distribution refers to how widely spread a given display is in different species. Reliability means how readily and/or frequently the animals of a given species react to a signal when displayed by nonconspecifics. It seems to be a general rule that the more primitive the signal, the greater the distribution and reliability. Primitiveness means in this case (a) that the behavior can easily be performed by animals of more or less different bodily organization, i.e., that its performance does not depend on size, species-specific peculiarities of anatomical structure (e.g., movability of the neck), presence or absence of special and specialized organs, etc., and (b) that the behavior in question has not been subject to deviating processes of elaborate species-specific ritualizations.

There are a number of expressive behaviors that fulfill these criteria in hoofed mammals. As examples, we may name the just-mentioned sudden phenotypic increase in size or breadth as a frequent principle of dominance displays, and the structure—loud, short, abruptly beginning and ending—of many alarm calls. Of course, in accordance with Darwin's famous principle of the opposite, behaviors which are the opposite of those mentioned above are also "internationally" understood. Thus, e.g., soft, long, and continuous vocalizations often calm down an excited animal. In intraspecific communication, certain contact vocalizations are of this type and have this effect. However, it also works with partners of different species, e.g., a man may calm down a spooky horse by persistently and slowly talking to it in a soft voice. Depending on the situation, of course, this does not always work, but it works often enough that—if I am correctly informed—the American Indians gave their children this rule for handling animals: "You can make 'good medicine' with your voice." (Even if it should not be historically correct, the statement in itself is very true.) Interestingly enough and very typical of expressions, these structural features and their effects are largely the same in acoustical, visual, and tactile (and possibly/probably also olfactory) means of communication. With strong, short, and/or abrupt touching one can drive almost any animal crazy, whereas soft, long and continuous petting strokes may calm it down. Likewise, vehement, abrupt, and short movements often have alarming effects, while moderate, slow and continuous ones are suitable to make an animal relax. However, the slowness of movements does have its limits. When a movement is performed so slowly that it very strikingly differs from normal speed, it may attract attention and make animals alert, since extremely slow movements are typical of rather severe threat and dominance displays in quite a number of the species under discussion.

Perhaps the signals with the widest interspecific distribution and the greatest reliability in interspecific communication are those which are linked to the sender's orientation relative to the recipient. They are largely independent of species-specific peculiarities in body structure and, although there certainly are species-specific ritualizations of the corresponding displays, these usually do not affect the basic message of the orientation. For example, a frontal orientation and, especially a frontal approach are rather universal indications that the sender has "something in mind" with respect to the recipient, and very frequently it is indicative of more or less hostile intentions, as extensively discussed in previous chapters. Thus, in a great number of species, the recipients react by flight or aggression—depending on circumstances—to the sender's frontal orientation or approach, including senders from other species. *Mutatis mutandis*, the same reactions as with conspecific senders can also be observed with respect to lateral, reverse, etc. orientations in interspecific encounters. It may be remembered from previous discussions that the orientation of the sender's head is often of particular importance in this regard and can substitute for that of the body to a certain extent. Perhaps one could even say more generally that the orientation of a part of the body can have the same effect as the orientation of the entire body. The orientation of the head is only a special, although very frequent and prominent, case of this general rule which, in principle, is also applicable to movements and orientations of other parts of the body. In short, it is the old expression principle: the structure of the movement is the most important thing, and the means by which this structure is brought about are of secondary importance. Thus, if the forward or sideward or backward component of such an orientation movement is expressed clearly enough, it is of minor importance whether it is a movement of the head, the neck, the leg, etc., or whether it is the torso that leans forward, backward, sideways. In the special case of man-animal relationships even such things as tools, sticks, and brooms, held in the hand, may play a role of body parts and thus be used for orientation and direction signaling. Since hoofed mammals do not make much use of tools in their natural lives (there are some indications of it but it is minor in extent as compared to certain primates and, above all, to humans) and their "tools" are bodily organs (e.g., horns or antlers), tools do not exist in their subjective world, their *Umwelt*—in the sense in which von Uexküll and Kriszat (1934) used this term. Consequently, the animals—to put it somewhat anthropomorphically but simply—do not "realize" that a tool is a thing on its own but "consider" it as part of man's body when he has it in his hands.

Because the message and meaning of such orientation movements are so generally understood by animals of different species, man can use them when handling or training animals. In addition, animals such as carnivores and ungulates are often especially adept at learning in this "special field," as pointed out above. All of this becomes particularly important when a human has to deal with relatively big animals, be it domestic stock—cattle, horses, sheep, goats—or wild animals, such as deer or antelopes, in a zoo or national park or something of the sort, which are not tame enough to touch but will tolerate man's presence at a relatively close range and pay attention to his signals, so that a certain communication can take place. By changes of position and orientation relative to the animals (placing himself in front, behind, or sideways; approaching or withdrawing; leaning the torso forward or backward; facing them or facing away), as well as by corresponding movements of his arms or legs and even utilization of sticks, whips, clothing, etc., a human can maneuver the animals in a definite direction, stop them from advancing in another direction, make them withdraw or follow him. This corresponds to the way a territorial buck of Grant's gazelle controls the movements of the females in his territory, or a plains zebra stallion "steers" his mares, or the "master bull" of a migratory oryx herd keeps the group together and directs its movements, etc.

When animals are together with people for a long while, they may also learn to react to corresponding human signals, so that eventually a herdsman may stand among the animals and direct their movements by waves of his raised hand, as Baskin (1974) describes from studies of the management practices of Siberian natives with animals such as reindeer, sheep, goats, camels, and yaks (*Poëphagus mutus*). In principle, these techniques are known to anyone handling ungulates under ranch conditions. Perhaps it is because these things are so well known to people who deal with animals on a daily basis that they have rarely been scientifically investigated; Baskin's paper (1974) is the single scientific contribution known to me that treats this subject at least to a moderate extent. Baskin is inclined to derive the obedience of ungulates toward signals by human herdsmen from the reactions of prey animals toward predators. In my opinion, this is an error, since animals which are themselves predators—dogs, for example—also react or learn to react to corresponding human signals. When the preyed-upon ungulates react to predators in a comparable way, in my opinion, it is a secondary process based on the primary intraspecific communication, as is the case with reactions to signals of humans.

Typically, man has only been able successfully to domesticate big animals like ungulates when they were (a) gregarious and (b) not territorial. Besides the territorial competition among the animals themselves, which certainly creates additional problems in keeping and breeding them, an advanced assimilation tendency causes the territorial bucks or bulls to respond to those human individuals with whom they have become particularly familiar as conspecific rivals. This means that they attack their caretaker as soon as he enters the "territory," and to a captive territorial ungulate male, the "territory" is the place where he is kept. I have described elsewhere (Walther 1966a) how troublesome it can be, with even such a small animal as a dorcas gazelle, when a captive buck has become so familiar with people that he defends the zoo enclosure as his territory against them. The ancient Egyptians tried to domesticate various antelope species, such as addax, scimitar-horned oryx, north-African hartebeest, and dorcas gazelle—species in which the males are known or presumed to become territorial. All these attempts failed. Of course we are not informed of the details of these failures, but there are ancient Egyptian paintings that depict instruments used and procedures taken to cut or deform the horns of these animals. Thus it does not take too much fantasy to imagine what had happened. I should add here that territoriality per se is not a handicap for domestication; it depends on the form of territoriality. When a species has group territories, man can become a member of the pack (speaking from the animal's point of view), and then the animal may defend its master's property as the mutual group territory, as is the case with dogs. In certain ungulates, however, only the males become territorial and each of them defends his territory against other conspecific males, and thus, also against humans when they are so familiar to him that he treats them as (male) conspecifics (regardless, by the way, of the sex of the person).

On the other hand, gregarious ungulates are accustomed to react to signals of their conspecifics and particularly to those of very dominant herd members. When they are not territorial and have "zoomorphized" man, he may easily take the role of an alpha animal in such a group, and then the herd members obey his signals or at least cause him no more trouble when he is herding them than they would a dominant conspecific. Thus, for example, when a cowboy directs the cattle precisely in the direction in which he wants them to go, or stops them from moving ahead in a given direction, or separates a herd member from the others by cutting its way, or brings a straggler back to the herd, he may be justifiably proud of his skills. On the other hand, his skills only work because he is doing something that is very familiar to the cattle from their social relations with each other. From the cow's standpoint, the herdsman is nothing but a very dominant bull.

In short, if one wishes to put it in a somewhat humorous way, primary interspecific communication works because of an "error" on both sides. The sender treats and addresses the recipient as if the latter were a conspecific (which he is not), and the recipient reacts as if the sender were a conspecific (which he is not). However, since (a) the expressive structure of a signal is more important than the means by which it is brought about, and (b) the message and the meaning of such signals can be the same in several species due to homologous or analogous developments, communication between animals of different species works in quite a number of cases. Of course, failures and mistakes are possible, and they are by no means exceptional, as stated above. However, successful cases of primary interspecific communication based on "mutual error" are much more numerous than many people would expect.

These "mutual errors," which are the direct consequence of Hediger's assimilation tendency, form the natural basis for interspecific communication in animals of the organizational level of ungulates. They also are the natural basis of man-animal communication. Certainly, man's tendency to anthropomorphize such animals is strong, and when one has to deal with them on a practical basis (of course, outside of a laboratory, an experimental station, or the engineered livestock facilities of modern agriculture), one can hardly avoid some form of anthropomorphism. On the animal's part, the tendency to zoomorphize humans after it has become sufficiently familiar with them is equally great—and man and animal may communicate on this basis to some extent.

Most scientists think of anthropomorphism as one of the worst mistakes that can be made in animal psychology. Certainly, one can give many arguments in support of this view. However, I can hardly avoid the impression that scientists have overreacted in this case, only seeing the negative aspects of anthropomorphism and completely ignoring the positive. Such positive aspects do exist, and they are by no means of minor importance. It is true that man-animal communication can be considerably improved when we learn to recognize and to avoid the mistakes and errors involved in anthropomorphism. On the other hand, anthropomorphism was, is, and will remain the natural basis of man's communication with animals. In particular, "man's greatest biological experiment," the domestication of large mammals—particularly some ungulate species—at a time when the human race was still in a rather primitive state of technical development, would have been impossible without man's anthropomorphizing these animals, and the animals' zoomorphizing man. Thus, instead of constant condemnation, anthropomorphism, or, more generally speaking, the assimilation tendency, deserves a monument.

Appendix:
A Classification List of
Hoofed Mammals

NOTE: The classification of hoofed mammals, particularly the ruminants, presents many difficult problems, but this is not the place to discuss them. It is sufficient for the reader to know that quite a number of classification lists of hoofed mammals have been published over the years, each of them having its advantages and disadvantages, and that a final, absolutely satisfactory solution has not been found up to now for some of these problems. Thus, there are differences of opinion among the taxonomists, and the reader should not be too surprised when he finds a classification in another book which differs more or less from that presented here.

In order to make things as simple as possible I have omitted two categories of modern classification systems, the supraorders and the tribes. The supraorders have no bearing on our previous discussions. Likewise, some of the tribes do not contribute anything to the understanding of differences or similarities in the behavior. In other cases, certain tribes are identical with certain subfamilies of older classification systems. I think a classification system which uses these old subfamilies is much easier to grasp for a reader who does not have a special training in taxonomy—and besides, it is by no means impossible that taxonomists may reconsider at least some of the tribes under discussion and replace them by subfamilies again.

Presented below are the common and the scientific names of the recent ungulate species (fossil forms are not mentioned), classified according to subgenera (as far as necessary), genera, subfamilies (as far as necessary), families, infraorders (as far as necessary), suborders, and orders. As is well known, each scientific species name consists of a generic name and a specific epithet. For example, in the case of the Malayan tapir, *Tapirus* is the scientific name of the genus, *indicus* is the specific epithet, and the full species name is *Tapirus indicus*. The subgenus is a taxonomic category between the genus and the species. Thus, in the scientific name, it is placed in parentheses between genus and species name. For example, the sika deer is *Cervus (Sika) nippon*, indicating that the species *nippon* belongs to the subgenus *Sika* within the genus *Cervus*. When scientific animal names are quoted in a text which does not particularly deal with the problems of classification, the subgenus is often left out. I also did so in a number of cases in the previous text. For example, I always wrote *Equus zebra* instead of *Equus (Hippotigris) zebra*. In the following classification list, I primarily included those subgenera which were considered to be genera by older taxonomists. These subgenera often are extremely useful under behavioral aspects. As a matter of fact, they are so convenient in a discussion on problems of behavior that I have frequently used them in lieu of generic names in the previous chapters of this book. For example, instead of *Kobus kob* or *Kobus (Adenota) kob*, I wrote *Adenota kob* in the text.

383

Subspecies names are excluded from the following classification list because it is only meant to convey general information to the reader who is not familiar with the classification of the species under discussion, and mentioning the subspecies would have made this list unduly long. However, I have occasionally mentioned subspecies in the previous text. In the scientific names, the subspecies name is put (without parentheses) after the species name. For example, the blesbok is *Damaliscus dorcas phillipsi* (*phillipsi* being the subspecies name). Since all domestic animals can, in the best case, only be considered to be subspecies of wild species, names of domestic animals do not show up in the following classification list (with the sole exception of the dromedary, because its wild ancestors have been extinct since prehistoric times).

Order: Odd-toed Ungulates (Perissodactyla)
    Suborder: Rhinoceros-related Animals (Ceratomorpha)
        Family: Tapirs (Tapiridae)
            Genus: Tapirs (*Tapirus*)
                Lowland Tapir, *Tapirus terrestris* (Linné, 1766)
                Mountain Tapir, *Tapirus pinchaque* (Roulin, 1829)
                Central American Tapir, *Tapirus bairdi* (Gill, 1865)
                Malayan Tapir, *Tapirus indicus* Desmarest, 1819
        Family: Rhinoceroses (Rhinocerotidae)
            Genus: Asiatic Two-horned Rhinoceroses (*Dicerorhinus*)
                Sumatran Rhinoceros, *Dicerorhinus sumatrensis* (Fischer, 1814)
            Genus: Great Indian Rhinoceroses (*Rhinoceros*)
                Indian Rhinoceros, *Rhinoceros unicornis* Linné, 1758
                Javan Rhinoceros, *Rhinoceros sondaicus* Desmarest, 1822
            Genus: Black Rhinoceroses (*Diceros*)
                Black Rhinoceros, *Diceros bicornis* Linné, 1758
            Genus: Square-lipped Rhinoceroses (*Ceratotherium*)
                Square-lipped or White Rhinoceros, *Ceratotherium simum* (Burchell, 1817)
    Suborder: Horse-related Animals (Hippomorpha)
        Family: Equids (Equidae)
            Genus: Horses (*Equus*)
                Subgenus: Zebras (*Hippotrigis*)
                    Mountain Zebra, *Equus* (*Hippotigris*) *zebra* Linné, 1758
                    Plains Zebra, *Equus* (*Hippotigris*) *quagga* Gmelin, 1788

Subgenus: Grevy's Zebras (*Dolichohippus*)
　　Grevy's Zebra, *Equus (Dolichohippus) grevyi*
　　　Oustalet, 1882
Subgenus: African Wild Asses (*Asinus*)
　　African Wild Ass, *Equus (Asinus) asinus*
　　　Linné, 1758
Subgenus: Asiatic Wild Asses (*Hemionus*)
　　Asiatic Wild Ass, *Equus (Hemionus) hemi-*
　　　onus Pallas, 1775
Subgenus: Horses (*Equus*)
　　Przewalski's Wild Horse, *Equus (Equus)*
　　　przewalskii Poliakov, 1881
Order: Even-toed Ungulates (Artiodactyla)
　Suborder: Nonruminants (Nonruminantia)
　　Family: Swine (Suidae)
　　　Genus: Bush Pigs (*Potamochoerus*)
　　　　Bush Pig, *Potamochoerus porcus* (Linné, 1758)
　　　Genus: Hogs (*Sus*)
　　　　Subgenus: Hogs (*Sus*)
　　　　　Bearded Pig, *Sus (Sus) barbatus* Müller, 1838
　　　　　Javan Pig, *Sus (Sus) verrucosus* Müller and
　　　　　　Schlegel, 1842
　　　　　Wild Boar, *Sus (Sus) scrofa* Linné, 1758
　　　　Subgenus: Pigmy Hogs (*Porcula*)
　　　　　Pigmy Hog, *Sus (Porcula) salvanius* (Hodg-
　　　　　　son, 1847)
　　　Genus: Warthogs (*Phacochoerus*)
　　　　Warthog, *Phacochoerus aethiopicus* (Pallas,
　　　　　1767)
　　　Genus: Forest Hogs (*Hylochoerus*)
　　　　Giant Forest Hog, *Hylochoerus meinertzha-*
　　　　　geni Thomas, 1904
　　　Genus: Barbirusas (*Babyrousa*)
　　　　Babirusa, *Babyrousa babyrussa* (Linné, 1758)
　　Family: Peccaries (Tayassuidae)
　　　Genus: Peccaries (*Tayassu*)
　　　　Collared Peccary, *Tayassu tajacu* (Linné,
　　　　　1758)
　　　　White-lipped Peccary, *Tayassu albirostris* (Il-
　　　　　liger, 1811)
　　Family: Hippopotamuses (Hippopotamidae)
　　　Genus: Pigmy Hippopotamuses (*Choeropsis*)
　　　　Pigmy Hippopotamus, *Choeropsis liberiensis*
　　　　　(Morton, 1844)
　　　Genus: Hippopotamuses (*Hippopotamus*)
　　　　Hippopotamus, *Hippopotamus amphibius*
　　　　　Linné, 1758
　Suborder: Tylopods (Tylopoda)
　　Family: Camel-related Animals (Camelidae)
　　　Genus: Camels (*Camelus*)
　　　　Two-humped Camel, *Camelus bactrianus*
　　　　　Linné, 1758

Dromedary, *Camelus dromedarius* Linné, 1758[1]

Genus: Llamas (*Lama*)

Guanaco, *Lama guanicoë* (Müller, 1776)

Vicuna, *Lama vicugna* (Molina, 1782)

Suborder: Ruminants (Ruminantia)

Infraorder: Chevrotain-related Animals (Tragulina)

Family: Chevrotains (Tragulidae)

Genus: Chevrotains (*Hyemoschus*)

Water Chevrotain, *Hyemoschus aquaticus* (Ogilby, 1841)

Genus: Mouse Deer (*Tragulus*)

Larger Malayan Mouse Deer, *Tragulus napu* (F. Cuvier, 1822)

Lesser Malayan Mouse Deer, *Tragulus javanicus* (Osbeck, 1765)

Indian Mouse Deer, *Tragulus meminna* (Erxleben, 1777)

Infraorder: Horned and Antlered Ruminants (Pecora)

Family: Deer (Cervidae)

Subfamily: Musk Deer (Moschinae)

Genus: Musk Deer (*Moschus*)

Musk Deer, *Moschus moschiferus* Linné, 1758

Subfamily: Water Deer (Hydropotinae)

Genus: Water Deer (*Hydropotes*)

Chinese Water Deer, *Hydropotes inermis* Swinhoe, 1870

Subfamily: Muntjacs (Muntiacinae)

Genus: Muntiacs (*Muntiacus*)

Muntjac, *Muntiacus muntjac* (Zimmermann, 1780)

Genus: Tibetan Muntjacs (*Elaphodus*)

Tufted Deer, *Elaphodus cephalophus* Milne-Edwards, 1872

Subfamily: American Deer and Roe Deer (Odocoileinae)

Genus: Roe Deer (*Capreolus*)

Roe Deer, *Capreolus capreolus* (Linné, 1758)

Genus: American Deer (*Odocoileus*)

Subgenus: American Deer (*Odocoileus*)

White-tailed Deer, *Odocoileus* (*Odocoileus*) *virginianus* (Zimmermann, 1780)

Mule Deer, *Odocoileus* (*Odocoileus*) *hemionus* (Rafinesque, 1817)

South American Marsh Deer, *Odocoileus* (*Odocoileus*) *dichotomus* (Illiger, 1811)

Subgenus: Pampas Deer (*Blastoceros*)

Pampas Deer, *Odocoileus* (*Blastoceros*) *bezoarticus* (Linné, 1766)

---

[1]No recent wild form.

Subgenus: Guemals (*Hippocamelus*)
    Peruvian Guemal, *Odocoileus (Hippocamelus) antisiensis* (D'Orbigny, 1834)
    Chilenian Guemal, *Odocoileus (Hippocamelus) bisulcus* (Molina, 1782)
Genus: Brocket Deer (*Mazama*)
    Red Brocket, *Mazama americana* (Erxleben, 1777)
    Grey Brocket, *Mazama gouazoubira* (Fischer, 1814)
    Lesser Brocket, *Mazama nana* (Lesson, 1842)
    Grey Dwarf Brocket, *Mazama bricenii* Thomas, 1908
Genus: Pudus (*Pudu*)[2]
    Northern Pudu, *Pudu mephistopheles* De Winton, 1896
    Southern Pudu, *Pudu pudu* Molina, 1782
Subfamily: Moose Deer (Alcinae)
Genus: Moose Deer (*Alces*)
    Moose, *Alces alces* (Linné, 1758)
Subfamily: Reindeer (Rangiferinae)
Genus: Reindeer (*Rangifer*)
    Reindeer and Caribou, *Rangifer tarandus* (Linné, 1758)
Subfamily: Deer (Cervinae)
Genus: Fallow Deer (Dama)[3]
    Fallow Deer, *Dama dama* (Linné, 1758)
Genus: Axis Deer (Axis)[3]
    Subgenus: Hog Deer (*Hyelaphus*)
    Hog Deer, *Axis (Hyelaphus) porcinus* (Zimmermann, 1780)
    Subgenus: Axis Deer (*Axis*)
    Axis Deer, *Axis (Axis) axis* (Erxleben, 1777)
Genus: Red Deer (*Cervus*)
    Subgenus: Sambars (*Rusa*)
    Indian Sambar, *Cervus (Rusa) unicolor* Kerr, 1792
    Sunda Sambar, *Cervus (Rusa) timorensis* De Blainville, 1822
    Philippine Sambar, *Cervus (Rusa) mariannus* Desmarest, 1822
    Subgenus: Barasinghas (*Rucervus*)
    Barasingha, *Cervus (Rucervus) duvauceli* Cuvier, 1823
    Eld's Deer, *Cervus (Rucervus) eldi* McClelland, 1842

[2]According to some taxonomists, *Pudu* is a subgenus of *Mazama*.
[3]According to some taxonomists, *Dama* and *Axis* are subgenera of *Cervus*.

Subgenus: Sika Deer (*Sika*)
Sika Deer, *Cervus (Sika) nippon* Temminck, 1838
Subgenus: Red Deer (*Cervus*)
Red Deer, *Cervus (Cervus) elaphus* Linné, 1758
Elk, *Cervus (Cervus) canadensis* Erxleben, 1777[4]
Subgenus: Tibetan Deer (*Przewalskium*)
Thorold's Deer, *Cervus (Przewalskium) albirostris* Przewalski, 1883
Genus: Pere David's Deer (*Elaphurus*)
Pere David's Deer, *Elaphurus davidianus* Milne-Edwards, 1866
Family: Giraffe-related Animals (Giraffidae)
Subfamily: Forest Giraffes (Okapiinae)
Genus: Okapis (*Okapia*)
Okapi, *Okapia johnstoni* (Sclater, 1901)
Subfamily: Steppe Giraffes (Giraffinae)
Genus: Giraffes (*Giraffa*)
Giraffe, *Giraffa camelopardalis* (Linné, 1758)
Family: Pronghorns (Antilocapridae)
Genus: Pronghorns (*Antilocapra*)
Pronghorn, *Antilocapra americana* (Ord, 1815)
Family: Horned Ungulates (Bovidae)
Subfamily: Duikers (Cephalophinae)
Genus: Grey Duikers (*Sylvicapra*)
Grey Duiker, *Sylvicapra grimmia* (Linné, 1758)
Genus: Duikers (*Cephalophus*)
Maxwell's Duiker, *Cephalophus maxwelli* (H. Smith, 1827)
Black Duiker, *Cephalophus niger* Gray, 1846
Banded Duiker, *Cephalophus zebra* (Gray, 1838)
Ogilby's Duiker, *Cephalophus ogilbyi* (Waterhouse, 1838)
Red-flanked Duiker, *Cephalophus rufilatus* Gray, 1846
Bay Duiker, *Cephalophus dorsalis* Gray, 1846
Gaboon Duiker, *Cephalophus leucogaster* Gray, 1873
Black-fronted Duiker, *Cephalophus nigrifrons* Gray, 1871
Harvey's Duiker, *Cephalophus harveyi* Thomas, 1893
Blue Duiker, *Cephalophus monticola* (Thunberg, 1789)

---

[4]According to some taxonomists, *Cervus canadensis* is a subspecies of *Cervus elaphus*.

Red Duiker, *Cephalophus natalensis* A. Smith, 1834

Jentink's Duiker, *Cephalophus jentinki* (Thomas, 1892)

Yellow-backed Duiker, *Cephalophus sylvicultor* (Afzelius, 1815)

Abbot's Duiker, *Cephalophus spadix* True, 1890

Subfamily: Dwarf Antelopes (Neotraginae)
Genus: Royal Antelopes (*Neotragus*)
Subgenus: Royal Antelopes (*Neotragus*)
Royal Antelope, *Neotragus (Neotragus) pygmaeus* (Linné, 1758)
Subgenus: Sunis (*Nesotragus*)
Bate's Dwarf Antelope, *Neotragus (Nesotragus) batesi* De Winton, 1903
Suni, *Neotragus (Nesotragus) moschatus* Von Düben, 1847
Genus: Dikdiks (*Madoqua*)
Subgenus: Dikdiks (*Madoqua*)
Salt's Dikdik, *Madoqua (Madoqua) saltiana* (Desmarest, 1816)
Red Belly Dikdik, *Madoqua (Madoqua) phillipsi* Thomas, 1894
Swayne's Dikdik, *Madoqua (Madoqua) swaynei* Thomas, 1894
Subgenus: Long-nosed Dikdiks (*Rhynchotragus*)
Günther's Dikdik, *Madoqua (Rhynchotragus) guentheri* Thomas, 1894
Kirk's Dikdik, *Madoqua (Rhynchotragus) kirki* (Günther, 1880)
Genus: Beiras (*Dorcatragus*)
Beira, *Dorcatragus megalotis* (Menges, 1894)
Genus: Klipspringers (*Oreotragus*)
Klipspringer, *Oreotragus oreotragus* (Zimmermann, 1783)
Genus: Steenboks (*Raphicerus*)
Subgenus: Grysboks (*Nototragus*)
Grysbok, *Raphicerus (Nototragus) melanotis* (Thunberg, 1811)
Subgenus: Steenboks (*Raphicerus*)
Steenbok, *Raphicerus (Raphicerus) campestris* (Thunberg, 1811)
Genus: Oribis (*Ourebia*)
Oribi, *Ourebia ourebi* (Zimmermann, 1783)

Subfamily: Spiral-horned Antelopes (Tragelaphinae)
Genus: Spiral-horned Antelopes (*Tragelaphus*)
Subgenus: Spiral-horned Antelopes (*Tragelaphus*)
Greater Kudu, *Tragelaphus (Tragelaphus) strepsiceros* (Pallas, 1766)
Lesser Kudu, *Tragelaphus (Tragelaphus) imberbis* (Blyth, 1869)

Mountain Nyala, *Tragelaphus (Tragelaphus) buxtoni* (Lydekker, 1910)

Nyala, *Tragelaphus (Tragelaphus) angasi* Gray, 1849

Sitatunga, *Tragelaphus (Tragelaphus) spekei* Sclater, 1864

Bushbuck, *Tragelaphus (Tragelaphus) scriptus* (Pallas, 1766)

Subgenus: Eland Antelopes (*Taurotragus*)

Eland, *Tragelaphus (Taurotragus) oryx* (Pallas, 1766)

Bongo, *Tragelaphus (Taurotragus) euryceros* (Ogilby, 1837)

Genus: Nilgai Antelopes (*Boselaphus*)

Nilgai, *Boselaphus tragocamelus* (Pallas, 1776)

Genus: Four-horned Antelopes (*Tetracerus*)

Four-horned Antelope, *Tetracerus quadricornis* (De Blainville, 1816)

Subfamily: Oxen (Bovinae)

Genus: Water Buffaloes (*Bubalus*)

Subgenus: Anoas (*Anoa*)

Anoa, *Bubalus (Anoa) depressicornis* (H. Smith, 1827)

Subgenus: Water Buffaloes (*Bubalus*)

Water Buffalo, *Bubalus (Bubalus) arnee* (Kerr, 1792)

Genus: African Buffaloes (*Syncerus*)

African Buffalo, *Syncerus caffer* (Sparrmann, 1779)

Genus: Oxen (*Bos*)

Subgenus: Gaurs (*Bibos*)

Gaur, *Bos (Bibos) gaurus* H. Smith, 1827

Banteng, *Bos (Bibos) javanicus* D'Alton, 1823

Subgenus: Koupreys (*Novibos*)

Kouprey, *Bos (Novibos) sauveli* Urbain, 1937

Subgenus: Oxen (*Bos*)

Aurochs, *Bos (Bos) primigenius* Bojanus, 1827[5]

Subgenus: Yaks (*Poëphagus*)

Yak, *Bos (Poëphagus) mutus* (Przewalski, 1883)

Genus: Bisons (*Bison*)

American Bison, *Bison bison* (Linné, 1758)

European Bison, *Bison bonasus* (Linné, 1758)[6]

Subfamily: Hartebeest-related Antelopes (Alcelaphinae)

Genus: Wildebeests (*Connochaetes*)

Brindled Wildebeest, *Connochaetes taurinus* (Burchell, 1823)

---

[5] Wild form extinct; ancestor of domestic cattle.
[6] According to some taxonomists, *Bison bonasus* is a subspecies of *Bison bison*.

Black Wildebeest, *Connochaetes gnou* (Zimmermann, 1780)
Genus: Hartebeests (*Alcelaphus*)
Hartebeest, *Alcelaphus buselaphus* (Pallas, 1766)
Red Hartebeest, *Alcelaphus caama* (G. Cuvier, 1804)[7]
Lichtenstein's Hartebeest, *Alcelaphus lichtensteini* (Peters, 1852)[7]
Genus: Topi-related Antelopes (*Damaliscus*)
Topi and Tsessebe, *Damaliscus lunatus* (Burchell, 1823)
Hunter's Antelope, *Damaliscus hunteri* (Sclater, 1889)[8]
Bontebok and Blesbok, *Damaliscus dorcas* (Pallas, 1766)
Subfamily: Reedbucks and Waterbucks (Reduncinae)
Genus: Waterbucks (*Kobus*)
Subgenus: Waterbucks (*Kobus*)
Common Waterbuck, *Kobus (Kobus) ellipsiprymnus* (Ogilby, 1833)
Defassa Waterbuck, *Kobus (Kobus) defassa* (Rüppell, 1835)[9]
Subgenus: Kob Antelopes (*Adenota*)
Kob, *Kobus (Adenota) kob* (Erxleben, 1777)
Puku, *Kobus (Adenota) vardoni* (Livingstone, 1857)[10]
Subgenus: Lechwe Antelopes (*Hydrotragus*)
Lechwe, *Kobus (Hydrotragus) leche* Gray, 1850
Subgenus: Nile Lechwes (*Onotragus*)
Mrs. Gray's Waterbuck, *Kobus (Onotragus) megaceros* (Fitzinger, 1855)
Genus: Reedbucks (*Redunca*)
Southern Reedbuck, *Redunca arundium* (Boddaert, 1785)
Bohor Reedbuck, *Redunca redunca* (Pallas, 1767)
Mountain Reedbuck, *Redunca fulvorufula* (Afzelius, 1815)
Genus: Rheboks (*Pelea*)
Rhebok, *Pelea capreolus* (Forster, 1790)

---

[7] *Alcelaphus buselaphus* includes many subspecies. According to some taxonomists, *Alcelaphus caama* and *Alcelaphus lichtensteini* are also subspecies of *Alcelaphus buselaphus*.

[8] According to some taxonomists, *Damaliscus hunteri* is a subspecies of *Damaliscus lunatus*.

[9] According to some taxonomists, *Kobus defassa* is a subspecies of *Kobus ellipsiprymnus*.

[10] According to some taxonomists, *Kobus (Adenota) vardoni* is a subspecies of *Kobus (Adenota) kob*.

Subfamily: Roan-related Antelopes (Hippotraginae)
Genus: Roan Antelopes (*Hippotragus*)
Roan, *Hippotragus equinus* (Desmarest, 1804)
Sable Antelope, *Hippotragus niger* (Harris, 1838)
Genus: Oryx Antelopes (*Oryx*)
South African Oryx, *Oryx gazella* (Linné, 1758)
East African Oryx, *Oryx beisa* (Rüppell, 1835)[11]
Scimitar-horned Oryx, *Oryx dammah* (Cretzschmar, 1826)[11]
Arabian Oryx, *Oryx leucoryx* (Pallas, 1777)[11]
Genus: Addax Antelopes (*Addax*)
Addax, *Addax nasomaculatus* (De Blainville, 1816)
Subfamily: Gazelle-related Antelopes (Antilopinae)
Genus: Gazelles (*Gazella*)
Subgenus: Larger Gazelles (*Nanger*)
Dama Gazelle, *Gazella (Nanger) dama* (Pallas, 1766)
Sömmering's Gazelle, *Gazella (Nanger) soemmeringi* (Cretzschmar, 1826)
Grant's Gazelle, *Gazella (Nanger) granti* Brooke, 1872
Subgenus: Small Gazelles (*Gazella*)
Mountain Gazelle, *Gazella (Gazella) gazella* (Pallas, 1766)
Dorcas Gazelle, *Gazella (Gazella) dorcas* (Linné, 1758)
Loder's Gazelle, *Gazella (Gazella) leptoceros* (F. Cuvier, 1842)
Pelzeln's Gazelle, *Gazella (Gazella) pelzelni* Kohl, 1886
Red-fronted Gazelle, *Gazella (Gazella) rufifrons* Gray, 1846
Thomson's Gazelle, *Gazella (Gazella) thomsoni* Günther, 1884
Speke's Gazelle, *Gazella (Gazella) spekei* Blyth, 1863
Subgenus: Goitered Gazelles (*Trachelocele*)
Goitered Gazelle, *Gazella (Trachelocele) subgutturosa* (Güldenstaedt, 1780)
Genus: Central Asiatic Gazelles (*Procapra*)
Tibetan Gazelle, *Procapra picticaudata* Hodgson, 1846
Mongolian Gazelle, *Procapra gutturosa* (Pallas, 1777)

---

[11] According to some taxonomists, *Oryx beisa*, *Oryx dammah*, and *Oryx leucoryx* are subspecies of *Oryx gazella*.

Genus: Blackbuck Antelopes (*Antilope*)
  Indian Blackbuck, *Antilope cervicapra* (Linné, 1758)
Genus: Gerenuks (*Litocranius*)
  Gerenuk, *Litocranius walleri* (Brooke, 1878)
Genus: Dibatags (*Ammodorcas*)
  Dibatag, *Ammodorcas clarkei* (Thomas, 1891)
Genus: Springbucks (*Antidorcas*)
  Springbuck, *Antidorcas marsupialis* (Zimmermann, 1780)
Subfamily: Impalas (Aepycerotinae)
  Genus: Impalas (Aepyceros)
    Impala, *Aepyceros melampus* (Lichtenstein, 1812)
Subfamily: Saiga-related Antelopes (Saiginae)
  Genus: Tibetan Antelopes (*Pantholops*)
    Chiru, *Pantholops hodgsoni* (Abel, 1826)
  Genus: Saigas (*Saiga*)
    Saiga, *Saiga tatarica* (Linné, 1766)
Subfamily: Goats and Sheep (Caprinae)
  Genus: Goats (*Capra*)
    Ibex, *Capra ibex* Linné, 1758
    Spanish Ibex, *Capra pyrenaica* Schinz, 1838
    Markhor, *Capra falconeri* (Wagner, 1839)
    Wild Goat, *Capra aegagrus* Erxleben, 1777
  Genus: Tahrs (*Hemitragus*)
    Himalayan Tahr, *Hemitragus jemlahicus* (H. Smith, 1826)
    Nilgiri Tahr, *Hemitragus hylocrius* (Ogilby, 1838)[12]
    Arabian Tahr, *Hemitragus jayakiri* Thomas, 1894[12]
  Genus: Barbary Sheep (*Ammotragus*)
    Barbary Sheep or Aoudad, *Ammotragus lervia* (Pallas, 1777)
  Genus: Blue Sheep (*Pseudois*)
    Blue Sheep or Bharal, *Pseudois nayaur* (Hodgson, 1833)
  Genus: Sheep (*Ovis*)
    Argali, *Ovis ammon* (Linné, 1758)
    Mouflon, *Ovis musimon* (Pallas, 1811)[13,14]
    Urial, *Ovis orientalis* Gmelin, 1774[14]
    Snow Sheep, *Ovis nivicola* Eschscholtz, 1829[14]
    Thinhorn Sheep, *Ovis dalli* Nelson, 1884[14]
    Bighorn Sheep, *Ovis canadensis* Shaw, 1804[14]

---

[12] According to some taxonomists, *Hemitragus hylocrius* and *Hemitragus jayakiri* are subspecies of *Hemitragus jemlahicus*.
[13] According to some taxonomists, *Ovis musimon* is a subspecies of *Ovis orientalis*.
[14] According to some taxonomists, all these *Ovis* species are subspecies of *Ovis ammon*.

Subfamily: Chamois-related Species (Rupicaprinae)
Genus: Chamois (*Rupicapra*)
Chamois, *Rupicapra rupicapra* (Linné, 1758)
Genus: Mountain Goats (*Oreamnos*)
Mountain Goat, *Oreamnos americanus* (De Blainville, 1816)
Subfamily: Goral-related Species (Nemorhaedinae)
Genus: Gorals (*Nemorhaedus*)
Goral, *Nemorhaedus goral* (Hardwicke, 1825)
Genus: Serows (*Capricornis*)
Serow, *Capricornis sumatraënsis* (Bechstein, 1799)
Subfamily: Takins (Budorcatinae)
Genus: Takins (*Budorcas*)
Takin, *Budorcas taxicolor* Hodgson, 1850
Subfamily: Musk Oxen (Ovibovinae)
Genus: Musk Oxen (*Ovibos*)
Musk Ox, *Ovibos moschatus* (Zimmermann, 1780)

References

Aeschlimann, A. 1963. Observations sur *Philantomba maxwelli* (Hamilton-Smith) une antilope de la forêt éburnée. *Acta tropica* 20:341–368.

Alexander, G. 1960. Maternal behaviour of the Merino ewe. *Proc. Austral. Soc. Anim. Prod.* 3:105–114.

Altmann, M. 1963. Naturalistic studies of maternal care in moose and elk. In: *Maternal Behavior in Mammals*, ed. H. L. Rheingold, pp. 233–253. New York: John Wiley.

Anderson, J. L. 1980. The social organisation and aspects of behaviour of the nyala *Tragelaphus angasi* Gray, 1849. *Z. Säugetierk.* 45:90–123.

Antonius, O. 1937. Über Herdenbildung und Paarungseigentümlichkeiten der Einhufer. *Z. Tierpsychol.* 1:259–289.

———1938. Nachtrag zu dem Aufsatz "Über Herdenbildung usw." *Z. Tierpsychol.* 2:115–117.

———1939. Über Symbolhandlungen und Verwandtes bei Säugetieren. *Z. Tierpsychol.* 3:263–278.

——— 1940. Beobachtungen an Einhufern in Schönbrunn. Über das Damara-Zebra. *Zoolog. Garten* 12:247–257.

Autenrieth, R. E. and Fichter, E. 1975. *On the Behavior and Socialization of Pronghorn Fawns. Wildl. Monogr. No. 42.*

Backhaus, D. 1958. Beitrag zur Ethologie der Paarung einiger Antilopen. *Z. Zuchthygiene* 2:281–293.

———1959. Beobachtungen über das Freileben von Lelwel-Kuhantilopen (*Alcelaphus buselaphus lelwel*, Heuglin 1877) und Gelegenheitsbeobachtungen an Sennar-Pferdeantilopen (*Hippotragus equinus bakeri*, Heuglin 1863). *Z. Säugetierk.* 24:1–34.

———1960a. *Beobachtungen an Giraffen in Zoologischen Gärten und in freier Wildbahn.* Brussels: Inst. Parcs Nat. Congo et Ruanda-Urundi.

———1960b. Über das Kampfverhalten beim Steppenzebra (*Equus quagga* H. Smith 1841). *Z. Tierpsychol.* 17:345–350.

Barette, C. 1977. The social behaviour of captive muntjacs, *Muntiacus reevesi* (Ogilby 1839). *Z. Tierpsychol.* 43:188–213.

Baskin, L. M. 1974. Management of ungulate herds in relation to domestication. In: *The Behaviour of Ungulates and Its Relation to Management*, ed. V. Geist and F. R. Walther, pp. 530–541. IUCN Publ. No. 24. Morges: IUCN.

Bell, C. 1844. *The Anatomy and Philosophy of Expression.* London: John Murray.

Benz, M. 1973. Zum Sozialverhalten der Sasin (Hirschziegenantilope, *Antilope cervicapra* Linné 1758). *Zoolog. Beiträge* 19:403–466.

Bergerud, A. T. 1974. Rutting behaviour of Newfoundland caribou. In: *The Behaviour of Ungulates and Its Relation to Management*, ed. V. Geist and F. R. Walther, pp. 395–435. IUCN Publ. No. 24. Morges: IUCN.

Beuerle, W. 1975. Freilanduntersuchungen zum Kampf- und Sexualverhalten des europäischen Wildschweines (*Sus scrofa* L.). *Z. Tierpsychol.* 39:211–258.

Bigalke, R. C. 1972. Observations on the behaviour and feeding habits of the springbok, *Antidorcas marsupialis. Zoolog. Afric.* 7:333–359.

Blakeslee, C. K., Rice, C. G., and Ralls, K. 1979. Behavior and reproduction of captive brow-antlered deer, *Cervus eldi thamin* (Thomas, 1918). *Säugetierk. Mitt.* 27:114–127.

Bourlière, F. and Verschuren, J. 1960. *Introduction à l'écologie des ongulés du Parc National Albert.* Brussels: Inst. Parcs Nat. Congo et Ruanda-Urundi.

Brander, A.A.D. 1923. *Wild Animals in Central India.* London: E. Arnold.

Bromley, P. T. and Kitchen, D. 1974. Courtship in the pronghorn *Antilocapra americana.* In: *The Behaviour of Ungulates and Its Relation to Management,* ed. V. Geist and F. R. Walther, pp. 356–364. IUCN Publ. No. 24. Morges: IUCN.

Brooks, A. 1961. *A Study of the Thomson's Gazelle (Gazella thomsoni Günther) in Tanganyika.* London: H.M. Stat. Ofc.

Bubenik, A. B. 1965. Beiträge zur Geburtskunde und den Mutter-Kind-Beziehungen des Reh- und Rotwildes. *Z. Säugetierk.* 30:65–228.

———1971. Geweihe und ihre biologische Funktion. *Naturw. u. Medizin* 8:33–49.

Buechner, H. K. 1961. Territorial behavior in Uganda kob. *Science* 133:698–699.

Buechner, H. K. and Schloeth, R. 1965. Ceremonial mating behavior in Uganda kob (*Adenota kob thomasi* Neumann). *Z. Tierpsychol.* 22:209–225.

Burckhardt, D. 1958a. Observations sur la vie sociale du cerf (*Cervus elaphus*) au Parc National Suisse. *Mammalia* 22:226–244.

———1958b. Kindliches Verhalten als Ausdrucksbewegung im Fortpflanzungszeremoniell einiger Wiederkäuer. *Rev. suisse Zool.* 65:312–316.

Bützler. W. 1974. Kampf- und Paarungsverhalten, soziale Rangordnung und Aktivitätsperiodik beim Rothirsch. *Z. Tierpsychol.* Suppl. 16.

Cadigan, F. C. 1972. A brief report on copulatory and perinatal behaviour of the lesser Malayan mouse deer (*Tragulus javanicus*). *Malay. Nat. J.* 25:112–116.

Carpenter, C. R. 1942. Societies of monkeys and apes. *Biol. Symp.* 8:177–204.

Cary, E. R. 1976. Territorial and reproductive behavior of the blackbuck antelope (*Antilope cervicapra*). Ph.D. diss., Texas A&M Univ., College Station.

Chance, M.R.A. 1962. An interpretation of some agonistic postures; the role of "cut-off" acts and postures. *Symp. Zool. Soc. Lond.* 8:71–89.

Cherry, C. 1957. *On Human Communication.* Cambridge: MIT Press.

Cowan, J. McT. and Geist, V. 1961. Aggressive behaviour in deer of the genus *Odocoileus. J. Mammal.* 42:522–526.

Cronwright-Schreiner, S. C. 1925. *The Migratory Springbucks of South Africa.* London: T. Fischer.

Daanje, A. 1950. On locomotory movements in birds and the intention movements derived from them. *Behaviour* 3:48–98.

Darling, F. 1937. *A Herd of Red Deer.* London: Oxford Univ. Press.

Darwin, C. R. 1872. *The Expression of the Emotions in Man and Animals.* Reprint 1965, Chicago: Univ. of Chicago Press.

David, J.H.M. 1973. The behaviour of the bontebok, *Damaliscus dorcas dor-*

cas (Pallas 1766), with special reference to territorial behaviour. Z. *Tierpsychol.* 33:38–107.

Davis, J. A. 1965. A preliminary report of the reproductive behavior of the small Malayan chevrotain *Tragulus javanicus* at the New York Zoo. *Int. Zoo Yb.* 5:42–44.

Dittrich, L. 1965. Absetzen von Voraugendrüsensekret an den Hörnern von Artgenossen bei Gazellen und Dikdiks. *Säugetierk. Mitt.* 13:145–146.

Dittrich, L. und Böer, M. 1980. *Verhalten und Fortpflanzung von Kirks Rüssel-Dikdiks im Zoologischen Garten.* Hanover: Freimann & Fuchs.

Dönhoff, C. 1942. Zur Kenntnis des afrikanischen Waldschweins. *Zoolog. Garten* 14:193–200.

Downing, R. L. and McGinnes, B. S. 1969. Capturing and marking white-tailed deer fawns. *J. Wildl. Mgmt.* 33:711–714.

Dowsett, R. J. 1966. Behaviour and population structure of hartebeest in the Kafue National Park. *Puku* 4:147–154.

Dubost, G. 1965. Glande préputiale du chevrotain aquatique *Hyemoschus aquaticus* Ogilby (Tragulidae, Ruminantia). *Biol. Gabon* 1:313–318.

———1971. Observations éthologique sur le muntjak (*Muntiacus muntjac* Zimmermann 1780 et *M. reevesi* Ogilby 1839) en captivité et semi-liberté. Z. *Tierpsychol.* 28:387–427.

———1975. Le comportement du chevrotain africain, *Hyemoschus aquaticus* Ogilby (Artiodactyla, Ruminantia). Z. *Tierpsychol.* 37:403–501.

Eibl-Eibesfeldt, I. 1957. Die Ausdrucksformen der Säugetiere. *Handb. Zool.* 8, 10(6):1–26.

———1970. *Ethology—The Biology of Behavior.* New York: Holt, Rinehart & Winston.

Einarsen, A. S. 1948. *The Pronghorn Antelope and Its Management.* Washington, D.C.: Wildl. Mgmt. Inst.

Espmark, Y. 1964. Rutting behaviour in reindeer (*Rangifer tarandus* L.). *Anim. Behav.* 12:159–163.

———1971. Mother-young relationship and ontogeny of behaviour in reindeer. Z. *Tierpsychol.* 29:42–81.

Estes, R. D. 1967. The comparative behaviour of Grant's and Thomson's gazelles. *J. Mammal.* 48:189–209.

———1969. Territorial behaviour of the wildebeest (*Connochaetes taurinus* Burchell, 1823). Z. *Tierpsychol.* 26:284–370.

———1972. The role of the vomeronasal organ in mammalian reproduction. *Mammalia* 36:315–341.

———1974a. Social organization of the African Bovidae. In: *The Behaviour of Ungulates and Its Relation to Management,* ed. V. Geist and F. R. Walther, pp. 166–205. IUCN Publ. 24. Morges: IUCN.

———1974b. Biology and conservation of the giant sable antelope (*Hippotragus niger variani* Thomas, 1916). *Proc. Acad. Nat. Sc. Philadelphia* 126:73–104.

Ewer, R. F. 1968. *Ethology of Mammals.* London: Logos Press.

Faatz, W. C. 1976. Mother-offspring relations and ontogeny of behavior in white-tailed deer. Ph.D. diss., Texas A&M Univ., College Station.

Fall, B. A. 1972. On social organization and behavior of nilgai, *Boselaphus tragocamelus* (Pallas) in South Texas. M.S. thesis, Texas A&M Univ., College Station.

Feist, J. D. and McCullough, D. R. 1976. Behavior patterns and communication in feral horses. Z. *Tierpsychol*. 41:337–371.

Flerov, K. K. 1954. *Musk Deer and Deer*. Eng. trans. 1960, U.S. Dept. Commerce, Clearinghouse Fed. Sc. & Tech. Inf., Springfield, Va.

Frädrich, H. 1964. Beobachtungen zur Kreuzung zwischen Schwarzrückenducker, *Cephalophus dorsalis*, Gray, 1846, und Zebraducker, *Cephalophus zebra* (Gray, 1838). Z. *Säugetierk*. 29:46–51.

———1965. Zur Biologie und Ethologie des Warzenschweins (*Phacochoerus aethiopicus* Pallas), unter Berücksichtigung des Verhaltens anderer Suiden. Z. *Tierpsychol*. 22:328–393.

———1967. Das Verhalten der Schweine (Suidae, Tayassuidae) und Flusspferde (Hippopotamidae). *Handb. Zool.* 8, 10(26):1–44.

———1968. Tapire. In: *Grzimeks Tierleben*, ed. B. Grzimek, Vol. 13, pp. 17–35. Zurich: Kindler, English ed.: 1972. Tapirs. In: *Grzimek's Animal Life Encyclopedia*, Vol. 13, pp. 17–33. New York: Von Nostrand Reinhold.

———1974. A comparison of behavior in Suidae. In: *The Behavior of Ungulates and Its Relation to Management*, ed. V. Geist and F. R. Walther, pp. 133–143. IUCN Publ. No. 24. Morges: IUCN.

Franklin, W. L. 1974. The social behavior of the vicuna. In: *The Behaviour of Ungulates and Its Relation to Management*, ed. V. Geist and F. R. Walther, pp. 477–487. IUCN Publ. No. 24. Morges: IUCN.

Fraser, A. F. 1957. The state of fight or flight in the bull. *Br. J. Anim. Behav.* 5:48–49.

———1968. *Reproductive Behaviour in Ungulates*. New York: Academic Press.

Freye, H. A. und Geisler, H. 1966. Das Ohrenspiel der Ungulaten als Ausdrucksform. *Wiss. Z. Univ. Halle* 5:893–915.

Fuchs, E. R. 1976. Behavior patterns of axis deer (*Axis axis*) in Texas. M.S. thesis, Texas A&M Univ., College Station.

Gauthier-Pilters, H. 1959. Einige Beobachtungen zum Droh-, Angriffs- und Kampfverhalten des Dromedarhengstes, sowie über Geburt und Verhaltensentwicklung des Jungtieres, in der nordwestlichen Sahara. Z. *Tierpsychol*. 16:593–604.

Geist, V. 1963. On the behaviour of the North American moose (*Alces alces andersoni* Peterson 1950) in British Columbia. *Behaviour* 20:377–416.

———1965. On the rutting behaviour of the mountain goat. *J. Mammal.* 45:551–568.

———1966a. Ethological observations on some North American cervids. *Zoolog Beitr.* 12:219–250.

———1966b. The evolution of hornlike organs. *Behaviour* 27:175–214.

———1968. On the interrelation of external appearance, social behaviour and social structure of mountain sheep. Z. *Tierpsychol*. 25:199–215.

———1971. *Mountain Sheep*. Chicago: Univ. of Chicago Press.

———1978. *Life Strategies, Human Evolution, Environmental Design*. New York: Springer.

Gilbert, B. K. 1968. Development of social behavior in the fallow deer (*Dama dama*). Z. *Tierpsychol*. 25:867–876.

Goethe, F. and Goethe, E. 1939. Aus dem Jugendleben des Muffelwildes. *Zoolog. Garten* 11:1–22.

Gosling, L. M. 1969. Parturition and related behaviour of Coke's hartebeest, *Alcelaphus buselaphus cokei* Günther. *J. Reprod. Fert. Suppl.* 6:265–286.

—————1972. The construction of antorbital gland marking sites by male oribi (*Ourebia oribi*, Zimmermann, 1783). *Z. Tierpsychol.* 30:271–276.

—————1974. The social behaviour of Coke's hartebeest *Alcelaphus buselaphus cokei*. In: *The Behaviour of Ungulates and Its Relation to Management*, ed. V. Geist and F. R. Walther, pp. 488–511. IUCN Publ. No. 24. Morges: IUCN.

Graf, W. 1956. Territorialism in deer. *J. Mammal.* 37:165–170.

Grau, G. A. 1974. Behavior of mountain gazelle in Israel. Ph.D. diss., Texas A&M Univ., College Station.

Grau, G. A. and Walther, F. R. 1976. Mountain gazelle agonistic behaviour. *Anim. Behav.* 24:626–636.

Gray, D. R. 1973. Social organization and behaviour of muskoxen (*Ovibos moschatus*) on Bathurst Island, N.W.T. Ph.D. diss., Univ. of Alberta, Edmonton.

Gregg, A. A. 1955. Summer habits of Wyoming antelope. Ph.D. diss., Cornell Univ., Ithaca, N.Y.

Griffin, D. G. 1976. *The Question of Animal Awareness*. New York: Rockefeller Univ. Press.

Grubb, P. 1974. Social organization of Soay sheep and the behavior of ewes and lambs. In: *Island Survivors*, ed. P. Jewell, C. Milner, and J. Boyd, pp. 131–159. London: Athlone Press.

Grzimek, B. 1949. Die 'Radfahrer-Reaktion.' *Z. Tierpsychol.* 6:41–44.

—————1958. Über das Verhalten von Okapi-Müttern. *Säugetierk. Mitt.* 6:28–29.

Gubernick, D. J. 1981. Mechanisms of maternal 'labelling.' *Anim. Behav.* 29:305–306.

Haas, G. 1959. Untersuchungen über angeborene Verhaltensweisen beim Mähnenspringer (*Ammotragus lervia* Pall.). *Z. Tierpsychol.* 16:218–242.

Hafez, E.S.E. and Signoret, J. P. 1969. The behavior of swine. In: *The Behavior of Domestic Animals*, ed. E.S.E. Hafez, pp. 349–390. Baltimore: Williams & Wilkins.

Haltenorth, T. 1963. Klassifikation der Säugetiere: Artiodactyla. *Handb. Zool.* 8, 1(18):1–167.

Hamann, U. 1979. Beobachtungen zum Verhalten von Bongoantilopen (*Tragelaphus euryceros* Ogilby, 1836). *Zoolog. Garten* 49:319–375.

Hammen, H. J. van der, and Schenk, P. 1963. Waarnemingen over het gedrag van Saane-geiten. *Tijdschr. Diergeneesk.* 88:34–44.

Hassenberg, L. 1977. Zum Fortpflanzungsverhalten des mesopotamischen Damhirsches, *Cervus dama mesopotamicus* Brooke, 1875, in Gefangenschaft. *Säugetierk. Mitt.* 40:161–194.

Hediger, H. 1941. Biologische Gesetzmässigkeiten im Verhalten von Wirbeltieren. *Mitt. Naturf. Ges. Bern:*37–55.

—————1946. Zur psychologischen Bedeutung des Hirschgeweihs. *Verh. Schweiz. Naturf. Ges. Zürich:*162–163.

—————1949. Säugetierterritorien und ihre Markierung. *Bijdr. Dierk.* 28:172–184.

—————1950. *Wild Animals in Captivity*. London: Butterworth.

—————1951. *Observations sur la psychologie animale dans les Parcs Nationaux du Congo Belge*. Brussels: Inst. Parcs Nat. Congo et Ruanda-Urundi.

—————1954. *Skizzen zu einer Tierpsychologie im Zoo und im Zirkus*.

Stuttgart: Europa. English ed.: 1968. *The Psychology and Behaviour of Animals in Zoos and Circuses*. New York: Dover.

———1980. *Tiere verstehen*. Munich: Kindler.

Heinroth, O. 1910. Beiträge zur Biologie, insbesondere Psychologie und Ethologie der Anatiden. *Verh. 5. Int. Ornith. Kongr., Berlin*: 589–702.

Hendrichs, H. und Hendrichs, U. 1971. *Dikdik und Elefanten*. Munich: Piper.

Hennig, R. 1962. Über das Revierverhalten der Rehböcke. *Z. Jagdwiss.* 8:61–81.

Hinde, R. A. 1966. *Animal Behaviour*. New York: McGraw-Hill.

Hirth, D. H. 1977. *Social Behavior of White-Tailed Deer in Relation to Habitat*. *Wildl. Monogr. No. 53*

Hunsaker, D. and Hahn, T. C. 1965. Vocalization of the South American tapir, *Tapirus terrestris*. *Anim. Behav.* 13:69–74.

Huth, H. H. 1970. Zum Verhalten der Rappenantilope (*Hippotragus niger* Harris, 1838). *Zoolog. Garten* 38:147–170.

———1980. Verhaltensstudien an Pferdeböcken (Hippotraginae) unter Berücksichtigung stammesgeschichtlicher and systematischer Fragen. *Säugetierk. Mitt.* 28:161–245.

Jarman, P. J. 1974. The social organization of antelopes in relation to their ecology. *Behaviour* 48:215–267.

Jarman, P. J. and Jarman, M. V. 1974. Impala behaviour and its relevance to management. In: *The Behaviour of Ungulates and Its Relation to Management*, ed. V. Geist and F. R. Walther, pp. 871–881. IUCN Publ. No. 24. Morges: IUCN.

Joubert, S.C.J. 1970. A study of the social behaviour of the roan antelope, *Hippotragus equinus equinus* (Desmarest, 1804), in the Kruger National Park. M.S. thesis, Univ. of Pretoria, Pretoria.

———1972. Territorial behaviour of the tsessebe (*Damaliscus lunatus lunatus* Burchell) in the Kruger National Park. *Zoolog. Afric.* 7:141–156.

———1974. The social organization of the roan antelope *Hippotragus equinus* and its influence on spatial distribution of the herds in the Kruger National Park. In: *The Behavior of Ungulates and Its Relation to Management*, ed. V. Geist and F. R. Walther, pp. 661–675. IUCN Publ. No. 24. Morges: IUCN.

———1975. The mating behaviour of the tsessebe (*Damaliscus lunatus lunatus*) in the Kruger National Park. *Z. Tierpsychol.* 37:182–191.

Jungius, H. 1970. Studies on the breeding biology of the reedbuck (*Redunca arundium* Boddaert, 1785). *Z. Säugetierk.* 35:129–146.

Kakies, M. 1936. *Elche zwischen Meer und Memel*. Giessen: Brühl.

Kiddie, D. G. 1962. *The Sika Deer in New Zealand*. *New Zeal. For. Serv. Inf. Ser., No. 44*.

Kiley, M. 1972. The vocalizations of ungulates, their causation and function. *Z. Tierpsychol.* 31:171–222.

Kitchen, D. and Bromley, P. T. 1974. Agonistic behaviour of territorial pronghorn bucks. In: *The Behaviour of Ungulates and Its Relation to Management*, ed. V. Geist and F. R. Walther, pp. 365–381. IUCN Publ. No. 24. Morges: IUCN.

Klages, L. 1936. *Grundlegung der Wissenschaft vom Ausdruck*. Leipzig: J. A. Barth.

Klingel, H. 1967. Soziale Organisation und Verhalten freilebender Steppenzebras. *Z. Tierpsychol.* 24:580–624.

———— 1968. Soziale Organisation und Verhaltensweisen von Hartmann-und Bergzebras (*Equus zebra hartmannae* und *Equus z. zebra*). *Z. Tierpsychol.* 25:76–88.

———— 1969. Zur Soziologie des Grévyzebras. *Zoolog. Anz.* 33:311–316.

———— 1972. Das Verhalten der Pferde (Equidae). *Handb. Zool.*, 8, 10(24):1–68.

———— 1974. A comparison of the social behaviour of the Equidae. In: *The Behaviour of Ungulates and Its Relation to Management*, ed. V. Geist and F. R. Walther, pp. 124–132. IUCN Publ. No. 24. Morges: IUCN.

———— 1975. Die soziale Organisation der Equiden. *Verh. Dtsch. Zoolog. Ges.* 1975:71–80.

———— 1977. Communication in Perissodactyla. In: *How Animals Communicate*, ed. T. A. Sebeok, pp. 715–727. Bloomington: Indiana Univ. Press.

Klopfer, P. and Gamble, J. 1966. Maternal "imprinting" in goats: the role of the chemical senses. *Z. Tierpsychol.* 23:588–593.

Knappe, H. 1964, Zur Funktion des Jacobsonschen Organes. *Zoolog. Garten* 28:188–194.

Koford, C. B. 1957. The vicuna and the puna. *Ecol. Monogr.* 27, (2):153–219.

Kok, O. B. 1975. Behaviour and ecology of the red hartebeest (*Alcelaphus buselaphus caama*). *Or. Free St. Prov. Adm., Nat. Cons. Publ. No.* 4:1–59.

Kortlandt, A. 1940. Eine Übersicht über die angeborenen Verhaltensweisen des mitteleuropäischen Kormorans. *Arch. Neerl. Zool.* 4:401–442.

Krämer, A. 1969. Soziale Organisation und Sozialverhalten einer Gemspopulation (*Rupicapra rupicapra* L.) der Alpen. *Z. Tierpsychol.* 26:889–964.

Krieg, H. 1948. *Zwischen Anden und Atlantik.* Leipzig: C. Hauser.

Kuelhorn, F. 1955. Säugetierkundliche Mitteilungen aus Süd-Mattogrosso. *Säugetierk. Mitt.* 3:77–82.

Kurt, F. 1968. *Das Sozialverhalten des Rehes (Capreolus capreolus L.).* Berlin: P. Parey.

Lang. E. M. 1956. Haltung und Brunft von *Okapia* in Epulu. *Säugetierk. Mitt.* 4:49–52.

———— 1980. Erfahrungen mit Somaliwildeseln. *Lib. Amic. W. Van den Bergh*, 1980:1–9.

Lent, P. C. 1965. Rutting behaviour in a barren-ground caribou population. *Anim. Behav.* 13:259–264.

———— 1966. Calving and related social behaviour in the barren-ground caribou. *Z. Tierpsychol.* 23:702–756.

———— 1969. A preliminary study of the Okavango lechwe (*Kobus lechwe lechwe* Gray). *E. Afr. Wildl. J.* 7:147–157.

———— 1974. Mother-infant relationships in ungulates. In: *The Behaviour of Ungulates and Its Relation To Management*, ed. V. Geist and F. R. Walther, pp. 14–55. IUCN Publ. No. 24. Morges: IUCN.

———— 1975. A review of acoustic communication in *Rangifer tarandus. First Intern. Reindeer and Caribou Symp. Biol. Pap. Univ. Alaska, Spec. Rpt.* No. 1:398–408.

Leonhard, K. 1949. *Ausdruckssprache der Seele.* Berlin: K.F. Haug.

Leuthold, W. 1966. Variations in territorial behaviour of Uganda kob (*Adenota kob thomasi* Neumann, 1896). *Behaviour* 27:214–257.

———— 1967. Beobachtungen zum Jugendverhalten der Kob-Antilopen. *Z. Säugetierk.* 32:59–62.

————1971. Freilandbeobachtungen an Giraffengazellen (*Litocranius walleri*) im Tsavo-Nationalpark, Kenya. *Z. Säugetierk.* 36:19–37.

————1977. *African Ungulates*. Berlin: Springer.

————1979. The lesser kudu, *Tragelaphus imberbis* (Blyth, 1869). Ecology and behaviour of an African antelope. *Säugetierk. Mitt.* 27:1–75.

Leyhausen, P. 1956. Verhaltenstudien an Katzen. *Z. Tierpsychol. Suppl. 2.* English ed.: 1979. *Cat Behavior*. New York: Garland STPM Press.

————1967. Biologie von Ausdruck und Eindruck. *Psychol. Forsch.* 31:113–227.

Lind, H. 1959. The activation of an instinct caused by a 'transitional action.' *Behaviour* 14:123–135.

Lindsdale, J. and Tomich, P. A. 1953. *A Herd of Mule Deer*. Berkeley: Univ. of California Press.

Lorenz, K. 1935. Der Kumpan in der Umwelt des Vogels. *J. Ornith.* 83:137–413.

————1949. *Er redete mit dem Vieh, den Vögeln und den Fischen*. Wien: Borotha-Schoeler, English ed.: 1952. *King Solomon's Ring*. New York: T. Y. Crowell.

————1951. Ausdrucksbewegungen höherer Tiere. *Naturwiss.* 38:113–116.

————1963. *Das sogenannte Böse*. Wien: Borotha-Schoeler. English ed.: 1966. *On Aggression*. New York: Bantam.

Lott, D. F. 1969. Postural aspects of threat and submission signalling in mature male American bison. *Am. Zool.* 9:50.

————1974. Sexual and aggressive behaviour of American bison *Bison bison*. In: *The Behaviour of Ungulates and Its Relation to Management*, ed. V. Geist and F. R. Walther, pp. 382–394. IUCN Publ. No. 24. Morges: IUCN.

Lynch, C. D. 1974. A behavioural study of blesbok. *Damaliscus dorcas phillipsi*, with special reference to territoriality. *Mem. Nas. Mus. Bloemfontain*, 8:1–83.

Manski, D. A. 1979. Reproductive behaviour of addax antelope. M.S. thesis, Texas A&M Univ., College Station.

Marjoribanks-Egerton, P. 1962. The cow-calf relationship and rutting behaviour in the American bison. M.S. thesis, Univ. of Alberta, Edmonton.

McHugh, T. 1958. Social behaviour of the American buffalo (*Bison bison bison*). *Zool.* 43:1–40.

Metzger, W. 1954. *Psychologie*. Darmstadt: Steinkoppf.

Mohr, E. 1960. *Wilde Schweine*. Wittenberg-Lutherstadt: A. Ziemsen.

Moynihan, M. 1955. Some aspects of reproductive behaviour in the black-headed gull (*Larus ridibundus ridibundus* L.) and related species. *Behaviour* Suppl. 4.

Müller-Schwarze, D. 1967. Social odours in young mule deer. *Am. Zool.* 7:807.

————1969. Complexity and relative specificity in a mammalian pheromone. *Nature* 223:525–526.

————1971. Pheromones in black-tailed deer (*Odocoileus hemionus columbianus*). *Anim. Behav.* 19:141–152.

————1974. Social functions of various scent glands in certain ungulates and the problems encountered in experimental studies of scent communication. In: *The Behaviour of Ungulates and Its Relation to Management*, ed. V. Geist and F. R. Walther, pp. 107–113. IUCN Publ. No. 24. Morges: IUCN.

———1980. Chemical signals in alarm behavior of deer. In: *Chemical Signals*, ed. D. Müller-Schwarze and R. M. Silverstein, pp. 39–52. New York: Plenum Press.

Müller-Using, D. und Schloeth, R. 1967. Das Verhalten der Hirsche (Cervidae). *Handb. Zool.* 8, 10(28):1–60.

Mungall, E. C. 1978. *The Indian Blackbuck Antelope: A Texas View*. College Station, Texas: Kleberg Stud. Nat. Res.

———1980. Courtship and mating behavior of the dama gazelle (*Gazella dama* Pallas 1766). *Zoolog. Garten* 50:1–14.

Murie, A. 1944. *The Wolves of Mount McKinley*. U.S. Nat. Park Serv. Fauna Ser. No. 5.

Naaktgeboren, C. and Vandendriesche, W. 1962. Beiträge zur vergleichenden Geburtskunde. *Z. Säugetierk.* 27:83–110.

Owen-Smith, R. N. 1974. The social system of the white rhinoceros. In: *The Behaviour of Ungulates and Its Relation to Management*, ed. V. Geist and F. R. Walther, pp. 341–351. IUCN Pub. No. 24. Morges: IUCN.

———1975. The social ethology of the white rhinoceros *Ceratotherium simum* (Burchell 1817). *Z. Tierpsychol.* 38:337–384.

Pedersen, A. 1958. *Der Moschusochs* (*Ovibos moschatus Zimmermann*). Wittenberg-Lutherstadt: A. Ziemsen.

Pfungst, O. 1907. *Das Pferd des Herrn von Osten*. Leipzig: J. A. Barth.

Pilters, H. 1954. Untersuchungen über angeborene Verhaltensweisen bei Tylopoden, unter besonderer Berücksichtigung der neuweltlichen Formen. *Z. Tierpsychol.* 11:213–303.

———1956. Das Verhalten der Tylopoden. *Handb. Zool.* 8, 10(27):1–24.

Pitcher, T. 1979. He who hesitates, lives. Is stotting antiambush behavior? *Am. Nat.* 113:453–456.

Pitzman, M. S. 1970. Birth behavior and lamb survival in mountain sheep in Alaska. M.S. thesis, Univ. of Alaska, Fairbanks.

Player, I. C. and Feely, J. M. 1960. A preliminary report on the square-lipped rhinoceros (*Ceratotherium simum simum*). *Lammergeyer* 1:3–24.

Prenzlow, E. J. 1964. Doe-kid behavior of pronghorns in north-central Colorado. *Col. Coop. Wildl. Res. Unit Tech. Pap. No. 1.*

Pruitt, W. O. 1960. Behavior of the Barren-Ground Caribou. *Biol. Pop. Univ. Alaska, No. 3.*

Quay, W. B. and Müller-Schwarze, D. 1970. Functional histology of integumentory glandular regions in black-tailed deer (*Odocoileus hemionus columbianus*). *J. Mammal.* 51:675–694.

Raesfeld, F. von 1957. Das Rotwild. Berlin: P. Parey.

Ralls, K. 1969. Scent-marking in Maxwell's duiker, *Cephalophus maxwelli*. *Am. Zool.* 9:1071.

———1974. Scent-marking in captive Maxwell's duiker. In: *The Behaviour of Ungulates and Its Relation to Management*, ed. V. Geist and F. R. Walther, pp. 114–123. IUCN Publ. No. 24. Morges: IUCN.

Ralls, K., Barash, C. and Minkowski, K. 1975. Behavior of captive mouse deer, *Tragulus napu*. *Z. Tierpsychol.* 37:356–378.

Richter, W. von 1966. Untersuchungen über angeborene Verhaltensweisen des Schabrackentapirs (*Tapirus indicus*) und des Flachlandtapirs (*Tapirus terrestris*). *Zoolog. Beitr.* 12:67–159.

———1971. The black wildebeest (*Connochaetes gnou*). *Or. Free Stat. Nat. Cons. Misc. Publ.* 2:1–30.

Robin, N. P. 1979. *Zum Verhalten des Kleinkantschils* (Tragulus javanicus Osbeck 1765). Zurich: Juris.

Schäfer, E. 1960. Über das Moschustier. *Jb. G. von Opel-Freigehege* 1959/60:61–63.

Schaffer, J. 1940. *Die Hautdrüsenorgane der Säugetiere.* Berlin: Urban & Schwarzenberg.

Schaller, G. B. 1967. *The Deer and the Tiger.* Chicago: Univ. of Chicago Press.

———1977. *Mountain Monarchs.* Chicago: Univ. of Chicago Press.

Schaller, G. and Mirza, Z. B. 1974. On the behaviour of Punjab urial *Ovis orientalis punjabensis*. In: *The Behaviour of Ungulates and Its Relation to Management,* ed. V. Geist and F. R. Walther, pp. 306–323. IUCN Publ. No. 24. Morges: IUCN.

Schenkel, R. 1947. Ausdrucksstudien an Wölfen. *Behaviour* 1:81–129.

———1958. Zur Deutung der Balzleistungen einiger Phasianiden und Tetraoniden. *Ornith. Beob.* 55:65–95.

———1966a. Zum Problem der Territorialität und des Markierens bei Säugern—am Beispiel des Schwarzen Nashorns und des Löwen. *Z. Tierpsychol.* 23:593–626.

———1966b. On sociology and behaviour in impala (*Aepyceros melampus suara* Matschie). *Z. Säugetierk.* 31:177–205.

Schenkel, R. and Lang, E. M. 1969. Das Verhalten der Nashörner. *Handb. Zool.* 8, 10(25):1–56.

Schloeth, R. 1956a. Zur Psychologie der Begegnung zwischen Tieren. *Behaviour* 10:1–79.

———1956b. Quelques moyens d'intercommunication des taureaux de Camargue. *Terre et vie,* 2:83–93.

———1958. Über die Mutter-Kind Beziehungen beim halbwilden Camargue-Rind. *Säugetierk. Mitt.* 6:145–150.

———1959. Das Scharren bei Rind und Pferd. *Z. Säugetierk.* 23:139–148.

———1961a. Das Sozialleben des Camargue-Rindes. *Z. Tierpsychol.* 18:574–627.

———1961b. Einige Verhaltensweisen im Hirschrudel. *Rev. suisse Zool.* 68:241.

Schlosser, M. 1887. Beiträge zur Kenntnis der Stammesgeschichte der Huftiere und Versuch einer Systematik der Paar- und Unpaarhufer. *Morph. Jb.* 12:1–136.

Schneider, K. M. 1930. Das Flehmen (1. Teil). *Zoolog. Garten* 3:183–198.

———1931. Das Flehmen (2. Teil). *Zoolog. Garten* 4:349–364.

———1934. Das Flehmen (5. Teil). *Zoolog. Garten* 7:182–201.

Schumacher-Marienfrid, S. von. 1939. *Jagd und Biologie.* Berlin: Springer.

Schweinsburg, R. E. 1969. Social behavior of the collared peccary in the Tucson Mountains. Ph.D. diss., Univ. of Arizona, Tucson.

Schweinsburg, R. E. and Sowls, L. K. 1972. Aggressive behavior and related phenomena in the collared peccary. *Z. Tierpsychol.* 30:132–145.

Seitz, A. 1940. Die Paarbildung bei einigen Zichliden. *Z. Tierpsychol.* 4:40–84.

Seton, E. T. 1929. *Lives of Game Animals.* New York: Doubleday.

Signoret, J. P., Mesnil du Buisson, F. du, and Busnel, R. G. 1960. Rôle d'un signal acoustique de verrat dans le comportement réactionnel de la truie en oestrus. *Compt. rend. Sc. Acad. Sc.* 250:1355–1357.

Simpson, C. D. 1964. Observations on courtship behaviour in warthog (*Phacochoerus aethiopicus* Pall.). *Arnoldia* 1:1–4.

Simpson, G. G. 1945. The principles of classification and a classification of mammals. *Bull. Am. Mus. Nat. Hist.* 85:1–350.

Sinclair, A.R.E. 1974. The social organization of the East African buffalo. In: *The Behaviour of Ungulates and Its Relation to Management*, ed. V. Geist and F. R. Walther, pp. 676–689. IUCN Publ. No. 24. Morges: IUCN.

Smith, J. W. 1977. *The Behavior of Communicating*. Cambridge: Harvard Univ. Press.

Snethlage, K. 1957. *Das Schwarzwild*. Berlin: P. Parey.

Sowls, L. K. 1974. Social behavior of the collared peccary. In: *The Behaviour of Ungulates and Its Relation to Management*, ed. V. Geist and F. R. Walther, pp. 144–165. IUCN Publ. No. 24. Morges: IUCN.

Steinhardt, J. 1924. *Vom wehrhaften Riesen und seinem Reiche*. Hamburg: Alster Verl.

Stringham, S. F. 1974. Mother-infant relations in moose. *Nat. can.* 101:325–369.

Talbot, L. M. and Talbot, M. H. 1963. *The Wildebeest in the Western Masailand, Tanganyika*. Wildl. Monogr. No. 12.

Tembrock, G. 1959. *Tierstimmen*. Wittenberg-Lutherstadt: A. Ziemsen.

———1963. *Grundlagen der Tierpsychologie*. Berlin: Akademie.

———1964. *Verhaltensforschung*. Jena: G. Fischer.

———1965. Untersuchungen zur intraspezifischen Variabilität von Lautäusserungen bei Säugetieren. *Z. Säugetierk* 30:257–273.

———1968. Artiodactyla. In: *Animal Communication*, ed. T. A. Sebeok, pp. 383–404. Bloomington: Indiana Univ. Press.

Tener, J. S. 1965. *Muskoxen in Canada, a Biological and Taxonomic Review*. Ottawa: Queen's Printer.

Thenius, E. 1969. Stammesgeschichte der Säugetiere. *Handb. Zool.* 8, 2(1):1–722.

Thenius, E. and Hofer, H. 1960: *Stammesgeschichte der Säugetiere*. Berlin: Springer.

Thomas, J. W., Robinson, R. M., and Marburger, R. G. 1965. Social behavior in a white-tailed deer herd containing hypogondal males. *J. Mammal.* 46:314–327.

Tinbergen, N. 1940. Die Übersprungbewegung. *Z. Tierpsychol.* 4:1–40.

———1951. *The Study of Instinct*. London: Oxford Univ. Press.

———1952. Derived activities; their causation, function and origin. *Quart. Rev. Biol.* 27:1–32.

———1953. *Social Behaviour in Animals*. London: Methuen.

———1959. Einige Gedanken über "Beschwichtigungsgebärden." *Z. Tierpsychol.* 16:651–665.

Tinley, K. L. 1969. Dikdik *Madoqua kirki* in South West Africa; notes on distribution, ecology, and behaviour. *Madoqua* 1:7–33.

Trumler, E. 1958. Beobachtungen an den Böhmzebras des Georg von Opel-Freigeheges für Tierforschung e.V., Kronberg in Taunus, 1. Das Paarungsverhalten. *Säugetierk. Mitt.* Sonderheft: 1–48.

————1959. Das "Rossigkeitsgesicht" und ähnliches Ausdrucksverhalten bei Einhufern. *Z. Tierpsychol.* 16:478–488.

Tschanz, B. 1962. Über die Beziehungen zwischen Muttertier und Jungen beim Mouflon (*Ovis aries musimon*, Pall.). *Experimentia* 18:187–191.

Tyler, S. J. 1972. The behaviour and social organisation of the new forest ponies. *Anim. Behav. Monogr.* No. 5:87–106.

Uexküll, J. von, and Kriszat, G. 1934. *Streifzüge durch die Umwelten von Tieren und Menschen.* Berlin: Springer.

Ullrich, W. 1964. Zur Biologie der Panzernashörner (*Rhinoceros unicornis*) in Assam. *Zoolog. Garten* 28:255–250.

Verheyen, R. 1954. *Monographie éthologique de l'hippopotame.* Brussels: Inst. Parcs Nat. Congo et Ruanda-Urundi.

Walker, D. 1950. Observations on behaviour in young calves. *Bull. Anim. Behav.* 8:5–10.

Walther, F. R. 1958*a*. Zum Kampf-und Paarungsverhalten einiger Antilopen. *Z. Tierpsychol.* 15:340–380.

————1958*b*. Ausdrucksstudien an Elenantilopen (*Taurotragus oryx* Pall.). *Jb. G. v. Opel-Freigehege* 1958:108–119.

————1960*a*. Beobachtungen zum Sozialverhalten der Sasin (*Antilope cervicapra* L.). *Jb. G. v. Opel-Freigehege* 1959/60:64–78.

————1960*b*. "Antilopenhafte" Verhaltensweisen im Paarungszeremoniell des Okapi (*Okapia johnstoni* Sclater, 1901). *Z. Tierpsychol.* 17:188–210.

————1961*a*. Einige Verhaltensbeobachtungen am Bergwild des Georg von Opel-Freigeheges. *Jb. G. v. Opel-Freigehege* 1960/61:53–89.

————1961*b*. Entwicklungszüge im Kampf- und Paarungsverhalten der Horntiere. *Jb. G. v. Opel-Freigehege* 1960/61:90–115.

————1961*c*. Zum Kampfverhalten des Gerenuk. *Natur u. Volk*, 91:313–321.

————1962. Über ein Spiel bei *Okapia johnstoni*. *Z. Säugetierk.* 27:245–251.

————1963. Einige Verhaltensbeobachtungen am Dibatag (*Ammodorcas clarkei* Thomas, 1891). *Zoolog. Garten* 27:233–261.

————1964*a*. Einige Verhaltensbeobachtungen an Thomsongazellen (*Gazella thomsoni* Günther, 1884) im Ngorongoro-Krater. *Z. Tierpsychol.* 21:871–890.

————1964*b*. Verhaltensstudien an der Gattung *Tragelaphus* De Blainville, 1816, in Gefangenschaft, unter besonderer Berücksichtigung des Sozialverhaltens. *Z. Tierpsychol* 21:393–467.

————1965*a*. Psychologische Beobachtungen zur Gesellschaftshaltung von Oryxantilopen (*Oryx gazella beisa* Rüpp.). *Zoolog. Garten* 31:1–58.

————1965*b*. Verhaltensstudien an der Grantgazelle (*Gazella granti* Brooke, 1872) im Ngorongoro-Krater. *Z. Tierpsychol.* 22:167–208.

————1966*a*. *Mit Horn und Huf.* Berlin: P. Parey.

————1966*b*. Zum Liegeverhalten des Weisschwanzgnus (*Connochaetes gnou* Zimmermann, 1780). *Z. Säugetierk.* 31:1–16.

————1968*a*. *Verhalten der Gazellen.* Wittenberg-Lutherstadt: A. Ziemsen.

————1968*b*. Kuhantilopen, Pferdeböcke und Wasserböcke. In: *Grzimeks Tierleben*, ed. B. Grzimek, Vol. 13, pp. 437–471. Zurich: Kindler. English ed.: 1972. Hartebeests, roan and sable antelopes, and waterbucks. In: *Grzimek's Animal Life Encyclopedia*, Vol. 13, pp. 399–430. New York: Van Nostrand Reinhold.

————1969*a*. Ethologische Beobachtungen bei der künstlichen Aufzucht eines Blessbockkalbes (*Damaliscus dorcas phillipsi* Harper, 1939). *Zoolog. Garten* 36:191–215.

————1969*b*. Flight behaviour and avoidance of predators in Thomson's gazelle (*Gazella thomsoni* Günther, 1884). *Behaviour* 34:184–221.

————1972*a*. Territorial behaviour in certain horned ungulates, with special reference to the examples of Thomson's and Grant's gazelles. *Zoolog. Afric.* 7:303–307.

————1972*b*. Social grouping in Grant's gazelle (*Gazella granti* Brooke, 1872) in the Serengeti National Park. *Z. Tierpsychol.* 31:348–403.

————1974. Some reflections on expressive behaviour in combats and courtship of certain horned ungulates. In: *The Behaviour of Ungulates and Its Relation to Management*, ed. V. Geist and F. R. Walther, pp. 56–106. IUCN Publ. No. 24. Morges: IUCN.

————1977*a*. Artiodactyla. In: *How Animals Communicate*, ed. T. A. Sebeok, pp. 655–714. Bloomington: Indiana Univ. Press.

————1977*b*. Sex and activity dependency of distances between Thomson's gazelle (*Gazella thomsoni* Günther, 1884). *Anim. Behav.* 25:713–719.

————1978*a*. Quantitative and functional variations of certain behaviour patterns in male Thomson's gazelle of different social status. *Behaviour* 65:212–240.

————1978*b*. Mapping the structure and the marking system of a territory of the Thomson's gazelle. *E. Afr. Wildl. J.* 16:167–176.

————1978*c*. Forms of aggression in Thomson's gazelle; their situational motivation and their relative frequency in different sex, age, and social classes. *Z. Tierpsychol.* 47:113–172.

————1978*d*. Behavioral observations on oryx antelope (*Oryx beisa*) invading Serengeti National Park, Tanzania. *J. Mammal.* 59:243–260.

————1979. Das Verhalten der Hornträger (Bovidae). *Handb. Zool.* 8, 10(30):1–184.

————1980. Aggressive behaviour of oryx antelope at water-holes in the Etosha National Park. *Madoqua* 11:271–302.

————1981. Remarks on behaviour of springbok, *Antidorcas marsupialis* Zimmermann, 1780. *Zoolog. Garten* 51:81–103.

Waser, P. 1975. Spatial associations in a "solitary" ungulate; the bushbuck *Tragelaphus scriptus* (Pallas). *Z. Tierpsychol.* 37:24–36.

Wemmer, C. Murtaugh, J. 1980. Olfactory aspects of rutting behavior in the Bactrian camel (*Camelus bactrianus ferus*). In *Chemical Signals*, ed. D. Müller-Schwarze and R. M. Silverstein, pp. 107–124. New York: Plenum Press.

Wilson, E. O. 1975. *Sociobiology*. Cambridge: Harvard Univ. Press.

Wünschmann, A. 1968. Die Rinder. In: *Grzimeks Tierleben*, ed. B. Grzimek, Vol. 13, pp. 368–436. Zurich: Kindler. English ed.: 1972. The wild oxen. In: *Grzimek's Animal Life Encyclopedia*, Vol. 13, pp. 331–398. New York: Van Nostrand Reinhold.

Zeeb, K. 1959. Die "Unterlegenheitsgebärde" des noch nicht ausgewachsenen Pferdes (*Equus caballus*). *Z. Tierpsychol.* 16:489–496.

————1961. Der freie Herdensprung beim Pferd. *Wiener tierärztl. Mschr.*, 48:90–102.

————1963. *Equus caballus* (Equidae), Paarung. *Encyclopaedia cinematographica*, Göttingen, Film E 509.

Zeeb, K. and Kleinschmidt, S. 1963. Beobachtungen zum Paarungsverhalten des Grévyzebras in Gefangenschaft. *Z. Tierpsychol.* 20:207–214.

Index

The index includes the common names of ungulate species, genera, families, etc., mentioned in the text. Animal names that occur only in the classification list and/or in Tables 3–6 are excluded. So are scientific species names. The latter can be taken from the classification list in the appendix.